STUDIES AND DOCUMENTATION IN THE HISTORY OF POPULAR ENTERTAINMENT
edited by
ANTHONY SLIDE

1. *Stage Dust: A Critic's Cultural Scrapbook from the 1990s*, by Charles Marowitz. 2001.
2. *The Rise of the Crooners: Gene Austin, Russ Columbo, Bing Crosby, Nick Lucas, Johnny Marvin, and Rudy Vallee*, by Michael Pitts and Frank Hoffmann. 2001.
3. *Thelma* Who?: *Almost 100 Years of Showbiz*, by Thelma White, with Harry Preston. 2002.

The Rise of the Crooners

*Gene Austin, Russ Columbo,
Bing Crosby, Nick Lucas,
Johnny Marvin, and Rudy Vallee*

by Michael Pitts and Frank Hoffmann
with the assistance of
Dick Carty and Jim Bedoian

Introduction by Ian Whitcomb

*Studies and Documentation in the History of Popular
Entertainment, No. 2*

The Scarecrow Press, Inc.
Lanham, Maryland, and London
2002

SCARECROW PRESS, INC.

Published in the United States of America
by Scarecrow Press, Inc.
4720 Boston Way, Lanham, Maryland 20706
www.scarecrowpress.com

4 Pleydell Gardens, Folkestone
Kent CT20 2DN, England

British Library Cataloguing-in-Publication Information Available

Library of Congress Cataloging-in-Publication Data

Pitts, Michael R.
    The rise of the crooners / by Michael Pitts and Frank Hoffmann, with the assistance of Dick Carty and Jim Bedoian ; introduction by Ian Whitcomb.
       p. cm.—(Studies and documentation in the history of popular entertainment ; no. 2)
    Includes bibliographical references, discographies, and index.
    Contents: Introduction : The coming of the crooners / by Ian Whitcomb—Gene Austin—Russ Columbo—Bing Crosby—Nick Lucas—Johnny Marvin—Rudy Vallee.
    ISBN 0-8108-4081-2 (alk. paper)
    1. Singers—United States—Biography.   2. Popular music—United States—History and criticism.   I. Hoffmann, Frank W., 1949– II. Title.   III. Series.
ML400 .P64 2002
782.42164′092′273—dc21
  [B]   2001034858

Contents

Acknowledgments   vii

Editor's Foreword *by Anthony Slide*   ix

Introduction: The Coming of the Crooners *by Ian Whitcomb*   1

1   Gene Austin   51

2   Russ Columbo   85

3   Bing Crosby   97

4   Nick Lucas   131

5   Johnny Marvin   159

6   Rudy Vallee   185

Discography   217

Filmography   295

Bibliography   303

Index   309

About the Authors   321

Acknowledgments

Many subject experts, collectors, and fans of the pioneer recording industry have contributed in some manner to this work. Don Peak, a leading authority on Gene Austin, donated much time to proofing various prepublication drafts. Tor Magnusson, a discographer based in Goteborg, Sweden, provided resource material regarding Austin's recordings and public appearances. His monograph devoted to Austin remains one of the finest discographical studies ever produced. Miles Krueger, head of the Institute of the American Musical, Inc., supplied valuable guidance throughout the project. The institute, founded in 1972 and based in Los Angeles, is one of the largest known archives devoted to cinematic and staged musicals; it also includes materials on theatrical productions in general, the film industry, broadcasting, and world's fairs.

Tim Gracyk, on-line entrepreneur, researcher, writer, and journal editor specializing in the field of pioneer recording, contributed contacts and recording data. George Blau, an Atlanta-based judge, supplied a wealth of recordings and factual information on Art Gillham. Blau's dedication to the preservation of the Gillham legacy runs in the family; his father was the architect of Gillham's home in Atlanta.

Contemporary recording artists greatly assisted in the research process. Ray Campi, early rockabilly and roots music stylist, offered a wealth of anecdotal insights. Paul Dandy contributed an enormous amount of recordings and printed material on all of the book's featured artists. Carrying on in the rich musical tradition of Cliff Edwards, Johnny Marvin, Rudy Vallee, Bing Crosby, and Gene Austin, twenty-year-old Dandy has recorded several albums, including *Vaudeville* (SDG, 1998) and *Wizard Oil* (Unit Three, 1999; distributed by Atlantic Records). They feature many of the classic songs of these artists as sung, yodeled, and crooned by Dandy. Accompanying himself on guitar and ukulele, as well as with a "hot" jazz band, his releases are highly recommended for all who love vaudeville, ragtime, hot jazz, and Dixie blues.

Many thanks go out to my fellow collaborators. Ian Whitcomb generously devoted time and energy that would otherwise have gone into his varied writing, recording, and performing projects. His career as an interpreter of ragtime, crooner standards, and vintage Tin Pan Alley pop music now spans five decades. Jim Bedoian, record collector and head of Take Two Records, provided information on a wide range of recordings from the crooning era. Michael Pitts, a longtime author and expert on film and popular music history, contributed essays on three of the crooners covered in this book. Dick Carty is well known to many record collectors and enthusiasts as a facilitator of research and publication concerned with furthering our understanding of pioneer recording. His selfless dedication within this field—including literature searching, chasing down valuable contacts, and the dissemination of rare recorded material—is legendary to those who share similar interests.

Others contributing recordings and background information on key artists included Mike Kieffer, Jeff Sherman, Way Clark, Bob Henderson, Gary Dial, Bob Pye, and Marc Friend. A special thanks to all family members and other close associates of these people, who have long provided the support necessary to carry out the project.

Editor's Foreword

The series Studies and Documentation in the History of Popular Entertainment provides readers with biographical and autobiographical studies concerning all areas of the genre. The emphasis here is on popular entertainment in the twentieth century, be it the theater, revue, musical comedy, the recording industry, or dance.

In *The Rise of the Crooners*, Michael Pitts and Frank Hoffmann examine the lives and careers of six pioneers in the field: the legendary Gene Austin, Bing Crosby, Rudy Vallee, and Russ Colombo and the underrated Nick Lucas and Johnny Marvin. Lengthy essays document the professional and private worlds of the entertainers, and each chapter is complemented by a complete discography and filmography. The book is prefaced with an entertaining and personalized history of the crooner by singer and musicologist Ian Whitcomb.

Anthony Slide
Series Editor

Introduction: The Coming of the Crooners

Certainly they've gone, like a murmur in the wind. Today in Australia shopping malls are cleared by the playing of crooner tunes. At least, that's what I caught a TV newsperson reporting in a comic-relief item at the end of the usual litany of worldwide death and destruction: "In Sydney, Australia, mall people have solved the problem of teenage loitering after closing time; Bing Crosby recordings are blasted out on big speakers and the result is a kid stampede for the nearest exit."

How low has the once-mighty crooner fallen! A vanished supremacy. Time was, in the early 1950s, when he seemed still secure as the staple of pop music—almost a quarter century since the start of sweet nothings whispered into a microphone for the pleasure of the masses. The year 1925 had seen both the triumph of pop song (as an aid to the selling of products on radio) and the advent of the intimate singer (made possible by electrification). In 1955, with rock already rolling, the crooner was still at it, draped around the mike, mooing his tried and tested balladry—the old story of love gained or lost, of love requited or unrequited, set in the traditional thirty-two bars and supported by those wailing saxophones, squashed brass, and ever so lightly tished and brushed drums. This was the drooping tailgate of the big band era, the comforter of shop-girls and secretaries as they mooned around the ballroom. It was also the

1

bane of old-time British songwriters, stout fellows who'd written for big-chested music hall artistes and for properly trained vocalists. Sensible men, who loved the great outdoors.

My great-uncle Stanley Damerell was one of them. He could never match the slick American stuff so he wrote "Lady of Spain" and "Let's All Sing Like the Birdies Sing." Stanley's attitude toward the Yankee invaders was expressed pithily and frequently by his red-faced colleague Ralph Butler, a songwriter specializing in such subjects as farming and hiking: "This imported drivel consists of nothing more than a continuous lugubrious lamentation by a disappointed lover!" The tirade was delivered in a roast-beefy voice echoing his forebears from the days of Nelson and Drake. All those present in the pub would cheer, and if my great-uncle was present, he'd lift high his beer mug and add something like: "Exactly, old man, these crooners simply won't do! They're not real men, are they? And they're sapping the national virility!" Of course, he and Butler and a host of other interested parties had been mouthing off these sentiments for donkey's years—at least since the 1930s when Crosby had almost boo-boo-booed them out of business.

A revolution was soon to arrive that would wipe them all—drooping crooners and disgruntled songwriters—off the face of pop: rock 'n' roll. It was heralded by Bill Haley, the square dance caller of "Rock Around the Clock," who told of the Great Coming. And then Elvis arrived full of tingling-fresh gargling and hiccuping. Things would never be the same again.

I remember it well. I bought Haley and Presley on 78 rpm and LP disks. I withstood the jeers of the jazz fans at my school. I couldn't express in cold words what attracted me to the rockers. They weren't stating anything of significance, but they shouted it with passion and élan, and they kept on rolling along. At that time nothing else moved.

Oddly enough—or so it seemed to my intellectual side at the time—when Elvis released a slow song, a ballad called "Are You Lonesome Tonight?," I spontaneously fell for this stylistic shift: the sweetly descending melody, the solid supporting chords, and the sincerity of his voice, especially in the narration. The "King of Rock 'n' Roll" had sold me on a 1920s ballad, from the soft underbelly of the Jazz Age. I didn't realize the antiquity of the song at the time, not until I discovered—in the family collection of 78s that accompanied boating trips and picnics on summer days before the war—the records of Gene Austin.

A major event in my life, Austin's voice massaged me with the most glorious oil all through those uneasy last years of adolescence when things my elders said annoyed me. I would go so far as lash out at dear uncles and aunts who had regularly given me presents, accusing them of rampant capitalism and racism and other "isms." When, rightfully banished to my room, I placed the needle on the battered old disk "The Sweetheart of Sigma Chi," I knew I was in for what would later be described as an "instant high." Only this particular needle shot me up into a land of unearthly balm.

So I haunted second-hand shops for more Gene Austins. In so doing I came across his brethren, "Whispering" Jack Smith and "Ukulele Ike." The search continued after I arrived in America in the early 1960s and grew apace even as I passed through a swift life as a rock 'n' roll star. In fact, the rock that followed my era—the whining and finger-pointing, the polemics of Bob Dylan and other journalistic inheritors of the Woody Guthrie tradition of protest and complaint—turned me even more toward the balladeers of the late 1920s, the pioneer crooners. I seemed to be seizing up, to be turning into a reactionary.

But then, as the century turned, I made the surprising and reassuring discovery that Gene Austin, the first million-selling crooner, had employed one Tom Parker as his advance man (i.e., publicist) for his tent show tours of the South. This was the very same Tom Parker who later called himself "Colonel" and managed King Elvis. Maybe that was why Presley recorded "Are You Lonesome Tonight?" Undoubtedly, Parker knew the worth of the solid old songs and their low-breathing interpreters, thereby helping forge a continuum between rock and the crooners of yesteryear. Provided with the right vehicle, Presley could transform the anguished "ouch" of rock into the still, sweet voice of calm.

I hope, by now, I've established my love of pioneer crooners. It seems to me that, like everything fine and rare in our world, this ethereal music scene had a butterfly life: stagnation set in during the 1930s, followed by deterioration in the 1940s and, as already noted, decimation in the 1950s. By and large, the 1920s crooners were free spirits, splendid individualists who were generally permitted to go their idiosyncratic ways, Art Gillham and "Little" Jack Little being notable examples. The reason was probably because the record companies and radio stations had little idea about what exactly was happening—thus, freedom by default. And so all manner of odd charac-

ters were invited to record, including some whose melodies
wobbled but whose pizzazz shined (witness Gillham or Biff Hoffman).

The finest moment for these early crooners came in 1929, just before the stock market crash and the Great Depression that followed.
In the deep night of the 1930s big showbiz corporations, like shep-
herding uncles, took over and provided safe and homogenized entertainment for the whole family. Yet for that brief but glorious prior
period, the croon of pop ruled: songs were still simple and peppy,
bands were still jaunty, and the records sold in the millions. True, it
was an ingenuous time, for the singers had not yet become standardized and the bands not yet steamrollered into the flat chug of
Swing. It was a time of plenty, a violent and corrupt time perhaps,
but also one in which the crooners were able to play a pacifying role.
This could entail restraining musicians who, given half a chance and
a pint of hooch, might break out with dissonant toots of hot jazz,
thus messing up the melodies and rocking the boat till it capsized.

In the corporate 1930s came the first appearance of what would
later be a pop formula—that is, the process of squeezing diversity
through the strainer of familiarity. The resulting familiar figure,
avuncular to a fault, was Bing Crosby, who effectively wiped out
the eccentrics. His astounding success begat a host of little Crosbies,
groaning and trilling and whistling away. It's a nightmare of
crooner-clones all the way through the 1930s and into the 1940s. A
little relief was supplied by the rhythm and blues shouters of the
1940s, and then, in the mid-1950s, came the welcome cold water
splash of unruly rockers.

Quickly, however, the formula reasserted itself and Presley, wild
as he was, defeated diversity by inspiring a host of copycats. The
process had come full circle. This, sadly, is the way mass culture
works.

*   *   *

From a lofty height overlooking the plain of sweeping statements,
it is high time we descended into the lush valley of detail. Our story
begins in the nineteenth century where, in parlors, drawing rooms,
and minstrel shows, the American vernacular singing style was
gradually emerging. It took the technology of the twentieth century
to transform a casual and natural mode of singing into a hot com-
modity that still retained the musical and lyrical sentiments of the
Victorian romantic tradition. Flowers and trees, birds and bees, all

hymned by a friendly modern troubadour, would become perfect material for radio and records. And the American voice, conversational in tone but with a hint of gentility, would be taken up as the lingua franca of popular music. By the 1930s every pop singer tried to sound American. In Britain, however, there was a movement, started by John Buchan (the famous novelist), to hold back the tide.

This is significant. The American accent, like Italian phrasing in opera, became the basis of the classic pop tradition. Even today, few will accept a love song performed, say, in a cut-glass British accent. In nineteenth-century America, the problem was too much of the Italian operatic school and not enough nativism. Society, inclined to be imitative of the Old World, urged singers to develop large and loud voices with lots of ornamentation—appogiature, mordents, portamenti, trills, and so on—and to exult in virtuosity and exhibitionism, forgetting that early Italian opera had been plain and simple, a sort of speak-singing.

In the nineteenth century, not only was there no native school of singing, but refined society tended to view natural, untrained singing as low culture, something associated with saloons and drunks and the ever-threatening mob. Charles Dickens, for example, couldn't abide the noisy and wretched street musicians who continually gathered below his window. They were fine within a music hall, but here, close to his house, they were undermining the bourgeois refinement of his drawing room. Vox populi, it appeared, was not to be tolerated if it desecrated hearth and home.

The seeds of destruction, however, could be discerned beneath the surface of the American popular music scene. The experience of British entertainer Henry Russell, one of the most successful parlor and concert singers of his age, sheds light on this situation. Although he possessed a range of only five notes, they were pearly ones deriving from years of formal training. From 1833 to 1841 he worked the genteel circuit with his songs at the piano; for example, "A Life on the Ocean Wave" and "Woodman, Spare That Tree." Like so many of his European contemporaries, he was shocked by instances of American barbarism, such as rustics who opined that these classical musicians spend the entire concert "jest tunin' up." In New Orleans he was furious at being upstaged by what he described as a "nigger fiddler." Venturing into a Negro church service in New York, he was startled to hear the choir swiftly garble an Old-World psalm into a brand new melody ("The original tune simply ceased to exist!'')[1] As for the Native Americans he came into contact with, they were beyond the pale. He judged their songs to be "hideous noises."

For Louis Frederic Ritter, the Alsatian author of *Music in America* (1883), the defining question was: "Are the Americans up to European standards? Can they emulate us?" His investigations failed to turn up a national folk music. He concluded, "The American landscape is silent; the American country people are not in possession of deep emotional power." And yet many later accounts would describe a crowded and jumping folk culture. These observers would describe a bubbling crucible of embryonic ragtime, jazz, and blues. Country music was in its prehistory, with fiddles and banjos in the hills and mountains and Jew's harps all over the place. At revivalist tent meetings the fervor of the singing was palpable. Then there were songs from mining camps, hobo gatherings, and sailing ships; there were railroad shouts, the call-and-response of the cotton fields, the cowboy ballads of the cattle trail, and even the songs of the anthracite and bituminous industries. And further up the social scale, one mustn't forget the singing societies, the serenaders with their mandolins and guitars, and the barbershop quartets. There certainly was plenty of American music.

What of the singing styles? Was there an embryonic form of crooning? We read that the country folk of hill, mountain, and range sang plainly and without affectation. They stood straight and sang down the nose, often with their eyes shut in modesty. The Hutchinson family from New Hampshire, for example, achieved recognition as a popular touring folk group, singing together in simple harmony. They specialized in morality songs, ranging from the sanctimonious, through the sentimental, to the downright humorous. Their political agenda included temperance and Negro rights. As was pointed out at the time, they "vibrated to every popular breeze."[2]

In the early years of the twentieth century the straightforward, unadorned singing style—the plain truth approach—was to be marshaled for the dissemination of revolutionary socialism. Joe Hill, the songster-martyr of the Wobblies (Independent Workers of the World), appropriated the apolitical singalong and distorted it into an instrument for building a new world out of the ashes of the corrupt American political system. For Hill and his colleagues, songs were the weapons of change. His *Little Red Song Book* was full of tin-der ("to fan the flames of discontent"),[3] and he wasn't squeamish about seizing a current Tin Pan Alley hit and politicizing the lyrics. Thus, Irving Berlin's 1910 ragtime hit "Everybody's Doing It Now" was altered to "Everybody's Joining It—One Big Union."

Such re-working demonstrated the power of song as polemic: the Utah authorities executed Joe Hill in 1915 and he soon became a folk legend, exerting a profound influence on Woody Guthrie, Pete Seeger, and other leaders of the urban folk movement. He anticipated the American protest movement, with songs fired as bullet-notes, and no laughing, no relaxing, no simple happiness.

At the outset of the twentieth century, though, the voices described here—some plain, some angry, some praising the Lord so fervently that the notes got bent and twisted—were operating in an underground; voices in the social wilderness, music not yet in print, let alone recorded. Now we must turn to the great American public, the Everyman and Everywoman who make up that all-important mass market: the middle class and those who aspire to be middle class.

The story of American pop is the story of the city and of the objects you are enticed to buy there. In the parlors and drawing rooms of late Victorian America one could always find a piano, its bench stuffed with sheet music. This material was supplied by a burgeoning music publishing industry based in New York and soon to be called "Tin Pan Alley," the place where the hits are manufactured.

Here inside the Victorian piano bench we can see the Old World giving way to the New, the stiff and starchy to the racy and slangy. First, we find ballads peppered with "thees" and "thous," and lines like "When Aurora empurples the morn"—numbers advertised as "tender, elegant and chaste, and designed to produce a sob."[4] Ladies, mostly younger women, bought this music to perform at social gatherings; many hoped that they might thereby attract a male suitable for husbandry.

Digging deeper, however, we find raunchier items for the males, perhaps acquired as a souvenir of a recent night on the town; for example, "If You Ain't Got No Money Then You Needn't Come Around," "All Coons Look Alike to Me," "Who Dat Say Chicken in De Crowd?" What these earthy songs have in common is the incorporation of the street vernacular—its colloquialisms, quaint phrases, and vulgarities. They reflect the vitality of the big city with its riotous racket created by a throbbing, jostling throng, babbling in countless unknown tongues but united in song by a raggy tune with words like "ain't" and "gonna" and "getcha." This is the real America of the post–Civil War era. Rather than a stilted copy of European high culture, these songs give us the mob, experienced from the safety of the parlor.

To meet the demand for this new type of song, the Tin Pan Alleymen created material that caricatured the immigrants comprising the new America; for example, "Happy Heinie," "Marie from Sunny Italy," "The Yiddish Society Ball." However, the foreigners providing the most highly visible characters for the voice of American pop had resided in the country since its creation: the African Americans. Since its origins in the 1840s, minstrelsy had depicted the black man as an exciting outsider, a devilishly attractive rebel with an equally attractive lackadaisical attitude. Because he'd been denied the main playing field, he could indulge in the sort of fun and games prohibited in mainstream white culture. So "Zip Coon" (a popular minstrel character) was allowed to pleasure himself with any girl in town, while "Old Black Joe" (another favorite) could laze under a Dixie tree, eating possum until he burst in ecstasy. These fantasy characters were necessary for a nation desperately in need of instant mythic heroes (e.g., the frontiersman) and antiheroes (the fantasy Negro).

The slang utilized in the minstrel song became the basis of the "coon" songs of the ragtime era in the late nineteenth century. At the same time, the love ballad flowed sweetly alongside antic ragtime. Stephen Foster, the spiritual father of the two primary streams of pop (the rapid and gurgling, as in "Camptown Races," and the slow and reflective, as in "Beautiful Dreamer"), had died in 1854. Irving Berlin, a master of both genres, is reputed to have kept a framed picture of Foster on the wall above his office desk.

We are now ready for an examination of the singers who performed these twin sides of American pop. Did they use a native style? Or did they still ape the American model? Was it not time to stop being declamatory and start being a little intimate? Was there yet any crooning?

The only crooning in overground pop was that of mammy to baby on the old plantation. You find such material in many a turn-of-the-century sheet; Al Jolson was still mining this vein in the World War I era when he cried for his mammy to "croon a tune" in "Rockabye Your Baby with a Dixie Melody." As to whether singers actually crooned—that is, sang softly in a person-to-person mode—we shall never know, due to the rude intrusion of a mechanical device that converted most Americans into listeners, rather than performers. The phonograph significantly altered the way music was presented to the public; although it provided a permanent audio snapshot, it gives historians a somewhat biased view of the past. We will never know firsthand what the slight or tender of voice sounded like in those days. The recording horn of the pre-1925 acoustic era required leather-lunged belters and shouters, accompanied by vibrant instrumentation.

The recording business bosses had initially assumed (and hoped) that the American public would embrace opera singers and symphony orchestras. They soon learned, however, that the real money was in the "coon shouters" of ragtime—like May Irwin and, later, Sophie Tucker—or the middle ground. The latter consisted of precise renditions of current pop sheet music by a noble band of general utility men, lead by Billy Murray, who handled largely comic material like a hopping, chirrupy bird, and Henry Burr, who took care of sentimental ballads with a trained, dulcet voice in the best drawing room manner. Both of these singers were throw-backs to the post–Civil War popularity of Irish-American tenors, complete with a characteristic high-collar vocal quality and a tendency to roll an awful lot of rrrr's.

Twin pillars of the acoustic era, Murray and Burr barged through the tin horn with a Celtic tenacity. They delivered everything Tin Pan Alley had to offer in workmanlike fashion, varying little from the printer's ink. The talking machine loved them, and they produced thousands of recordings reflecting the many strains of contemporary pop.[5]

If a little subtlety and variety were lost in the heat of the studio encounter, then so be it. Theirs was a tough job, with tremendous stamina needed for the vocal hurling. Poor Murray would later relate that he was sometimes directed to make as many as forty versions of the same song. Understandably then, his characteristic "ping" and sharp accent, which cut nice thick grooves in the wax, were subject to flagging and even ennui. His machine-gun drooped. This was mechanical work in the worst sense of the word—as bad as having a regular job down in the mine, on the farm, or at the conveyer belt. The worker-singers would face a cold horn projecting from a blank wall and try to inject some degree of excitement and conviction into the sheet music facing them. A generally plodding band, jammed into the background space behind the vocalist, would do its job; however, there was little interaction between singer and players in this icy, invisible world. When the operation was over (the wax had not been overrun), there'd be not a clap or congratulatory word, for fear of ruining the master. No wonder that few personality quirks spark out of the finished disks. Sometimes, though, Murray would tweak up the ends of phrases or break into speech, just to show that the recording process was driven by real live folks rather than an army of mechanical midgets.

Still, wasn't it part of the daily struggle, a vital element of the great American work ethic? John Philip Sousa, the renowned American March King, didn't think so. In a journal article entitled "The Menace of Mechanical Music," he spoke for a significant portion of his contemporaries, arguing that talking machines were no substitute for the true-to-life sound of a nightingale's song. "It is the living, breathing example alone that is valuable to the student and can set in motion his creative and performing abilities." He added that these machines, while ingenious, "offer to reduce the expression of music to a mathematical system of megaphones, wheels, cogs, discs, cylinders and all manner of revolving things." Amateur music-making in the home will wither and die, "until there will be left only the mechanical device and the professional executant."[6]

Sousa depicts a future landscape where millions of Murray and Burr records are spinning around the once-singing United States of America, obliterating the amateur parlor singer. In such a setting, those without large larynxes and belligerently thrusting vocal cords would be warned to keep well away. Finally, working himself up into a righteous frenzy, Sousa asks, "Then what of the national throat? Will it not weaken? What of the national chest? Will it not shrink? When a mother can turn on the phonograph, will she croon her baby to slumber with sweet lullabies, or will the infant be put to sleep by machinery?"[7]

Women—at least those within the entertainment world—were not in the vanguard of the crooning movement. The leading female vocalists, most notably Sophie Tucker and Blossom Seeley, were to continue "coon shouting" until it became known as jazz singing. They, not their male counterparts, put the roar into the Roaring Twenties. Thus, on disk, we hear Miss Patricola boasting "I've Got My Habits On," and that she's ready for the "Hot Lips" of a dusky

Southern dude called "Lovin' Sam." Margaret Young, counters with claims concerning the prowess of "Dancin' Dan" and how "He May Be Your Good Man Friday (but He's Mine on Saturday Night)." Marion Harris, who often favored material from African American writers, joined this regiment of red hot jazz babies with such spirited complaints as "I Ain't Got Nobody" and "A Good Man Is Hard to Find."

Why were women, who only a few years back had been quiet and slow-moving ships of stateliness, now so strident and fast? Leaving aside the limitations of acoustic recording (which required a stentorian approach), the answer lies outside of show business. It also proves that good pop mirrors society (albeit with a touch of exaggeration for entertainment purposes). We need to examine the march of the women because, as we shall see, they played a crucial part in the establishment of crooning as a commercial enterprise.

The end of World War I also marked the final dash to victory by the Women's Movement after almost a century of social and political agitation. For a few years, beginning with the "go" of enfranchisement, women had the license to run wild. Some of them did, especially the young ones (named "flappers" from the way they flapped their elbows in jazzy dances like the Charleston). The flapper sported knee-length skirts, taped-down breasts, and boyish short hair. In a more direct assault on public mores she smoked and swore and applied lipstick in public. In 1922—when flappers, vamps, and shebas seemed to be on every movie screen, in every novel and newspaper, and the subject of countless songs—an editorial in *The Pittsburgh Observer* spoke of "a change for the worse, during the past year, in female dress, dancing, manners, and general moral attitudes."[8] Clearly, after a war climaxing decades of reticence and self-sacrifice, the gentler sex wanted in on the action. After all, as recently as the ragtime era women had been arrested for turkey-trotting, smoking, and failing to wear a corset.

Entrenched America need not have worried. Outright rebellion was not on the agenda. The noisy flapper in the tight cloche helmet-hat would soon settle down, ready to become a good consumer in a nation that worshiped at the altar of Big Business. A *New York Times* article of July 1922 prophesied this development: "She'll don knickers and go skiing with you; she'll dive as well as you, perhaps better. . . . Watch her five years from now and then be thankful that she will be the mother of the next generation, with the hypocrisy, fluff, and other 'hookum' worn entirely off. You'll be surprised at what a comfort [she] will be in the days to come!"

By 1927, the year that Gene Austin's "My Blue Heaven"—a hymn of praise to the joys of domesticity—became one of the biggest-selling records of all time, the flapper was consigned to history, replaced by the housewife presiding over a realm filled with creature comforts. The housewife's dedication was to marriage and children, especially when modern family life offered beauty parlors, electric irons, washing machines, and hot water heaters. For an overall enhancement, she turned to entertainment and, in 1927, her hand commanded the radio dial and electrically recorded disks that fed the combination music machine, a beautiful piece of furniture sitting squarely in the living room, an essential for any well-appointed household.

The American female now outnumbered the American male; furthermore, she had become the major purchaser of consumer goods. Almost one quarter of the national income was being spent on leisure activities. The women were paying the piper and, by the late 1920s, they were favoring high-pitched pipers with honeyed voices, men who gently persuaded from radio and record as if whispering mash words into your ear while dancing cheek to cheek.

What sort of a man could act in this manner? What had happened to the pioneer tradition of hardship and danger, of manly men with hair on their chests, of cigar smokers and tobacco chewers? Where was the rugged spirit of Boone, Crockett, and Custer? Gone with the closing of the frontier and inexorable rise of the city. By 1930, only one citizen in four lived in rural areas. Manual workers were in a minority; suited men who worked in offices were the heroes who brought home the bacon (although they'd have been squeamish if forced to witness the killing of the pig). The urbanites of 1927 looked to urbanity as a required quality for the up-to-date American male model. A Yale man would certainly fill the bill. And, in fact, a Yale man with a sweetly sophisticated voice would soon be pleasing the wives greatly. On January 8, 1928, Rudy Vallee opened at New York's Heigh Ho Club. Although he is undyingly associated with the megaphone, he was created by the microphone.

*   *   *

It is now time to move to the technical realm, to a new device lighting up the homes of America, voiced by a magnificent and impressive word: *Superheterodyne*. This heroic vacuum tube, an essential of the blossoming radio and record industries, was the magic aura that allowed the crooner to enter the homes, and capture the hearts, of America's housewives.

Our new world is populated by transmitters, amplifiers, patch bays, line equalizers, modulators—and enunciators. The latter would occupy the central place in this empire of gadgetry; soon it would be known as the microphone. Human voices—first, the announcer, then the general utility singer, and finally the crooner— were soon issuing from this totem pole of mass entertainment.

The radio was an immediate beneficiary of these technological developments. In the early years, however, there were no mellow tones, only a storm of crackle, whistle, and hum. Radio evolved out of the wireless, useful as a form of telephone for ship-to-shore communication and other sensible, practical matters. Operators wore headsets rattling with tinny noises as they tried to make sense out of this static.

Even then, though, seers noted the potential of the wireless. One broadcast technician predicted that the airwaves were likely to become "the ultimate extension of personality in time and space."[9] More to the business point was an extraordinary memo in 1916. David Sarnoff, a Marconi employee who would later go on to build the Radio Corporation of America into a media empire, sent his superiors a description of a vision he'd had about developing the wireless into a "household utility" much like the piano or phonograph. In essence, he viewed the instrument as a means for cultural advancement: "The idea is to bring music into the home by wireless. The receiver can be designed in the form of a simple radio music box. . . ." High culture could be conveyed to the masses, with the result that "the oldest and newest civilizations will throb together at the same intellectual level and to the same artistic emotions."[10]

A fine vision, never to be realized. By 1922, there were indeed plenty of these new "household utilities"—radio sets with proper speakers rather than headsets—pumping out a fairly decent sound. But the sound was not generally that of "good" music. Such music had been offered earlier when the airwaves were full of arias and art songs. The result had been a shattering of vacuum tube filaments and the recoiling of terrified carbon mikes. Radio technology was too sensitive for the likes of serious music.

The trial-and-error of the early 1920s revealed that a natural type of voice—effortlessly modulated rather than classically trained—

was best suited to the radio mike. An everyday, casual, off-the-street and into-your-living room voice. So it was that all manner of folks, including street singers and other rank amateurs, were invited to step up to the mike and deliver. Sometimes, if the scheduled professional performer failed to show up, the engineer filled in with the latest pop hit, accompanied no doubt by a ukulele or some such popular string instrument. Radio, it was soon discovered, needed neither the skills of the concert hall nor those of the vaudeville stage. Rather, it preferred friendliness.

The carbon mike responded best when the voice was projected from a mere six inches away. Accordingly, pop singers and announcers became the mainstay of radio, along with an army of salesmen. By 1925 radio sales and revenue exceeded that of the recording industry, and programming was rapidly becoming standardized. At virtually every station one heard friendly presenters promoting the benefits of goods you never knew you needed, before smoothly segueing into a sweet singer. From snake oil to velvet tones in one easy move.

While Vaughn De Leath could rightly claim to be "The Original Radio Girl" (she had participated in test broadcasts from inventor Lee DeForest's laboratory to an audience of wireless operators at sea in 1920), she was not to reap the benefits of the new medium. First to profit were Tin Pan Alley song pluggers who took to radio like little boys to a lollipop and, in so doing, fashioned a new kind of American vernacular singing that wasn't really jazz, wasn't really folk, and certainly kept a suave distance from the still-bleating minstrel show.

The first plugger-cum-performer to fit the crooner mold and enjoy a notable degree of fame was Jack Smith, "The Whispering Baritone." A tall fellow with almost saturnine features (but tempered by a winning smile) and dark hair slicked back from a well-defined widow's peak, he cut an immaculate and sophisticated figure when completed by his uniform of white tie and tails. But it was not his appearance that made him a stand-out in the overcrowded radioland of New York in 1925, when the airwaves were hot for simple songs from confidential singers who could also double as salesmen. Smith was famous for his sound: a deep-dish voice of clear and quiet authority with an amiable unctuousness that could sell a song or soap without leaving a trace of oil. He talked and sang with such an insinuating seductiveness that female performers found it hard to tell where the song ended and the sales pitch began. Not that it mattered; radio, like the rest of twentieth-century mass media, was really just a new kind of commercial traveler. Unlike the old-time salesman, who had to establish a foot in the door before commencing the oleaginous pitch, the radio personality flew into the home like Santa Claus without a chimney.

Jack Smith was a natural baritone, but it was a German gas attack in World War I that made him a whisperer. His parents, ironically enough, were German immigrants. It wasn't until after the war, when he was an entertainer-at-the-piano in New York cafes and cabarets, that he changed his name from Jacob Schmidt to Jack Smith. His widowed mother had worked hard as a laundress to pay for his piano lessons. Where his perfect diction, clipped but rounded, originated is not known. Certainly, there was still a place in the business for the gentleman performer. Another factor was the absence of public address systems, making it necessary for those with small voices to project with a high degree of enunciation. It's said that Smith's diction was so well developed that he could be heard clearly not only in intimate niteries but in large theaters as well.

As yet he was still one of many entertainers scurrying around the showbiz mecca, trying to be heard in a big way. To make ends meet, he became a song demonstrator at the relatively new music publishing company owned by Irving Berlin. In a little booth, at a studio piano, he plugged his company's products to selected members of the music trade deemed susceptible to his sly and subtle charms. His presentations were diametrically opposed to the hard and passionate selling of an Al Jolson. In order to keep the customer's attention trained on words and melody—rather than the dance possibilities—of the song in question, Smith would restrict his piano playing to the right hand, leaving the left hand free to cup his cheek, thereby completing a picture of good-humored nonchalance.

This ultra-simple performing style was perfect for the ultra-simple type of song being developed for broadcasting needs. Radio executives informed Tin Pan Alley that a range of no more than five melody notes around the middle of the keyboard was most suitable for quality radiophonics.

Expansive vaudevillians, concerned primarily with bludgeoning their audience into loving submission, were generally too loud and intense—as well as too expensive—for the new medium. Furthermore, a considerable number of vaudeville acts were one-dimensional (e.g., animal stunts, jugglers), possessing little or no relationship to singing. Smith, on the other hand, was perfect for radio. In the spring of 1925, after an apprenticeship as an on-the-air plugger, he was invited to become a regular "delineator of song and story" on New York's WMCA, based in the Hotel McAlpin. Here, in a studio the size of an average drawing room (and decorated like one, too), he would go to work by removing the mike from its usual place atop a raised flowerpot stand and placing it on the closed lid of the baby grand piano. When the broadcast light flashed, he'd place his left hand on the industry-approved keyboard range and his other hand on the mike. Then he'd lean in ever so close and start confiding his songs and other wares.

Smith's popularity, particularly among the important ranks of housewives and working girls, impressed Eddie King, manager of the Victor label's popular music division. A sharp operator, with a keen ear for money music, King reckoned that Smith could be marketed nicely as an artist, using the recently developed electrical recording process. In the race to be first, Columbia, a rival outfit, had beaten them to the post by exactly one day with a disk by a hokum performer from the midwest, one Art Gillham, billed as "The Whispering Pianist." Victor would eat them alive. After watching Gillham's version of "Cecilia" sell well, King released a "cover" by his discovery Smith, who was now billed as "The Whispering Baritone." The recording consisted of just a soft voice and a simple piano, along with a crisp sibilance that could be heard deliciously above the usual disk hiss. "Cecilia" was a big hit, and Smith was on his way for a few precious years as a novelty recording artist. He remained a specialty act, not yet referred to as a "crooner" and certainly no vagabond lover oozing out of the ether.

New York, as the center of the entertainment industry, gave Smith a head start over song pluggers with similar stylistic deliveries in other cities. Also, his dapper manner and urbanity fitted him neatly into the requirements of the day. He was to become something of a celebrity, albeit short-lived, featured in movies, sponsored on radio, and an international star. In Britain he became (and still remains) a household name. He would play cabaret and revue in London, record with the Bert Ambrose Orchestra, and become a favorite of the Prince of Wales. The Germans adored him, too.

As previously noted, Smith's ticket to fame, "Cecilia," was not peculiar to him. Art Gillham's story illuminates the hitherto dark passage between the end of ragtime and the beginning of electronic media. Gillham would emerge as a fully wired modern minstrel.[11]

Like Smith, Gillham had been a song plugger, but he'd been operating in the hinterlands years before the New Yorker got in on the act. Gillham was active in local radio as a casual, almost nutty, confider of song and patter, a perambulating character similar to the wandering troubadours of yore.

Chicago, where Gillham headquartered in 1922, considered itself a modern urban center with an entertainment machine every bit as efficient as New York's and with the advantage of a certain rustic edge lacking in the effete civilization of the East Coast. Chicago was situated smack dab in the middle of America's heartland. WLS's National Barn Dance would be started up on Chicago radio; the program invited interpreters of hill and range songs to perform for the public at large via the microphone. It soon became clear that money could be made serving this large radio audience, as listeners tended to remain loyal to what they liked.

Gillham had the right musical roots. Raised in St. Louis, long a hotbed of ragtime, he'd thrown off the regimentation of classical music training by his early teens in order to concentrate on mastering a gut-bucket piano style. In 1914, at the height of the ragtime dance craze, he joined a traveling band. The next year found him in Louisville where, years before, ragtime's first star entertainer, Ben Harney, had cobbled together hit songs from scraps of old Negro refrains. Gillham played a part in publishing a version of "Hesitation Blues,"[12] in direct competition with W. C. Handy, the chief stenographer of this extraordinary art form built around three flattened notes, three notes, and a devilish power to cause otherwise decent people to writhe and squirm.

Art tempered his blues with humor ("I had a sweet mama, so bashful and shy, when she mends her underwear, she plugs the needle's eye") because he was not an anguished soul but a merry minstrel who read *Variety* and followed the trends. In 1919, while temporarily in Los Angeles, he organized Art Gillham's Society Syncopators and had them pose for publicity photos in crazy positions similar to the Original Dixieland Jazz Band, which was then enjoying huge record sales as a trailblazer of the new music.

In 1922, he landed a position as plugger, demonstrator, and part-owner of the Ted Browne Music Company in Chicago.[13] He spent most of his time outside of the office, which was situated above a noisy chop-suey house. One of his responsibilities consisted of dropping by radio station WDAP in the Drake Hotel and demonstrating the latest Ted Browne songs at the piano, live on the air. One afternoon, when the staff singer failed to show up, Art attempted to fill the void on a dare from one of the radio staff members. Although aware that he couldn't hold a note, Gillham was a game little fellow and, setting the mike on the piano, he got real close and affected a combination of singing and conversation. He'd always been a silver-tongued sales patterer, and now he showed off his new trick of playing the tune accurately at the same time that he monologued. When the instrumental passage came up, he exclaimed, "C'mon fingers—percoolate!" This was something novel, yet down-homey.

Listener response was positive and he became a fixture, talking his way into each new plug as if the song he was putting across to his "customers" (as he liked to call his radio audience) had popped into his brain on the way over to the station. He was creating a persona right there on the air; "I'm a broken-down piano player jest tryin' to get by. . . . I'm a fat, bald old fellow who wants his coffee."[14] After a well-clunked piano vamp redolent of Midwest prairie ragtime, he'd launch into a current Ted Browne plug such as "I'm Drifting Back to Dreamland." From nostalgia for the older set, he'd rip into something suggestive for the young folks; for example, "The Deacon Told Me I Was Good" (so says the young maiden after a closed session with her minister), with Art inserting a little scatting—"Doo-di-do-doo!"—during the instrumental break.

Those were the days before network radio and Art took it upon himself—with Ted Browne's blessing—to sally forth on a swing tour of individual stations, ranging from big beamers to one-lung operations, scattered around the country. The radio craze was at its height, and it seemed that everybody was setting up his very own broadcasting outlet. When Art set off on his trip in early 1923, there were stations owned by newspapers, department stores, drug outlets, hospitals, and even a dry-cleaning business. All welcomed the modern troubadour in his guise as a quaint, self-deprecating, bald, and roly-poly salesman, the man with the bag full of hokum and old-time sentiment who could work the mike.

On February 23, 1924, he announced his arrival at WSB, Atlanta, a powerhouse beamer. His persona having preceded him, the WSB staff was taken aback by Gillham in the flesh. He was neither fat nor bald and was certainly no slave to coffee. He was, in fact, trim, thick-haired, and partial to orange juice. And far from being a loser in affairs of the heart, he was happily married, to Mrs. Louisa Canada Gillham, the coloratura soprano, formerly with the San Carlo Opera Company. Getting straight down to business, Art, now titled "Sales Manager," demonstrated two "instant hits": "I Had Someone Else before I Had You (and I'll Have Someone after You're Gone)" and, after the laughter had subsided, "You May Be Lonesome (but You'll Be Lonesome Alone)." During the latter number, Art delivered a beautifully articulated recitation that knocked the station staff dead. Although he smiled and winked after the finish, those who looked closely could make out a pair of worldly wise eyes behind those owlish spectacles.

Mr. Lambdin Kay, director and chief announcer at WSB, recognized a fellow operator. Known to his listeners as "The Little Colonel" (he was, in fact, neither), he shrewdly sized up the situation and, in his capacity as radio editor of *The Atlanta Journal,* published a piece on Art that featured the first use of the sobriquet "The Whispering Pianist." Henceforth, that was his name, and while there would be other "whisperers" in his wake, he was—as he never tired of telling the world—the very first.

Gillham now had his eyes set on a conquest of New York, where other media might avail themselves of his talent and business acumen. As a one-man band who required no help from either agent or manager, he sent telegrams to every recording engineer upon his arrival there in August 1924. The telegrams indicated that "The Whispering Pianist"—the popular radio star whose credits included appearances on more than fifty U.S. stations and fan letters from as far away as New Zealand—would be heard on half-hour programs at noon and 9 P.M. on WJZ for a week. It admonished them to sign him to a contract while he was still available.

Pathé and Okeh took up his offer and cut a few acoustics. It was Frank Walker's experiments at Columbia with Gillham, however, that were to make pop music history. The company had acquired the secrets of the new electrical process and was anxious to show off what they could achieve. Gillham's quirky intimacy was right on the money. Even his lisp on "Cecilia" could be picked up clearly.

Hot on the heels of Gillham's "Cecilia," as previously noted, came the version by Jack Smith. When Smith went on to fame and fortune, Art was accused in some quarters of imitating and a little feud ensued. Columbia ran a trade ad proclaiming its artist to be "Famous

Enough to Be Imitated," while Art himself wrote to *The Music Trade Indicator*, protesting this state of affairs: "I have received word from good authority that this new artist was 'dug up' and promoted for the prime purpose of competing with me and affecting the sales of my phonograph records."[15] Obviously, there was big money to be made in the new "confidential style," especially when it was mass-marketed through electric recordings.

Art needn't have worried unduly; there was room enough for them both. While Smith became the darling of the New York cocktail set and a perennial favorite abroad, Gillham would be cherished by rural audiences, particularly in the Deep South. He remained an exclusive Columbia artist through 1933, even as Bing Crosby and his peers were sweeping the field clean.

A third member of this radiophonic band of song pluggers was Little Jack Little. Born John Leonard in London, England, he was raised in Iowa. Like Gillham, he later moved to Chicago, where he was a demonstrator for local publishers (as well as contributing many of his own compositions) before becoming a radio song salesman. As we have noted, the carbon mike responded best when the singer was close, and Leonard almost caressed it with his lips. A slow exhalation of breath would preface his interpretation of some mundane ballad, the sort of stuff cut by the yard. The music and radio trade appreciated his tongue-in-cheek approach to the clichés of the newly streamlined pop song. They were especially impressed by his simple (but never simplistic) piano playing, with its fiery bursts of Chinesy phrases and ear-trilling cross-hand thumb melodies close to the bass keys.

Soon he was going by the moniker "Little Jack Little, the Friendly Voice of the Cornfields" and establishing himself as a radio fixture of the Midwest. Like Gillham, he coined a collection of signature catch phrases in order to distinguish himself from the clamoring voices already filling the air. A Little Jack Little presentation always opened with "Here 'tis," and closed with "Yours very truly, Little Jack Little." Radio led to records, and these capture the essential pixie-like quality of Little Jack and his featherweight slivers of song.

Eccentric, and often comic, our trio of pioneer crooners was able to romp free for only a few years.[16] As the electronic media of radio and records grew mightier, so the inevitable standardization set in. By 1929 the first wave of crooners had been swept aside on the airwaves by the sudden rise of Rudy Vallee, an authentic Ivy League gentleman with a voice exuding sex appeal—a quality noticeably lacking in Smith, Gillham, and Little.

Unfortunately, there's not much laughter in the sex game. Although Vallee would later develop into a first-class comic character actor, he maintained a poker face as a crooning sensation, letting his wavy voice match his wavy hair. Off the record, he claimed his sex appeal was due to a phallic quality deep in his throat. Be that as it may, his was a voice that began life in his upper head and, proceeding down his nose and into the mike, arrived in American homes with all the authority of lavender and lace. Originally a bandleader broadcasting as a radio "remote" from a New York club, he was being networked around the entire country by 1930. A national institution, he drew sighs from the women and snorts of derision from the men. He was the first swooner-crooner. The word *crooner* was at last established as a part of everyday speech.

By 1932 a backlash had set in against crooners. Rudy Vallee was one thing—a civilized fellow you could invite to the club for a cocktail. But Vallee's chief competitors, Bing Crosby and Russ Columbo, came from more humble stock. Furthermore, a swarm of copycat vocalists was pursuing the big stars, scooping and swooping at melody lines, adding silly little trills and boo-boo-boos, diluting any originality that might have been left in the genre. Mr. and Mrs. America considered this kind of "mechanical toy" crooning to be a social menace, especially now that radio was an essential home appliance. Why, they'd have sold their bathtub before they got rid of the Godlike box, their vital connector to the outside world.

The press had a field day disseminating attacks on the "crooning boom" by moral authorities. In January 1932, newspapers scrambled to quote Boston-based Cardinal O'Connell: "Crooning," he thundered, "is a degenerate form of singing. . . . No true American would practice this base art. I cannot turn the dial without getting these whiners and bleaters defiling the air and crying vapid words to impossible tunes." The New York Singing Teachers Association chimed in, "Crooning corrupts the minds and ideals of the younger generation."[17] Lee DeForest, one of radio's inventors, regretted that his dreams for the "music box" as a dispenser of "golden argosies of tone" had become "a continual drivel of sickening crooning by 'sax' players interlaced with blatant sales talk."[18]

Among these "uncouth sandwich men" was our own Whispering Jack, sonorously pitching a medicated cream especially designed for seniors afflicted in their private parts. In his broadcasts, Jack would skillfully slide from the cream pitch into his next sweet old song: "Can you remember back a few years when I sang this one?" Very hard to remember that far back when there was so much new and exciting stuff pulsing out of the radio, when songs and singers were here today and gone tomorrow.

High in the splendid RCA skyscraper—a "Cathedral of Commerce" solidly imbedded in downtown Manhattan, the capital of both the show and the business—sat, at any hour of the day, David Sarnoff, captain of the industry. He could remember the old days when radio was a muddle of too many stations and too few receivers with good loudspeakers; when most customers were content with old-fashioned horns that made broadcasting sound no better than a wind-up phonograph. As for the murmurings, groanings, and moanings of Crosby and his ilk, Mr. Sarnoff didn't give a fig. In fact, he never listened to the invention he'd steered into the marketplace and thence into the homes of the masses. It was a pity they didn't care for classical music, but one had to respect the rule of numbers. Let them wallow in their sloppy schlock—he would look to the future, gazing out from his paper-free polished desk, past the white oak paneling and fluted Greek columns, to a twinkling skyline made possible by the man-handled miracle of electricity. Sarnoff's mind was not on radio at the moment or on the future of the record company he'd purchased in 1929. He was preoccupied with the next inevitable step in the never-ending effort to keep America constantly buying new technology. Novelty machines for which, no doubt, the public would be sold the same old song and dance. The particular novelty he was setting his mind on was television.

Meanwhile, down below in the battlefield lighting up the Depression, the crooners continued to be winnowed out until only those who sounded sufficiently Bing-like were left in the game of providing the soft soap necessary for easing the nation through the harsh realities of everyday life. Where did a whimsical character like Art Gillham fit in such a womb-like world?

In 1932, a lucrative year for radio, record sales hit an all-time low. Gillham was, by a hair, still represented in the Columbia catalog with the aptly titled "Just a Minute More to Say Goodbye." Wisely, he chose this time to realign the focus of his life, remarrying and settling in Atlanta. He went on to become head of a business college and, at a later date, the owner of an office space rental firm, the Representative's Center.

Jim Walsh, the indefatigable music researcher and contributor to *Hobbies—The Magazine for Collectors,* began corresponding in 1957 with Gillham, who was then retired and residing in an Atlanta suburb with his wife, Gertrude. This was a vintage year for rock 'n' roll with hits by Elvis Presley, Little Richard, Chuck Berry, Jerry Lee Lewis, and other stars. It was also a time, however, for mellow balladeers like Pat Boone and Connie Francis, who successfully revived hits of the 1920s and 1930s. Even Gene Austin, a pioneer crooner, managed to squeeze into the *Billboard* chart with his own composition, "Too Late." Gillham would have made a great narrator on "The Shifting, Whispering Sands," a smash of that year. Jack Smith might have made a more urbane version, but he'd died in 1951, forgotten and alone in a deep melancholy.

Gillham comes across as chipper and modest in his correspondence with Walsh. In his first letter he expresses surprise that anybody would be interested in "my corny recordings." Noting the quality of 1957 releases, he commented, "When I hear the beautiful jobs that are on the market now, I just don't tell anyone that I made records back in the dark ages." However, he was proud to state that he was the artist and writer on the "first electrically recorded record, No. 328-D, for Columbia."

Art's historic disk "You May Be Lonesome (but You'll Be Lonesome Alone)" reflects the fact that disks, not radio, constitute the legacy—the documentary evidence—of the pioneer crooners. That so many of the disks remain both fascinates and moves me. Somebody paid good money for these records back in the 1920s or early 1930s, when the singers could have been heard on radio for free. Somebody had to have and hold these performances as they might a loved one. To possess and perhaps to be possessed. To use alone in a cold water flat or to share with family and friends at a house party. Whatever the function of the records, their crooners were viewed at the time as a passing fancy, a mere fad. In 1932, the *New York Times* reassured its readers: "They sing like that because they can't help it. Their style is beginning to go out of fashion. . . . Crooners will soon go the way of tandem bicycles, mah jongg and midget golf."[19]

So much for ephemeral radio. But the black shellac 78 rpm disks with their appetizing graphics can live forever, if handled with care. Material objects with wise old facial lines in their grooves, quite unlike the smooth and bland compact disk. You can't see the sound of a CD, so how can you be sure it isn't just magic? Grooved disks, however, testify—and not only when revealed by a needle. Many are worn and scarred by years of giving pleasure—joy, comfort, laughter, grateful tears—so that they now present the listener with a monster bacon-and-egg frying noise. Clearly, somebody loved them.

Walsh, in the September 1957 issue of *Hobbies*, provides a glimpse of one such record lover. He recalled a chat with a "veteran record dealer" about how silly the young girls were becoming over Elvis the Pelvis. "Did I ever tell you," smiled the dealer, "about the girl who had a crush on 'The Whispering Pianist,' Art Gillham?" One summer morning in 1929, she entered his store and asked to audition the new Gillham release. The dealer, considering it to be "a syrupy thing," merely sniffed. In a stifling air-tight booth she played that record over and over, from nine o'clock until two-thirty in the afternoon. Once or twice she came out for water. "I thought I'd go nuts!" said the dealer. The title was "I Love You—I Love You—I Love You, Sweetheart of All My Dreams."

Now I happen to be very partial to the Gillham version of this much-recorded song, a straightforward, no-conditions-attached declaration of utter and complete love. Rudy Vallee had the big hit, while Johnny Marvin turned in a workmanlike job with his light tenor tripping along to a bouncy accompaniment. Gillham's interpretation, though, is captivating because, as usual, he begs winsomely for our attention. He clearly got one girl's attention on that summer day in 1929, and I believe he'll continue to work his skills into the new millennium and beyond.

Here's the tableau: With the violin taking care of the melody, Art is free to mold the rather mundane verse into an inspired monologue—a plea that only the coldest-hearted listener can resist. Away go the printed lyrics and in comes Art with a personal entreaty: "Listen sweetheart, why are you sad and blue? Please come over here dear. . . . Sit down real close to me. . . . Let me tell you how I feel. . . ." With the melting well under way, he heads into the chorus, his trademark quavering singing made acceptable by the sincerity of his delivery. A cleanly picked guitar supplies Art with all the sweet harmony he needs. Then suddenly, in the last chorus, he surprises with a special patter lyric, doubling the word flow, pledging to love her morning, noon, and night; promising to let her do anything she likes and—what's even more important—to *say* anything she likes.

Note that Art keeps his lovey-dovey talk down to earth (e.g., he employs the phrase "real close" rather than the grammatically correct "really close") in keeping with his disk persona as a folksy downhomer of the old school who, although still loaded with prewar pathos, can nevertheless play some pretty peppy barrelhouse piano should the occasion arise. He bends the Jazz Age over to embrace the old-time verities.

Gillham's claim to the contrary, apparently nobody knows for certain when the first commercial electric recordings appeared; I'm not about to risk a pin-pointing, only to be raspberried later by some dedicated disk sleuth armed with facts and figures to prove me wrong. Somehow I want to trust Art; perhaps it's the avuncular honesty of his recorded voice.

A number of facts, however, can be ascertained concerning the evolution of "ortho" recordings. By "ortho" I mean sound that shoots straight as an arrow into one's heart, sound that is "right" in the ethical sense of "honest and faithful." The Victor label, which coined the word *orthophonic* may have inferred a different meaning, but to me it is synonymous with the warm, tubby electric 78s of the late 1920s onward. With the arrival of hi-fi the expansiveness shrinks; today's CDs seem thin, reedy, and shrill. Perhaps the secret of the warmth lies in the human sound box of the period; that is, in cultural considerations, rather than the cool and clever science of mankind.

It appears that the first electric recording was made in Britain in 1920 as a limited pressing by Columbia. The session was supervised by two unlikely engineers, the Honorable Lionel Guest and his friend Captain H. O. Merriman. Their offering was the hymn "Abide with Me," performed at Westminster Abbey by a choir and congregation, with instrumental accompaniment by the band of His Majesty's Grenadier Guards. I've no idea how the record sounded. I only know what it looks like and that the engineers employed a telephone mouthpiece rather than a microphone. That may have been a fatal mistake. Suffice it to say that the British effort led to no further progress along these lines. (This may have been due in part to the fact that, being upper-class Englishmen, they were amateur explorers rather than professional exploiters.)

Over in America, however, at the Western Electric research division of Bell Telephone Laboratories (part of the mighty AT&T combine), scientists took note of the British experiment. The trick was to convert real sounds into electrical impulses via the medium of the microphone and thence through an amplifying vacuum tube (like radio) and finally back to life again as seemingly real (or even improved) sound.

Sometime in 1924, with the sales of both records and phonographs plunging to unprecedented lows, the scientists demonstrated their electric test disks to Victor executives. It was an astonishing experience; for the first time you could hear the high end of the sound spectrum (a little shrill, it is true) and a gut-shaking bass response (rather boomy, to be sure). Above all, the sound was amazingly loud and brimming with energy. The scientists pointed out that their electrics reproduced $5^1/2$ octaves as opposed to the mere 3 of the then-current acoustics. It was all mind-boggling, but there were other considerations pressing in on the executives once they'd left the lab and returned to their desks.

Victor was burdened with loads of hardware and software sitting in warehouses (not to mention stock in retail outlets). So its executives hummed and they hawed. While they procrastinated, the scientists took their formula over to Columbia Records, a company sorely in need of a sales attraction. A licensing deal was struck and Columbia was experimenting with the new process by the fall of 1924. (Gillham volunteered to act as a guinea pig, participating in a week of tests under the supervision of Frank Walker, the label's music chief.) Victor finally saw the light and made a hasty deal. The other record industry giant, Edison Records, gamely stuck to its trusted acoustic process.

Owner Thomas A. Edison—who operated with a hands-on policy, preferring the talking machine to all his other inventions—loved machinery far above electronics. He loved to see the music go round and round. He loved music more than money-making because, as he said (and said again, as electronics and big corporations engulfed his simple world of shining individuals):

> Of all the various forms of entertainment in the home, I know of nothing that compares with music. It is safe and sane; appeals to all the finer emotions; tends to bind family influences with a wholesomeness that links old and young together. If you will consider for a moment how universally the old heart songs are loved in the home, you will realize what a deep hold music has in the affections of the people.[20]

The old man professed to know what his people ought to like. Why, the selfsame parlor songs he's sung and cherished as far back as the Civil War. Pretty melodies with moving lyrics: "Beautiful Dreamer," "Silver Threads among the Gold," and "I'll Take You Home Again, Kathleen" (he'd requested this one for his funeral). Songs of nostalgia for a better time in a better place, far from today's madcap cash chase to a syncopated jazz rhythm.

Even as late as 1926, when almost every label had gone electric, Edison was still holding out despite pleas from his employees to reconsider. A Mr. Miller wrote him in Memo #749: "Don't you think we could make some royalty arrangement with A.T. & T. for the use of this system?" The old gent scribbled his reply straight onto the note: "I could have taken this up without paying anybody. . . . They cannot record without distortion."[21] He chose instead to introduce Diamond Discs for playing in beautifully crafted cabinets such as the Louis XVI model in Circassian Walnut.

Edison would eventually surrender to the blessed vacuum tube, but shortly thereafter his precious company gave up the ghost, a victim of the stock market crash of 1929. The new system, perfect for tearing hot dance bands and intimate warblers, represented a trend that couldn't be bucked. Nevertheless, I admire Edison for his tenacity and strong moral stance. I'm sure that if he'd lent an ear to a Gillham, Smith, or Little, he would soon have succumbed to their mother's milk music. After all, they, too, were advocates of simple, clear melodies, with the added bonus (thanks to electricity) of a thick bed of harmony set on wheels by a sturdy bass line.[22]

Electric recording couldn't have arrived at a better time. The record industry, which had enjoyed peak sales of more than 100 million in 1921, was in a frightful slump by 1925. Why buy a tinny disk when you got better fidelity on radio, and for free? In the spring of 1925 the first electric releases from Columbia and Victor hit the market, but existing phonographs made them sound harsh at the top and muddy at the bottom. New hardware was necessary—another boon for the industry. Victor led the sales parade, proclaiming November 2 to be "Victor Day." Long lines formed outside stores for the heavily advertised demonstrations of the Orthophonic Victrola. Record sales started rising once more, continuing an upward swing through 1929 but still way below the 1921 high-water mark. Radio was the mass medium of preference; the Talkies were hot on their tail.

The label managers and their vocal talent recognized that it was a whole new ballgame. Embryonic crooners were ready to display hitherto unrequired talents—their sss's and hhh's. But what of the battle-scarred veterans from the days of tinhorn penetration? What about Billy Murray, Henry Burr, Irving Kaufman, Frank Crumit, and Cliff Edwards, to name a few of those noble warriors? One of their number, Franklyn Baur, was greatly relieved regarding the turn of events. In 1927 he found new fame as first tenor of the mellifluous close harmony group the Revelers. Now he could sing unencumbered. Later, he told the press: "The strain on the singer is immeasurably eased. A record can be made in exactly one-third the time it used to take, and no longer is it necessary for us to nearly crack our throats singing into that hated horn."[23] Nor would there be any more of the physical humiliation of the old days, when singers had to duck down during an instrumental passage or be shoved by the recording director so as to be close enough to the horn for low notes (and then yanked back for the high ones).

In the new age, there were new reasons for the recording managers—not known for their gentleness and consideration in the handling of artists—to goad and intimidate their charges. Victor's Eddie King, pushing for more breathiness from Murray during the "Roll 'Em Girls" session, was countered by a remonstration from the venerable vocalist: "Heck, I'm no crooner!"[24] Unfortunately, the results proved him right; Murray was obviously holding back, a self-bridling horse, once so free and frisky, now so stilted.[25]

The same applied to Burr and the rest of those stout-hearted men. By reining in their former attacking style, they lost their potency. There was, furthermore, the harsh reality that the great days of the Irish-American tenors—the kind who rigidly punched out sentimental ballads or else comic songs of the ethnic and minstrel variety—were over and done with, despite Mr. Edison's dream wishes. True, the early electrics didn't do justice to the old-fashioned, leather-lunged tenors. Nat Shilkret, the Victor musical director, admitted as much: "Tenors gave us plenty of grief for a while. At first they sounded rather thick, like baritones; at times they were hollow. But all voices were finally conquered."[26]

The conquest by condenser, vacuum, and amplifier revealed starkly that certain veteran voices were married for life to the old horn; no amount of play-acting could endow them with the geniality and naturalness of a Smith, Gillham, or Little. An electric Murray sounds like an acoustic Murray, except that now the band is plump and spread nicely around the room, while Murray is a rail-thin pixie trapped in a box.

Musically speaking, it must have been galling for Burr, a master of perfect intonation, to be outsold by Gillham, with his trail of wounded notes. But the fact was that the Whispering Pianist's small voice and limited range were assets as far as the all-important lady customers were concerned. For here was humanity, here was vulnerability, here was a fellow clearly suffering (e.g., the 1928 Columbia release "Nobody's Lonesome but Me") and, therefore, in need of succoring. On the other hand, Burr has a high-collar concert platform manner as he sings of foraging in a cheap store and eventually lighting on an ideal chicken behind the counter in the china department ("I Found a Million Dollar Baby [in a Five and Ten Cent Store]," Victor, 1926). He simply cannot be believed.

While the sharp-eared mike made some of the old gang from the acoustic era sound like charlatans trapped in a lead pipe, others were liberated by the new conditions. Frank Crumit is a case in point. From 1919 onward, he'd been belting out Alley material with the best of them and seemed like one of the boys.[27] Now, thanks to modern magic, he was metamorphosed into a sophisticated man-about-town, a character of silky charm with a voice of attractive nasality, redolent of the cigarette holder and the nineteenth hole. His subtle phrasing and pleasing timbre, delivered easily by the mike, allowed him to move smoothly from Stephen Foster to the Gershwin brothers, with time for such novelties as "Nettie Is the Nit-Wit of the Networks."

Crumit's freedom extended to radio, where he went on to become a network fixture on quiz shows with his singing wife, Julia Sanderson. It's odd that Gene Austin, another acoustical artist freed by electricity, never made it big in radio. Of all the pioneer crooners, Austin had, I believe, the most beautiful voice and the most relaxing style. He also sold more records than any other performer of the late 1920s. Why no regular radio show for him? Perhaps he loved the road too much, taking his trail-blazing to excess. Despite his million-selling anthem of domestic bliss "My Blue Heaven" (1927), he was a rolling stone, gathering and shedding quite a few wives along the way. Happily, they all remained in his circle of friends. It seems he had a very generous nature (and was an easy touch). He comes across as an all-round good fellow in his recordings.

Cliff Edwards ("Ukulele Ike") also made the great electrical leap. Unlike the other early crooners, he had a reputation for jazziness and it was all his own, owing nothing to black Americans. His special trick was to break into nonsense syllables, later to be termed "scat" singing. However, Edwards insisted on calling it "eefing," a continuation of Gene Greene's ragtime pig Latin that dated back at least to the 1890s, when Ben Harney introduced the ragtime song onstage at Tony Pastor's vaudeville house in New York.

Edwards's "eefing" adds a nicely sour aspect to the otherwise sweet portrait of domesticity in "Halfway to Heaven" (Columbia, 1928). He sings of a "cottage small," surrounded by flirting butterflies where, inside, the little lady is cooking and also looking out the window for Cliff's return, signaled by his guttural moaning, his "eefing." Unfortunately, the lovely picture painted on record was not reflected in Edwards's real life. Like Gene Austin, he had a string of ex-wives, but in his case they weren't all friendly. Chicago, for example, was forbidden territory because there lurked an ex-wife with a judgment out against the cheerful crooner.

Unlike the previous entertainers, "Whispering" Jack Smith had no experience as an acoustical artist. His urbane murmurings would have made little impression on the needle. The mike, though, was ready for every shade of his breathing and he took full advantage of that, often insinuating a little wicked humor into otherwise standard songs. His version of "Baby Face" rolls merrily along until the tail, when Jack suddenly stings with "But at the break of dawn, with all your make-up gone, oh! What a face!"

Off the record, Smith was deeply disturbed about something. So much so that he took to the bottle and was the despair of his manager. At one point, in the early 1930s, he threatened to throw himself out of his hotel window. Saved in the nick of time by his manager and valet, the next thing they knew he'd disappeared from the face of the earth, only to reappear the worse for drink. Was he reacting to the domination of Crosby and company? Or was it something deeper, an insight into the ultimate chaos of life? Behind Jack's svelte and steady tones I detect a hint of the sinister. In 1951 he died, alone and forgotten, watching a basketball game in his New York apartment.

Little Jack Little was to become a melancholic, probably due to neglect. Shifting styles left him stranded, like others gifted with a fragile, will-o'-the-wisp talent. His recordings capture a rather hyper personality with a pronunciation so precise you fear there's a break-down on the horizon. His extraordinary reading of "Are You Lone-some Tonight?" (Columbia, 1927) shows him at his most impish, leaning on his words, tilting them for fun (or devilishness?), and dis-playing a split personality at the keyboard: his legato lower register lines are suddenly and brutishly assaulted by cascades of chromat-ics. Clearly, it's Jack who's lonesome to the bone. In 1956 he commit-ted suicide at his home in Hollywood, Florida.

None of our early microphone masters paid any attention to sex appeal. Here we are in the late 1920s, with Clara Bow as the "It Girl" on the screen, while Mae West, on Broadway, is celebrating the flesh in her play *Sex*. Yet our crooners come across as whimpering wets! The masculine ideal had changed considerably since the turn of the century, when the muscular type held sway over women's hearts. In the 1920s the male star prototype softened, melting from He-Man into Dream-Boy, from husky George O'Brien into pretty Buddy Rogers. *Variety*, always aware of trends, explained the rise of the softer image as an effort to "compensate for the hard sexiness of fe-males, on-screen and off."[28]

Songwriters, often good mirrors of mass opinion, were already poking fun at what appeared to be a very un-American androgyny: girls with boyish short hair, boys in billowing baggy pants falling just short of skirtdom. Lyricist Edgar Leslie, a seasoned Alleyman, documented the situation in his 1925 hit "Masculine Women! Femi-nine Men!" Sister Susie's learning to shave, while her brother adores his permanent wave: "Once you used to kiss your little sweetie in the hall—Now you'll find that you are kissing her brother Paul." Leslie's Alley associate Con Conrad, composer of "Margie" and "Ma! He's Making Eyes at Me," was soon in demand as a provider of "special material" for the proliferating "drag" and "pansy" en-tertainment circuit of New York and other big cities.

Surprisingly, there had been a general tacit open-mindedness concerning the more outlandish aspects of homosexuality, going back at least as far as the Victorian era. "Fairies" and "sissies" (as they were termed) were "worthy of mercy," provided they were ob-vious and out there—and not in the home. The New York of the 1900s had enjoyed drag balls at Madison Square Garden, attended by high society (including Astors and Vanderbilts). During the Jazz Age, there was a vogue for "pansy" clubs and revues, highlighted in 1927 by Mae West's theatrical extravaganza *The Drag*, which featured forty fruity chorus boys tossing off one-liners like "When I walk up 10th Avenue, I can smell the meat sizzling in Hell's Kitchen" and describing a ball gown as "trimmed with excitement in front." In mainstream vaudeville, stars like Frank Fay and Jack Benny displayed the limp wrist and undulating walk for laughs and, in Benny's case, for character creation.[29]

Now this is not to suggest that America was going gay (in fact, there was to be a mighty backlash during the 1930s); rather, I am simply setting the scene for the social acceptance of high-pitched male singers, even as microphone technology was making possible the broadcast and recording of deeper and wider tones. How else could one account for this golden age of the high tenor? Or the heaven-stroking sound of a Nick Lucas or a Morton Downey? A possible explanation: For centuries the high voice had been the hallmark of both the Italian bel canto (Lucas) and the Irish ballad (Downey) style. Could the tenors simply have been continuing the great traditions? Yes, but now we're in ethnic and specialty fields. Our story is about mass appeal.

None of the previous factors can completely explain the grip that Rudy Vallee had on millions of American females—from girls and wives to elderly matrons—as 1929 sank from an everybody-happy high through the stock market crash and into the Great Depression. Such a grip had this seemingly epicene boy of wavy hair and wavy voice that bosums stirred and real men expectorated when radios poured him out, that newspapers warned of the "Vallee Peril" caused by this "punk from Maine" with the "dripping voice," that mounted police were called up to beat back crowds of screaming and swooning females at his vaudeville appearances, that the trailer for his first movie, *The Vagabond Lover*, exclaimed, "Men Hate Him! Women Love Him!" Jimmy Durante, an earthy entertainer of the old school, put the men's complaint succinctly: "He became an epidemic or national calamity or something, because your girl friends were always wondering why you don't croon the way he does."[30]

Martha Gellhorn—who later married Ernest Hemingway, paradigm of machismo—argued, in a 1929 magazine article entitled, "Rudy Vallee, God's Gift to Us Girls," that the gift was actually nonthreatening. In truth, he was a sweetie who meant no harm, right from the moment he announced that floating "Heigh ho, everybody" at the opening of his popular radio show, beamed in from the New York nightclub where, surrounded by a nice-looking collegiate band, he stood like a statue and crooned—almost keened—with eyes closed tight and head up at the ceiling. In his arms he cradled only a saxophone. Afterward, he was always available for interviews. The boy liked to talk. He was, he said, "pouring out [my] soul" into the song. All he was interested in were songs and saxophones.

Indeed, there was nothing very sexy in his face, hair, or body. He was the epitome of the clean-cut college boy. The secret of the allure lay in his supremely radiophonic voice, a perfect match for the mikes, amps, and loudspeakers of the period. Hardware was getting better all the time—the latest offering being an all-electric radiophonograph, a great improvement on every old radio or record player. Watch out for announcements of new developments! So, for the moment, Rudy was in the right place at the right time, both sociologically and technologically. This point was underscored by a 1929 *Literary Digest* article called, "New Rudy Vallee Voice Is Catnip."

The way the catnip worked was effectively described at the time by William Bolitho:

> By the divine accident or miracle, that is what makes art nearer religion than science, the voice that starts its strange journey at the microphone hardly more than banal fills the air at its destination with some sort of beauty, and with that rarest charm of beauty—uniqueness, novelty. His voice is a new sound.[31]

The sweeping success of this novelty voice inevitably leveled the field. The quirky Gillhams and Smiths were to be sidelined. On came a host of soft modulators, singing excessively of arms and charms and moon and June, following the lead role played by the well-bred, almost bland, New Englander Vallee.

Chester Gaylord was "The Whispering Serenader," so they made Nick Lucas "The Crooning Troubador." Eddie Walters introduced a modernistic tone of campiness, while Les Backer brought the old chestnut "You Tell Me Your Dream" up-to-the-minute in a creamy treatment. Bostonian Jack Miller, later to be a noted conductor, was rumored to be a pseudonym for Vallee, so like the star did he sound on his self-penned "From Sunrise to Sunset." "Crooning" Andy Razaf was really Fats Waller's songwriting partner. Freddie Rose, riding high and smooth on disk, would later adapt his Alley abilities to publishing, where he cofounded the pioneer Nashville firm of Acuff-Rose. Sam Coslow, who had demonstrated for Edison and would go on to write Crosby anthems like "Learn to Croon," was joined by Alley colleague Sammy Fain, then billed on disk as "The Crooning Composer" and hot with "Wedding Bells (Are Breaking Up That Old Gang of Mine)." As Jimmy Durante was fond of saying, "Everybody wants to be in the act!"

During that fateful year of 1929, "Whispering" Jack Smith, holding fast in his inimitable manner, released a superb sermon in song, "She's a New Kind of Old-Fashioned Girl," reassuring parents that the dangerous jazz baby had been successfully reformed and was now saying the same prayers as her mother. But what did the women themselves have to say about their situation? After all, they were past masters: they'd been crooning to their babies since the closure of the Garden of Eden. And in the early Jazz Age they'd been extremely vociferous, if not downright noisy.

For the most part they were trudging along, carrying torches for unattainable loved ones, moaning low even as their men sang high. Of all those brash Jazz Age babies, only Sophie Tucker still stood high and proud. She'd been a star since the days of "coon shouting," introducing her ragtimey signature tune "Some of These Days" back in 1910. Here in 1929 she was boasting, "I'm the Last of the Red Hot Mamas" and claiming that her kisses could burn off a guy's mustache. In the Tucker world, men were submissive creatures. Her accompanist, the loyal Ted Shapiro, would often hum and murmur alongside her, like a sailboat bobbing in the shadow of a battleship.

Blossom Seeley, the lone rival to Tucker, had also come up through ragtime and then burst out as a jazz baby. She, too, employed a male assistant, in this case her husband, Benny Fields. A Vitaphone short of the period shows them at work; Seeley is demonstrative and brassy, while Fields fans her dotingly, singing responses to her fevered vocal in a distinctly croonerish way. He'd been doing this for years. His husky, easy-going delivery leads one to believe he was a Crosby forerunner, favoring the deeper register as opposed to the characteristic 1920s tenor. In other ways, Fields is quite unlike Crosby—the fawning places him squarely in the Vallee camp as just another emasculated male.

The hits of the day continued to speak of male submission; for example, "Guilty," "I'm Confessin'," "Just One More Chance," and "Prisoner of Love." Furthermore, one Ellen O'Grady, in a letter to the *New York Times* responding to the news that President Hoover had invited Rudy Vallee to "sing a song to chase depression," claimed that crooners were creating a "depression of spirit." In her opinion, this wasn't surprising since *Webster's Dictionary* defined crooning as "a continuous hollow sound, as cattle in pain; to bellow."

Interestingly, the image of the effete male in popular culture starts to be shattered during the Great Depression. On the cinema screen, tough guys appear: James Cagney squashes a grapefruit into his girl's face because she's talking too much during breakfast; Clark Gable reveals he's wearing no undershirt; and Humphrey Bogart is getting ready to sneer and snarl. In real life the public exhibition of homosexuality is made taboo.

Leaving the bigger picture to social historians, it's now time to concentrate on the new breed of crooners, tracing how and why public taste shifted from high tenors to husky baritones. By 1932, a crooning triumvirate was generally acknowledged. Dick Robertson's recording "Crosby, Columbo & Vallee" (Romeo, 1931) had satirized this sorry state of affairs, telling bachelors and married men to "stick together" and fight these "public enemies" who, sneaking in over the radio, are "stealing all our blondes" and "breaking up our happy homes." In the days before radio ruled, recalls Dick Robertson with manly nostalgia, you threw a gigolo out into the alley, but "now you can't say a word."

Rudy Vallee was soon to drop out of the triumvirate, and he knew it. Besides, he had other talents and he wanted to display them, rather than being remaindered as a lover-boy. The picture of the soulful youth, with golden hair and blue eyes, piping in a garden of classic columns and splashing fountain (a favorite setting for movies and stage appearances), he represented a hangover from the 1920s, a romantic ideal of gentility and inaction.

In contrast, Bing Crosby and Russ Columbo looked and sounded like they might have the right tools for plumbing the Great Depression. They made no pretenses about having Ivy League credentials; they did not sport Frenchified surnames. They were men who worked, and they showed it.

Columbo had a solid working-class Italian Catholic background. His violin playing was offset by a great physique, especially evident in broad shoulders more typical of a halfback.[32] As a sideman with Gus Arnheim's orchestra in the late 1920s, he'd played the obedient member of the vocal trio—a then-fashionable adjunct to nightclub ensemble—warbling like a trained canary. When Crosby hit it big in the early 1930s, Columbo, following the fashion, lowered his voice to sound more virile.

Bing Crosby, of course, never seemed to make any conscious changes. Training was not in his line—he just naturally sang as he did. Unlike Gillham, Austin, Smith, Little, Vallee, or Columbo, he played no instrument—unless you count kazoo and sock cymbal. He never bothered to read music, not even a top line melody. Nor did he ever rehearse a song all the way through. He was a stroller and a whistler, an average all-round good guy. The women set their sights on this casual creature. The men weren't jealous—they could identify with him, whereas Vallee was high up on a damned Greek pedestal.

Bing (what a sensibly low-faluting name!) was Irish-Catholic and, like Columbo, from the lower class. Yes, he'd been to college, but, unlike Vallee with his obsession over the classical meanderings and ragtimey novelties of famed saxophonist Rudy Wiedoeft (he even took the star's first name), Bing had followed the more masculine pursuit of hot jazz. For hot jazz involved not only music but also girls and booze. He and his buddy Al Rinker (later his partner in Paul Whiteman's Rhythm Boys) had snapped up every "eefing" Cliff Edwards record immediately upon release. In their vaudeville act Bing scatted the "bop-bop-de-do-do" like any wild and crazy jazz boy should do. Off-stage he behaved likewise, liquoring up and running into cop trouble. The avant-garde crowd at Berkeley, a hep campus down the road apiece from Crosby and Rinker's Northwest home stomping ground, relished Bing's lazy but heated stage manner. He was in the vanguard of "cool" and "laid back." He was way ahead of the game.

Rudy Vallee, no slouch when it came to spotting trends, recognized the Crosby insouciance early on. In 1927 Vallee was gigging as a Ben Bernie sideman at a debutante party in a Baltimore gym; the band was taking a break, letting the Rhythm Boys entertain off on the side. Nobody was paying much attention until Bing stepped into the center of the gym and sang a solo ballad. There was no mike, not even a megaphone. Vallee would later write: "When he had finished, there was a deafening roar of applause which would have called for at least one or two encores. Instead, he walked off the floor past where we sat, his classic features expressionless, his patrician nose just a bit up in the air. You might have thought him deaf, so unaware he seemed of the sensation he had created."[33]

Bing's walk may have seemed snooty, but clearly he had the common touch. After a stint with Gus Arnheim at the Cocoanut Grove in Hollywood (where he lived up to his nickname of "Binge" in hoarse readings of ballads spiced with ribald interpolations, most notably on "What Is It?"), he quickly rose to network radio fame, movie stardom, and, most important, a pivotal role as a savior of the record industry. On the eve of World War II, when the public was sorely in need of a reassuring presence, Bing was established as a corporate image: an all-round entertainer, safe and fully tested, perfect for the entire family. Gone were the melodramatic night cries for "Just One More Chance"; instead, listeners were presented with a carefully packaged, happy-go-lucky chap who wore sloppy clothes and loved sports. Crosby Inc. covered every base; you could buy him singing Irish, Hawaiian, Dixie, Hillbilly, and even Christmas songs. He would also be the first king of World Music, tourist-style. Whatever the category, Crosby, like an alchemist, transformed his songs into easy-listening. Wherever you were, you could be sure that, like a McDonald's in Moscow, the fare would be normal and standard in tone.

Crosby would escape the confines of the 1930s school of crooning, something none of his contemporaries were able to do. In later years, resting comfortably as an institution, he poked fun at his days as a crooning sensation. He talked of a "hot mush" in a throat containing frogs caused by late night carousing.[34] He would protest that he was really nothing special because "most people who've ever sung in a kitchen quartet or in a showerbath sing like me."[35] But behind the relaxed vocals stalked another Crosby, a shrewd and canny business tycoon with eyes always alert to the main chance: old Rhythm Boy pals were discarded when no longer useful and reporters were treated with kid gloves. When asked for advice on breath control, diction, and intonation by a neophyte singer, "The Groaner" replied, "Sing from the belly—That's where the money is."[36] This public manner took a private toll. Hotel rooms where Crosby had stayed were littered with broken or chewed pencils.

As a vocal heavyweight and acceptable Average Joe of the Depression, Crosby was safe from the humiliations suffered by Vallee. The press could imagine Crosby and Columbo as working stiffs, but Vallee and the other high tenors had all the earmarks of drones. Could they mend a fuse or change a tire? On January 23, 1931, the *New York Times* reported gleefully that among the important events of the last few days had been a Boston concert at which Mr. Rudy Vallee was the "target for two large grapefruits that had seen better days." The perpetrators, the reporter was happy to state, "got off with a police lecture." The number that had triggered the incident was "Oh Give Me Something to Remember You By." Had the guilty parties, Ivy League undergraduates, been offended by the dangling preposition? Or by the preposterous figure of Vallee, limp of bearing and singing like a contented nanny goat, performing piffle while the world whirled into an abyss?

Vallee would reflect on the grapefruit matter in his memoir, *My Time Is Your Time*, "I was pretty damn shaken, I can tell you." Nevertheless, he ordered the show to carry on, and then: "I launched into an all-out impression of Al Jolson, theorizing that my previous vocalizing perhaps had been lacking in virility and masculinity." If he couldn't persuade the public that he was "one of the guys," at least he could attempt to show that he was a real guy and not a nancy-boy. But what the hell—there were other ways to make a living, and Vallee proved his worth in a subsequent career as a network radio show host and a comic character actor of stage and screen. A listening session with a stack of Crosby records later in 1931 had convinced him that "this young man was going to push Pappy Vallee right off his throne!"[37]

His time was up, and so, almost, is mine. I could examine every document of this age of crooners, could read every newspaper item, watch every newsreel, listen to every transcription of old-time radio shows, and gaze at photos in the hope that they'd speak but never reach the heart of popular taste in order to discover the exact cause of the pumping.[38] Vox populi cannot give answers; the entertainers speak for the people, and then only obliquely, mysteriously.

After Russ Columbo was killed in 1934, it was clear sailing for Crosby. He would, of course, be followed by the aforementioned little Bings, tootling along in imitation.[39] And so, over the years the parade of pop moved efficiently through the ooze until, in the mid-1950s, in a Sargasso Sea of its own making, the righteous wrath of another America sent down the Great Flood of Rock 'n' Roll.

*   *   *

Completing the evolutionary cycle described here, I return to my passionate friendship with the frozen voices of long ago. To at last being given permission by the vice-headmaster of my prep school to—very carefully—place the tone arm of his radio-gram (a beautiful piece of polished walnut, glowing from its front panel with names of faraway places like Hilversum and Moscow, and humming from the back, should you crawl there, with a yellow ochre city of vacuum tubes that we knew as "valves") onto a fragile 78 rpm disk, to watch the disk revolve placidly until, after a few reassuring crackles and clicks, the magic unwound.

Then to stretch out on his carpet and wallow in the comfy, tubby sound as Frank Crumit (pronounced "Croomit" in England and beloved there by every class) and his guitar took me "Riding Down to Bangor" in a tale of boy-meets-girl, but which didn't attract me half as much as the silky lure of that singular voice. Outside, the weather was, as so often in those gloomy postwar years, "inclement" (the preferred word of vice-headmaster Captain T. D. Manning, which took on a distinctively blurred tone when growled through the clenched jaw holding his ever-present pipe), but the dinning of the rain on the corrugated iron of Manning's study only served to reinforce the siren call of the 78, commanding me somewhere far from the bitter, sighing coast of Seaford, Sussex, England, the World, 1949.

On a summer afternoon a few years later, I'm lying at the bottom of a punt on a little man-made lake at a holiday village by the Suffolk coast. The water laps around me in a romantic manner, but I'm paying no attention because, from a portable wind-up HMV gramophone, Bing Crosby is winning me to "Galway Bay" and, on the other side, to a "Home on the Range." Both spots seem considerably more appetizing than my current position as an overweight schoolboy enjoying none of the perks of being a teenager. Where did Crosby and Crumit live? Inside the gramophone, of course, behind the curtain.

Now I'm on the edge of the 1960s, having put away the conceit of the previous as childishness and confronting the question of what on earth to do in life. Why, go back to school, but to a school hiding behind the name of "university." I decided on an odd institution but one that was easy to enter: Trinity College in Dublin. Gene Austin inspired the move, singing from a snappy electric Dansette portable, bouncing around the thick-carpeted family flat on Putney Heath, London: "Each sweet co-ed like a rainblown trail . . . ("The Sweetheart of Sigma Chi").

Crooners even accompanied me in the midst of a rock 'n' roll career as a "One Hit Wonder," their records a solace to the pressures
of trying to keep on the charts, telling me the same old story of love
under the moon and the stars, in a shady nook, by a waterfall, in a
gypsy tea room, in a little hula heaven, in a shelter from a shower, on
a dream ranch, or by the seaside, where the waves are whispering
goodnight so sweetly that I'll forget they've changed my name to a
number. . . .

Such a dangerously mawkish attachment to pop music long past
its shelf life was tempered by encounters in the 1970s with still-liv-
ing crooners. There was also the incident with Vicki, a girlfriend of
the time. We were walking hand in hand along a beach, and I, as
was usual when conversation had ground to a halt, started murmur-
ing the words to an old song—in this case, the chorus of "You Were
Meant for Me." I had reached "You were all the sweet things rolled
into one," when Vicki stopped dead in her tracks, fixed me straight
in the eyes, and said, "You really meant that! How wonderful!" I
was stunned and terribly embarrassed, all the while dreading that
the next move expected of me might well be an engagement pro-
posal. Thus was I warned of the dangers inherent in unconsidered
crooning.

Safely back in America, and deep into research for *After the Ball*,
my book on the history of pop music, I had the opportunity to spend
a crowded day with Rudy Vallee, an expert on the potency of lyrics.
I had been staying in Hollywood with music business friends;
they'd suggested I simply ring the old man up. His number, after
all, was listed in the phone book. He craved an audience, said my
friends. Recently, he'd been in the papers as a result of his campaign
to get the name of his street changed from Pyramid Drive to Rue de
Vallee. When the authorities refused his request, Vallee threatened
to change his name to Rudy Pyramid.

I rang him up and, in a hearty voice, he invited me up to his house
for tennis and dinner. Arriving on the dot at the wild and wooded
estate located on the peak of a Hollywood hill, I saw no sign of the
Vagabond Lover. No doubt he was out and about, living up to his
name. I wandered the grounds, under the watch of Latino servants,
admiring the garage's revolving driveway and the tennis court
perched on the hilltop's edge, over the official Rudy Vallee museum
and library. I noted the public pay telephone, kiosks scattered about,
and the metal signs stuck in flower beds informing smokers to mind
their manners.

Eventually, the crooner, accompanied by his glamorous blonde wife, made a breezy entrance. He was fresh from ocean cruising and ready for champagne and caviar. Following this morning snack, we knuckled down to some tennis. Vallee made up the rules as we played, and they were generally in his favor. He did, however, grant me a few points. Afterward, he led me on a tour of the archives under the tennis court, where he lectured boomingly on the collection of megaphones, saxophones, and stacks of scrapbooks documenting every known reference to the Vallee name in print.

Inside the mansion was more champagne, followed by a one-man show starring my host: now telling how he'd made love to a famous silent screen siren on her floor, now tooting a saxophone in the manner of Rudy Wiedoeft, now singing of his bedding Dolores Del Rio, now reciting "How Fights Start in Bars," and finishing with a virtuoso performance of "The Old Sow," compete with realistic pig and whistle noises. At long last, with midnight approaching, we had dinner at a banquet table that seemed a mile long. Just Rudy, his wife, and me. He was at the other end of the table; I knew he must be there because his red plaid dinner jacket shone brightly and I could occasionally make out bits of gossip concerning the sex lives of certain household names in the world of show biz. When I heard snoring, I knew it was time to leave. There were an awful lot of dogs to negotiate my way through, but their mood was friendly.

Many years—and several dogs—later I inherited a delightful mixed-breed from Vallee's widow, the blonde of that memorable day. Inspector, she said, had been Rudy's favorite and was at his master's side, licking his face, when he died watching his old friend Ronald Reagan deliver a presidential speech on television. The animal came with a few meager belongings—a red leather leash and matching collar, a packet of frankfurters, a megaphone, and a portfolio of photos showing the dog munching tapes of Vallee's radio shows, cocking an ear at the star as he lay slumped in an armchair, and attempting to terrorize a pant-suited Dorothy Lamour. He indicated no interest at all when I screened *The Vagabond Lover.*

My relationship with Nick Lucas was friendlier, but nothing like so grand. We met in professional circumstances at the Mayfair Music Hall in Santa Monica, where we were both appearing as performers. He was always spruce, clear-spoken, and chipper in spirit. In 1975, I arranged for Nick to be filmed as part of a television series on which I was working, a British-made history of popular music called, *All You Need Is Love*. News of his camera-ready perkiness spread, and I was able to get him into an Irish-made documentary on Hollywood characters. We filmed him in the garden of his apartment building, a suitable spot for tiptoeing through the tulips despite being encircled by a growing, vociferous army of ne'er-do-wells and graffiti artists. In addition to his signature song, "Tiptoe," he sang "Baby Face," inviting me to join him with my ukulele on the second chorus. "Remember to play the right chords," he admonished me as the clapper was about to crash down on its board.

A few years later we were on the same bill at the Variety Arts Roof Garden in downtown Los Angeles. Again, he invited me to play along with him. Again, he mentioned the chords, underlining their importance because tonight we would be playing "Tiptoe": "A lot of artists don't use the correct chords, you know." But I must have done OK because he gave me the wink. I was touched by his on-stage reference to not minding Tiny Tim's version: "You see, folks, I smile every time I go to the bank." As a songwriter, I knew that he never received a penny in royalties from "Tiptoe" because he'd had no part in its composition or publication. Unlike many other star singers of his day (including Vallee and Austin), Lucas refused to take a cut-in as reward for exposing a song to a mass audience.

Compared to the splendor of the Vallee lifestyle, Lucas lived quite modestly. I believe he had a lady admirer who lived out in Hemet. I remember he would drive out there from time to time. Every so often we'd meet for lunch at the place of his choice, a cafeteria patronized by senior citizens on limited budgets. Over chicken pot pie or Salisbury steak, I'd pepper Nick with questions concerning his glory days. But he never seemed particularly interested; he wasn't forthcoming and couldn't remember dates (I had to supply them). He expressed only mild surprise when I informed him that his guest shot on Nashville's *Grand Ole Opry* in its earliest days had had a tremendous influence on future generations of country-western performers. Nick quickly turned the table talk to more immediate matters, like how much I was currently being paid for gigs at the Mayfair or Roof Garden. The last time I sang with him was outdoors at a Republican rally of some kind on the lot of a Ford auto dealership in a rather insalubrious part of Hollywood.

I had a brief encounter with Sam Coslow (our Edison assistant, side-of-the-mouth crooner, and Crosby songwriter). By this time—the early 1970s—he was a wealthy retired music executive living in

Florida and a regular traveler to London, Paris, Rome, and what-have-you. We were having cocktails and canapés at the Savoy Hotel when I congratulated him on his kinship with hippiedom: he'd written one of the first overground druggie songs, "Marahuana," for the 1930s Paramount picture *Murder at the Vanities.* He quickly lowered his cocktail. What *was* I talking about? And then he changed the subject. But he was very kind to me later on when, back in Hollywood, I found myself on the wrong side of an exposé news rag editor who threatened me with a sleaze attack. I called Sam at his Florida home and he arranged for some large men to pay a visit to the muckraking editor. Nothing more was heard; nor did I ever see or hear from Coslow again. I wish I'd asked him more questions about those crooning years.

And I wish I'd known that Cliff Edwards was a few blocks down the street from me, ending his days in virtual poverty. He died in July 1971, a charity case, at the Virgil Convalescent Hospital in Hollywood. I wish I'd known that Gene Austin was not far away, over in nearby Palm Springs, entertaining strangers at the electric organ of his mobile home. He was to die in January 1972; Nick Lucas was one of the pallbearers. These men of song could have steered me straight, wised me up, dressed me down. I could have learned a lot.

Now I'm something of a lone contender in an empty ring. Of course, the recordings of the dead masters lie waiting and ready to prove their point; meanwhile, I battle on as a live performer, singing out of style in a confidential, conversational manner. Am I merely retro, or am I simply expressing myself in the only way I can, following in the steps of the great masters?

Is crooning an art in the aesthetic sense? Can it be a thing of beauty with universal appeal and significance? Can it be transcendental? All I know is that I keep coming back to the singers and songs of this tradition whenever I'm caught in a wave of happiness or sadness. Fortunately, sadness rhymes with gladness, and jolly with melancholy, and so it goes, beautifully and naturally. This funny little self-contained world—archaic, no doubt, and far from the rant and cant and brown of today—continues to hold me, for better or worse, in peaceful captivity.

And when, lying at rest, I try to conjure up the essence of that world, I start with a memory from years ago: A muggy summer night in North London, after a quick storm. Streets slippery with grease, lined with rows of nondescript Victorian attached houses, grim and forbidding. I'm hurrying to catch the tube train for home, weighed down with old records just purchased from local dealers, 78 rpm buffs of uncertain age, wearing stained clothing and with remains of meals stuck to their faces and beards. Glancing to my left, through an open door and into a parlor, I spy an old woman sitting in profile on a sofa. She's leaning forward, hands clasped in front, listening intently while nodding and smiling, to music from a wind-up gramophone facing her. I recognize the voice of Al Bowlly, but I don't know the song. From the shadows I watch her in what seems to be a moment of precious lost time recaptured. The lyrics have something to do with a past longing at a dance. When the waltz comes to an end, the woman turns around and stares out the front door, into the wet and steamy street, straight through me. She is silently crying. I hurry on, moved and slightly embarrassed. I make a mental note to check up on this spellbinding waltz.

It turned out to be "I'm Saving the Last Waltz for You," written by Jos. Geo. Gilbert and Horatio Nicholls (two old hands at the British pop ballad) and recorded in London on July 1, 1938, by Felix Mendelssohn & His Orchestra, with vocal refrain by Al Bowlly. A catchy tune in a time-honored pattern, with old warhorse words like *arms* and *longing* and *forsake,* as well as two redundant uses of *just* and a pseudo-poetic line construction ("In your arms I'm just longing to be"). So says the critical self.

But the emotional self—the one that unabashedly accepts love, pity, and nostalgia—knocks down the critical self and takes in the sincerity of Bowlly and the poignancy of the song's story: He's been looking at her all evening through, as she dances with everyone but him. Even so, he's saved the last waltz especially for her. A forlorn but brave hope. Yes, the critical self gets up off the floor to demand why Al didn't simply go over and ask her for a dance much earlier in the evening. Very sensible, but beside the point in the world of the sentimental song. When you're enraptured, you don't reason why, you let your emotions transport you to that ineffable place from which you hope never to return.

*   *   *

NOTES

1. Ian Whitcomb. *After The Ball: Pop Music from Rag to Rock.* London, 1972, p. 17.

2. George McDonald-Brown. *Song-Catching in America*. Edinburgh, 1846, p. 38.

3. Joe Hill. *The Little Red Song Book*. Seattle, 1914, p. 1.

4. Catalog of latest songs published by White, Smith & Perry, 1876.

5. Mention must be made of Gene Greene, the self-styled "Ragtime King." A maverick of the acoustic era, his extraordinary recording of "King of the Bungaloos" reveals little respect for the composer's ink, tearing the sheet into ragtime tatters and providing us with the earliest example of "scat" singing on disk. Here is no Murray or Burr—here is a wonderful madness. Since he'd co-written "Bungaloo" (with his friend and piano accompanist Charley Straight), he was entitled to destroy it by the use of gobbledygook. But in the process he builds a startling eccentric, part human, part animal, part bubbling baby.

In no way is he anticipating the crooner. Like the other horn blasters, he knows about the necessity to bleat and bluster in order to make that needle vibrate. His originality lies in the asides; a free spirit emerges between the official phrases when, playing an exalted African ruler riding across the Nile on his very own crocodile, he ejaculates a "zumm-zumm!" and an "uh-huh!" with all the roar of an early motorcycle. Indulging himself in an orgy of odd sounds made purely for their own sake and not for sense, an assault of hot flourishes that reel and rock us with delight, he is the very essence of what true jazz should be. Vernacular gone crazy.

During the second chorus Greene proves he's far from finished, employing a sort of Pig Latin ("When I ri-ger-dide across the mighty Niger-dile") followed by a volley of pure blather ("Im-bong-bung-bung zoodle-um-bo!") and punctuated by his taxi horn impression. Or is it something else? Maybe I'm being too wordy in trying to analyze the objects in Greene's wonderland. Maybe I should simply lie back and luxuriate in his tub of abstraction. At this point in the record, however, there's a reference to *eefin'*, the word later used by Cliff Edwards (a jazzy singer-cum-crooner best known as "Ukulele Ike") to describe scat.

Greene was a vaudeville headliner during the heyday of the ragtime craze (the decade prior to America's entry into World War I). He was particularly popular in England, where he headlined at London music halls and recorded extensively for Pathé. A true ragtimer, never a balladeer, his energy and easy—if eccentric—flow of language comes across as modern, whereas other American ragtime invaders of the period sound stilted and unnatural. Take, for example, the American Ragtime Octette, the rage of London in 1913, and its recording of "Oh, You Beautiful Doll," a vehicle for rag vernacular if there ever was one: "fire" is pronounced as "fie-yore" and "desire" as "dee-zy-yore." The octette, like most of the theatrical ragtimers, seemed unable (or unwilling) to shake off the European conservatory style of the nineteenth century.

Greene is notable in that he sings squarely in a truly American manner, albeit within the hidebound "darky" conventions of the minstrel show. Owing little to European models, his gurgling hustle-bustle breaks through the grim castle walls of the tin horn recording device, proving that true personality could be registered on an acoustic disk. But you had to be noticed. You had to do battle.

"The Ragtime King" continued to battle to be noticed well into the late 1920s, when the Jazz Age was giving way to softer sounds. Although his approach had fallen out of fashion in the trendy urban centers, he could still find fans in the South who treasured that old rag pizzazz. All around Dixie he toured in a vast auto emblazoned with a hand-painted sign, stating that he was "The Human Singing Machine," which, of course, he certainly was *not* in his heyday. But an old vaude dog has to bark for attention, and so there was Greene, in a clashingly colored carpet suit, animatedly informing dull-eyed theater managers how he'd fill their houses to bursting point. On stage, he gave all he'd got, strutting about in a tried-and-true outfit of straw hat, blue blazer, and white trousers, testifying to the supremacy of anything below the Mason-Dixon line, and making the point quite clear with his cane.

A *Billboard* reviewer wrote that Greene's act was "old and decrepit" and in need of updating (June 13, 1928, p. 34). You had to be "modernistic"— this was the general trade consensus in the late 1920s, when electronic media (radio, records, talkies) were in the process of destroying vaudeville. In 1930 Greene was in New York, appearing at a tucked-away venue calling itself the Grand Opera House. Now he was billing himself as "The Western Al Jolson." The trouble was that there was only one Al Jolson, and he, too, would soon be having box-office problems. The 1930s demanded smaller egos with gentle and caressing voices. A sound to take to bed and help see one through the long, dark night. "Actor Dies as He Leaves Stage" read a small item in the *New York Times* for Sunday, April 6, 1930.

6. H. Watts. *Gramophone Topics*. London, 1912, p. 113.

7. Watts, *Gramophone Topics*, p. 113.

8. *Pittsburgh Observer*, September 2, 1922.

9. Byron T. Hawkins quote: *The Marconi Telegram* (April 19, 1916).

10. Internal memo by David Sarnoff, June 5, 1916. Quoted in Ian Whitcomb, *After The Ball: Pop Music from Rag to Rock*. London, 1972, p. 110.

11. I am indebted to George Blau of Atlanta for a goldmine of information regarding Art Gillham. As a boy he knew Art and soon started collecting his records, as well as taping his piano playing at parties and gatherings. Blau recently inherited Gillham's scrapbook, a worthy addition to his collection of Gillham acetates, sheet music, and a final taped interview.

12. I assume Art was in Louisville at this point, but the problem is that the 1915 version, published by Billy Smythe (a pal of Art's) only credits

Smythe and a certain Scott Middleton. Reputedly, Smythe and Middleton went on to California with Gillham, but there the trio's trail disappears. Smythe turns up playing piano on Gillham's last commercial release, a Bluebird record made at a hotel in San Antonio, Texas, in 1934. Meanwhile, Art's name was added to the writer credits of "Hesitation Blues" on its republication in 1924 by the Jack Mills Company of New York, an outfit specializing in blues and black music in general. (Jack Mills's brother Irving cowrote "Lovesick Blues" and went on to manage Duke Ellington.) By this time Gillham had recorded his first version of "Hesitation" for Gennett, the feisty little label in Richmond, Indiana, specializing in jazz, gospel, Klan anthems, and hillbilly. It may never have been released, since copies haven't showed up as yet. In February 1925 he recorded "Hesitation" again, this time as an electric for Columbia, and it was released. A rollicking version full of amusing couplets and backed by cracking good piano, it's not quite the same as the original 1915 Billy Smythe publication. Nor is it the same as W. C. Handy's. This is probably because, like so much early and rootsy pop, "Hesitation" (or "Hesitating," as Handy had it) was a "floating" folk song (i.e., of no known authorship). Performers, amateur and professional, contributed their own lines and melody switches to the tried-and-true blues, a form that seems to have surfaced around the first years of the century as a ribald "slow drag" dance-song accompaniment to the inviting movements of a sporting house tart. Variations of "Hesitation" can be found in collections of black folk songs published in the middle 1920s, and they are noted as having been found or collected in Southern states between 1915 and 1917. Indeed, the Smythe publication invites customers to write in for ninety-nine extra "all funny" couplets. Had these Southerners learned "Hesitation" from the published versions or were they re-creating by polishing and then passing on their efforts to the world in the time-honored folk process, in which copyright and royalties play no part?

My guess is that Gillham and Smythe picked up a version of the song while they were living in St. Louis in 1914. That was the year when "Hesitation" waltzes were the rage and, therefore, our blues is probably a saucy comment on the dance fad (which is, anyway, suggestive of a lover teetering on the brink of a dive into sex). We know that Art met Billy shortly before 1914, when Art was enrolled at St. Louis University and Billy was already a local music publisher (he'd published his "Ten Penny Rag" in 1911). Maybe Billy, the older of the two pals, taught Art how to rag at the piano, for Billy was an active St. Louis pianist and the city was known for its ragtime. (Tom Turpin, pioneer rag composer and performer, ran a popular saloon there in the 1890s, and before that he'd played at the notorious Castle Club, a luxurious brothel patronized by the local big-wigs, where songs like "Ta-Ra-Ra-Bom-Deray," "A Hot Time in the Old Town Tonight," and "Frankie and Johnny" had been introduced in all their original dirtiness. In addition, John

Stark, publisher of Scott Joplin, moved his business to St. Louis in the early 1900s.)

13. Ted Browne's real name was Fred Brownold. He'd been a ragtime composer in turn-of-the-century St. Louis, when John Stark published his "Manhattan Rag" (1905). Two years later he wrote "That Rag," a collection of melodies that had been floating around the ragtime world of saloons and sporting houses. Sometime later he moved to Chicago and started his own publishing company. The trail of Browne, Smythe, and Gillham shows the connection between Victorian ragtime and Jazz Age electronics, from music paper to radio's ether.

14. *RadioDoings* (Los Angeles), (March 17, 1922): 36.

15. *The Music Trade Indicator* (New York) (October 1924): 27.

16. It's nice to learn from Art Gillham (on his home recordings of the 1950s) that he considered Jack Smith and Jack Little to be his good pals. Gene Austin was part of the gang, too, joining Art for a chin-wag on Atlanta radio station, WQXI, in 1953. I wonder if record and radio executives were as fraternal. Somehow I doubt it.

17. "These Pesky Crooners," *Air Time* (Los Angeles) (December 5, 1932): 13.

18. "These Pesky Crooners," p. 14.

19. *New York Times*, November 2, 1932, p. 18.

20. Edison Records catalog (Spring 1925), p. 43.

21. Internal Edison Company memo, January 14, 1926 (source: Dick Carty archives).

22. My surmise is compromised somewhat by the fact that Edison had no ear for harmony. Sam Coslow—later to become an arch-crooner (with a way of mooing from the side of his mouth) and a writer of the Crosby hit "Learn to Croon"—writes in his memoirs that he worked as Edison's song-scout in the early 1920s. The great inventor judged a new song by its tune alone; harmonies were forbidden. When Coslow picked out "Carolina in the Morning" (soon to become a smash hit in 1923), the naked melody sounded so see-saw monotonous that Edison rejected it, just as he'd rejected Rachmaninoff for playing too loudly ("You call yourself a pianist?!") and Al Jolson's brother Harry for being a "Jew trying to sound like a Negro" (internal memorandums from Thomas Edison, February 24, 1923).

23. "An Hour with Franklyn Baur," *The Long Beach Press-Telegram*, May 10, 1927, p. 68.

24. Frank Hoffmann, Dick Carty, and Quentin Riggs. *Billy Murray: The Phonograph Industry's First Great Recording Artist*. Lanham, MD: Scarecrow, 1997, p. 110.

25. Victor soon replaced Murray—both as a premier solo artist and Aileen Stanley's singing partner—with the more orthophonic Johnny Marvin.

26. Nat Shilkret interview, *Record Spinner* (London) (July 10, 1949): 37.

27. Crumit's delivery on "My Honey's Lovin' Arms" (Columbia, 1922) reflected a self-conscious effort to mimic the big-voiced acoustic era singers. He is dead on the beat, military style, rolling his r's and exhibiting a pronounced nasal tone.

28. *Variety* (New York), October 6, 1929, p. 51.

29. A Paramount musical short from that period featured Frances Williams gaily singing of problems with her current boyfriend, who keeps demanding, "Let's don't and say we did." John Gilbert, then a handsome screen idol, is her delight, but "It seems my boyfriend likes him, too."

30. Jimmy Durante. *Night Clubs*. London, 1936, p. 115.

31. Edward B. Marks. *They All Sang*. New York, 1935, p. 217. William Bolitho quote.

32. In the 1933 movie *Broadway through a Keyhole,* a young woman intently appraises Columbo during a nightclub scene as he leads the band, fiddle tucked underneath his arm. Approvingly, she delivers her verdict: "He doesn't *look* like a crooner."

33. Rudy Vallee. *My Time Is Your Time*. New York, 1962, p. 76.

34. Max Jones interview, *Melody Maker* (London) (April 1, 1956): 28.

35. Max Jones interview, p. 28.

36. Max Jones interview, p. 28.

37. Rudy Vallee, op. cit., p. 80.

38. A simple technological point may provide one answer. Around 1932, condenser microphones and loudspeakers with a warmer bass response were introduced; this favored baritones. In particular, jukebox sound cones seemed to resonate with loving sympathy whenever a Crosby vocal provided them with that certain huff of sugared energy.

39. Not all 1930s crooners were Crosby imitators. Notable among the few originals was Britain's Al Bowlly, the African–born singer who recorded over 1,000 sides between 1927 and 1941 (when he was killed in his London flat by a bomb blast during an air raid). His material ranged from standard Tin Pan Alley material to the comparative exoticism of Africaan and Jewish numbers (even including a couple of Shakespeare sonnets). His voice had a steady quality all its own, with a hint of Cockney, and women in great swarms were overcome. A simple soul who was fond of boxing and always wore a gold crucifix, he reportedly was so moved by some of the ballads he was assigned to record that he'd dissolve into tears during the studio session. Good for him! A shining example of the ability of pop songs to be as powerful as "serious" music.

Much as I admire him, Bowlly played an unfortunate part in my romantic life. In the 1980s I was dating a voluptuous Malibu woman who was attracted to all things British and kept telling me so. One night, when our affair had hit the rocks, she dismissed me from her court with the taunt that my singing couldn't touch Al Bowlly's: "That man is a master of the bedroom!" To be beaten by a phantom lover! Again, evidence of the power of pop.

1

Gene Austin

Lemuel Eugene Lucas, better known as Gene Austin, was born June 24, 1900, in Gainesville, located in the Red River Valley of north Texas. He was the only child of Nova and Belle Lucas, both Missouri natives. Nova, the son of George Washington and Kate Lucas, would die in 1943, long after he and Belle were divorced. Belle, the daughter of Alva and Elmansa Hearrel, was a descendent of a famous Shoshone maiden, Sacajawea, her great-great grandmother. Sacajawea—known as the "Bird Woman" and celebrated for her courage, resourcefulness, and good humor—accompanied Lewis and Clark in their expedition from North Dakota to the Pacific Coast, 1800–1806. Belle would die August 3, 1956, and be buried alongside Nova in Gainesville.

In his autobiography, Gene would recall those early developmental years with considerable fondness.

My Texas childhood . . . was rich in the stuff that mattered most to a small boy at the start of the twentieth century. Plenty of room to grow in, fresh air and sunshine, nourishing simple food, friendly neighbors, pleasant climate, horses, cattle, rabbits, chickens; and most of all, first-hand contact with the singing cowboys. It was a typical Mark Twain childhood.[1]

Gainesville was located in cattle country crossed by the Chisholm Trail, the fabled thoroughfare traveled by cowboys and steers on the way to the stockyards of the Upper Midwest. While still a toddler, Gene would wander off to the Trail while his mother was engaged in chores, drawn to the Western trail songs sung by the cowboys during the cattle drives. His access to this music, however, was cut short by Belle, who, upon hearing these songs re-enacted at home by Gene, denied him access to "that dreadful trail where any bolting steer could trample my child to death, or gore him!"[2]

Restricted from enjoying one form of forbidden fruit, Gene substituted another in short order, gravitating to the parlor houses located on a few side streets of the town, which presided over a thriving prostitution trade. Hearing the exotic improvisations of the piano-playing "professors," he inched his way up to the stoop, eventually being invited inside by the friendly occupants. This district became the new center of Gene's life, and he curried favor by running errands for the professors and attractive ladies of the night. His mother's suspicions were again aroused when he echoed this new music at home; despite his evasive responses to her inquiries, she soon discovered the source of his new material, and once again he was denied access to what he perceived to be an innocent pleasure.

Gene, however, had greater distractions to deal with at this time. His parents didn't get along. The headstrong Belle, who longed for adventure and travel, had tired of life with Nova, a gentle soul who was unwilling to assert his preordained authority. Acquiring a divorce, Belle took Gene off for a prolonged visit with her relatives, an unruly lot given to extended bouts of arguing and fighting. She eventually returned to Gainesville and, in short order, decided to marry a blacksmith named Jim Austin. Jim insisted soon after the marriage that his young stepson adopt the Austin family name.

Although a county seat, Gainesville was small enough to afford daily encounters between Belle, Jim, and Nova. It appears that this circumstance played a large role in Jim's decision to move his family to Louisiana and open his own "smithy." Gene would later relate that he instantly disliked his new home in the swampy village of Yellow Pine.

> The air was heavy, the shadows thick and plentiful, the sky visible only in patches, the rains frequent, the insects, heat and humidity unbearable; this could never replace what I had left behind. What a change! Then and there whatever feeling I could have had for Big Jim vanished. To me it seemed my adventurous days were over, because

the area was infested with snakes and alligators, creatures I didn't like; and there were bogs, quagmires and quicksand. Also, I couldn't understand the people, who spoke unlike us Texans; and worst of all, I couldn't hear any of my favorite music. . . . All I heard was Mother nagging me to go to school; and after school, Big Jim ordering me to make myself useful around the shop.[3]

To make matters worse, Jim began drinking heavily, and "nice" families shunned the Austins due to their humble working-class background. As a result, Gene instinctively withdrew into a shell.

While loitering after school in order to delay the inevitability of chores in the forge, Gene discovered the songs of cotton pickers working the nearby plantations. One of the workers, a kindly old black man named Esau, befriended Gene after hearing him singing along to the music. Over his parent's protestations, Gene regularly visited Esau's shanty in "The Quarter" for the next ten years. "Uncle Esau" provided the human dignity and understanding Gene required in the face of a steady stream of beatings and verbal abuse at home.

By his early teens, Gene had become big and strong enough to stand up to his stepfather. When Jim came at him one day, threatening to beat the music out of him, Gene's rebellious spirit surged to the fore. "You an' that ol' smithy can go to the devil! I've taken my last punishment from you," Gene snarled back.[4] After an evening stopover with Uncle Esau, Gene went to the local railroad yard in order to catch the first freight train passing through Yellow Pine. His brief adventure as a runaway took him back to Gainesville, where he became reacquainted with his natural father, Nova Lucas. A fracas with one of the town's leading businessmen, a Colonel Mills, however, resulted in his father advising him to return to Jim and Belle.

But Gene's inability to submit to his stepfather's enforced regimen of physical labor, without the pleasures of Uncle Esau's company and plantation music, caused him to leave home again shortly after his return. Hopping a train that carried him deep into the heart of Texas, he began fraternizing with the professors with the hope of adding to his repertoire of songs. He moved on to a wide array of jobs, including selling balloons for a circus and playing a calliope for a traveling carnival. Gene would later provide the following assessment of this period of his life:

In my wildest imagination, I had never thought that the wanderlust of
my mother had rubbed off on me. But I soon developed a restlessness
that kept me on the go; fortunately for me I was always able to hustle
some grub and a place to sleep. I became good at my job, but not want-
ing to limit myself as a parlour-house professor, I decided to try my
luck in cabarets, which today would be considered honky tonks, singing the songs of Uncle Esau's people, as well as songs I had picked up
from the cowboys on the trail, and the parlour-house "blues." I became an itinerant entertainer, and my wanderings took me all over the
country.[5]

Gene eventually matriculated to New Orleans. Associates always
seemed to be touting that city, arguing that if you could make it
there as a singer, then you could succeed anywhere. He soon located
the parlor-house district and, shortly thereafter, joined the army as
one of General Pershing's recruits for the ill-starred Mexican expedition in pursuit of the elusive Pancho Villa. Gene's army service—
which largely consisted of suffering through inclement weather,
treachery from civilians, and ambush from guerrillas—was abruptly
terminated when fellow soldier Tom Mix, the future film cowboy
star, instigated a check on his date of birth.

Discharged from the military and back in New Orleans, Gene
picked up where he'd left off. Becoming a top entertainer in parlor
houses, he moved on to the cabaret circuit. On the eve of his seven-
teenth birthday, he received a special delivery letter from his
mother, indicating that she and Jim were coming to take him back
home. In the face of this dilemma, Gene again enlisted in the army
and was assigned to the 156th Infantry of the 39th Division. After
four months of guard duty on the New Orleans docks, with most
of his off-duty time spent performing in the parlor houses, he was
transferred to Camp Merritt, New Jersey, where he did stevedore
work in the depot detail.

Wishing for more adventure, Gene—responsible for getting a
company onto a troopship headed for France—absentmindedly-on-
purpose remained aboard until the boat had sailed out well beyond
docking area. Following an obligatory reprimand by the commanding officer, he was rewarded with immediate assignment to a company scheduled to leave for the front. Surviving a year of battle in
the trenches, Gene became a victim of the 1918 Spanish flu epidemic. During his convalescence, he met a Medical Corps dentist,

Lieutenant Knapp, who had admired his singing at the military "Y" hut. Knapp convinced him that becoming a dental assistant would be a good trade to learn, not only while in the army but as a civilian.

He stayed in Paris for a year after the signing of the Armistice, working as Lieutenant Knapp's assistant. On the way home, Knapp offered to take Gene on as an associate if he would go to dental school. Following a stint in a preparatory school, Gene enrolled in the University of Maryland dental program. In addition to working in Knapp's office, he continued performing in obscure nightclubs, which helped in financing his education. By now familiar with the problems of getting some patients to pay their bills, Gene switched to law school, convinced he'd be of greater use if he could help Dr. Knapp collect outstanding accounts.

One night another performer, Roy Bergere, who'd been impressed by Gene's singing during a nightclub engagement, suggested that they work together in vaudeville. It didn't take much persuasion for Gene to begin rehearsals for a piano-and-song act with his new partner, after apologizing to Knapp that the entertainment business would always be his first love. A break-in date at a Philadelphia theater, however, was so poorly received that the manager felt impelled to cancel the balance of the engagement. Undeterred, the duo headed to New York City, spending several lean months there in an attempt to secure vaudeville bookings.

During his free hours, Gene began developing another dimension of his musical talent, that of songwriting. He relates that the inspiration behind his first successful song composition came while sitting on a city park bench, watching people walk by as sparrows in the trees engaged in morning singing.

> Before long, I became bothered by a tune in my subconscious mind that seemed to be crying to be written. The unknown tune soon found its way to the surface. The rhythmic sound of high heels fell into place with the "tweet-tweets" of the sparrows. Without much knowledge of what I was doing, I pulled out a pencil and some paper and wrote these words, "When my sugar walks down the street, all the birdies go tweet-tweet-tweet." I continued to write until I had completed the entire chorus and a verse.[6]

Several days later, Gene came up with the idea for another song while riding the elevator up to his hotel room. When he absentmindedly dropped the shells of the peanuts he was eating on the floor, the elevator operator groaned, "Mistuh Gene, how come you do me like you do?"[7] Feeling that these words succinctly expressed his misgivings about the recent months of futility in New York, Gene quickly improvised a melody to complete the song.

"How Come You Do Me Like You Do?" was not only accepted by the song publisher, Mills Music, Inc., but Austin and Bergere were engaged to help promote it. This work enabled the duo to make valuable contacts with performers and cabaret owners. After the song became a big hit, they began a successful run playing at Lou Clayton's Mahjong Club. When Bergere started working professionally with his new wife, Gene continued there as a single until prohibition agents found sufficient liquor on the premises to have it shut down.

Hoping to eventually break into the vaudeville circuit, Gene began working for the song publishers Stark & Cowan as a general demonstrator. (The firm would publish the Austin and Bergere composition "Tell Me If You Want Somebody Else," in 1924.) During one appointment in April 1924, he met his future wife, a vaudeville dancer still in her teens named Kathryn Arnold. Despite the awkward arrangement of having to include her mother as a chaperone on all of their dates, the courtship proceeded smoothly and on June 16, 1924, they were married.

The August 16, 1924, issue of *Billboard* would report that Austin was employed as a songwriter and contact man with the recording companies by Jack Mills, Inc., an up-and-coming music publisher. The first week on the job proved unproductive; Gene, who'd always subscribed to the conventional wisdom that "songs write themselves," found himself pressing in trying to come up with a decent song. He was rescued from his immediate dilemma when directed to demonstrate the Mills catalog to the Vocalion label. After listening to a few songs, the executive—recognizing Gene's regional dialect—confided to him about a "Southern problem" facing the company: "There's a chain of music stores in Nashville that sent up a blind man to record some hill-billy songs. They happen to be one of our largest accounts and we can't afford to offend them. But this George Reneau's voice sounds absolutely impossible."[8]

Sympathetic about the plight of Vocalion and the blind musician, who wanted nothing more than to return home, Gene agreed to try lending his voice to some recording sessions. The approach clicked, and Austin cut a series of records to Reneau's guitar and harmonica accompaniment between April 1924 and February 1925, including "The Wreck on the Southern 97"/"Lonesome Road Blues" (#14809); "You Will Never Miss Your Mother until She Is Gone"/ "Life's Railway to Heaven" (#14811); and "Turkey in the Straw"/ "Little Brown Jug" (#14812). The labels on these releases read as follows: "Sung & Played by George Reneau—The Blind Musician of the Smoky Mountains—Guitar and Mouth Harp."[9] Although Austin professed no great affinity for country music, the credibility of his singing and yodeling reflected his close proximity to country music during his youth, as well as his natural skills for mimicry. The success of these releases spurred Edison to bring the duo into the studio to record many of the same songs during September 1924.

In the meantime, Reneau confided that he was on the "Oregon Short Line" (out of money). Gene suggested that Reneau play his guitar and harmonica on New York street corners while Gene kept a lookout for the cops. This ploy proved so successful that the blind musician had second thoughts about returning home; only Gene's warnings that they would inevitably be apprehended by the law convinced Reneau to board a train headed back to Nashville.

Austin's big break as a recording artist came when Mills asked him to select some songs and demonstrate them to Victor's star singer, Aileen Stanley. After being introduced to Miss Stanley and musical director Nat Shilkret at the Victor Company studios, he ran through his first selection, the self-penned "When My Sugar Walks Down the Street." He couldn't believe his ears when Stanley responded, "Don't bother with the others, this is just what I wanted. Thank you, young man." After listening to the song one more time, Shilkret then took him aside and said, "You're going to sing on [Miss Stanley's] record. You know, young man, I have a hunch if you cut some recordings alone, we may be able to start a new style of singing in popular records, I'm going to take a chance on you. I'll give you a hundred dollars a record. If they sell, we can talk about a contract."[10]

When asked what gave him the idea for his type of singing, Austin replied, "Well, Mister Shilkret, when I came to New York, all the singers were tryin' to follow the great Al Jolson. I knew I could never sing as loud or perhaps as good as Mister Jolson, so since he was always talkin' about how his mammy used to croon to him, I just croon like his mammy."[11]

This conversation would appear to have Austin placing himself in the vanguard of the crooning tradition. Although crooning didn't become a full-fledged movement within the record industry until the introduction of electronic microphones by the major labels in mid-1925, Austin's soft, laid-back style translated well using the acoustic process. However, he was not the only singer to achieve success employing this type of understated vocal technique prior to the advent of electronic recording. In 1924 Cliff Edwards, popularly known as "Ukulele Ike," enjoyed success with "It Had to Be You," "All Alone," and other releases for Pathé and the American Records conglomerate, as did Nick Lucas, "the Crooning Troubador," with the Brunswick label. Furthermore, Whispering Jack Smith, Johnny Marvin, and others possessing a crooning delivery were extremely popular with record buyers shortly after the electronic process became widely used. Nevertheless, Austin's immense success—among singers, he was rivaled in popularity only by Al Jolson during the 1920s—made it inevitable that he would be viewed as the figurehead, if not the actual originator, of the crooning genre.

Austin accompanied Stanley on "When My Sugar Walks Down the Street" in Victor's New York City studio, January 30, 1925. On the strength of this performance, more sessions followed over the next three months, including a duet with country performer Carson Robison, comic sketches accompanied by Billy "Yuke" Carpenter, and "tenor with orchestra" fare. His first hit release of note, "Yearning," backed by "No Wonder" (Victor 19625), was recorded March 12, 1925.

Austin felt confident enough about his prospects to quit his job with Mills Music. While waiting for the public's verdict on his first group of releases, he and his wife put together an act and hit the road. By the time they hit Columbus, Ohio, however, Nat Shilkret was on the phone, exclaiming, "For heaven's sake, Gene, why did you run off without letting us know where you were going? I spent over a week trying to locate you. I have good news for you. All I've heard for the last month is, 'More Gene Austin records!' I want you to leave immediately and get back to New York as fast as you can."[12]

One hit record seemed to follow another during Austin's early years as a Victor recording artist. He claims that royalties during the first three months for his first four records under the Victor contract totaled $96,000; he carried the uncashed check around for a considerable period of time in order to impress skeptics. Nurtured by his wife, and—in view of the uniqueness of his singing style—given free rein by his label to select song material, Austin would look back on this period as the happiest of his life. He prided himself on his ability to find first-rate material that often had been ignored or rejected by established singers. Notable choices from that first year included "Yes Sir, That's My Baby" (composed by Gus Kahn and Walter Donaldson), "The Flapper Wife" (Beatrice Burton-Carl Rupp), "Five Foot Two, Eyes of Blue" (Young-Lewis-Henderson), "Sleepy Time Gal" (Alden-Egan-Lorenzo-Whiting), and "Sweet Child" (Whiting-Lewis-Simon). However, he remained uneasy over his inability to convince Victor officials of his need to interpret the soulful music he'd learned from Uncle Esau. But for the time being, he and Kathryn focused on adjusting to a significantly more lavish lifestyle, punctuated by a beautiful new home, a large car, expensive clothes, and access to the best that New York nightlife could offer.

Eventually, the pressures that are a natural by-product of success began to undercut his peace of mind. He became defensive when told that the Tin Pan Alley denizens were convinced he could turn any song into gold. Decades later, he would comment, "They were so wrong. I'd always told them hit songs don't care who sings them. They wouldn't take no for an answer; and when I refused to be pushed into a song I didn't think suited me, I got the reputation of being high hat and hard to get along with."[13]

Austin decided that an automobile tour back to his hometown of Yellow Pine would be just the ticket for regaining a fresh perspective on a career that seemed to be rapidly spinning out of control. On the way down to Louisiana, he pointed out the milestones of his life to Kathryn. The visit with Jim and Belle, who had relocated to the nearby town of Minden, went smoothly; they both seemed to be deeply impressed by Gene's newfound celebrity. As soon as he had finished an informal performance for houseguests on the first evening home with his parents, he slipped off to visit his beloved mentor, Uncle Esau. Esau, refusing Gene's offer to buy him a new home, proved as kindly and helpful with his counsel as he had in the past. Austin's chief regret was that he still hadn't shared the secret of this special relationship with his wife.

The next morning, Austin was awakened from a deep sleep by a phone call from Nat Shilkret in New York, who exclaimed, "We are flooded with so many orders for new Gene Austin records, I want you to come back as fast as you can make it. Can you leave immediately?"[14] Austin hastily made preparations to return back East but not before arranging the purchase of a large farm house for his parents, as well as providing funds for Esau's immediate needs.

After meeting his recording obligations, Austin formed his own music publishing company, with the aim of placing African American songs in a position to be recorded by Victor and the other major labels. He also began booking personal appearances as a means of funding his new venture, as well as popularizing this music. Caught up in a whirlwind of conferences with songwriters, booking agents, theatrical managers, bankers, and record company executives, Austin agonized that Kathryn always seemed to be stuck with either "a moody husband or an absent one." He justified the situation to her by noting that in the uncertain world of show business, it was best to "get it while the getting's good."[15]

One day not long after Austin's return from Louisiana, the latest batch of records he'd sent Esau was returned with the word *Deceased* stamped across the package. Despite his outward success, Austin relates that his personal life fell into complete disarray.

> For months to come, I tried to cling onto a form of communication with Esau's spirit. The practice of spiritualism left me shaken and lost in a solitariness of forsaken gloom. This was the beginning of such gnawing doubts and fears that I turned to another spirit, alcohol, to bolster my imagination into believing that I was a complete individual and did have the power and initiative to carry on without the help of the one I believed had supreme authority and held the key or controlling influence over my voice, deeds and person.[16]

He added that heavy drinking, rather than numbing the pain, made him temperamental, arrogant, and belligerent. In the process, he disappointed, even hurt, those closest to him. Realization of the impact of his behavior led to further self-recrimination.

By mid-1925, his records were so popular in England that London's prestigious Princess Club made Austin an offer to perform there. He eagerly accepted, in part to escape the stifling atmosphere of New York but also to hopefully make contact with British scientists then investigating survival after death. The English reserve, combined with his own extreme shyness, dictated against Austin's wishes to gain entry to a scientific séance. In his words, "The net result of my three months in London was that the supply of Gene Austin records was sold out in England as well as in America; and

'Nipper' was yelping for his star to hurry back; and I picked up some English songs for my music company's catalog, which turned out to be hits."[17]

Upon his return to the States, Austin, thirsting for the blues music of his youth, began frequenting the Harlem club scene. One of his new associates was pianist Fats Waller, who had first approached Austin with songs to publish while he was employed at Mills Music. Austin also was attracted by Harlem's reputation for "conjur" activity, believing that it accounted for his career. Looking only for proof of the continuation of the bond between Esau and himself, he gave any "prince" or "princess" a fair trial, stipulating only that he be treated as any other client from downtown.

One of his recordings from this period, "Me Too" (Victor 20143)—coupled with "For My Sweetheart," has baffled more than one fan of early sound recording history. Recorded in New York on August 12, 1926, the song exhibits a considerable amount of rumbling noise, a feature one wouldn't expect of a release from a major artist on the label then known for the highest-quality sound reproduction. One researcher, Don Peak, consulted the August 13, 1926, issue of the *New York Times* for clues. The front page headlines read, "STORM TIES UP CITY TRAFFIC, FLOODS SUBWAYS, KILLS BOY" and "LIGHTNING STARTS 15 FIRES." Other records recorded on that day do not display similar background noise. However, Austin's cut included a spare accompaniment (violin and piano, only), whereas some of the other releases featured a fuller band arrangement. Furthermore, the full impact of the storm may have been limited to the Austin session. Regarding the aesthetic judgment of the Victor brass in deciding to release the track, *The New Amberola Graphic* (no. 47, Winter 1984) observed that "most [sound reproduction] machines in use in 1926 were not sensitive enough to reproduce the low frequency of rumbling thunder, so it is safe to assume that the customers never even noticed it."

Following another stage tour, while his wife remained back home with her family in St. Louis, expecting their first child, Austin entered the Victor studios resolved to record a song that had been in the files of a leading publishing company for several years. As noted by David Ewen, in *All the Years of American Popular Music,*

"My Blue Heaven" . . . was written in 1924, three years before its publication; [Walter] Donaldson wrote it one afternoon at the Friars Club in

New York while waiting for his turn at the billiard table. George Whiting, then appearing in vaudeville, adapted the lyrics to the melody and used it in his act, but the song failed to attract much attention. For three years it lay in discard until Tommy Lyman, a radio singer, picked it up for use as his theme song.[18]

By now, Austin's arrangement with Victor had soured, regarding the choice of material to record. He was convinced that the best material that he brought to the company's attention was going to other artists. In view of his own family situation, he felt that this was one song he had to commit to disk. He pleaded and finally gave Nat Shilkret an ultimatum that he wouldn't do another session unless his interpretation was commercially released. According to Austin, an agreement was reached for "My Blue Heaven" to be coupled with "Are You Thinking of Me Tonight?," the most highly regarded song among those he was planning to record at that time.

Austin relates that it was scheduled last on the September 14, 1927, recording agenda, in order minimize potential conflicts with the Victor brass. However, as soon as satisfactory takes had been achieved for the other songs, the orchestra members put away their instruments and filed out of the studio. When Austin complained, Shilkret replied, "I'm sorry, Gene. I didn't know at the time I made you that promise that the musicians had another date and would have to leave. We can make it another day."[19] H. Allen Smith, in *A Short History of Fingers*, documents the singer's refusal to back down: "I grabbed an old guy with a cello and talked him into standing by. Then I grabbed a song plugger who could play pretty fair piano. And the third fellow I got was an agent who could whistle— bird calls and that sort of thing. I made the record with those three."[20]

When Austin proved intractable, Shilkret resigned himself to the possibility of Austin's first major flop. To the contrary, however, the song immediately struck a chord with the American public. Austin would later claim, in an interview published by the *Los Angeles Times* (March 8, 1959, part 5), that the record sold over eight million copies. The song would also have an unhappy postscript: Ready to leave for St. Louis to be united with his family and carrying a freshly pressed copy of "My Blue Heaven," Austin received a telegram notifying him of the death of his newborn son.

Following an interlude of healing, which consisted primarily of

"soaking up the blues and booze" with Waller and other musicians
in Harlem, Austin was able to return to his apartment and once
again deal with responsibilities of his career and everyday life. Kathryn finally agreed to return from St. Louis, provided that he maintain certain standards of sober behavior. Gratified at his improvement, she agreed to accompany him to activities involving New
York's social elite. Since Kathryn seemed to particularly enjoy week-
end excursions on their stockbroker's yacht, Gene suggested they
purchase one of their own. The process of gathering information on
boats and navigation helped bring the couple closer together. They
submitted blueprints to a custom boat builder in Maryland who'd
come highly recommended. The yacht, paid for in full by a certified
check for $75,000, was delivered to a Hudson River mooring directly
alongside the couple's apartment. Austin convinced his wife that a
whopping party was needed to launch the boat, christened *My Blue
Heaven,* in style. He would recall,

> What people came to see us off! Songwriters and music publishers,
> vaudeville and night club headliners, agents, stockbrokers, newspaper
> columnists. Walter Donaldson, Benny Davis, composer of my first big
> hit record, "Yearning," Harry Warren and I took turns at the little
> piano rolled out on the deck. Aileen Stanley and I re-created our duet
> of "All the birdies go tweet-tweet-tweet." The fun was endless, there
> was a spirit of friendship; and even Jimmy Walker, popular mayor of
> New York, dropped in for a couple of choruses of his famous song,
> "Will You Love Me in December as You Do in May?"![21]

The Austins' planned itinerary—sailing to New Orleans and then
up the Mississippi, across the Great Lakes and the St. Laurence, and
completing the voyage down the North Atlantic back to New York—
was widely covered by the media. With the boat setting sail in a
southerly direction, the first few days were spent touring the Atlantic coast. Nights were spent in ports along the way. Upon reaching
Southport, North Carolina, Captain Ott told Austin that a storm
warning had been issued on the receiving radio; the Coast Guard
was advising those in the vicinity that the winds could reach hurri-
cane force. Due to the danger of floundering in shallow waters if
they stuck to the inland route, Ott recommended that they head out
to sea and ride out the bad weather.
The storm hit with intense fury almost immediately after the boat

had left the harbor. With no sending equipment on their radio, the captain focused his efforts on locating one of the small islands in the area in order to beach the vessel. With Kathryn in near hysterics, Austin retreated to his liquor cabinet and poured out his troubles to the steward inside the galley.

When calm weather finally appeared, it came with astonishing suddenness. Surrounded by heavy blankets of fog and unsure of their location, the crew retreated to the cabinet radio set. Out of the static they heard a voice say, "Those were three more songs introduced and made famous by Gene Austin. Once again, we repeat, the Coast Guard [has] abandoned the search for the famous crooner's boat, *My Blue Heaven*, and all the hands aboard must be presumed to be drowned."[22]

Captain Ott turned off the radio in disgust. Austin, however, was probably not as surprised over hearing his own obituary. Earlier in the year, *Variety* (February 22, 1928) had included a news note stating, "Austin was last week reported killed in a Milwaukee automobile smash-up, the Boston 'Transcript' carrying a report to that effect. It is merely one of the recurring popular pastimes of killing off recording artists." Perhaps this is why Austin turned the radio back on. The voice was now telling listeners that a storm-battered cruiser—its crew evidently washed overboard—had been found on a Carolina beach. It went on,

> The wrecked boat is believed to be the *Blue Heaven*. Coast Guard headquarters give little hope that the man who sang his way into America's heart could have survived the terrible hurricane. Will each of you just tuning in, join me as we continue our memorial program for Gene Austin. The beloved singing star lives in our hearts as we take a musical tour back through the years, back over the career that brought fame, success and wealth. Only five short years ago, Austin came out of the relative obscurity of vaudeville and music publishing to become the brightest star of the new phonograph record business. Here is one of his most recent hits and the song his yacht was named for, "My Blue Heaven."[23]

The crew's reverie was interrupted by the captain's announcement that the fog had lifted. A Coast Guard cutter was spotted on the way back to the mainland. The Austins were given a lift ashore, wishing to return to New York as soon as possible. They obtained a ride to the railroad station before their identity was public knowledge.

Back in New York, Austin had to contend with "questions, wise-cracks, and comments" from the public; the fear of losing his voice (perhaps not unwarranted, considering the abuse—heavy drinking, irregular hours, and inclement weather—it had taken); and Kathryn's worries over their expected child.[24] Nevertheless, he had much to be thankful about. The February 22, 1928, issue of *Variety* reported, "The biggest selling popular vocal artist on all records now is Gene Austin, exclusive Victor artist whose 'Forgive Me' recording went over 500,000 disks and 'My Blue Heaven' will exceed that. Austin's records sell 100,000 blind to the dealers without [being] previously heard." The September 14–16, 1927, recording sessions for Victor had yielded a bumper crop of hits; besides "My Blue Heaven," "There's a Cradle in Carolina" (#21015-A), "My Melancholy Baby" (#21015-B), "The Sweetheart of Sigma Chi" (#20977-B), and "The Lonesome Road" (#21098-A) all qualified as best-sellers. (The last song would be the only composition not written by Hammerstein and Kern to be included in the 1929 Universal production of the immensely successful musical *Show Boat*.)

Furthermore, the latest series of Victor releases—culled from sessions spread over the March–May 1928 period—seemed likely to keep Austin at the forefront of contemporary popular music. "Ramona," backed by "Girl of My Dreams" (#21334), would prove to be his strongest coupling ever. "Ramona," the theme song of a successful motion picture bearing the same name, would eventually sell nearly as many copies as "My Blue Heaven." Around this time, Austin's accountant allegedly informed him that Victor had thus far paid him royalties representing the sale of more than seventy-five million records. While he may have been tormented by feelings that his success was undeserved, there seemed to be little doubt that his popularity would continue undiminished for some time into the future.

Victor's willingness to allow Austin to selectively record blues-flavored material represented yet another positive development in his life. He was particularly attracted to Fats Waller's compositions; in 1929 alone he recorded his old friend's "I've Got a Feeling I'm Falling" (Victor 22033-B), "Ain't Misbehavin' " (Victor 22068-A), and "My Fate Is in Your Hands" (Victor 22223-A). The recording of the latter song, which included Waller on piano, has been the subject of a number of widely told anecdotes.

Shortly after his harrowing experience on the high seas, Austin received a special delivery letter with the news that Waller had been incarcerated for failing to pay his back alimony. As related by Ed Kirkeby, in his Waller biography *Ain't Misbehavin'*, Austin rushed to court with the necessary bail money. The judge, pointing to Waller in the dock, noted sternly, "This man has been before this court too many times for failure to pay his alimony dues—this cannot go on any longer. Is there any special reason why I should release this man on bail?" Austin, seemingly taken aback by the question, nimbly responded, "Well, your honor, I do have a record session this afternoon, and if this man is not there to play the piano for me, it will put quite a few other musicians out of a job—and jobs are hard to come by these days." According to Austin's own biography, the judge replied, "Gene, I doubt your incredible story. However, I'll give Waller a reprieve on these conditions, that you be responsible to see he pays up his alimony . . . and I want those records as soon as they are available and YOU are to be the presenter." Waller and his benefactor then stopped off at a nearby speakeasy, where he demonstrated two songs he claimed to have just written in the Hotel Alimony: "My Fate Is in Your Hands" and "Ain't Misbehavin'." Upon hearing them, Austin exclaimed, "You've got yourself a couple of hits there, boy. I knew some day you would do it. I'm glad you forgot to pay that back alimony. You just keep runnin' outa dough so you get thrown back in the pokey, if that's where you can write these kind of songs. I'm recordin' tomorrow, so let's go to my boat where we won't be disturbed." There, with the help of a bottle, Waller spent most of the night orchestrating the songs.

Although in close agreement with Kirkeby regarding the events in this episode, Austin's recollection of the matter is flawed in at least one respect. According to Victor session ledgers, Waller's signature work, "Ain't Misbehavin'," was recorded in three takes by Austin on July 30, 1929. "My Fate Is in Your Hands" was the next Waller song to be recorded by Austin, on November 25, 1929. According to the ledger, the session consisted of only this song because of a fuse blowing in the studio switch box; Austin had to leave before the electrician could correct the problem. In that Austin did not record another Waller song until June 9, 1930 (i.e., "Rollin' Down the River"), it appears that his friend had nothing else of sufficient merit to interest him in late November 1929.

During the November 25 session, an argument started when the musicians learned that Austin planned to have Waller play the piano part. Austin recalled,

When they found out that Fats didn't belong to the musicians' union, there was an uproar. I assured the musicians that before the day was out, he'd become a member. More and more objections were fired at me, till I finally insisted, "Dammit! He's gonna play! These are his songs, an' he's the only one who can improvise on the piano like I want them played."[25]

Kirkeby states that racial considerations were behind the session musicians' initial refusal to work with Waller. He adds, "The record was eventually made with the accompanying orchestra grouped around one microphone, while Fats was placed at the opposite end of the studio by himself." Austin's account of the session portrayed both himself and the studio accompanists in a more favorable light.

All else failing, I announced I refused to go through with the date. Fats seemed to be embarrassed by all this, and suggested for me to go ahead without him, that he would sit down and show the piano player what he had in mind. After the musicians heard his first run-through, each one stood up and applauded, and I could see their heads nodding to the leader that they would take a chance and play with a non-union musician, making me the guarantor that it would be taken care of.[26]

Whatever actually took place, Austin could rightly take credit for having helped Waller join the Victor family of recording artists. The two would remain close friends for the rest of their lives.

In the meantime, Austin's voice did not improve sufficiently during the several months beginning in December 1928 to enable him to go back into the studio. He became heavily involved in the stock market as a means of keeping his mind occupied. When his daughter Anne was born in December, he used this happy event to justify a new round of heavy drinking. Thoroughly disgusted by his behavior, Kathryn took Anne to St. Louis to live with her parents.

Austin engaged a nose, ear, and throat specialist, who told him, "Gene, it could be . . . cancer. We in the medical field know so little about this dread disease. Your throat looks very angry. I suggest you give it a long rest. Quit smoking and drinking. Stay out of the night air for awhile. I can only recommend just what I told you."[27]

With both his life and his career at risk, Austin traveled back to Louisiana to visit his mother. His mother's eccentricities, however, ruined whatever hopes he might have had about finding a haven for relaxation. Annoyed at what she perceived to be price gouging by the utilities, Belle had adopted tactics that left her without oil and gas service. Austin later recalled his frustration with this situation:

> I never felt so da'gone weary in my entire twenty-nine years. "Why can't things be easy an' nice once in a while?" I moaned to myself. The money I sent and the bills I paid each month could keep them in luxury. I was so disgusted over her not paying the measly light bill. Why, those dozen [oil] lanterns cost more than three times the amount of the bill! I had always hoped that some day my little mother would conquer her wild spirit so she could acquire the normalcy of average intelligence and pride that could rule out forever her gift of creating scenes and the crafty scheming that brought trouble to her and those around her.[28]

After sorting out what problems he could, Austin paid his respects at Esau's grave and pointed his automobile back to New York.

Upon his return, he found a letter from his wife's attorney, finalizing their divorce. Unable to live in the apartment that held so many memories of better days with his family, Austin moved to a suite in a mid-Manhattan hotel. He adopted a routine of drinking and listening to music on the radio alone in these new surroundings.

One morning in October 1929 Austin awoke to the sound of loud rapping at his door. Four unidentified men entered his suite, begging for a drink. As they downed a bottle of whiskey, Gene was informed of the recent stock market crash. Although his losses were great, he was far from destitute. He would later reflect,

> I had certain assets, thanks to the foresight of Victor Herbert, Gene Buck and that wonderful attorney, Nathan Burkan, along with Silvio MacDonough, George Maxwell and Jay Witmark, who had organized the American Society of Composers, Authors and Publishers, to assure that no member need ever meet the fate of unfortunate Stephen Foster.[29]

Although his recording and music publishing activities proved far less lucrative in the 1930s, Austin found some measure of success through radio and film work, as well as concert performing. In 1934 alone he performed in the film short *Ferry-Go-Round* (RKO) and the features *Sadie McKee* (Metro-Goldwyn-Mayer) and *Gift of Gab* (Universal). While Austin performed on many of the leading radio shows—including *Hollywood on the Air* and *The Magic Key Show*—he professed not to have cared much for the medium during its infancy. However, he took credit for pioneering the use of microphones in concert venues.

> I had heard presidential candidate Warren G. Harding speak over an apparatus in an auditorium, which gave me the idea of using a sound amplifying system in my personal appearances. I had the Victor engineers develop a portable compact model for me to take along on tours, thus becoming, I think, the first performer to use such a set-up. Rudy Vallee, who had become very popular, asked me about it, and I made him a present of the duplicate emergency set I always had taken with me on tour.[30]

One of Austin's more interesting live appearances resulted from a Long Island socialite's offer relayed through a prominent society orchestra leader, Meyer Davis. According to the terms, he was to receive $1,000 for a brief fifteen-minute performance at a party in the man's mansion. After a brief altercation with a male heckler, Austin was led back to the music room by an apologetic host, who stated, "The hell with them. I've been a great admirer of yours, Gene, and I invited you here for my own entertainment."[31] Austin was happy to perform in that setting solely for his host.

One of Austin's chief activities during tours consisted of making appearances at local stores to autograph records. During one such session, he smugly told the clerk, "Looks like they still come out for me, eh, ol' buddy." He received his comeuppance when the young man hesitantly replied, "I play your records all the time, Mistuh Austin, and love them, and recommend them to my customers. But when Saturday comes, people crowd in here from farms miles around to get the latest Vernon Dalhart records. They say that's the kind of music they understand."[32]

At the height of the Depression, Austin decided to settle in Chicago. The Windy City, then famous as a haven for gangsters such as Al Capone and John Dillinger, featured a diversified night scene that attracted musicians of every stripe. Austin was able to rent a large home, lavishly furnished and located in the fashionable part of town, for a very reasonable price. In addition to performing in Syndicate-controlled clubs, he again opened his house to "wine, women, and jam sessions."[33] During this period, Gene met his second wife, Agnes Antelline, on a blind date.

Wishing to share his Southern homeland with Agnes, Austin combined their honeymoon with a concert tour. While on tour, he learned that the Suburban Gardens in New Orleans were available for leasing. He asked his manager at the time, Bob Kerr, to make arrangements for taking over the club. He then hired jazz musician Wingy Manone, a New Orleans native then active in Chicago, to organize a house band. One of these musicians, bass player Johnny Candido, caught Austin's fancy, and they began performing together live. After a few weeks at the club, Candido coaxed Gene out into the streets to audition a talented but bashful guitarist. Austin later recalled,

> I knew guitar players were a dime a dozen, and at the same time had enough respect for Johnny, who wouldn't waste time with ordinary musicians, so we went outside. I watched Otto Heimel pick up his guitar and, holding it in his left hand, set off at a run across the strings with an art and knowledge of this instrument denied any other man at that time. It was this man from whom, in my opinion, all the great guitar players of today learned. I hired him that night, and formed an act, Gene Austin and his Candy and Coco.[34]

The group proved extremely successful, with Candy and Coco developing a unique sense of comedy that audiences loved. Their popularity, which led to many tempting offers for out-of-town live performances, helped re-ignite Austin's wanderlust. Receiving a good offer for the club, Gene sold out and relocated to Charlotte, North Carolina, which was closely situated to many of the venues interested in securing his services. Shortly thereafter, Agnes gave birth to a daughter who was named Charlotte after their place of residence. Charlotte would later make a name for herself as an actress under contract with 20th Century-Fox.

Austin's luck soured a few months later when he collapsed from exhaustion while performing onstage. The theater owner, undoubtedly aware of Austin's past reputation for carousing and noting the bottle of booze standing on the singer's dressing table (which Austin claims to have kept around as a gesture of hospitality to guests), immediately fired him and issued the edict, "I'm goin' to blast you to every theatre owner all over the country. You'll never play another date! I'll see to that! You're through!"[35]

With a potential blacklist by clubs facing him, Austin took his wife's advice and moved to Hollywood in hopes of finding steady work in motion pictures. Considering the area a perfect place to raise a family, Gene succeeded in getting his mother—by then married a third time and raising a daughter, Irene—to settle nearby. He offered the owner of the failing Clover Club on Sunset Strip his services, along with those of Candy and Coco, free of charge for a couple of weeks, banking on the likelihood that the act would be good for business. His hunch proved correct, with the clientele including many movie stars, directors, writers, and producers, some of whom made offers for the act to appear in films.

When Austin refused to accede to the club owner's demand that his group perform in a smaller area in order to accommodate more customers, he was fired. The act was immediately signed by the renowned Cocoanut Grove in the Ambassador Hotel and went on to even greater success. Wishing to keep both his career and his second marriage together, Austin abandoned his former drinking habits, earning that sobriquet "the sarsaparilla kid" in the process.

Although the money associated with film offers proved hard to resist, Austin soon decided that this medium was not his "cup of tea." Lacking the dark handsome looks in the Valentino mold that were required of matinee idols, as well as the patience and discipline to become a good dramatic actor, he focused on the songwriting and performing side of movie production.

A major break came Austin's way in the summer of 1935 when close friend Mae West—aware that he had composed songs tailored to performers with a diversified array of styles, from Broadway belter Sophie Tucker to dance-oriented bandleader Ted Lewis—asked him to provide a sexy Oriental blues number for her upcoming film *Klondike Annie*. Having been told that it was needed by the following afternoon, he immediately sat down and wrote "I'm an Occidental Woman in an Oriental Mood for Love." When West and producer William LeBaron heard the piece, Austin was given the assignment of writing the rest of the songs for the picture. By the time the film went into production on September 16, 1935, he was also penciled in as a performer, playing the organ and singing in a scene depicting a Nome, Alaska, settlement house. The role seemed tailor-made, in that it reminded him of his early days as a parlor-house professor.

Despite numerous offers to tour with Candy and Coco, Austin took over a defunct nightclub on Vine Street in order to have the semblance of a normal family life. Named My Blue Heaven, the club became a popular hangout for tourists and Hollywood stars.

This success led to a series of guest appearances on the *Joe Penner Show*, beginning in the fall of 1936. The radio program was broadcast on WABC at 6 P.M. each Sunday for network distribution. The popularity of these spots resulted in his being billed as a regular artist for two full seasons beginning January 17, 1937. Each program usually featured Austin for one song, along with Candy (now Russell Hall on string bass) & Coco. The duo was now billed as "Coco & Malt" because the show sponsor, Coco-Malt, didn't want to give listeners the impression that it was marketing a candy product.

Dividing his time and energy between the club and the radio program (which alone entailed three or four days of rehearsals) soon proved overtaxing to Austin, in addition to severely disrupting life at home. This dilemma was solved when jazz singer Louis Prima, an old friend who—like Austin—had spent much of his early career in New Orleans, agreed to take over the club. This venue, renamed the Famous Door, would play a significant part in launching Prima's successful career as a live performer and recording artist.

When the second season with the Penner show proved less taxing (one day for rehearsal and one for the broadcast), Austin purchased another defunct nightclub, this one located on Beverly Boulevard in Hollywood. The second My Blue Heaven was also a commercial success, attracting many patrons who fondly recalled their courtship rituals in the parlor, with Austin's classic recordings playing in the background.

The film vogue for singing cowboys provided Austin with his next challenge. Given his background—listening to authentic Western songs and observing the range riders as they passed by on the Chisholm Trail, combined with his years as an assistant to Big Jim at the forge—Gene was captivated when offered a chance to star in this type of picture. Selling his club for a solid profit, he went on a crash diet in order to properly fit the seat of a saddle and immersed himself in the technical details of shooting Westerns. The resulting film, *Songs and Saddles,* was made by Road Show Pictures as an independent venture, with Austin contracted to receive a portion of the profits.

Austin's deep involvement with the project assured his receptiveness to producer requests that he stimulate business by making personal appearances at theaters showing the picture. The tour was continually on the go, some days taking in as many as three or four cities. Despite its commercial viability, the stress and exhaustion ensuing from these appearances caused Agnes to return to Hollywood with Charlotte.

During the tour Austin met Billy Wehle, the owner of a traveling tent show. Wehle tried to talk Austin into joining him in this enterprise, promising to deliver vast audiences for his performances. Austin would later recall, "With my gullible nature, Waley's [sic] con hit me in my vulnerable spot, memories of Uncle Esau's prophecy that people would come from far and near to hear me. I told him to let me think it over, and if he'd come back the next day I'd give him my answer."[36]

Austin's manager, Bob Kerr, was not in the least bit intrigued by Wehle's proposition, preferring to quit rather than get involved with a tent show. Austin, however, decided to become a part of the venture, promising to meet up with Wehle in Albany, Georgia, after finishing his film tour commitments. The March 4, 1939, issue of *Billboard*, which carried the dateline February 25, Valdista, Georgia, reported that Wehle had signed Austin and Candy & Coco to appear in his show. The April 15, 1939, issue of *Billboard* (dateline April 8) indicated that the show, entitled "Star-O-Rama of 1939" and featuring Gene Austin, had opened in Moultrie, Georgia. Further news briefs from the publication between May 6 and June 17 noted Austin's involvement with the show at stops in Chattanooga, Tennessee; Staunton, Virginia; and Jacksonville, Florida.

After several months on the road with the tent show, Wehle asked Austin to consider taking over the enterprise. The July 8, 1939, issue of *Billboard* reported that the singer would be taking over on July 10; three weeks later, the publication referred to the show, then playing in Raleigh, North Carolina, as the "Ball of Fire Revue." The show's continual name changes—the September 9, 1939, issue of *Billboard* referred to it as "Models and Melodies"—would seem to indicate that Austin was struggling with marketing considerations. Remembering his positive impressions of a young press agent and manager he'd met in Tampa, Florida, while plugging *Songs and Saddles*, Austin now asked Tom Parker to come aboard as manager of the show. He remembered, "It was obvious Tom knew his business by the way he went about things. In a short while he had the show going full blast, attendance was great, and it looked like we would never know anything but success and money. Bookings poured in."[37]

Despite the generally good turnouts, the tent show was embroiled in controversy by the end of the season. According to Austin, most of the ample profits were attached for back taxes owed by Wehle. Although Austin hadn't been aware of this liability, the federal government insisted that he was responsible for the bill. *Billboard's* pages, however, told a different story; the September 23, 1939, issue indicated that Wehle had filed an attachment suit against the enterprise for alleged back payments due. The trial was scheduled to begin in Mobile, Alabama, on February 1, 1940.

As a result, Austin found it necessary to head back to Hollywood with Candy and Coco to earn the money needed for his trial defense and to reopen the show the following season, while Parker and a skeleton crew managed to scrape by in winter quarters in Gainesville, Texas. The act headlined at Sardi's, while also participating in the film *My Little Chickadee,* beginning November 12. He began assembling a company of performers early in 1940 for the upcoming tent show season. In the meantime, the performers warmed up for the tour with engagements at Spokane, Portland, Denver, and elsewhere.

The bad luck returned once Austin reunited with Parker in his old hometown in early May 1940. He recalled,

> The second season barely started before the threats of war began to slow down attendance. We were saddled with the obligation of paying back taxes, which had to be met on time; this caused me to fall behind in meeting the weekly payroll. When some of the hands became unmanageable and insisted on their money to satisfy their imbibing habits, hell broke loose. It was only Tom's knack of handling people that kept them from coming after me, by telling them I was an openhanded guy and they'd all get bonuses when the money started rolling in. Other shattering misfortunes like storms, tornadoes and hurricanes contributed to our hard times.[38]

Austin's troubles were compounded when Wehle won a judgment against the show in early July. Matters became so desperate that Austin found it necessary to close the show on July 30 in Newport News, Virginia. Wehle appears to have gained little satisfaction from these developments. The August 17, 1940, issue of *Billboard* reported that he had been unable thus far to collect any judgment money from Austin. On September 7, 1940, the periodical noted that the U.S. Bureau of Internal Revenue planned to auction the physical property associated with the Models and Melodies show. This decision was necessitated by nonpayment of assessed taxes due from both Wehle and Austin.

Before Austin headed for New York, where he planned to renew his professional contacts, his wife informed him of her plans to obtain a divorce in Las Vegas on grounds of nonsupport. The split became official October 12, 1940, with Agnes being awarded custody of their seven-year-old daughter.

Taking a train back East, Austin became more closely acquainted with Doris Sherrell, a sixteen-year-old who had performed the second season with his tent show. Before disembarking, he offered to provide her with singing lessons free of charge. While making the rounds in New York, Austin made a point of visiting the Sherrell home in New Jersey. After he provided Doris with some vocal pointers, the family issued him a standing invitation. Although there was a twenty-four-year difference in age, the two were shortly head over heels in love. However, two obstacles—the likelihood that her parents would be against marriage at such a tender age and the opposition of her church to such a relationship with a divorced man—kept the couple apart for the time being.

While co-headlining with vaudevillian showman Ken Murray at the Earle Theatre in Washington, D.C., the two developed the concept for a show to be entitled "Blackouts." At the close of the Washington engagement, Murray left for Hollywood to secure financial backing and Austin returned to New York with a double proposition for Doris: a secret marriage and a spot in the show, teamed with her sister Grace.

They worked with the show until Austin again felt the urge to take on new challenges. He assembled a troupe consisting of the Sherrells and the Whippoorwills—four musicians he'd first hired for the 1940 tent show tour when Candy and Coco left after a dispute over wages—and toured the country. He also found time in the early 1940s to perform in a series of three-minute music clips for the Soundies Distributing Corporation of America and Murray Hollywood Productions; several of these featured Doris.

Following a year of secrecy, Austin informed the Sherrells that he was their son-in-law. Thus liberated, the couple headed for a brief vacation in Las Vegas prior to returning to Hollywood. After winning a considerable sum of money at the gaming tables, however, Austin decided to open a new Blue Heaven club on the strip. This time, however, his venture was compromised by the war effort, which had created many problems in acquiring food, liquor, and other necessities associated with running a successful club and gaming facility. Furthermore, on one particular night a patron won big at the dice tables; Austin suspected foul play but couldn't substantiate his suspicions. As a result, he was forced to accept concert bookings in order to keep the club afloat. Bad publicity proved to be the last straw leading to the club's closing. While en route to one of his performance venues, Austin noticed the following headline on a newspaper resting on a train seat: "GAMBLER'S WIFE SHOT AT HIM OUTSIDE GENE AUSTIN'S BLUE HEAVEN CLUB IN LAS VEGAS."

Due to his wife's own career aspirations, Austin saw little of her for the next couple of years. He spent the time touring and carousing in much the same fashion as before. While performing in St. Louis, he met the woman who would eventually become his fourth wife. Austin had always made it a point to wander around a club where he was playing, asking guests if they had any special requests. An extremely attractive woman wearing a pink outfit asked to hear one of his early recordings, "I Wish I Had Died in My Cradle." After the show, the woman—by now he'd learned her name was LouCeil Hudson—explained to him why the song had a special meaning:

> My dearest girl friend was working in a record shop and I used to drop in after school and listen to your records. As I had used up most of my allowance, she promised to buy this one. We would visit each other many a night and have us a Gene Austin concert. I never dreamed I'd have the experience of the artist in person singing the song for me.[39]

The couple was married in 1949, following a whirlwind three-month courtship. The record that LouCeil's girlfriend had saved many years before was presented to them as a memento. Regarding the marriage, Austin would later reflect, "Perhaps it was because I was more mature or I had a constant companion; or rather because I had a feeling of being understood. Whatever the secret, it built a solid relationship between us that formed a strong foundation to our marriage as the years went by."[40]

Since both of them found Las Vegas to their liking when Austin played there, they decided to settle there in the early 1950s. Gene continued to tour on a regular basis. His only recording activity between 1948 and 1957 took place in New York on November 23–24,

1953. During the sessions, he re-cut twelve of his vintage hits for RCA Victor. Austin was featured on vocals and piano; further accompaniment was provided by George Barnes, electric guitar, and Frank Carroll, string bass.

Austin's career underwent a significant revival when NBC-TV broadcast "The Gene Austin Story" on *The Goodyear Television Playhouse*, Sunday, April 21, 1957. The program featured George Grizzard in the title role, with Austin dubbing the vocals. At the end of the hour show Austin made an appearance, singing his latest composition, "Too Late." The RCA release of the song (#20-6880) became his first hit—reaching number 75 on the *Billboard* pop singles chart in early June 1957—since "Ridin' Around in the Rain" (Victor 24663) in July 1934. He was also in demand on network television, appearing on *The Ed Sullivan Show* (NBC), *The Jimmy Dean Show* (CBS), *The Red Skelton Show* (CBS), *The Today Show* (with Dave Garroway; NBC), *The Jack Payne Show* (BBC), *The Woolworth Hour*, and Patti Page's *The Big Record* (CBS).

Austin continued performing in clubs, hotels, and other venues throughout the 1960s. He also purchased another club, the Chalet, located in a Dallas shopping center, in December 1961. According to longtime friend John Dunagan, an Anheuser-Busch distributor based in the Missouri area, the royalties from songs he wrote and recorded proved to be his main source of income during this period. He began taking a special interest in the careers of two successful country singers, godson David Houston and cousin Tommy Overstreet.

Austin entered politics briefly in 1962, opposing incumbent Nevada Governor Grant Sawyer in the Democratic primary. An article appearing in the May 17, 1962, issue of the *New York Post,* offered the following take from the singer regarding his campaign prospects: "Campaigning is nothing new to me. After all, it's just like show business." The ticket, which included Eddie Jackson (of Clayton-Jackson-Durante fame), lost to Sawyer and his running mate, former film star Rex Bell.

Austin and LouCeil were divorced in June 1966. Shortly thereafter, in early 1967, he married Gigi Theodora, a woman decades his junior who reportedly was born in Greece and attended Cambridge University in Great Britain. By this time, Austin had relocated to the Miami area. Florida Governor Haydon Burns proclaimed June 24, 1966, his sixty-sixth birthday, "G Austin Day" in recognition of his "distinguished career."

Other honors followed. In February 1971 he appeared on Merv Griffin's CBS-TV tribute to popular music composers, and later in the year he stated in a published interview that he'd assisted in establishing the Museum of Jazz, based in New Orleans, sometime around 1956. His final live performance took place at the Jack London Club in Palm Springs, California, where he ushered in 1972 by singing his old hits.

Austin died on January 24, 1972, at the age of seventy-one, in Palm Springs' Desert Hospital. He had been suffering from cancer for ten months. Five of his recordings comprised the music at the funeral, including "My Blue Heaven" and a song written by him especially for this event and recorded two years earlier, "There's a New Blue Heaven in the Sky." The pallbearers included Dunagan, Bill Putnam, Rick Adams, Jon Antelline, Dave Covey, Harry Segal, Phillip Moody, Jack Pepper, Hartley Cassidy, and fellow recording artist Nick Lucas.

Table 1.1.   Music and Lyrics Composed and Copyrighted by Gene Austin

How Come You Do Me Like You Do? (1924)
Tell Me If You Want Somebody Else, 'Cause Somebody Else Wants Me (1924)
A Thousand Miles from Here (1924)
Just about Sundown (1924)
I Had a Good Gal but the Fool Laid Down and Died (1924)
I'm Going Where the Climate Fits My Clothes (1924)
Wanted, Someone to Love (1924)
Charleston Charley (1924)
When My Sugar Walks Down the Street, All the Little Birdies Go Tweet-Tweet-Tweet
    (1924)
What Makes Me Love You Like I Do? (1925)
I Had a Sweet Mama, but She's Turned Sour Now (1925)
Abie's Irish Nose (1925)
I Wonder Why I Love You (1925)
The Gambler's Sweetheart (1926)
When the Moon Shines Down upon the Mountain (1926)
All That You Left Me Were Two Empty Arms (1926)
Why Do You Tell Me, You Love Me? (1927)
The Voice of the Southland (1927)
'Til I Found You (1928)
Old Pals Are the Best Pals after All (1928)
I've Changed My Mind (1928)
The Lonesome Road (1928)
Please Come Back to Me (1929)
Trying, to Love You (1930)
Whippoorwill, Go Tell My Honey That I Love Her (1931)
My Success (1931)
When the Roll Is Called by the Fireside (1931)
Git Along (1933)
When a St. Louis Woman Comes Down to New Orleans (1934)
Ridin' around in the Rain (1934)
Out of the Blue (1935)
Mister Deep Blue Sea (1935)
It's Never Too Late to Say No (1935)
That May Not Be Love, but It's Wonderful (1935)
I Hear You Knockin' but You Can't Come In (1935)
Open Up Your Heart and Let the Sunshine In (1935)
I'm an Occidental Woman in an Oriental Mood for Love (1935)
It's Better to Give Than to Receive (1935)
Little Bar-Butterfly (1935)
Cheer Up Little Sister (1935)
Occidental Woman (1936)
Under the Spell of a Voodoo Drum (1936)
I'm in a Mellow Mood (1938)

Take Your Shoes Off, Baby, and Start Runnin' through My Mind (1942)
Oh, What a Mess I'm In (1943)
I've Given My Life to the Business (1944)
I'm a Rootin', Shootin', Tootin' Man from Texas (1944). First recorded in 1936 as
    "Rootin', Shootin', Tootin' Man from Texas"
Nothin' Doin' (1944)
Crazy Song (1944). Also known as "But I'm Alright"
Keep a-Knockin', but You Can't Come In (1948)
(Bad Boy) Dream on, Little Plowboy (1949)
Oh, These Lonely Nights (1953)
Too Late (1957)
Please (1957)
The More I See of Somebody Else (1957)
Sounds in the Night (1957)
Wise Guy (1957)
My Restless Heart (1957)
I'm Not the Braggin' Kind (1957)
My Rosita, My Own (1957)
If You Only Had a Heart for Me (1957)
Wonder (1957)
There's a New Blue Heaven (1957)
Goofin' (1958)
Sweetheart of Demolay (1958)
The Jass Story; an original musical play by Gene Austin [text only] (1958)
Lovely Lou'siana Moon (1963)
Here's to You (1964)
This Life of Mine (1965)
I Don't Want Nobody (1965)
Miami in the Morning (1968)
Let Me Lean against Your Shoulder (1968)
The Trip (1968)
Dora (1968)
Golden Wedding Waltz (1968)
Texas (1968)
That Fatal Day in Dallas (1968)
What Happens to My Friends on Sunday? (1968)
Somebody Lied (1968)
I'm All In, Out, and Down (1968)
On a Rainy Afternoon (1968)
Back Street (1968)
I Know Why (1968)
The Moment I Found You (1968)
Lonesome Train (1968)
Springtime, Ringtime, and You (1968)

Table 1.2. Songs Published by Gene Austin, Inc.

Someday You'll Pass This Way Again (1928)
Then Came the Dawn (1928)
Down by the Old Front Gate (1928)
Divine Lady (1928)
Wear a Hat with a Silver Lining (1928)
Anyone Can See with Half-an-Eye, I'm Crazy over You (1928)
Blowing Kisses over the Moon (1928)
On Riverside Drive (1928)
She's Got a Great Big Army of Friends (1928)
Long, Long Ago (1928)
Daddy o' Mine (1929)
A Garden in the Rain (1929)
Peace of Mind (1929)
I Gotta Have You (1929)
At Twilight (1929)
I Knew We Two Were One (1929)
Blue Morning (1929)
Keep Your Overcoat Open (1929)
Who's the Who (1929)
Maybe I'm Wrong (1929)
What Do I Care? (1929)
Please Come Back to Me (1929)
Dreary Night (1929)
Trying (1929)
When You Dance with an Old Sweetheart (1929)
With Love and Kisses (1930)
You're Flying High—But You'll Do a Tail-Spin for Me (1930)
Be Careful with Those Eyes (1930)
Would You Care (1930)
Lonely Stowaway (1930)
To-Night or Never (1931)
I Wish I Knew a Bigger Word Than Love (1931)
My Success (1931)

Table 1.3.   Sheet Music Featuring a Picture of Austin on the Front Page

Carolina Mammy (Leo. Feist Inc., 1922)

It's Not the First Time You Left Me (but It's the Last Time You'll Come Back) (Waterson, Berlin & Snyder Co., 1923)

Montmartre Rose (Edw. B. Marks Music Co., 1925)

I Wish I Had Died in My Cradle (before I Grew Up to Love You) (Shapiro, Bernstein & Co., 1926)

Since I Found You (Shapiro, Bernstein & Co., 1926)

Yesterday (Ted Browne Music Co., 1926)

I'm Still in Love with You (Austin, Bloom & Koelher, Inc., 1927)

My Melancholy Baby (Joe Morris Music Co., 1927)

My Blue Heaven (Leo. Feist Inc., 1927)

So Tired (Harold Rossiter Music Co., 1927)

Tomorrow (Forster Music Pub. Inc., 1927)

The Voice of the Southland Keeps Callin' Me Home (Austin, Bloom & Koelher, Inc., 1927)

Why Do You Tell Me, You Love Me (When You Don't Mean a Word You Say) (Ted Browne Music Co., 1927)

After My Laughter Came Tears (Shapiro, Bernstein & Co., 1928)

Ashes of Love (M. Whitmark & Sons, 1928)

Bluebird Why Don't You Call on Me? (J. W. Jenkins Son's Music Co., 1928)

Carolina Moon (Joe Morris Music Co., 1928)

Dream River (Joe Morris Music Co., 1928)

Old Pals Are the Best Pals after All (Irving Berlin, Inc., 1928)

The Saint Louis Blues (Revised Edition) (Handy Bros. Music Co., Inc., 1928)

I Got a Woman, Crazy for Me: She's Funny That Way (Villa Moret Inc., 1928)

Then Came the Dawn (Gene Austin, Inc., 1928)

You Wanted Someone to Play with (I Wanted Someone to Love) (Empire Music Co., 1928)

All That I'm Asking Is Sympathy (Joe Morris Music Co., 1929)

Dream Mother (Joe Morris Music Co., 1929)

I Ain't Got Nothin' for Nobody but You (Empire Music Co., 1929)

My Fate Is in Your Hands (Santly Bros., Inc., 1929)

On Riverside Drive (Gene Austin Inc., 1929)

Please Come Back to Me (Gene Austin Inc., 1929)

Wedding Bells (Are Breaking Up That Old Gang of Mine) (Waterson, Berlin & Snyder Co., 1929)

I Have a Sweetheart (and Mother Is Her Name) (Red Star Music Co., Inc., 1930)

Moonlight (Frank Capano & Co., Inc., 1930)

You Cried Your Way into My Heart (but Laughed Yourself Right out Again) (Frank Capano & Co., Inc., 1930)

Building a Home for You (Santly Bros., Inc., 1931)

Me Minus You (Leo. Feist, Inc., 1932)

The Night When Love Was Born (Leo. Feist, Inc., 1932)

To-ward Morning (Dancing with You) (Bibo-Lang, Inc., 1933)

Blue Sky Avenue (Harms Inc., 1934)

Talkin' to Myself (Harms, Inc., 1934)

NOTES

1. Ralph M. Pabst, *Gene Austin's Ol' Buddy* (Phoenix, Ariz.: Augury, 1984), 5.
2. Pabst, *Gene Austin's Ol' Buddy*, 6.
3. Pabst, *Gene Austin's Ol' Buddy*, 9.
4. Pabst, *Gene Austin's Ol' Buddy*, 12.
5. Pabst, *Gene Austin's Ol' Buddy*, 26.
6. Pabst, *Gene Austin's Ol' Buddy*, 49–50.
7. Pabst, *Gene Austin's Ol' Buddy*, 51.
8. Pabst, *Gene Austin's Ol' Buddy*, 60.
9. Tor Magnusson, comp. "The Gene Austin Recordings," *Skivsamlaren* 15 (February 1983): 5.
10. Pabst, *Gene Austin's Ol' Buddy*, 67–68.
11. Pabst, *Gene Austin's Ol' Buddy*, 68.
12. Pabst, *Gene Austin's Ol' Buddy*, 71.
13. Pabst, *Gene Austin's Ol' Buddy*, 76.
14. Pabst, *Gene Austin's Ol' Buddy*, 88.
15. Pabst, *Gene Austin's Ol' Buddy*, 91.
16. Pabst, *Gene Austin's Ol' Buddy*, 92.
17. Pabst, *Gene Austin's Ol' Buddy*, 96.
18. David Ewen, *All the Years of American Popular Music.*
19. Pabst, *Gene Austin's Ol' Buddy*, 101.
20. H. Allen Smith, "A Friend in Las Vegas," in *A Short History of Fingers and Other State Papers* (Boston: Little, Brown and Company, 1964), 47.
21. Pabst, *Gene Austin's Ol' Buddy*, 111–112.
22. Pabst, *Gene Austin's Ol' Buddy*, 120.
23. Pabst, *Gene Austin's Ol' Buddy*, 121.
24. Pabst, *Gene Austin's Ol' Buddy*, 124.
25. Pabst, *Gene Austin's Ol' Buddy*, 126.
26. Pabst, *Gene Austin's Ol' Buddy*, 127.
27. Pabst, *Gene Austin's Ol' Buddy*, 129.
28. Pabst, *Gene Austin's Ol' Buddy*, 131–132.
29. Pabst, *Gene Austin's Ol' Buddy*, 141.
30. Pabst, *Gene Austin's Ol' Buddy*, 144.
31. Pabst, *Gene Austin's Ol' Buddy*, 143.
32. Pabst, *Gene Austin's Ol' Buddy*, 147.
33. Pabst, *Gene Austin's Ol' Buddy*, 149.
34. Pabst, *Gene Austin's Ol' Buddy*, 158.
35. Pabst, *Gene Austin's Ol' Buddy*, 159.
36. Pabst, *Gene Austin's Ol' Buddy*, 168.
37. Pabst, *Gene Austin's Ol' Buddy*, 170.
38. Pabst, *Gene Austin's Ol' Buddy*, 172.
39. Pabst, *Gene Austin's Ol' Buddy*, 181.
40. Pabst, *Gene Austin's Ol' Buddy*, 181.

2

Russ Columbo

Russ Columbo's career reads like a metaphor of unfulfilled promise, for what might have been. By the time of his tragic death at age twenty-six, he was generally conceded to reside at the pinnacle of the crooning genre, the chief rival to the hegemony enjoyed by Rudy Vallee and Bing Crosby. Like these stars, his popularity cut across fan publications, sound recordings, radio, and the cinema. Yet Columbo's legacy—a body of recorded work intermittently spread over a mere five years—provides slim evidence in support of such a lofty assessment. As a result, he has received only passing mention from the vast majority of sources concerned with chronicling the popular music of that era.

Born January 14, 1908, Ruggerio Eugenio de Rodolpho Colombo came from a large Catholic family. His parents, Nicholas and Julia Colombo (died May 1942 and August 1944, respectively), gave birth to numerous children, including Albert (d. August 1946), Anthony (d. February 1965), John (d. August 1967), Alonzo (death date unknown), Fiore (d. 1929), Florence Colombo LoDuca (d. 1919), Anna Colombo (d. September 1940), and Carmela Colombo Tempest (d. January 1986), and an unidentified number who died as infants.

Evidence differs as to whether the place of birth was in San Francisco or Camden, New Jersey; at any rate, he seems to have spent portions of his early childhood in both locations. As his Italian-born father was a theater musician, Russ grew up in an atmosphere permeated by music. He was provided with guitar and violin lessons beginning as a young boy.

While he was a teenager, his family moved from the Napa Valley, California, town of Calistoga to Los Angeles. There, Russ joined his high school's orchestra as a violinist. In addition, he was able to secure additional experience playing "mood music" in small combos on silent movie sets. Film companies of that day utilized musicians as a means of helping actors achieve the proper frame of mind for interpreting their respective roles. One of these gigs resulted in actress Pola Negri taking an interest in Columbo. Negri, one of the leading film stars of the 1920s, had been romantically involved with the famed Rudolph Valentino. Noting a physical resemblance between the two, she assisted Russ in landing small roles in a number of late 1920s movies.

At the same, Columbo regularly found work as a violinist in hotel and theater orchestras around Los Angeles. When a band singer became ill immediately prior to a CBS radio program being broadcast from the Hollywood Roosevelt, Russ was quickly recruited to go on as his replacement. As a result, he was able to secure a position with Gus Arnheim and His Cocoanut Grove Orchestra. The Arnheim association elevated Columbo to the big leagues. Arnheim—a widely known pianist, composer, and bandleader who'd played with Abe Lyman during 1921–1923—toured the United States and Europe heading his own ensemble in the mid-1920s. Notable musicians under his baton over the years would include Jimmie Grier, Woody Herman, Earl Hines, Stan Kenton, Bing Crosby, Shirley Ross, and actor Fred MacMurray. Arnheim began recording in 1928 (his first release was "I Can't Do without You"; Okeh 41057), and his 1931 release "Sweet and Lovely" would be one of the biggest hit recordings of all time. Russ would be regularly featured on records as Arnheim's lead vocalist between 1929 and 1931, prior to making it big on his own.

Although Columbo was officially signed as a violinist, Arnheim considered him a standby vocalist because Arnheim's featured singer, Bing Crosby, had exhibited erratic behavior brought on largely by bouts of heavy drinking. When Grove's manager, Abe Frank, attempted to levy a fine on Crosby for missing a show, the talented singer left for good. Tabbed to fill the void, Columbo immediately flourished as Arnheim's featured vocalist. Building on the bit movie parts filmed during the day to supplement his band work by night, Russ attracted considerable public attention for his scenes with the Arnheim band in the 1929 musical *Street Girl*.

After touring the East Coast with Arnheim, Columbo attempted to strike out on his own, forming a band and opening a nightclub with two of his brothers in Los Angeles. The Depression-era economy, however, greatly limited his success on both fronts. But his fortunes resumed an upward trajectory when Con Conrad—best known as the composer of "Ma, He's Making Eyes at Me" and the first song to win an Academy Award, "The Continental"—offered to manage him. Allegedly aggressive to a fault, Conrad used all of his persuasive powers to convince Columbo that he was, in the words of Crosby biographer Barry Ulanov, "the great singer of the time and would have no trouble with his career." Conrad took Russ out of his nightclub and band, in which he had been playing violin and guitar and singing a little in the Crosby style, bought him a top hat and resplendent dress suit, and had him photographed to best advantage. These efforts enabled Columbo to land a contract for an NBC radio program airing weekdays at 11 P.M.

When Bing Crosby was signed to head a comparable program for CBS in the same time slot, network executives saw the potential for a publicity bonanza. The rivalry—which was further fueled by Crosby's defection from RCA to record for Brunswick, followed by RCA's signing of Columbo—was billed as the "Battle of the Baritones" and some of the resulting coverage strained the boundaries of good taste. Ulanov notes,

> Columnists, taking advantage of a good story, began to quote the two men about each other in a manner and a parlance that neither of them would employ about anybody, much less about his chief rival. And then one very amusing story started going the rounds. "A lot of people seem to think Russ Columbo is Bing Crosby under another name," wrote one critic. Another asked, "Are Bing Crosby and Russ Columbo one and the same person?"[1]

The rivalry seemed convincing, in that their renditions of many songs—for example, "Stardust," "Goodnight Sweetheart," "Sweet and Lovely," "Street of Dreams," and "Paradise"—were only days apart. Columbo actually recorded Crosby's signature tune, "Where the Blue of the Night (Meets the Gold of the Day)," five days before Crosby did. Furthermore, Bob Weitman, manager of Paramount

Theatres, booked Columbo into the Brooklyn Paramount and then Crosby into the Manhattan Paramount, just a few miles away.

In reality, the singers remained on friendly terms. Crosby, in a newspaper column that appeared over his signature, praised a Columbo record. He also had played a part in the composition of Russ's theme song, "You Call It Madness, but I Call It Love," which was nevertheless paraphrased by wags as "You Call It Crosby, but I Call It Russ."

Columbo, undoubtedly sensitive to claims that he was a Crosby clone, attempted to focus on the differences between their vocal deliveries. The NEA Service carried the following self-appraisal in 1931: "I'm not a crooner—or a blues singer or a straight baritone. I've tried to make my phrasing different, and I take a lot of liberty with the music. One of the things [audiences] seem to like best is the voice obbligato on repeat choruses—very much as I used to do them on the violin."

The contrasting qualities of their voices were even more pronounced than this comment would suggest. Despite certain stylistic similarities, the timbres differed to a striking degree. Columbo possessed a soft, sweet, creamy voice that had a tendency to border on blandness. Crosby, on the other hand, had a rougher, stronger, more vigorous instrument, typically informed by jazz phrasing. Even his ballads were vehicles for the expression of greater rhythmic bite and a richer palette of tonal coloring. Hemming and Hajdu have noted further differences between two singers:

> [Columbo] almost always sounded deadly serious, sometimes even pretentious, about the romantic lyrics he sang—in contrast to Crosby's way of distancing himself from them with a degree of self-irony and occasional kidding. Yet there is no denying the gently nonthreatening appeal of Columbo's voice and approach—and the soothing effect his voice had on millions of listeners in the depths of the Depression. It's a style that also clearly influenced the most romantic of the big-band singers of the mid-1930s, such as Art Jarrett and Jack Leonard.[2]

In the meantime, extramusical qualities were a key ingredient in Columbo's success. His striking good looks—black hair, dark eyes, a smooth olive complexion, and athletic physique—graced a multitude of posters, sheet music covers, fan magazines, and trade publications. NBC billed him as "The Romeo of the Airwaves," while his

amorous image was augmented by a series of well-publicized romances, including singer Dorothy Dell, actress Sally Blane (Loretta
Young's sister), and Hannah Williams.

Columbo's considerable songwriting skills helped further his career as well. A number of his hit recordings were self-penned, including "Prisoner of Love," "You Call It Madness (but I Call It
Love)," and "My Love." Professing to enjoy composing almost as
much as performing, he told one interviewer, "I write late at night
mostly—and get some of my best ideas after I've gone to bed" (a
statement likely to have had additional layers of meaning to his legion of female fans).[3]

Columbo's popularity on the radio made it possible to surround
himself with first-rate talent. In the spring of 1932, for instance, a
rapidly maturing Benny Goodman was hired to front his dance
band. The offer proved sufficiently attractive to inspire Goodman to
fill his ensemble with excellent jazz musicians like Gene Krupa,
Babe Russin, and Joe Sullivan. He functioned as musical director
when the band was booked for the summer into the Woodmansten
Inn, a roadhouse located close to Manhattan, enabling Columbo to
mix with customers when he wasn't singing. Reviews of the engagement appear to have been decidedly favorable—the *Variety* review
of the May 5 opening called the band's music "dance inspiring"—
but Con Conrad was not happy with the results. According to
Goodman,

> It was a good little band, but Conrad wound up getting me because
> whenever we played for dancing[,] people seemed to really like it. I
> mean, we'd play "Between the Devil and the Deep Blue Sea" or some
> song like that, and all of a sudden the joint was rocking. He'd say,
> "Hey, wait a minute—you guys aren't supposed to be the attraction
> here," and he meant it.[4]

As a result, Goodman—temporarily stymied in his efforts at leading his own band—was left no recourse but to retreat to the ano-
nymity of radio studios, while Columbo would be mated with a suc-
cession of sweet orchestras that served merely to accentuate the
romantic qualities of his crooning style.

By 1933, during a lull in his recording activities, Columbo became
more actively involved in film acting. He was signed to his first starring role that year in a two-reeler titled *That Goes Double*, which had

him playing a dual role—as himself and as a look-alike office worker—in addition to singing three songs, "Prisoner of Love," "You Call It Madness (but I Call It Love)," and "My Love." Although his acting in this short was widely considered to be more self-conscious and less "natural" than Crosby's comparable efforts from the same period with Paramount, Columbo's rising celebrity—combined with his suave good looks and robust masculinity—assured him of further opportunities in Hollywood productions.

Broadway thru a Keyhole (1933) provided Columbo with his first romantic lead in a feature-length film. One of Darryl F. Zanuck's earliest productions for his recently formed Twentieth Century Pictures, it also starred Constance Cummings and included spot appearances by a host of Broadway and vaudeville veterans, most notably Blossom Seeley, Frances Williams, Texas Guinan, Eddie Foy, Jr., and Abe Lyman and His Band. Although Columbo received mixed reviews as an actor—he appeared wooden in contrast with the vitality displayed by many of the bit players—one of the songs he introduced in the picture, "You're My Past, Present, and Future," became a major hit. The film's box office performance was also helped by a windfall of unexpected publicity; Al Jolson, convinced that the Walter Winchell–based script depicted a situation in his romance with Ruby Keeler too faithfully for his liking, instigated a public altercation by punching the gossip columnist.

Perhaps due to his less-than-rave notices for his work in *Broadway thru a Keyhole,* Columbo was reduced to a cameo role in his next film, *Moulin Rouge* (Twentieth Century Pictures). Even during his brief segment onscreen, he was forced to share the spotlight with the Boswell Sisters and headliner Constance Bennett, performing the Harry Warren and Al Dubin–penned standard "Coffee in the Morning and Kisses at Night."

While Columbo's fledging movie career temporarily stalled, new opportunities arose in other venues. He was offered a new NBC prime-time radio series early in 1934. Emanating "deep in the heart of Hollywood," in the words of presenter Cecil Underwood, the program aired every Sunday night. Introduced as "the Romeo of songs, here with songs to delight your ears and heart," Columbo would open with the greeting "Good evening, my friends," followed by his theme, "You Call It Madness," which would also return as his closing number. His song selection featured a blend of hit recordings and plugs for material from current films, including "With My Eyes

Wide Open I'm Dreaming" from *Shoot the Works*, "I've Had My Moments" from *Hollywood Party*, and "Rolling in Love" from *The Old Fashioned Way*.

At the same time, Columbo signed a new recording contract with Brunswick (once again filling the void left by the departure of Crosby to another label, in this case, Decca). Despite the absence of precise sales figures, his releases from that period reputedly sold exceedingly well. According to Robert Deal, Columbo was reportedly earning more than $500,000 a year from all sources—a vast sum at the time.

These developments appear to have spurred Universal Pictures to select him for a major part (as Gaylord Ravenal) in the heavily publicized film version of the Kern-Hammerstein musical *Show Boat*. When that project was temporarily put on hold due to production problems, Columbo was assigned an interim lead in *Wake Up and Dream*, a low-budget, standard backstage musical also starring June Knight, Wini Shaw, and Roger Pryor.

Titled *Castles in the Air* in Great Britain and initially referred to in press releases as *The Love Life of a Crooner*, this film—which would be released a month after Columbo's untimely death—might well have proved a springboard to better roles in the future. Despite the inherent banalities of a run-of-the-mill script, his part seemed designed to reveal a darker side and wider acting range than that demonstrated by chief rival Crosby up until then. In contrast to the "good guy" roles characterizing Crosby's output at Paramount, Columbo played an egotistical singer who attempted to steal away his best friend's girl. The movie also showed his singing in a good light, as exemplified by the posthumously released hit "When You're in Love" (Brunswick 6972), with an accompaniment by Jimmie Grier & His Orchestra.

Universal's announcement in press releases while Columbo was still alive that his next film role would be as a toreador in *Men without Fear* gives some credence to the scenario that he was on the verge of challenging Crosby's hegemony as the leading crooner of the 1930s. Furthermore, he was rumored to be in line for choice roles in two other motion picture projects, Universal's *Glamour* (which would have reunited him with former co-star Constance Cummings, who, in personal correspondence in the late 1990s, fondly recalled her professional relationship with Columbo) and *Sweet Music*, which eventually was released in 1935 by Warner Bros. starring

Rudy Vallee. The latter film included the song "I See Two Lovers," which initially appeared in *Wake Up and Dream*.

Public interest in Columbo was further hyped by his romance with actress Carole Lombard. In the fall of 1933, a short time after her divorce from actor William Powell, Lombard fell in love with the singer. For his part, Columbo responded favorably to her zany behavior, as well as accepting her salty language, something that had offended a number of her male friends in the past. Although marriage seemed a distinct possibility, Lombard's close associates doubted that the affair would come to that. According to gossip columnist Hedda Hopper, "the couple's relationship was based on many things—but not sex."[5] Hopper cited a number of traits that caused her to question Columbo's masculinity, including the considerable trouble he spent on his hair and sun-tanning treatments, as well as his habit of carrying around a pocket-mirror that he produced on occasion to gaze at himself in public. It is indisputable, however, that Lombard was devoted to him and made every effort to help further his film career. She invited Columbo onto film sets to observe the filmmaking process and to pick up pointers on acting. He repaid this favor by coaching her in the two songs she was designated to sing in the movie *White Woman*.

By September 1934 it was clear that Crosby's career had thus far been more successful than Columbo's own. Columbo had appeared in only four films during 1933–1934, two of which he did not star in. Crosby, on the other hand, had starred in six features during the same time span. Furthermore, the material Columbo had been given to sing in films trailed far behind that provided Crosby, with regard to quality and sheer quantity. While Crosby's film music played a significant role in propelling him to stardom, Columbo's song hits were for the most part limited to recordings and radio broadcasts. Deal states, "He had the greater romantic appeal but very little chance to demonstrate any versatility and it seems likely that there were more sides of him to be seen on film than his presenters had up to that time revealed to the cinema audiences."

Columbo and Lombard continued to date up to his death; they could be seen dining and dancing at the Cocoanut Grove most Wednesday nights. His last recording session took place on August 31, 1934; he concluded with the Allie Wrubel and Mort Dixon composition "I See Two Lovers."

On September 2, just hours before his regular Sunday evening radio program, Columbo stopped by to see his lifelong friend Lansing V. Brown, Jr., who lived with his parents at 584 Lillian Way in Beverly Hills. Columbo was going to have some publicity shots taken by Brown, who was highly respected as a still cameraman and much in demand as a portrait photographer. After the photos had been taken, they talked about a common interest, antique pistol collecting. Brown then produced a pair of dueling pistols that dated from the Civil War, part of his own collection of curios. He placed the head of a match under the rusty hammer of one of the pistols with a flourish, then pulled the trigger to ignite the match in order to light a cigarette. The pistol, which evidently hadn't been used for over sixty-five years, still housed a charge of powder and an old bullet. The chick of the hammer caused the charge to explode and the corroded bullet struck the top of a table located between the two friends, ricocheted, striking Columbo in the left eye, then entered his brain.

Columbo was rushed to the Good Samaritan Hospital, and doctors discovered that the bullet, after piercing the center of the brain, had fractured the rear wall of the skull. A brain specialist summoned to the scene, Dr. George Paterson, counseled against the delicate operation being considered unless Columbo's rapidly waning strength could be restored. The singer lingered in agony for six hours before dying; the doctors were amazed that he hadn't been killed instantly. Bedside mourners included members of his family and his former girlfriend Sally Blane. Those outside in the hospital corridor included Lombard, who had heard of the tragedy by telephone at Lake Arrowhead, where Columbo was to have joined her to vacation the following week; film producer Carl Laemmle; and other film celebrities.

Brown would collapse following police interrogation; officers' suspicions had been aroused by a statement from a servant who alleged that he'd heard Columbo and the photographer arguing violently in the den. However, Brown was released after a court inquest. The verdict: "This jury finds that Russ Columbo came to his death by a gun wound accidentally inflicted by Lansing Brown. Brown is absolved of all blame. . . ." The singer's relatives and friends agreed with this ruling. A number of professional "dirt" diggers, an inevitable consequence of the Hollywood scene, spread stories of suicide due to an unrequited romance. Brown would grieve until his own passing decades later.

A crowd of 3,000 persons attended funeral services at the Sunset Boulevard Catholic Church in Hollywood. The pallbearers were Bing Crosby, Gilbert Roland, Walter Lang, Stuart Peters, Lowell Sherman, and Sheldon Keate Callaway.

Columbo's seven surviving brothers and sisters conspired to keep news about the death from their mother. With her having suffered a heart attack two days prior to Columbo's accident, they were concerned that the shock of hearing about his death would kill her. A story was concocted about Columbo agreeing to a five-year tour abroad. While money from his life insurance policy was used to support her, the deception was maintained for a decade until she died. The family employed a variety of stratagems during this period, including sending letters, allegedly written by the singer, which contained newsy accounts, tender sentiments, and reports of his many successes. Warren Hall noted, in the October 8, 1944, issue of *The American Weekly* (a Sunday supplement distributed in the Hearst syndicated newspapers), that they took the further precaution of imprinting each envelope with a rubber stamp to simulate a London postmark. The same stamp was conspicuous on the wrappings of the Christmas and birthday gifts that arrived "from your loving son."

The family also played records in order to simulate his radio program. The only radio shows actually heard in the Columbo household were those that made no mention of bandleaders. Even though his mother was almost totally blind, all newspapers coming into the house were carefully censored. Lombard assisted by corresponding with Mrs. Columbo, explaining that her son was unable to visit because he was performing in the major cities of Europe. All visitors were warned to speak as though Russ were still alive and more popular than ever. According to Hall, when Mrs. Columbo died in 1944 at the age of seventy-eight, her last words were: "Tell Russ . . . I am so proud . . . and happy."

Many music historians have openly questioned whether the "Battle of the Baritones" would have turned out differently if Columbo's life hadn't been tragically ended. According to Deal,

> Rudy Vallee was one man in the business who thought so, on account of Crosby's drinking habits in the early thirties, believing that Bing may have lost some popularity if Columbo's career had continued. Johnny Mercer disagreed for he took the view that Columbo did not

possess Crosby's original talent and did not have the type of personality that gave Crosby such a universal appeal. By 1934, if not before, Russ Columbo was the finest singer of love songs in the United States and the one who had the greatest attraction for women, although the timbre of his voice also appealed to men—as did Bing Crosby's and Al Bowlly's. Columbo phrased rather like Crosby, in a voice more silkily textured than that of his "rival" but it is doubtful if he could have handled the more rhythmic sort of number which Crosby excelled at or, indeed, the country and western type of song, such as "Home on the Range," "The Last Round-Up" or "Empty Saddles" that Bing featured so successfully. Russ Columbo did represent the most serious challenge to Crosby and at only twenty-six years of age—he was five years younger than Bing—it is reasonable to assume that his best years were still to come. It says something for the talent and popularity of the man that it was to be almost six years before another serious challenger—in the person of Frank Sinatra—forced his way into the reckoning.[6]

Despite the relatively limited number of recordings made by Columbo during his lifetime, Crosby is probably the only crooner predating the Sinatra era to have been honored by more reissues. Over the years there have been a notable number of tribute albums to Columbo, including those of Paul Bruno, Gordon Lewis, Steve Mason, and Jerry Vale. Although the project is not yet a reality, many singers—including Perry Como, Don Cornell, Johnny Desmond, and Tony Martin—have been considered for the leading role in a film biography of Columbo. In the 1950s a television drama featuring Tony Curtis as the crooner got as far as the planning stage.

NOTES

1. Barry Ulanov, *The Incredible Crosby* (New York: Whittlesey House, 1948), 130.
2. Roy Hemming and David Hajdu, "Russ Columbo," in *Discovering Great Singers of Classic Pop* (New York: Newmarket Press, 1991): 54.
3. "He's Thrilling, Girls, This Russ Columbo!" *Anderson (Indiana) Bulletin* [NEA Service] (November 28, 1931): 5.
4. James Lincoln Collier, *Benny Goodman and the Swing Era* (New York: Oxford University Press, 1989), 93.
5. Robert F. Deal, *The Story of Russ Columbo* (Middlesex, England: Hampton, Memory Lane, 1988), 10.
6. Deal, *The Story of Russ Columbo*, 13.

3

Bing Crosby

Considerable confusion exists regarding Bing Crosby's birth date; the singer himself, in his autobiography, *Call Me Lucky*, would state, "I've seen several dates listed for my birth in various publications, among them, 1901, 1903, and 1906. I'd like to take 1906, but 1904 is the one I was stuck with." Baptismal entries at St. Patrick's Church, combined with sister Catherine's Tacoma birth certificate (October 3, 1904) indicate that he was born Harry Lillis Crosby on May 2, 1903, at the family's home on 1112 North J Street. He was the fourth child of Harry Lowe and Catherine Helen Crosby (maiden name Harrigan). Besides Catherine and Bing, other offspring included Laurence Earl (Larry), January 3, 1895; Everett Nathaniel, April 5, 1896; Henry Edward (Ted), July 30, 1900; Mary Rose, May 3, 1906; and George Robert (Bob), August 25, 1913.

The Harrigan family had Irish-Catholic roots; Catherine, known as Kate, was born February 7, 1873, in Stillwater, Minnesota. Her family would later migrate to Tacoma, where she met her future husband.

The Crosby family appears to have been of Danish origin; its forebears were allegedly Vikings who settled the British Isles during the eighth through tenth centuries. Bing's brother Larry found that the *Mayflower* had included a Crosby, a damsel said to have married Thomas Brewster, one of the Pilgrim Fathers. Bing's paternal great-grandfather, Nathaniel, a sea captain hailing from Worcester, Mas-

sachusetts, traded in the Far East and helped found Portland prior
to helping settle Olympia, Washington.

Harry, born in Olympia on November 28, 1870, attended a year or
so of college before becoming a bookkeeper. A charming, easygoing
man from a good family and engaged in a good profession, he was
undoubtedly a solid catch for the pretty, level-headed Kate. His con-
version to Catholicism cleared any barriers to their union, and the
marriage took place in the early 1890s.

Harry was a bookkeeper for the county treasurer during Bing's
early years, but a change in political administration caused him to
lose his job. Like many other inhabitants along the Coast with limited prospects, he found Spokane enticing. Located two hundred
miles eastward near the Idaho border, Spokane was in a fertile
wheat belt and, as a railroad center, it was becoming the logging
and mining center of the region. Harry found work there as a bookkeeper for the Inland Brewery and sent for the family in July 1906.

The family residence, a two-story, four-bedroom rented house on
Sinto Avenue, was located on the northeast side of the city, across
the Spokane River from the business and manufacturing districts.
The home—comfortably equipped with indoor plumbing and electricity and located near stores and trolley lines that ran to the downtown sector—would become the hub of Bing's childhood years. A
number of the more formative institutions of his life—Webster, a
grade school; a Jesuit-administered high school-college complex
named Gonzaga; and the adjoining church, St. Aloysius—were located within three blocks of his home.

Bing received his famous nickname around 1910. At this time he
became a fan of the "Bingville Bugle," which occupied a full page
of the Spokane *Spokesman Review*'s Sunday edition. Taking the appearance of the front page of a newspaper published in the mythical
Bingville, the humor feature included short country-bumpkin stories about town citizens, sometimes illustrated by cartoon spots. A
next-door-neighbor friend, Valentine Hobart, noticed that carica-
tures of the cartoon residents had stocky, pear shapes and protrud-
ing ears exactly like those possessed by young Harry. Valentine
began calling him Bingo from Bingville. Other school peers picked
up the phrase, which soon was shortened simply to Bingo; eventually the *o* was dropped and the youngster was known to all thence-
forth as Bing.

Music was always a key ingredient of life within the Crosby

household. One memorable payday evening Bing's father returned home toting two large packages containing a phonograph complete with a large speaker horn, in addition to several records featuring baritone Denis O'Sullivan, marches by John Philip Sousa and other bandleaders, and a collection of songs from Gilbert and Sullivan's operetta *The Mikado*. On another occasion, Dad Crosby went without a new suit he had been saving for in order to purchase a piano. Kate made sure that her daughters received lessons on the instrument; however, none of the boys displayed an interest. Every Sunday evening the Crosbys would engage in a family songfest. Dad Crosby would bring out his mandolin and four-string guitar, and all would gather round their favorite pop standards. Kate possessed a rich contralto voice—she'd been a member of the church choir in Tacoma prior to the responsibilities of motherhood—and the children (except for Everett, who reputedly couldn't carry a tune in a bucket) did a creditable job of contributing the harmony parts.

It is perhaps not surprising that Bing's involvement in music typified his easygoing, albeit self-assured, approach to life in general. Donald Shepherd and Robert F. Slatzer have noted,

> Even in grade school, Bing . . . was . . . what is called a quick study in show business; he had something akin to total recall. This was true for people's names and faces, which ingratiated him with the adults in his early years and with the relatively unknown technicians or bit-part actors he met during his professional life. But at Webster and at Gonzaga High School and at college, his extraordinary ability was used to get ordinary grades with as little time and effort as he could get away with.[1]

Barry Ulanov, in *The Incredible Crosby,* has succinctly addressed the forces behind Crosby's increasing realization that music had the potential to become more than a mere hobby in his life.

> It was "life-worship" that impelled his musical career, organized it, carried it along. At no point in the early years, years of whistling and singing and beating almost aimlessly on doors and pots and pans and rude drum equipment, did Bing consciously imagine himself a singer or a musician. He was fascinated with music, as many of his school friends were. He was sufficiently interested to convert his whistling and singing and drumming, as he had his abilities to sweep up floors and push buttons and pick berries, into a job of work. When, during

the school years, he and his friends . . . knocked together a band, it was easy for him to make the band his major interest. The impulse was there; all that was needed was the organization of a vehicle to transport the impulse from whistling at work to working at whistling.[2]

Bing entered Gonzaga College in September 1920. In addition to the baseball team and cheerleading, his extracurricular activities included joining the college band. The latter activity gave him access to a bass drum and six like-minded musicians; in short order they formed a dance combo known as the Juicy Seven. Bing's contributions included drumming and periodic vocal turns. While the musicians apparently weren't very good—employing stock arrangements that were not only dated but called for instrumentation the outfit lacked—they managed to obtain gigs at school dances and occasional off-campus parties.

After a couple years with the Juicy Seven, Bing received a telephone call that was to prove a watershed development in his music career. Al Rinker, whose group, the Musicaladers, needed a competent drummer, asked Bing to come by for a tryout. Rinker would later recall the group's first practice session with Bing: "We went over a couple of tunes and we knew right away that this guy had a beat. Not only that, but he picked up his megaphone, and he could *sing!* So this was *great*, a real surprise to us."[3]

For his part, Bing was impressed that the Musicaladers performed the latest hits, utilizing the harmonies, phrasings, and voicings of the hot, avant-garde bands of the day.

Although not yet accomplished musicians, the Musicaladers became extremely popular in the Spokane area, most notably with the younger generation, who tended to dislike the "old-fashioned" music of their elders. By September 1925, however, three of the band members had left for college and another attempted to break into the Los Angeles music scene, leaving only Al and Bing. During the course of hanging out, playing golf, and going to parties, they began experimenting as a singing duo.

Hearing that the Clemmer Theater was looking for a quartet to perform between motion pictures, they acquired three singers, utilizing Al as an accompanist. The group was hired, but, following a week of lackluster results, the management fired all of the singers but Bing. After performing solo for a few shows, Bing convinced the management to let him sing with Rinker. Al would remember, "The audience loved us. So we stayed there about five weeks, making about thirty dollars a week each, and this was big money for us. That's how we began singing together professionally."

With Bing now earning more money on the side as a musician than beginning attorneys typically were paid for full-time work, he cast aside his earlier ambition of studying law. When the Clemmer Theater decided to revert back to showing films without a stage show, however, Al and Bing were suddenly unemployed in a town that appeared to be a dead-end for anyone harboring show business aspirations. Accordingly, they decided to try their luck in Los Angeles, where Al's sister Mildred Bailey was just beginning her career singing in speakeasies and Bing's brother Everett was selling trucks.

Arriving in Los Angeles in their 1916 topless Model-T Ford, the boys sought out Mildred Bailey, who used her show-business contacts to help them find work. In short order, they were hired at $75 a week each to perform in the Fanchon and Marco traveling variety show called *The Syncopation Idea*. The show included jugglers, comedians, dancing girls, and other vaudevillians and started out in small cities like Glendale and Long Beach, moving north to San Francisco and Sacramento, where the tour ended thirteen weeks later. The experience enabled them to polish their act and, by tour's end, they were doing encores.

Back in Los Angeles, Al and Bing caught on with a musical show called *Will Morrissey's Music Hall Revue* for $150 a week. Billed as "Two Boys and a Piano," they proved adept at stopping the show, with audiences demanding encores. Morrissey helped book the duo for a notable one-night engagement at the Olympic Auditorium, where they shared the stage with such established stars as Eddie Cantor, Fannie Brice, George Jessel, Jackie Coogan, Pola Negri, and Charlie Chaplin, and took them to exclusive Hollywood parties. After the Los Angeles run, the Morrissey Revue played in San Diego's Spreckels Theater, the Capital Theater in San Francisco, and the Lobero Theater in Santa Barbara for an additional eight weeks.

While the revue was still playing in Los Angeles, the Paramount Publix chain signed the duo to perform in stage shows that complemented film showings at two theaters, the Grenada in San Francisco and the Metropolitan in Los Angeles. The contract, which paid the act $300 a week, took effect as soon as the Morrissey Revue closed or when Al and Bing's affiliation with the show terminated, whichever came first. Billed as Crosby and Rinker, they played—along with the rest of the troupe—four shows a day, five on weekends. Although now playing in far more prestigious venues, they continued to be show stoppers. Their audiences didn't know what they were doing, from a technical standpoint—the jazz touches, variations on the melody, and flirtations with minor chords or the augmented and diminished facets of major chords prior to modulating back on track. However, people responded instinctively to Al and Bing's energy and enthusiasm.

While Crosby and Rinker were playing their second engagement at the Metropolitan, Paul Whiteman, leader of the most popular band in the world, arrived in Los Angeles to perform at Sid Grauman's Million Dollar Theater. According to Crosby biographer Charles Thompson, Jimmy Gillespie, Whiteman's manager, saw the duo and recommended them to his boss. Whiteman then sent viola player Matty Malneck and pianist Ray Turner to see the act. They brought back highly favorable reports; Malneck indicated that the duo had an infectious style, "like hearing a great jazz player for the first time."[4] Whiteman sent word for Crosby and Rinker to come back for a visit and immediately offered them a job with his organization. He went on, "I'll start you at $150 a week each, and you can make extra money from recordings and from a couple of Broadway plays we're going to be in; we're signed to do a show called *Lucky* and one called *Whoopee*."[5] Eleven months from the day they'd left Spokane to seek fame and fortune, they signed a contract to sing with Whiteman's band.

Many observers have attempted to ascertain why Crosby and Rinker achieved so much in such a comparatively short period of time. Certainly, at that time there were many talented duos comprised of young men who possessed fine voices, attractive personalities, and superb show-business instincts. More than one expert has posited that Al Rinker's arrangements are what enabled them to rise above the competition in a comparatively short period of time.

While Crosby and Rinker were completing their contractual arrangement with Paramount Publix, Don Clark, a former Whiteman sideman whose orchestra was playing at the Biltmore Hotel in Los Angeles, asked them to cut a record with his musicians. Music historians have speculated that news of duo's agreement with Whiteman may have been the primary reason Clark sought out their services. As a result, Al and Bing sang on two songs recorded October 18,

1926, in the giant ballroom of the Biltmore. One selection, "Don't Somebody Need Somebody?" was never released. The other, "I've Got the Girl," composed by Walter Donaldson (perhaps best known for pop standards such as "My Blue Heaven" and "Carolina in the Morning"), was issued by Columbia, backed by the instrumental "Idolizing."

The release proved to be something of an embarrassment. According to Bob Osborn and Vernon Wesley Taylor, whose comments appeared along with a limited-edition, 7-inch LP issued by the Bing Crosby Historical Society of Tacoma in 1980, Columbia apparently thought that the master cut of the record was slow. In an effort to achieve a jazzier sound, the recording was speeded up when duplicates were cut for release. Both Al and Bing would later admit that they sounded like a pair of chipmunks chattering in the background.

After a one-week engagement at Spokane's Liberty Theater, from November 21 through November 27, accented by visits with family and friends, Crosby and Rinker headed to Chicago to meet up with Whiteman. Despite at least one awkward moment—a piano they were pushing offstage following their segment in one particular concert tipped over, requiring the combined efforts of Al, Bing, and Whiteman himself to get it back on its wheels as the audience roared with laughter—the duo continued to elicit a favorable response. During the three-theater run in Chicago, they had the opportunity to cut another record, "Wistful and Blue," recorded December 22, 1926, at the Concert Hall on Michigan Avenue. Whiteman also went out of his way to take them around town, introducing them to important people. Rinker would later recall, "Whiteman seemed to be quite proud of us. We were young and eager, and I think it was because we were fresh and very enthusiastic that he took more than a casual interest in us."[6]

Crosby and Rinker's success continued in the cities where Whiteman played en route to the East Coast. Their New York City debut at the Paramount Theatre on Times Square in January 1927, however, brought them face-to-face with failure for the first time since they'd turned professional. By the time Whiteman opened his own club at 48th and Broadway on February 18, they had been reduced to performing during intermission; for most of the run they worked as stagehands. In 1980, Rinker offered the following explanation for their poor reception in the Big Apple:

People didn't seem to understand what we were doing! We'd go: bop-bop-de-do-do / de-doodle-eeaaaa [snapping his fingers while singing scat] and stuff like that. And they didn't know what the hell we were doing! And now that I think about it, I don't blame them. The New York audience was mostly Jewish—provincial in its own way—staid; you know what I mean. They were used to great entertainers of a certain tradition like Jolson, Cantor, and Sophie Tucker, who were *belting* out songs. [Imitating Jolson here] Mammmeee! Mammmeee! They *really* let you have it! But we were *intimate*. That wasn't what they expected, and they didn't like it.[7]

In February 1927, with Al and Bing's career in jeopardy, violinist Matty Malneck suggested they get together with Harry Barris, a singer and piano player who was in danger of being let go because Whiteman couldn't find a place for him in the organization. Having nothing to lose, all three were receptive to the idea. Rinker recalled the meeting arranged by Malneck,

We talked, then Barris played a couple of his songs. One of them was "Mississippi Mud," which he had composed—James Cavanaugh had done the lyrics—and we liked it. We talked some more, fooled around at the piano a bit, then we said, "Let's learn it." So we started harmonizing and arranging it, all four of us chipping in ideas, and then we finished, it sounded great to Bing and me because we had another voice there. And Barris could *really* swing, you know. So we learned "Mississippi Mud" and another number, "Ain't She Sweet," We thought that was great, too, because it was another song for us, and we were anything but intimate in our delivery.[8]

Malneck then herded the trio over to Whiteman's club for an audition, where it performed the two numbers. The trio sang in three-part harmony, with Barris and Rinker playing pianos, accented by Bing's filigrees on a hand-held cymbal. The bandleader was delighted and immediately put them on at the club, billed as Paul Whiteman's Rhythm Boys. They were enthusiastically received and were on their way to becoming one of the hottest trios ever to perform.

Back in Whiteman's good graces for the time being, Bing cut his first disk as a solo artist on March 7, 1927. The song, "Muddy Water," was recorded by Victor at Leiderkranz Hall in Manhattan, with accompaniment by the Whiteman Orchestra. Shortly thereafter, on April 29, 1927, the Rhythm Boys made their first record with Whiteman, "Side by Side" (Victor).

The Rhythm Boys also contributed a number, "Sam, the Accordion Man," to the musical *Lucky*, which ran for seventy-one performances at the New Amsterdam Theater, beginning March 22. After it closed, the Whiteman Orchestra toured the United States. Rather than taking the trio with him, Whiteman booked it as a headliner on the vaudeville circuit for forty-five weeks. His rationale for this decision remains a topic for conjecture. Rinker believed it was because Whiteman didn't consider their act suitable for concerts. Crosby biographers such as Thompson and Ulanov, however, repeated the Crosby organization's take on the issue, that the trio was relegated to the vaudeville tour in disgrace. Numerous people associated with Crosby at the time, including some of Whiteman's musicians, have argued that Whiteman—while fond of Bing and impressed with his talent—would get incensed at his irresponsible behavior, particularly his drinking binges and tendency to miss engagements.

It could easily be argued that headlining the Keith-Albee-Orpheum circuit—the top vaudeville venue at the time—was not a completely depressing experience. The trio was earning $1,000 per week for just two 12- to 15-minute shows a day. There was plenty of time left to play golf, attend college football games as they toured the Midwest, and enjoy the company of star-struck young women. Despite these distractions, the trio was on its best behavior, not missing engagements and earning uniformly positive reviews. The Rhythm Boys also participated in more than a dozen recording sessions independent of Whiteman; the first, on June 20, 1927, resulted in two records, "Mississippi Mud"/"I Left My Sugar Standing in the Rain" and "Sweet Li'l"/"Ain't She Sweet."

When the tour ended during the summer of 1928, the Whiteman office apparently continued to book the act into New York area venues for the next few months, occasionally with the orchestra itself. In the meantime, Whiteman was planning new challenges for his organization, with the Rhythm Boys as a featured attraction.

Whiteman had been one of last big-name holdouts with the radio medium, believing it would undercut record sales and personal appearances. The grind of producing a weekly show acted as another deterrent to such a move. However, when Old Gold cigarettes made him a lucrative offer, he approached NBC about doing a show.

Much to his surprise, the network turned him down, explaining, "We already have a cigarette account."

Whiteman immediately took his package over to CBS. *The Old Gold-Paul Whiteman Hour* was broadcast from New York City at 9 P.M., Tuesday, to an estimated fourteen million radio sets. Part of the arrangement had Whiteman and his various ensembles, including the Rhythm Boys, jump from the Victor label to Columbia. Old Gold also agreed to sponsor a radio tie-in for a projected motion picture featuring Whiteman, *King of Jazz.* An entire train was leased for the trip out to the West Coast, the Old Gold-Paul Whiteman Special, with stops at sixteen cities along the way.

Prior to the Western trip, Whiteman and the Rhythm Boys played in another Broadway musical, *Whoopee,* which opened December 4, 1928, at the New Amsterdam Theater. The Whiteman Orchestra replaced George Olsen's orchestra in the show and was then itself replaced when Whiteman headed for Hollywood. The Rhythm Boys also recorded the hit song from the musical, "Makin' Whoopee," for Columbia on December 11, 1928.

Bing's first solo recording for Columbia, "My Kinda Love"/"Till We Meet"—cut March 14, 1929 and featuring a piano, violin, and guitar accompaniment—represented yet another pivotal development in his career. In a May 1929 letter to his mother, he wrote that "my name is being prominently featured in the newspapers and in the broadcasts, and considerable invaluable publicity thus redounds to me." This could be interpreted to mean that Crosby was already thinking in terms of a solo career. Family biographers indicate that a successful agent offered him a personal management contract, promising him work in radio and possibly musical comedy. Although tempted, Bing opted for the status quo in view of the Rhythm Boys' success, his lack of confidence in his ability as a solo performer, and the speculative nature of the agent's offer.

When the Whiteman entourage reached Los Angeles on June 6, 1929, it was caught up in a swirl of preparatory activities: lighting tests, film tests, sound tests, and so forth. Whiteman's doubts about the project were compounded by the fact that Universal Pictures had yet to create a script. With the movie company picking up the tab for the Whiteman orchestra—close to $10,000 a week in all—individual members were left to pursue their own interests.

In addition to hosting parties in a large leased home on Fairfax Avenue and playing golf, Crosby made the rounds of the movie studios. According to Whiteman biographer Glenhall Taylor, the studios spent, collectively, more than $70,000 in screen tests on Bing, and none offered a contract. One casting director allegedly turned him down because of his protruding ears.

At some point during their West Coast residency, for several weeks the Rhythm Boys played the Montmartre Café—an exclusive dining and dancing spot on Hollywood Boulevard where film celebrities went to be seen. During this engagement, they became the "discovery" of the movie colony and the talk of the town. This popularity appears to have been a key factor in the trio's decision to part with Whiteman shortly after the completion of *King of Jazz* in March 1930. Furthermore, Bing—the spokesman for the group—seems to have harbored some resentment that a feature solo for the film "Song of the Dawn," originally promised to him, was shot with John Boles while Bing was locked up in the county jail for public intoxication. Shepherd and Slatzer's assessment of the forces behind the breakup, however, appears to have been closest to actual fact.

> The boys had never really been enthusiastic about going back with Whiteman after they finished their vaudeville tour. They had had more freedom as an individual act; they weren't subject to the discipline that Whiteman insisted upon; they didn't have to sit through hours of performance holding dummy instruments on the bandstand; they had had star billing, rather than being an appendage of a famous orchestra; and finally, they wanted to stay on the West Coast, where they felt assured of starring as a trio and of getting movie work as well.[9]

Whiteman had scheduled a tour up the West Coast that would continue into Canada and back to the East. In Seattle, the Rhythm Boys left the band for good. From all reports, the departure was amicable on both sides.

The trio returned to Los Angeles, signing on with booking agent Leonard Goldstein. A chance meeting with an executive from an oil company that sponsored a local radio variety show emceed by Walter O'Keefe resulted in a thirteen-week booking. This was followed by a stint at the prestigious Cocoanut Grove nightclub. Although their salary was no more than Al and Bing had made when they first signed with Whiteman, the club offered other advantages. The owner, Abe Frank, had installed a radio studio and his shows were broadcast nightly from ten to twelve along a Pacific Coast network reaching as far north as Seattle and east to Denver. Entertainment was diversified, featuring two full orchestras, conducted by Gus Arnheim and Carlos Molina, respectively, and a trio called the Three Cheers.

At the Cocoanut Grove, the Rhythm Boys became the hottest act in town. Besides the Montmartre fans who followed them there, they became very popular with the college crowd. The crowd's response to Crosby's singing led to solo stints—both live and in the recording studio—with the Arnheim orchestra. Shepherd and Slatzer have noted that Bing's success was largely due to his development of an innovative singing style.

> Prior to this time, Bing was delivering songs in a smooth manner not unlike the lyrical style used by Irish tenors of the day, concentrating on producing "pretty" pear-shaped tones and adhering to the melody, which resulted in his sounding much like the voicing of a technically correct but uninspired alto saxophone solo. But at the Grove, Bing seems to have brought all of his musical experience to bear on his delivery, and the result was the first stage of a totally new style of singing, different from that of any singer before him and much copied by all who followed.[10]

Vernon Wesley Taylor elicited the following insights from Kenny Allen, a vocalist with the Three Cheers Trio who had the opportunity to observe the Crosby phenomena firsthand during this period:

> I've given a lot of thought to the phenomenon of the popular singer. After all, I tried to be one myself. Well, Bing, besides that intonation of his, had a very nice sense of swing; that's hard to manage even once in a while. Most of us were not only afraid to do it, we hoped the whole idea of it would go away. But Crosby did it all the time—fast songs, slow songs, silly songs, sad songs. It didn't seem to matter with him. He didn't look like he gave a damn, and yet he still managed to make you think he did.[11]

With the premiere of *King of Jazz* at New York City's Roxy Theatre in June 1930, the Rhythm Boys received more film offers. Pathé engaged them in a couple of "two-reeler" musical shorts, *Ripstitch the Tailor* (never released) and *Two Plus Fours* (1930). They next appeared in the features *Check and Double Check*, a 1930 RKO release starring radio comedians Amos and Andy, and *Confessions of a Co-Ed* (Paramount, 1931). *Reaching for the Moon* (United Artists, 1931), starring Douglas Fairbanks, was notable for two Crosby firsts: a solo ("When Folks Up North Do the Mean Lowdown") and a spoken part (two words: "Hi, gang").

At this time, Bing had begun focusing on his solo work at the Cocoanut Grove to the detriment of the Rhythm Boys spots. His partners didn't seem particularly concerned about this state of affairs. Barris was able to put more energy into composing, supplying Crosby with some of the best material during his early career, including "I Surrender, Dear" and "It Must Be True." Rinker would reflect, "I had less and less to do at the Grove, but I had my own interests apart from work, and I really didn't give it much thought at the time."[12] He went on to success as a radio, then television, producer.

During the Grove residency, Bing met and wooed Dixie Lee (a.k.a. Wilma Winnifred Wyatt), a young actress felt by many film insiders to possess the potential to become the next blonde bombshell. Their marriage on September 29, 1930, at the Blessed Sacrament Church on Sunset Boulevard brought such newspaper headlines as: "20th Century Fox Star Married Obscure Crooner." Crosby's relative obscurity, however, was soon to become a thing of the past.

Clashes with Frank over missed engagements at the Grove had usually ended with Crosby's salary being docked. When Crosby walked out on one occasion—followed by Rinker and Barris—Frank retaliated by getting the Musicians' Union to blacklist the trio. The impossibility of finding work, combined with the members' outside interests, led to the breakup of the Rhythm Boys. Going on alone seemed like the only logical move for Crosby. "I Surrender, Dear," recorded for Victor on January 19, 1931, with accompaniment by the Arnheim band, had became Bing's first notable solo hit.

Bing's first step as a solo act was to have his personal manager, brother Everett, play a more active role in his career. Bing's wife brought John O'Melveny, a lawyer she had met at Fox, into the organization. O'Melveny effectively sorted out the ban, thereby enabling Crosby to find work. Bing was impressed enough to retain O'Melveny as his lawyer for forty-five years.

No longer hindered by the ban, Everett secured a contract from Mack Sennett for Bing to appear in six film shorts, each one to be based on songs with which he was associated. The films—all shot in

1931—included *I Surrender Dear, Just One More Chance, Billboard Girl, Dream House, Sing Bing Sing,* and *Where the Blue of the Night.*

Everett's next goal was to obtain a national radio show for Bing. William Paley, president of CBS, quickly signed him for $600 a week in the fall of 1931. Despite a three-day postponement due to throat problems, Bing was an immediate hit with radio listeners. As the broadcast grew in stature, Cremo Cigars came aboard as the show's sponsor.

If any doubt remained that Crosby was a smashing success as a solo artist, Everett got him a ten-week contract to headline at New York City's Paramount Theatre, where he had flopped along with Al Rinker during the Whiteman period. The stint, which began November 1931 and paid $2,500 a week, broke all house records and was extended to twenty-nine weeks, another venue first.

Paramount manager Bob Weitman also contributed to Crosby's rise in popularity. Thompson notes,

> The so-called Battle of the Baritones was another of Weitman's gimmicks to pull the crowds in. He put the handsome Russ Columbo with his Valentino looks into the Brooklyn Paramount a few miles from the Manhattan one. Russ, a former colleague of Bing's in the Gus Arnheim days at the Cocoanut Grove, was now making something of a name as a crooner. And an artificial rivalry was being whipped up purely for publicity. Bing and Columbo were really the best of friends—although the public were not led to think so.[13]

Some entertainment business observers, including fellow crooner Rudy Vallee, have argued that Crosby might never have achieved the success he did if Columbo had lived. Lyricist Johnny Mercer felt otherwise, stating, "Columbo would have done very well, but I don't think he had what Bing had. He didn't have Bing's original talent. He copied Bing. He didn't have Bing's line of talk and he didn't have Bing's personality. He was a different kind of man."[14]

With his popularity reaching new heights, Crosby returned to Hollywood to appear in the film *The Big Broadcast of 1932.* In contrast to the days when his ears had scared away many movie moguls, he was now considered money in the bank. In the midst of production, Paramount signed him to make five films over a period of three years for a fee of $300,000. Bing would end up making fifty-eight pictures with the studio, including some of the biggest box-office successes of all time. Paramount head Adolph Zukor, later recalling that Crosby had expressed reservations about his acting abilities, offered the following assessment: "He doesn't have to act; he can just be himself and that's enough. That's what he was and that's why he was different to anybody else, and yet he reached stardom and popularity not only in this country but all over the world."[15]

Crosby also found time to tour in 1932, hiring pianist-conductor Lennie Hayton and former Whiteman guitarist Eddie Lang. In New York, he met a young comic named Bob Hope, who was sharing the bill with him at the Capitol Theatre. Although they wouldn't formally team up for another seven years, Thompson notes that they immediately recognized the potential for working together professionally.

> It was there, between shows, that Hope and Crosby displayed their natural but competitive good humour. Many of the patrons thought they were indulging in plain old bar talk, but as Bob was to reveal more than forty years later, they knew it was the start of something big: "The chemistry was so good and it was a great piece of electricity, because things were happening all the time—new, fresh things and that's always great for anything."[16]

By 1934 Crosby was a major star on three fronts—radio, film, and sound recordings. He was receiving 10,000 letters per month and close to 100 fan clubs were established worldwide. Rudy Vallee himself allegedly saw the writing on the wall after hearing Bing singing "Beside a Shady Nook." Vallee provided his own interpretation of the song on his radio program and then announced to his eighteen million listeners: "This man Bing Crosby, who has recorded this number for Gus Arnheim, is going to push me off my throne."[17]

Despite Crosby's regular appearances in motion pictures and broadcasts (by the mid-1930s he was averaging three movies a year, along with the weekly radio show), his recordings were probably most responsible for the vast size of his audience. At the time of his death, he was estimated to have waxed some 4,000 songs, with combined sales of 400,000,000. (Furthermore, new recordings—in the latest electronic configurations—seem to appear almost daily.) Up to 1934, Bing had recorded extensively with both of the major U.S. labels—Victor and Columbia. On August 8, 1934, however, he became the first artist to sign with the newly founded Decca, headed by visionary Jack Kapp.

While Crosby virtually carried the fledging label on his shoulders during the mid-1930s, his career in turn owed much to Kapp's sound policies. Bing would later comment,

> He was tremendously competent. I was impressed with what he'd done and had great faith in him. He developed a recording programme for me that involved every kind of music. I sang with every kind of band and every kind of vocal group—religious songs, patriotic songs and even light opera songs. I thought he was crazy, but I had confidence and went along with his suggestions![18]

In 1935, the *Kraft Music Hall*, then radio's best-known program, invited Crosby to participate in an experimental broadcast. The December 5 show had host Paul Whiteman performing in New York, while Crosby, backed by Jimmy Dorsey's orchestra, sang from Hollywood. It was an immense success, and before the end of the year Bing was signed as the new host. The program, now based in Hollywood, quickly became the medium's number one offering, attracting a listening audience of roughly 50,000,000.

When Jimmy Dorsey—concerned that only one radio program per week was undercutting his identity as a major big band leader—expressed his wish to leave the Kraft organization after two years, John Scott Trotter was brought in as the orchestra leader. Trotter, who'd made a name as the arranger for the Hal Kemp band, became a major architect of the Crosby sound, staying with the Kraft show for more than 300 broadcasts. Bing took an immediate liking to the musical director and let him significantly modify the style of the orchestra. In essence, Trotter shifted the melody line from the band over to Crosby, making sure that the saxophones didn't interfere with his voice. He offered the following justification for this policy: "If you listen to some of his early records, they've got saxophones practically in exactly the same range as Bing—and that is lethal."[19]

During the 1930s, it could be argued that Crosby's film accomplishments lagged far behind his stature in radio, performing venues, and the recording industry. The "Road" series would change that perception in dramatic fashion. Beginning with *Road to Singapore*, the series—which encompassed seven films made over a twenty-year period—ultimately broke all existing box office records, as well as creating a new style of cinema. With Hollywood in the midst of a South Sea Island fad, calculated to provide escapist fare for a world facing the harsh realties of economic depression and global warfare, Paramount decided to team Bing and Bob Hope, a pairing that had already produced inspired comedy on the airwaves. The films were notable for enabling the two stars to ad-lib almost at will. Co-star Dorothy Lamour would later recall, "That's the way it was, the whole way through; you never knew what they were going to say. You kind of had that feeling that maybe they stayed home the night before and read their scripts to see who could out-do the other."[20]

Shortly after the second film of the series, *Road to Zanzibar*, was released, the United States became a direct participant in World War II. Cutting back on his radio and film activities, Crosby shifted the bulk of energies to raising money for the Armed Forces. One tour, which teamed him with Jimmy Van Heusen, covered more than 5,000 miles stateside as they performed for servicemen and visited hundreds of hospital wards. The trips, which lasted throughout the war years, were extremely taxing, with Crosby averaging three shows a day in camps across the nation.

In late summer 1944 Crosby traveled to Europe to help boost morale among American military personnel and the Allied citizenry. In addition to live performances and personal appearances, he was persuaded to broadcast to Germany from London. He talked and sang in phonetic German, expressing the hope that soon the German nation would know the freedoms enjoyed by Americans and Britons. From that time on, the enemy fondly referred to him as "Der Bingle."

While Crosby was less visible in the mass media during the war years, his work reached new heights for both commercial success and artistic achievement. *Holiday Inn*, released in 1942, became the top-grossing musical up to that time. Its Irving Berlin score included "Easter Parade" and "White Christmas"; Crosby's rendition of the latter song is probably the biggest-selling record of all time, estimated to more than 30,000,000 units at the time of his death.

The following year, Bing began work on *Going My Way;* cast as a Catholic priest, his performance earned him an Oscar for Best Actor in 1944. The film also won the New York critics' Golden Globe award as best motion picture and propelled Bing to the top of the box-office draw chart for the fifth consecutive year. In addition, the soundtrack included two of his most popular records ever, "Swinging on a Star" (which received an Oscar for Best Song) and an updated rendition of "Silent Night."

Bing's role as Father O'Malley was reprised in *The Bells of St. Mary's;* it went on to become the biggest money-maker of 1945. He also made brief film appearances in support of the war effort. He sang "Buy Bonds" in 20th Century-Fox's *All Star Bond Rally* and "We've Got Another Bond to Buy" in *Hollywood Victory Caravan.* During the war, he is estimated to have sold Victory Bonds worth over $14,500,000.

Crosby was now at the pinnacle of his popularity. Evidence of his popularity seemed to be everywhere:

- The National Father's Day Committee named him the "Number One Screen Father of 1945."
- GIs, in a poll sponsored by *Yank* magazine, voted him the person doing the most for their morale overseas.
- At a time when gold records were rare, three more of his releases reached that plateau (bringing the total to twelve): "Too-ra-loo-ra-loo-ral," "Don't Fence Me In," and "I Can't Begin to Tell You."
- At least two entertainment trade publications—*The Motion Picture Herald* and *Radio Daily*—voted him the most profitable star for the second consecutive year.
- *Box-Office Magazine* named him "the year's Top All-American Male Star."
- *The Motion Picture Daily Fame Poll* designated him the "Top Radio Master of Ceremonies" for the fourth consecutive year and "Top Male Vocalist" for the ninth straight year.
- *Billboard*'s poll of army camps had him receiving far more votes than the combined tallies of his chief singing rivals, Frank Sinatra, Perry Como, and Dick Haymes.

Despite these successes, the rise of Sinatra—particularly after his boffo appearances at New York's Paramount around Christmastime 1942, when girls allegedly screamed and swooned for the first time in show business annals—was viewed by some as a threat to Bing's hegemony within the entertainment field. Sinatra himself admitted that he had been inspired by Crosby, stating, "I don't believe that any singer has enjoyed the unanimous acclaim of the American public, as well as performers and musicians, as much as Bing." Rather than slavishly copying the latter's style, however, Sinatra made it clear he was seeking fame and fortune on his own terms. Likewise, Bing paid his respects to Sinatra's talent, even inviting the young singer to appear on the November 16, 1944, broadcast of the *Kraft Music Hall.*

Much in the same manner as the "Battle of the Baritones" in the early 1930s, the clash between "the Swooner versus the Crooner" was hype as a result of its box office appeal. Sinatra soon acquired his own radio show and his chief gag writer, Carroll Carroll, continued to function in this capacity for Crosby as well. Carroll would later outline the characterizations supplied to each star: "Bing was the avuncular elder man who wanted to see a young man come along and make it; Frank was the impatient newcomer who wanted to push everything aside and get in there."[21]

In the summer of 1946 Crosby negotiated a break with Kraft and signed on with the Philco Radio Corporation. The program was carried by ABC, which agreed to pay Bing $25,000 a week and stock. In addition, approximately 400 independent stations each provided him with $100 per broadcast, thereby supplementing his pay with another $40,000. Wednesday was promoted as "Bingsday" by the network. Philco went along with Bing's wish to transcribe *The Crosby Show,* as long as it maintained high ratings. This enabled him to stockpile shows, leaving relatively long periods of time free to pursue other professional and recreational interests. In short order, other radio stars began following his example.

During this period, Crosby became directly involved in a wide variety of activities outside of performing. His first notable investment of this type had been the Del Mar Turf Club, located north of San Diego, in 1937. He sold his one-third interest in the racetrack in April 1946 to avoid a conflict of interest relating to his part ownership of the Pittsburgh Pirates major league baseball franchise. His interest in professional sports continued with the purchase of a 10 percent interest in the Los Angeles Rams National Football League franchise on December 13, 1949. In 1948 Bing joined forces with Jock Whitney, at one time the U.S. ambassador to England, to market Minute Maid orange juice concentrate. He worked out an arrangement with Philco to tout the product on the radio, taking advantage of preferential options to purchase stocks and shares in the venture. Other investments included Bing's Things, Inc., which marketed toys, clothing, and other products; oil drilling in Louisiana and Oklahoma; banking in California and Arizona; livestock in both the United States and South America; ice-cream distribution; and the acquisition of real estate.

Crosby was no longer merely an entertainment giant but an American institution as well. *The Music Digest* estimated that his recordings filled more than half of the 80,000 weekly hours allotted to recorded radio music at the time, that his radio show was heard by 25 million listeners weekly, and that each film was seen by 250 million viewers. *Women's Home Companion* voted Bing the leading film star, an honor repeated for the next four years. The proliferation of Crosby references in films and other mass media attests to the fact that his name was a household word (e.g., in *Billy Rose's Diamond Horseshoe*, a 20th Century-Fox motion picture released in 1945, Betty Grable sings, "I'd love a double order of Bing").

Musicologists, journalists, and other cultural observers continued to devote considerable newsprint space and broadcast time to the dissection of Crosby's singing style. J. T. H. Mize discussed how Crosby might melt a tone away, scoop it "flat and sliding up to the eventual pitch" as a "glissando," sometimes "sting a note right on the button," and take diphthongs for "long musical rides." Mize argued that "some of his prettiest tones are heard on *ng's*" and inventoried the Crosby arsenal of vocal effects, including "interpolating pianissimo whistling variations," sometimes arpeggic, at other times trilling.[22] Osterholm would state,

> Prior to 1934 he sometimes displayed the brassiness of Jolson, Cantor, and Ted Lewis . . . and by 1946 these old-fashioned "plagues" still occasionally crept in. Henry Pleasants thinks Bing's best range was G to G or even lower and that only about this time was he able "slowly to sort out what worked on the microphone and to eliminate what was superficial or incompatible." Still, Bing's voice was incomparable, which Charles Henderson called "phonogenic" and Pleasants "microgenic." His early upper mordents, light and fast, produced a "slight catch, or choke, or sob which was to remain one of the most attractive of his vocal devices," according to Pleasants.[23]

By 1949, as the cultural changes were gathering momentum in postwar America, cracks began appearing in the firmament of Crosby, the institution. He slipped to second place in the film star poll, the first time since 1943 that he hadn't been voted most popular. The Philco show was losing its mass appeal; the last broadcast would take place on June 1. *A Connecticut Yankee in King Arthur's Court,* which cost more than $3 million to produce, earned only $3 million in America during its first year of release.

Nevertheless, many signs of outward success could still be found. British distributors named Bing the most popular international star in 1948. In November he made eight appearances in London's Empress Hall for $400,000. In Communist Czechoslovakia, an overflow crowd reportedly assembled in October 1949 in a Prague theater to hear—and applaud—Crosby records. In 1950 *Women's Home Companion* announced that Bing was voted the most popular male star for the fifth consecutive year. Between 1946 and 1950 he had nine more recordings achieve gold status—"McNamara's Band," "South America, Take It Away," the *Merry Christmas* album, "Alexander's Ragtime Band," "The Whiffenpoof Song," "Now Is the Hour," "Galway Bay," "Dear Hearts and Gentle People," and "Sam's Song," a duet with son Gary—making it twenty-one million sellers in his career overall.

During the early 1950s, Crosby's impeccable public image was tarnished somewhat by domestic problems. The May 9, 1950, issue of the *Los Angeles Times* reported that close associates, including brother Larry, had substantiated rumors that Bing and Dixie had "strained relations." Larry went on to say that he hoped for a separation and knew nothing about supposed divorce plans. While vacationing in Europe at the time—without Dixie—Crosby narrowly avoided a fifth stay in jail, on this occasion for violating the grass near the Champs Elysees while awaiting a luncheon appointment. In the spring of 1951 a Vancouver hotel clerk insultingly refused Bing and companion Bill Morrow a room because they were unshaven. In addition, son Gary was drawing attention for boorish behavior of his own, which included chaffing at his father's attempts to impose discipline.

Meanwhile, Bing Crosby Productions committed wholeheartedly to television. In early 1950, the organization produced the first ten 26-minute films at Hal Roach Studios, for a weekly series sponsored by Proctor & Gamble called *The Fireside Theater*. Another twenty-four shows would soon follow. Bing himself had first appeared on TV December 19, 1948, when he sang in "A Christmas Carol" for NBC. Beginning with his second appearance on February 27, 1951, when he sang several songs on *The Red Cross Program* (NBC), he became increasingly visible in the new medium. His third appearance took place on June 21, 1952, as he joined Bob Hope and Dorothy Lamour in a telethon concerned with financing the American Olympic team. Nevertheless, he stated his preference for radio and other projects, while allowing, "Sure, I'll get into television eventually, when I find the right format. I don't think radio is dead—nor ever will be."[24]

In 1952 Crosby signed with General Electric to host a radio program for $16,000 a week; the contract included a clause that he would receive about $50,000 as a package for a television show. In the meantime, his film schedule remained heavy as work commenced on *Road to Bali*, along with brief appearances in *The Greatest Show on Earth* and the Dean Martin–Jerry Lewis vehicle *Scared Stiff*. In September he set sail for Europe to film *Little Boy Lost*.

While abroad, Bing received word that Dixie was dying of ovarian cancer. He returned home on October 4, Dixie meeting him at Union Station, with the aid of daily blood transfusions. She had a relapse the following morning, as Bing prepared for the General Electric program, which premiered on October 9. Dixie died on October 31, one day before she was to have turned forty-one.

Crosby went into private mourning, with Judy Garland and Jimmy Stewart serving as guest hosts on the radio show for two weeks. By early 1953 he had returned to work on a full-time basis. When he began dating Mary Murphy, a Paramount starlet, and divorcée Mona Freeman, rumors began circulating in the mass media.

Crosby justified an April 1, 1953, appearance on a Bob Hope television show by stating, "I want to keep in touch with the public and if you're not on TV it appears you're out of touch."[25] Motion pictures occupied the bulk of his attention in the latter months of the year; he began filming *White Christmas* in August and *The Country Girl* in October. George Seaton, director of *The Country Girl*, touted Bing's performance as a drunken singer, asserting that it was more remarkable than the standard excellence expected of a Marlon Brando. He would be nominated for Best Actor at the March 30, 1955, Academy Awards; however, Brando won for his unforgettable performance in *On the Waterfront*.

The Bing Crosby Show, his first TV special, was broadcast January 3, 1954, on CBS. The reviews for the program, which featured Bing singing several songs and guests Jack Benny and Sheree North, were decidedly cool. Jack Gould of the *New York Times* stated, "Bing would be a natural for TV and will be when he takes a great interest in this medium's requirements." Crosby seemed unconvinced regarding television's potential. After filming his second special, which aired in April 1954, he announced that "it's my last. Why do

I do it? I don't need it. I won't do TV again, not unless I lose my job in the movies."[26]

Crosby's final radio show for General Electric occurred on May 30, 1954, with his son Gary taking over the show for the summer. In the fall Bing hosted daily fifteen-minute programs with the Buddy Cole Trio and Ken Carpenter, which ran on CBS until 1962.

Decca decided to honor Crosby by assembling a special album of eighty-nine songs, many re-recorded and all complemented by an audio commentary. The musical biography included the bulk of Bing's most popular—and most critically acclaimed—songs, as well as a 24-page illustrated biography and discography. In the meantime, his opinions regarding the rhythm and blues–inflected sounds then becoming popular were published in the November 2, 1954, issue of *Look*. In his essay, entitled "I Never Had to Scream," he noted that popular music had changed, "but not all for the better, by any fair means or foul."

Despite his reservations about the state of pop music at the time, Crosby remained a commercially viable recording artist. According to Osterholm, "each jukebox in America offered at least four Crosby songs." In early 1956, while Elvis Presley was becoming a national obsession, Bing earned two more gold records—his twenty-second and twenty-third—for the single "True Love," a duet with actress Grace Kelly, and the album in which it was featured. Nevertheless, during a brief trip to England in the summer of 1956, the *Daily Express* ran the following headline: "Is Bing Crosby Going Out—Or Has He Gone?"

Undoubtedly bowing to pressure to update his style, Crosby recorded a rock 'n' roll–inflected song, "Seven Nights a Week," in January 1957. However, he continued to champion the old guard. When music publishers and disk jockeys were being investigated regarding possible payola violations in the late 1950s, he made the following point in a letter to the Senate Commerce Committee: "It galls me exceedingly to see so much trash on our airlines and TV screens while the work of the talented and dedicated songwriters is crowded out of the picture."

Crosby remained busy making films in 1956. In February he began work on *High Society*, which featured a Cole Porter score. After a brief recuperation following surgery for kidney stones and a minor eye problem, he returned to the Paramount lot to finish filming *Anything Goes*. The TV film *High Tor* was aired March 10; despite generally high marks for the music, the overall production received cool reviews. He also learned that he'd been nominated once more for Best Actor, this time for *The Country Girl*.

After several postponements over a two-year period, Crosby secretly married actress Kathryn Grant in Las Vegas on October 24, 1957. Despite some adjustment problems—Kathryn would later relate that on returning to their Hollywood home, she had been shocked to find a portrait of Dixie in the bathroom and a blanket cover on their double bed bearing the initials D. L. C.—the marriage lasted up to Bing's death two decades later. Their union would produce three children: Harris Lillis Junior, born August 8, 1958; Mary Frances, September 14, 1959; and Nathaniel Patrick, October 29, 1961.

The second marriage and subsequent family appears to have spurred a marked change in Crosby. According to Army Archerd, an entertainment journalist who knew Bing for twenty-five years,

> I think it was the rebirth of his life and a new impetus for him to continue in show business. I doubt whether he would really have gone on—as successfully as he had in this second-half of his life—had he not married again and had this wonderful second family. I think he got the urge to be Bing Crosby again.[27]

Crosby finally committed himself to television in a big way when he signed a five-year contract with ABC in June 1958. Its terms included a $2-million payment to star in two one-hour shows per year, in addition to producing another ten on film. His first special per the agreement was aired in October 1958. Including Dean Martin, Mahalia Jackson, and Patti Page among the guests, it received uniformly high marks. The October 13 issue of *Time* noted, "Bing Crosby's topnotch ABC special last week swayed along with rocking-chair ease; its spare (but expensive) sets and casual tone made the usual frenetic TV variety shows look sick by comparison."

Throughout the 1950s the media seemed to carry stories about the misadventures of the four sons from Crosby's first marriage with alarming regularity. Furthermore, his marriage to Kathryn seemed to exacerbate the problems he had in communicating with them. Evidently feeling that the public deserved an explanation, Bing granted an interview to Joe Hyams of the Associated Press in late March 1959. In the two-part series, entitled "How Bing Crosby

'Failed' His Four Sons," he observed, "I guess I didn't do very well bringing my boys up. I think I failed them by giving them too much work and discipline, too much money, and too little time and attention." Other periodicals published their own take on the situation. All of the sons except Gary—who had been stunned at the public disclosure, which he chose to interpret as an apology—immediately came to their father's defense in the mass media. In the end, Bing's public reputation emerged largely unscathed by the episode.

By the 1960s Crosby was widely perceived as one of the entertainment industry's elder statesman. While still capable of boffo box office feats, his best days were considered to be long past. Like other Hollywood titans such as Bob Hope and Jerry Lewis, Bing lent his time and public persona to a variety of charitable causes. His Crosby Clambake, now a major international event, garnered further attention in January 1960 when Bing, prompted by a newspaper column written by baseball legend Jackie Robinson, forced the Professional Golfers Association to rescind certain racial discrimination practices. Honors from outside the show business community included having President John F. Kennedy as a house guest in his Palm Springs home.

On June 9, 1960, Crosby received a platinum record for "White Christmas" from the Hollywood Chamber of Commerce. The inscription noted that he had sold more than 200 million records and led the whole recording industry into prominence and profitability. *Variety* noted at the time that royalty figures seemed to indicate that Bing's rendition of "Silent Night" had outsold "White Christmas"; sales were so high that it was evidently hard to ascertain actual facts on a conclusive basis.

The following week, on June 15, Crosby was responsible for an interesting footnote in motion picture history, finishing three films in one day. The movies included *High Time,* in which he starred as a jaunty old college student, as well as cameo spots in *Let's Make Love* and *Pepe.*

Crosby's extracurricular activities—all of which typically combined work with pleasure—included travel, golf, and a charter membership in the Clan, better known in the mass media as the Rat Pack. Although the best-known members were Dean Martin, Sammy Davis, Tony Curtis, Peter Lawford, and nominal leader Frank Sinatra, there were evidently a number of other stars in the set-up when it began. Davis would later reflect,

Bing was a member based upon the fact that the Clan really started with Bogart and Betty Bacall. Crosby, though he wasn't at every party, would be there at certain times; he'd leave early if he had to go fishing or somewhere but he'd have dinner. . . . he made no bones about how much fun he was having. He used to say, "Do you guys live like this all the time?"[28]

This association would lead to Crosby's involvement in the film *Robin and the Seven Hoods* (1964), a tongue-in-cheek depiction of Chicago's gangster era during the Roaring Twenties, which co-starred Sinatra, Martin, Davis, and Peter Falk.

While Crosby now lived a life of, in Thompson's words, "less work and more play," his professional life would remain the envy of many a younger entertainer.[29] In late December 1960, for instance, he recorded 101 songs in eight marathon sessions. He also continued making films, commenced a daily radio program co-starring Rosemary Clooney for CBS in February 1960, and maintained his string of appearances in TV specials, including those starring show business colleagues (e.g., Perry Como's *Kraft Music Hall* aired on NBC March 16, 1960).

Crosby was asked to host the filmed premiere of *The Hollywood Palace*, a television variety show, which took place January 4, 1964, three days before his mother's death at the age of ninety. He continued to host the program every few weeks until the final production in February 1970. In late summer 1964 he began filming his only TV series, *The Bing Crosby Show*, which would air on ABC during the 1964–65 season. Co-stars of the sitcom included Beverly Garland as his wife, Carol Faylen and Diane Sherry as the children, and Frank McHugh as the live-in handyman. Critics gave positive reviews at the outset; however, their impressions became less enthusiastic as the season progressed. His television work also included hosting *The Grand Award of Sports* live from the New York City Theater in Flushing Meadow during the 1964–65 World's Fair.

In 1965 Crosby was cast in a nonsinging role as the drunken doctor in a CinemaScope remake of the classic John Ford Western *Stagecoach*. Considering the fact that the 1939 original had garnered three Oscars, including a Supporting Actor award by Thomas Mitchell as the character now being played by Crosby, many might have questioned the prudence of taking on such a challenge. Bing, however, had no reservations about signing aboard:

It was a chance to do a character and I wanted to try it. They had a big cast and I knew it had been a success before. There were some people who thought we were foolish to make the picture, because the original one was such a legend. I went to see it and great as it was it really isn't much of a film to look at any more. It's more dated than any picture I can recall ever seeing.[30]

The 20th Century-Fox production would be the last film for Crosby. In 1972 he would claim that he never officially retired from movie making. After turning down yet another script, he would explain, "If one came along, and it wasn't dirty or pornographic, or lascivious, or full of smut and was a good role, I'd do it. But I don't think there are many of those films around, unless you get one with Disney."[31]

Crosby occasionally went public during the last decade of his life regarding what he perceived to be the low standards of the entertainment media. The following comments, directed largely against the film industry in early 1972, were typical of his stance:

I really think its disgraceful what they're doing on the screen now, and they're starting to do it on television too. I think the entertainment media has got a lot of things to be responsible for. . . . I'm sure it's agreed that no other medium in the history of the world had had such a profound influence on manners, dress, coiffure, speech or behavior as the motion picture. And now they are selling, furiously, moral irresponsibility. I think it's wicked.[32]

Crosby's work output was indeed scaled back in the latter half of the 1960s. Aside from his regular stints in *The Hollywood Palace*, he appeared in only two or three television shows a year. He recorded a mere two songs in 1966 and was limited to one session in 1967, on October 31, which resulted in "Step to the Rear" and "What Do We Do with the World?" After waxing forty-one songs during seven sessions in 1968, he would record only three songs in 1969. His studio works would continue to be sporadic from 1970 through 1974 as well.

While Crosby's professional load became increasingly lighter in the early 1970s, he maintained a high level of involvement with charitable activities. He appeared on *The Bob Hope Show* on January 27, 1970, as part of a benefit for the Eisenhower Medical Center then under construction at Palm Springs. In 1971 he teamed with Hall of

Fame baseball player Ted Williams in a banquet dedicated to saving
the Atlantic salmon. The following year Bing served as the national
chairman of the fund drive for the Arthritis Foundation.

His successful December 9, 1973, TV special, *Bing Crosby's Sun
Valley Christmas Show,* provided evidence that he remained a show
business institution. The NBC broadcast attracted a then record audience of 49,270,000 viewers.

Crosby's public activities were halted for a time when a rapidly
growing cyst was found in his left lung on New Year's Day, 1974.
Nearly half of his left lung was removed on January 13; it was deter-
mined to have been caused by a rare fungal infection contracted
during a recent African safari. Back home on January 26, he resigned
himself to a long recovery pottering around his half-million-dollar
estate.

In the spring Bing began to cautiously test his voice. To his relief,
he found that it remained strong and possessed of the familiar mellow tone long considered a Crosby trademark. His renewed vigor,
combined with, in Thompson's words, "the special awareness that
comes with a close brush with death," inspired him to embrace a
new series of ambitious projects.[33] These activities included British
Decca's planned release of a series of his classic radio shows; the
scheduled August 1975 issue of a 7-disk set of the 100 best Crosby
songs by MCA, through the World Record Club; a jazz recording
session accompanied only by piano; and six 3-hour recording sessions in London aimed at producing 25 songs for two 50th-anniver-
sary albums to be released by the U.K. arm of United Artists.

In mid-1975 Bing assembled a road show, "Bing Crosby and
Friends," which included wife Kathryn, Rosemary Clooney, and the
Joe Bushkin Trio. The troupe would tour for the next two years,
gaining additional performers along the way. In addition, he made
a large number of TV appearances during the balance of 1975 and
the following year, including co-hosting *The Bell Telephone Jubilee*
with Liza Minnelli on March 21, 1976.

Crosby's only live album to be officially released during his lifetime was produced from a successful two-week engagement in June
1976 at the London Palladium. His British stay also included many
taped TV shows and public appearances.

On the heels of further concerts and charitable activities, "Bing
Crosby on Broadway" opened for a two-week run at the Uris Theater, beginning December 7, 1976. Osterholm provided the follow-

ing assessment of the stint for the December 15 issue of the *Worcester (Mass.) Evening Gazette*:

> Bing Crosby proves with little apparent effort that his baritone voice has gained far more in richness than the little steadiness it has lost in the highest register. . . . Bing's voice is still very strong, and he can turn up a lot of volume when he wishes. He still has a respectably high range, stopping at one high note to state that he had just invaded the territory of Andy Williams.

Crosby returned to world headlines when he fell into a twenty-foot-deep orchestra pit while taping a CBS special commemorating his fiftieth anniversary in the entertainment business at the Ambassador Auditorium in Pasadena, California, March 3, 1977. Although his grabbing for a piece of scenery helped to break his fall, it was found that he had ruptured a disk at the base of his spine. He underwent a prolonged recuperation. At his age, it was hard to determine how he would be affected. Eleven weeks after the accident, however, he appeared on the *Barbara Walters Special*, doing a little dance step with Barbara as they walked arm-in-arm and, because it was drizzling, singing a few bars of "Singing in the Rain."

He returned to the golf course in short order and his "Bing Crosby and Friends" did a concert at Concord, California, in mid-August as a tune-up for a planned tour of Norway, Sweden, and England. The troupe performed at Momarkedet August 25 in a benefit for the Norwegian Red Cross. In September Bing taped his last Christmas special, his forty-second (going back to radio), in London for CBS. The program, titled *Bing Crosby's Merrie Olde Christmas* and featuring guest star David Bowie, was aired on November 30. He also found time to record his last album, *Seasons*, with British producer Ken Barnes; it would become his twenty-fourth gold record.

"Bing Crosby and Friends" opened September 26 at the London Palladium, playing to sell-out crowds through October 10. The October 1, 1977, issue of *Variety* published the following review of the show:

> Undoubtedly, the highlight of this two and a half hour show, in for two weeks at this vaud flagship, is a stint when Bing Crosby and the Joe Bushkin Quartet glide smoothly through a medley of chestnuts including "White Christmas" and an up-beat arrangement of "Old Man River." . . . [Crosby] always looked relaxed and confident, whether

gagging with the capacity audience, duetting with wife, Kathryn, or
son, Harry, or singing along with Rosemary Clooney. . . . The audience
was predominantly middle-aged to elderly, and much of Crosby's
show is designed to take advantage of the singer's tremendous nostalgia appeal.

On October 13 Crosby flew to Spain for golf and game shooting.
His wife and family employee Alan Fisher remained behind to help
Harry, Jr., get settled in at the London Academy of Music and Dramatic Arts, where he would be a student for the next three years. At
the La Moraleja Golf Club the next day, Crosby challenged Valentin
Barrios, the former Spanish champion, and Cesar de Zulueta, president of the club. Teamed with Manuel Pinero, then Spanish champion, Bing was reportedly in the best of humor, joking and singing
throughout the match, which they won by one stroke. He collapsed
from a massive heart attack while walking away from the eighteenth
hole. He passed away without regaining consciousness as an ambu-
lance was taking him to the Red Cross Hospital in Madrid.

Television stations in Spain interrupted their programs with the
news, and word quickly spread across the globe. Tributes immediately began pouring in from a vast number of friends and admirers.
President Jimmy Carter offered the following eulogy:

> For all the roads he traveled in his memorable career, Bing Crosby re-
> mained a gentleman, proof that a great talent can be a good man de-
> spite the pressures of show business. He lived a life his fans around
> the world felt was typically American: successful, yet modest; casual,
> but elegant.

His crooning rival, Frank Sinatra, would comment,

> Bing's death is almost more than I can take. He was the father of my
> career, the idol of my youth, and a dear friend of my maturity. His
> passing leaves a gaping hole in our music and in the lives of everybody
> who ever loved him. And that's just about everybody. Thank God we
> have his films and his records providing us with his warmth and talent
> forever.

Harry, Jr., and Alan Fisher accompanied the casket containing
Bing's body back to Los Angeles on October 17. Funeral services
were held, unannounced, on October 19, at St. Paul's Church, near

the UCLA campus in Westwood. Crosby had wanted only his wife and seven children to be in attendance; however, Kathryn modified the request to include Bing's living brother and sister, Bob and Mary Rose, as well as a small number of close friends and associates. The body was then taken some five miles to Holy Cross Cemetery, with his six sons serving as pallbearers. His oak casket was placed alongside that of first wife, Dixie. With all adjacent plots taken, Bing had himself buried at a depth of eight to nine feet, thereby giving Kathryn the option of being buried in his plot, above him, if she wishes.

THE CROSBY LEGACY

Ample evidence exists to suggest that Crosby was the most popular entertainer in the twentieth century. From 1926, the date of his first commercial record release, until his death in 1977, he was constantly in demand as a recording artist, film actor, radio—and later, television—personality, and concert performer. Jose Ferrer offered the following assessment of his talent: "Bing Crosby is like Mr. Everything of all time."[34]

His singing, of course, was central to understanding his appeal. In addition to virtually defining the crooning tradition, he was widely held to be a premier jazz interpreter. Earl Orkin would write,

> Bing Crosby was one of the greatest of all jazz singers. Although he could and often did sing just about anything, he grew up in the world of Bix Beiderbecke and Hoagy Carmichael, and jazz was always what he loved best. (Unlike Sinatra, for instance, he always phrased the music, not the words.) Short of Louis Armstrong or Billie Holiday perhaps, there is no better role-model for an aspiring jazz singer than Bing.[35]

Osterholm attempted to ascertain Crosby's importance as a singer in commercial terms.

> Conceding for a moment that Elvis Presley, who died two months before Bing, sold 500 million records since 1954, and that Bing sold only 400 million since 1926, we could, for a simple method, compare relative sales in relation to population by comparing the nation's population at the mid-points of their careers. Adjusting Presley's sales by the audience in Crosby's time, it would be about 365 million, Crosby's

sales would be 508 million in Presley's time. Moreover, in the 1930s, when Bing was first popular, record sales were very low because of the Depression, and many people also maintain that Bing has actually sold more than 500 million records.[36]

This success was instrumental in enabling Crosby to assume a larger-than-life persona. According to Thompson,

> Bing Crosby is probably the most-loved character in the world apart from the creations of Walt Disney. For a half century he has dispensed much joy and much entertainment for the benefit of millions who were never ever to meet him but felt that they knew him and in him had a friend. A colossal, enveloping warmth of affection has justly come his way through the years. Even if the image of the casual, lazy pipe-smoking crooner was not completely true it would not matter. He was Bing, Mr. Family Man, Mr. Clean.[37]

The Crosby image was, in fact, the crooner image personified. The relaxed, gentle touch first defined by 1920s trailblazers such as Gene Austin and Rudy Vallee ultimately became identified with Crosby alone. The evolutionary process was largely completed by the mid-1930s, with Vallee's popularity on the wane and Columbo, who was widely acknowledged to be a Crosby clone, coming to a tragic end. From this point onward, the vitality of the crooning tradition was sapped by the Spokane supernova. Faced with a stylistic dead-end, the genre was easily pushed aside by the rhythm and blues–based sounds of the 1950s.

NOTES

1. Donald Shepherd and Robert F. Slatzer, *Bing Crosby: The Hollow Man* (New York: St. Martin's Press, 1981), 23.
2. Barry Ulanov, *The Incredible Crosby* (New York: Whittlesey House, 1948), 34–35.
3. Shepherd and Slatzer, *Bing Crosby: The Hollow Man,* 43.
4. Shepherd and Slatzer, *Bing Crosby: The Hollow Man,* 65.
5. Shepherd and Slatzer, *Bing Crosby: The Hollow Man,* 65.
6. Shepherd and Slatzer, *Bing Crosby: The Hollow Man,* 73.
7. Shepherd and Slatzer, *Bing Crosby: The Hollow Man,* 75.
8. Shepherd and Slatzer, *Bing Crosby: The Hollow Man,* 77.
9. Shepherd and Slatzer, *Bing Crosby: The Hollow Man,* 99.

10. Shepherd and Slatzer, *Bing Crosby: The Hollow Man*, 109.

11. Shepherd and Slatzer, *Bing Crosby: The Hollow Man*, 110–11.

12. Shepherd and Slatzer, *Bing Crosby: The Hollow Man*, 115.

13. Charles Thompson, *Bing: The Authorized Biography* (Litton, Yorkshire, U.K.: Magna Print Books, 1976), 114.

14. Thompson, *Bing: The Authorized Biography*, 117.

15. Thompson, *Bing: The Authorized Biography*, 128–129.

16. Thompson, *Bing: The Authorized Biography*, 134–135.

17. Thompson, *Bing: The Authorized Biography*, 141.

18. Thompson, *Bing: The Authorized Biography*, 152.

19. Thompson, *Bing: The Authorized Biography*, 178–179.

20. Thompson, *Bing: The Authorized Biography*, 200.

21. Thompson, *Bing: The Authorized Biography*, 280.

22. J. Roger Osterholm, *Bing Crosby: A Bio-Bibliography*. Westport, Conn.: Greenwood, 1994, 63.

23. Osterholm, *Bing Crosby: A Bio-Bibliography*, 64.

24. Osterholm, *Bing Crosby: A Bio-Bibliography*, 46.

25. Osterholm, *Bing Crosby: A Bio-Bibliography*, 48.

26. Osterholm, *Bing Crosby: A Bio-Bibliography*, 49.

27. Thompson, *Bing: The Authorized Biography*, 416.

28. Thompson, *Bing: The Authorized Biography*, 448–449.

29. Thompson, *Bing: The Authorized Biography*, 460.

30. Thompson, *Bing: The Authorized Biography*, 453–454.

30. Thompson, *Bing: The Authorized Biography*, 456.

32. Thompson, *Bing: The Authorized Biography*, 457.

33. Thompson, *Bing: The Authorized Biography*, 486.

34. Thompson, *Bing: The Authorized Biography*, 521.

35. Osterholm, *Bing Crosby: A Bio-Bibliography*, 64.

36. Osterholm, *Bing Crosby: A Bio-Bibliography*, 12.

37. Thompson, *Bing: The Authorized Biography*, 505.

4

Nick Lucas

Nick Lucas's contributions to a number of entertainment media make him unique among the crooners. In fact, he was one of the first singers to be billed as a crooner and was one of the few in the field who also accompanied himself on the guitar. Often credited with initiating the intimate style of singing, Lucas was also a major figure in popularizing the guitar in the twentieth century. He was the first to record using the instrument with an orchestra, his were the first important guitar instruction books, he was the first celebrity to endorse a guitar pick, and his Nick Lucas Special, manufactured by the Gibson Guitar Company, was the first guitar to be especially designed for a singing star. Nick Lucas was one of the most successful popular singers of the 1920s and 1930s, selling well over 80 million records, and he introduced some of the most enduring songs from that period. In tandem with his recordings was his success in vaudeville, where he went from making $250 per week in 1925 to $3,000 per week at the start of the Depression. He also found success in movies, radio, nightclubs, Broadway, and television. Like Rudy Vallee, he entertained almost until the end of his life in a professional career that spanned more than seventy years.

Nick Lucas was of Italian descent, being born Dominic Antonio Nicholas Lucanese on August 22, 1897, at 10 Gaslight Street in Newark, New Jersey. His father, Otto Maria Lucanese, was born in 1860 and his mother, Bella Ermiania Lucanese, was born in 1862. Natives of Italy, they were married in that country and their first child,

Frank, was born there in 1890. The family migrated to America in
1893 and settled in Newark, where a daughter, Tessie, was born in
1894. Two other sons, Librato (born in 1904) and Anthony (born in
1908), rounded out the family. Otto Lucanese worked for the Essex
County Parks Commission in Newark as a landscaper and tree sur-
geon and in 1900 the family, which also included the paternal
grandmother, moved to the small town of Silver Lake.

By the time Nick was four years old, his brother Frank taught him
to play the mandolin, and by the time he was eight the two brothers
were playing for money at social events. The two also picked up
extra money by performing in saloons and streetcars. While in
grammar school Nick starting playing the guitar, and he and Frank
continued to supplement the family income as entertainers.

In 1912 Nick Lucas made his first recordings when he and Frank
did a series of test pressings for Thomas A. Edison, who was experimenting with the use of string instruments on recordings. Although
they were not intended for commercial release, the cylinders were
the beginning of Nick Lucas's seventy-year recording career, which
made him one of the very few people to record on cylinders through
the acoustic and electrical eras up to the multichannel stereo recordings of the 1980s.

The year 1912 also saw Frank Lucas join a popular group called
the Three Vagrants, a trio that played the vaudeville circuit for several years. The next year Nick graduated from grammar school and
took a job in a leather tannery. By this time he had mastered not
only the mandolin and guitar but also the banjo and banjorin, and
during lunch breaks he would serenade his fellow workers. They
urged him to become a professional musician and to shorten his
name to Nick Lucas. He left the $2 a day tannery job for a position
as an instrumentalist in a trio at a Newark cabaret, where he was
paid $20 per week. He stayed at that job for two years, getting musi-
cal experience playing variety shows, and then obtained a $5 a week
raise.

In 1917 he married Catherine Cifrodella, who was eighteen at the
time, and six months later he began working at Newark's Iroquois
Club for $28 per week. He then put together a group called the Ken-
tucky Five, which included his friend Ted Fio Rito, and the five-
member act was signed at $300 per week to appear in vaudeville.
With this group Nick began singing professionally, as the Kentucky

Five toured the Interstate Circuit for six months during the 1917–18 season. When the tour ended, Nick returned to Newark for the birth of his daughter, Emily, in 1918. He then joined Vincent Lopez and His Peking Five, which performed at the Peking Cafe on 46th Street in New York City. The club featured four chorus girls and an emcee-comic, with Nick singing some of the production numbers before an audience that included the cream of New York City society, in addition to mobsters and racketeers. It was also during this time that Lucas began to record commercially, playing the banjo on a number of studio recordings such as "Lil' Liza Jane"/"Coon Band Contest" (Victor 18394) as a part of Earl Fuller's Jazz Band in 1917.

After staying with Vincent Lopez's band for several months, Nick Lucas joined the Vernon Country Club Orchestra in 1919. Sponsored by Paul Whiteman, the group had originated in Vernon, California, and Nick became the banjo player with the group when it debuted in New York. He stayed with the ensemble for nearly three years; the first year they played at Risenwhipper's Cafe and their second season was at the Boardwalk Cafe. Nick also recorded with the Vernon Country Club Orchestra in 1921 for the Pathé Actuelle and Columbia labels. For Pathé, he and his brother Frank also teamed for records as the Lucas Ukulele Trio and the Lucas Novelty Quartet.

In the summer of 1922 Nick waxed his own guitar compositions, "Pickin' the Guitar" and "Teasin' the Frets," for release on the Pathé, Perfect, and Silvertone labels. The influence of this record proved to be tremendous, as it had a big impact on future guitarists like Gene Autry, Merle Travis, and Chet Atkins. Nick re-recorded the two selections for Brunswick Records in 1924 and 1932. With two members of the Vernon Country Club Orchestra, alto saxophone player Don Parker and pianist Frank Banta, Nick played the banjo for a series of records released by Pathé Actuelle as the Don Parker Trio.

When Nick left the Vernon group in 1921, he joined Sam Lanin's orchestra at the Roseland Ballroom at 51st Street and Broadway in New York City, and he was paid $90 per week. The Lanin group would do a twenty-minute set and then be relieved by Mal Hallet's orchestra; this arrangement would continue throughout the evening. Among the members of the Lanin group were Miff Mole, Red Nichols, Arthur Fields, Rube Bloom, and Jimmy and Tommy Dorsey.

In addition to working with Lanin's band, Nick also played banjo for Lanin on studio recordings for the Gennett label. Known as Bailey's Lucky Seven, the group would have three-hour recording sessions in the morning and afternoon, as it took about three hours to record two sides, due to the wax cylinders that were used to make record pressings at the time. Nick Lucas was paid $20 for each record session. Lanin and his recording group also used the Bailey's Lucky Seven name for disks issued by Gennett Records, but on other labels they had different names. On Edison Bell Winner (a British label) and Westport, the group was called the Pavilion Players, Regent Orchestra, Diplomat Orchestra, and Diplomat Novelty Orchestra, while on the Cardinal label it was called the Cardinal Dance Orchestra. Bailey's Lucky Seven was also used for Apex Records and Starr, a Canadian label.

While doing these recordings, Nick Lucas got the idea of substituting the guitar in place of the banjo. When recording at the time, banjo and tuba players were placed far away from the recording apparatus because if their instruments were played too hard, it would make the needle jump on the wax cylinder and ruin a take. The banjo also had a metallic sound when recorded and was kept away from the recording device for this reason as well. Nick suggested to Sam Lanin that the guitar be placed very close to the sound horn, or even under it, and thus the rhythm would be retained in the record, with none of the worry of picking up the metallic tone of the banjo or causing the recording needle to jump. Although not convinced, Lanin decided to give it a try and it proved to be very successful, thus making Nick Lucas the first musician to use the guitar in recordings with a studio orchestra. Lanin then suggested that Nick use his guitar in their live shows; in doing so, the entertainer set another precedent by being the first musician to replace the banjo with a guitar in a big-name band.

In the early 1920s the guitar was not considered suited for commercial use. Nick Lucas proved this conception false, and his strumming the instrument in unusual rhythms, plinking grace notes, and carrying the melody, brought the guitar to the attention of bandsmen of the day. As a result, Nick found that his services were in great demand.

Toward the end of 1923 Nick Lucas accepted an offer from his old friend Ted Fio Rito to appear in Chicago with the Oriole Terrace Orchestra, which featured Fio Rito and Danny Russo. He was paid $150 per week for appearing with the group, which was headquar-

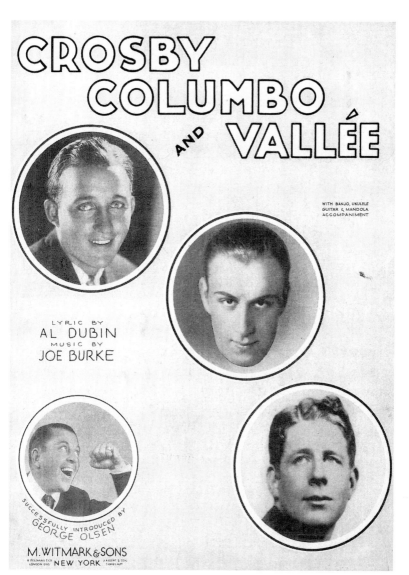

Sheet music cover circa 1931. *Source:* John Newton Collection

Bing Crosby: early 1930s. *Source:* Marc Friend Collection

Sheet music cover circa 1936. *Source:* Dick Carty Collection

Sheet music cover circa 1933. *Source:* Jim Bedoian Collection

XXC·8500·30

Russ Columbo: circa 1932. Twentieth Century Pictures, Inc. Photograph
Source: Marc Friend Collection

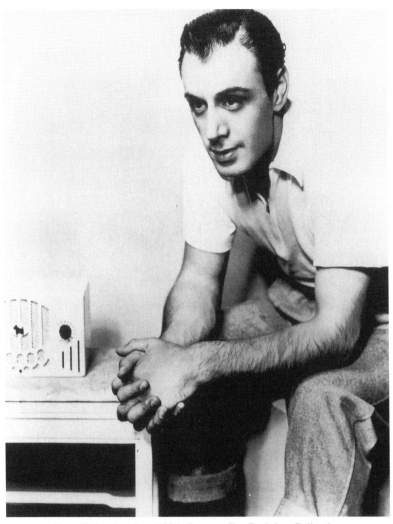

Russ Columbo circa 1934. *Source:* Jim Bedoian Collection

Rudy Vallee: circa 1936. *Source:* Marc Friend Collection

Rudy Vallee and Baby Rose Marie: circa 1930. *Source:* Marc Friend
Collection

Sheet music cover circa 1930. *Source:* Dick Carty Collection

Gene Austin circa late 1930s. *Source:* Jim Bedoian Collection

(L to R) Gloria Stuart, Gene Austin, and Ruth Etting. 1934 Universal Film *Gift of Gab. Source:* Michael Pitts Collection

Sheet music cover circa 1928. *Source:* Jim Bedoian Collection

Johnny Marvin circa 1934. *Source:* Jim Bedoian Collection

Johnny Marvin circa late 1920s. *Source:* Jim Bedoian Collection

Painting the Clouds with Sunshine.

Painting the blues beautiful hues,
    coloured with gold and old rose;
Playing the clown, trying to drown all of my woes,
    Tho' things may not look bright,
    They'll all turn out alright,
    If I keep painting the clouds
        with sunshine.

NICK LUCAS & ANN PENNINGTON
(WARNER BROS. STARS)
STARRED IN "THE GOLD DIGGERS of BROADWAY"

56

1929 Postcard. *Source:* Bob Henderson Collection

Nick Lucas: circa 1950s. *Source:* Marc Friend Collection

Newspaper publicity photo for Art Gillham's 1930 CBS radio program "Syncopated Pessimism." He used the phrase "Have you got a cup of coffee in your pocket?" on each program. *Source:* George Blau Collection

Art Gillham at the Piano in this 1920 photograph. *Source:* George Blau Collection

November 4, 29124: WEAF 18 Station "Hook-Up" Election night broadcast. Sitting on right is Carson Robison. Standing (R to L): Will Rogers, Art Gillham, Wendell Hall, and the Eveready Quartet. Orchestra is Waldorf Astoria, led by Joseph Knect (not pictured). Standing by microphone with violin is Ben Posner. The other individuals are unidentified. *Source:* George Blau Collection tered at the Edgewater Beach Hotel. Nick stayed with the ensemble for nearly two years, and during this period he began making appearances on radio station WEBH, whose studio was located next door to the hotel. Between sets he would take his guitar to the radio station and, for free, sing a song or two, later doing requests. He began to build a big following over the airwaves, and within a few weeks the station was deluged with hundreds of cards and letters from people from all over the country who wrote to say how much they enjoyed Nick's singing and guitar playing. At this time his picture also began to be featured on the sheet music covers.

WEBH was owned by Eugene MacDonald, who was a friend of the explorer Frederick Albert Cook. At the time, Cook was on an expedition to the Arctic and had become marooned in the ice off Iceland. The ship was frozen in ice for two months and the only outlet for communication to the outside world was by wireless. As a favor to MacDonald, once a week Nick would serenade the crew of the Cook expedition via radio, noting that he had a captive but appreciative audience.

While appearing with the Oriole Orchestra in Chicago, Lucas also recorded with the group on the Brunswick label. At the time Brunswick was one of the three largest record companies in the country, along with Victor and Columbia. Noticing Nick's Chicago and radio popularity, Brunswick officials signed him to make a solo disk with an option for a one-year contract if it proved successful. In November, 1924, singing to his own guitar accompaniment, Nick Lucas recorded the Walter Donaldson composition "My Best Girl," backed by a Ted Fio Rito–Danny Russo tune, "Dreamer of Dreams." The record proved so successful that Brunswick took up its option for a one-year contract, which paid the entertainer a recording fee and a royalty of one cent per disk sold. The contract also called for renewal options on a yearly basis, with annual increases in royalties.

The March 15, 1925, issue of *The Talking Machine World* noted,

Nick Lucas, widely known as "The Crooning Troubadour," who was recently added to the growing list of popular Brunswick artists, has achieved fame. His first Brunswick record, "My Best Girl," has enjoyed widespread demand. . . . Mr. Lucas sings to his own banjo or guitar accompaniment, and he is scoring in leading moving picture theatres and broadcasting stations of which he is now making a tour.

Billboard (February 21, 1925) said that Lucas "is selling reproductions of his peculiar style of singing in amounts undreamed of by the Brunswick when they signed him exclusively." On August 29, 1925, the same trade paper stated that Nick Lucas "is now one of the biggest sellers on the Brunswick label."

As a result of his newly found success, Nick Lucas left the Oriole Orchestra and became a solo act at the Tent Cafe in Chicago, early in 1925. Also appearing there was Bert Wheeler, who recommended Nick to his manager, Leo Fitzgerald, one of the most powerful agents in show business. Nick and Leo Fitzgerald came to an agreement and with a handshake began a professional association that lasted fifteen years. In the spring of 1925 Leo Fitzgerald began booking Nick Lucas into various locations in the Midwest, at places that would give him good publicity and at the same time reinforce his image as a guitarist-crooner, something quite new at the time.

When Nick signed with Brunswick Records, it was common for entertainers who made records to have a nickname. Gene Austin was dubbed "The Whispering Tenor" and there was "Whispering" Jack Smith, "Little Jack" Little, and Cliff "Ukulele Ike" Edwards, just to name a few. Brunswick dubbed Nick Lucas "The Crooning Troubadour," thus giving him the claim of being the first official crooner, although some sources credit female singer Vaughn De Leath as the first crooner. At any rate, Nick never liked the moniker and later changed it to "The Singing Troubadour."

Following a four-week stay at the Chicago Theatre in 1925, Leo Fitzgerald had requests for Nick's services from practically every major city in the country, and the entertainer got the feel of vaudeville and solo performing by appearing in cities like St. Louis, Des Moines, and Indianapolis, as he accustomed himself to working as a single act. He also had huge success in Philadelphia and Atlantic City, and it was announced that he would appear in the Aarons and Freedly show *A Night Out* in the fall of 1925. Instead, he was signed to appear in Rufus LeMaire's production of *Sweetheart Time*, which debuted on Broadway on January 19, 1926. In the second act he sang "Tahiti" and did a specialty number, "Sleepy Time Gal," which he also successfully recorded for Brunswick. *Variety* wrote, "Nick Lucas, the guitar-playing warbler, was spotted later in the show and went over for a sure hit." On January 30, 1926, *Billboard* said he was "the outstanding feature of the show. He actually stops the story in the second act."

As a result of his success on Broadway Nick was signed to appear at the Mecca of vaudeville, the Palace Theatre in New York City. His Palace debut, however, was not a success and he bowed out of the engagement to appear in a revue headed by Joe Howard in Cleveland, Ohio. In a flash act he was featured in a nightclub scene singing two songs, plus an encore, and he proved to be a big hit. As a result, he returned to Chicago, where he headlined at the Palace Theatre. *Billboard* (March 13, 1926) reported,

> Nick Lucas with his guitar and his crooning proved as popular as ever and he enjoyed encores galore. He sang one after another of the songs that he has sung to these same people so often before and they seem to never get enough of them. The demand was so great that Lucas stopped the show. His crooning is just as pleasing to listen to as it ever was. Personality is quite an asset to him.

Nick Lucas's dual successes in recordings and vaudeville complemented each other. Audiences would come to see him in person to hear him sing his latest recordings, which they had also purchased. *The Talking Machine World* noted in its October 15, 1926, issue, "Brunswick dealers are tying up effectively with the appearances of this artist, and in the cities in which he has appeared record sales have shown a marked increase."

Following his initial Brunswick disk, Lucas had a series of best-sellers, including "Because They All Love You," I've Named My Pillow after You," "Brown Eyes, Why Are You Blue?" and "Sleepy Time Gal." "Isn't She the Sweetest Thing?"/"By the Light of the Stars" was a dual-sided success. Of this pairing, *Variety* (July 27, 1925) said that Nick "does his stuff pretty," adding, "Lucas is an expert song salesman, his guitar accompaniment making for a novelty musical background."

When Nick Lucas began to have hit records, the making of the platters was not an easy task. When he began recording commercially in the late teens, Lucas learned that heavy-sounding instruments like the tuba and the banjo could easily disrupt the fragile recording mechanism used to capture the sound on wax. When he began making solo disks for Brunswick in the mid-1920s, the process had not improved to any extent. In those days before the microphone Nick had to sing into a horn, which in turn relayed the sound to the needle that imbedded it in wax for the master pressing. In order for his voice to be picked up for the pressing, Nick had to sing directly into the horn and also had to pitch his voice quite high for the delicate mechanical devices to record him properly. Thus, for the first couple of years that he recorded for Brunswick, Nick's voice sounded quite high on the acoustic disks.

With the coming of electrical recordings, the process improved, and by the late 1920s Nick's voice on disks was at a lower level, although he was still a high baritone or low tenor. Although he is best remembered for the many millions of records he sold in the mid- and late 1920s, with this somewhat high tenor voice, Nick Lucas never actually sounded that way in his personal appearances, where he sang more naturally an octave or two lower in his natural singing voice. Ironically, four decades later Tiny Tim developed his high singing voice and style by listening to these early Nick Lucas recordings, which in reality were not Nick's natural singing style but were necessitated by the primitive recording devices of that time.

The couplings of "No Foolin' "/"My Bundle of Love" and "Bye Bye Blackbird"/"Adorable" by Brunswick continued the Nick Lucas string of record sellers, as the crooner headlined the Keith-Orpheum vaudeville circuit in cities like Los Angeles, San Francisco, Oakland, and Denver. In the fall of 1926 Leo Fitzgerald received an offer for Nick to headline the Cafe de Paris in London, the top night spot in the British capital. In England, Nick's Brunswick records were big sellers and his latest hit there was "A Cup of Coffee, a Sandwich and You," which Jack Buchanan had introduced earlier on the London stage. Fitzgerald reckoned that a success for Nick in London would enhance his earnings when he returned to the United States. At the time London was the cultural capital of the English-speaking world, and good notices there for him would mean added luster to his already proliferating career.

Nick Lucas opened at the Cafe de Paris in London on November 8, 1926. The event was heavily publicized, and the first performance was for a closed audience of the elite, nobility, and big-name entertainers who were in London at the time. Among the guests were the Prince of Wales, the Queen of Spain, Fred and Adele Astaire, and Jack Buchanan. Not only did his opening play to a capacity audience, it was also broadcast all over England by radio and Nick was the only person on radio in that time period, thus giving him access to the entire British radio-listening audience. Lucas's singing and guitar playing made him an instant favorite; following his one-hour show, he received a five-minute standing ovation. After the show Nick autographed copies of his records for the guests as they left the Cafe de Paris. The Prince of Wales told him that he "was immensely entertaining and I especially enjoyed your extraordinary rhythm and your guitar playing."[1]

The next day he received laudatory reviews in all the London newspapers, and word of his success also reached his homeland. In its November 14, 1926, issue the *New York Times* reported,

> Because the Prince of Wales has heard and likes his playing and singing, after the manner of old Provencial Troubadours, Nick Lucas has suddenly become one of the most popular entertainers in London. . . . Accordingly, Lucas is in great demand, not only in theatres and cabarets, but also at the homes of society hostesses.

Of his Cafe de Paris opening, *Variety* (November 10, 1926) said that the entertainer "acclaimed one of the biggest receptions ever given any artist in that establishment." *Billboard* (November 20, 1926) noted that Lucas "was a riot at the Cafe de Paris," and the following week the same journal said that he "did consistently well at the Alhambra."

Following his overnight success at the Cafe de Paris, tickets were almost impossible to obtain for Nick's show. He quickly became the biggest sensation in London and was literally the talk of the town. In order to meet ticket demand for his show, Lucas had to give two performances each night. In addition, he was soon doing two matinee performances at the Alhambra Theatre, where *Variety* termed him "a sensational hit." He also appeared at private parties, including one for banking tycoon Otto Kahn, where he was paid about $750 for singing a few songs. He played the London Palladium twice to sold-out performances, as well as enjoying standing-room only appearances at the Kit Kat Klub, the Picccadilly Hotel, and the Coliseum Theatre, along with a successful week at the Victoria Palace. At the request of the Prince of Wales, Nick entertained at a private party given in honor of the prince's aunt, the Queen of Spain. Bandleader Jack Hylton wanted Nick to tour the provinces with him and Brunswick wanted him to record in London, but his hectic schedule prohibited these activities.

Originally, Nick Lucas was scheduled to remain in Great Britain for six months, but he was forced to cancel his stay early due to laryngitis. This illness also forced him out of a proposed four-week engagement in Cannes. Still, Nick's stay in London, perhaps the high point of his career, had been vastly rewarding for him, both financially and in added popularity. To show its appreciation, the management of the Cafe de Paris gave him a farewell party on the boat the night before he sailed for home. He suffered from seasickness on the voyage, however, and it took him a month to recover after returning home to his wife and daughter in Newark.

The London engagement established Nick Lucas as one of the top names in show business, and as a result Leo Fitzgerald was able to book him for eighty consecutive weeks on the Keith-Orpheum Circuit at a salary of $2,000 per week, a figure paid to only the top names in that medium. Years later, Bing Crosby told a group of radio disk jockeys, "I've been the luckiest guy in the world. If you disk jockeys had been on hand when Nick Lucas hit his stride he'd be the biggest name in show business."[2]

In the 1940s writers covering the Frank Sinatra craze stated that such a phenomenon had occurred once before, to Rudy Vallee in 1929. To an extent they were correct, but in actuality it had happened twice, previously; the first time was with Nick Lucas in London in 1926. The main difference was that Sinatra appealed to teenagers, while Lucas's and Vallee's popularity was with adults. Despite his success in London, Nick Lucas never appeared there again. Although plans for a British tour were announced in the late 1940s, it never materialized.

During this time, Mills Music asked Nick Lucas to write a guitar instruction book for beginning players, and *The Nick Lucas Guitar Method* proved so successful that he followed it with a second volume for advanced students. He later wrote *The Nick Lucas Plectrum Guitar Method Book* for Mills in 1932, followed by two more advanced volumes. For Mills, he also compiled the *Nick Lucas Chord, Rhythm and Fill-in Book for Guitar,* and for Robbins-Engel he did *Nick Lucas Comic Songs for Ukulele and Guitar* in 1926. In the 1930s he wrote a three-volume set, *The Nick Lucas Hawaiian Method,* for the Nicomede Music Company. He also compiled a number of song folios for Nicomede: *The Crown Folio, The Keystone Folio, The Liberty Folio, The Premier Folio, Six Original Nick Lucas Guitar Solos Folio, Nick Lucas Plectrum Guitar Solos, The Imperial Folio, The Waikiki Folio* (two volumes), and *The National Folio.* He also did the *Nick Lucas Collection of Neapolitan Love Songs* for Robbins Music in 1935.

In compiling his various guitar instruction books, folios, and songbooks, Nick Lucas composed scores of songs, many of them instrumentals for the guitar. He also composed a number of popular songs, including "I Might Have Known" and "Let Me Live and Love You Just for Tonight," both with Sam H. Stept; "I've Named My Pillow after You," with Fred Rose and Billy Waldron; and "Underneath the Stars with You," all of which he recorded for Brunswick Records.

In the mid-1920s Nick Lucas also lent his name to a line of guitars manufactured by the Gibson Guitar Company. While he was working at the Edgewater Beach Hotel in Chicago, Nick was asked by Gibson's general manager, Frank Campbell, to change from the Galliano guitar he was using to a Gibson model. Nick told him he would do so if the company built a guitar to his specifications, one with a wider neck, deeper sides, and a smaller body, which would be easier to use than the bulky Galliano. Nick was so pleased with the guitar Gibson built for him that he kept it for the rest of his career, although he had to have it repaired a few times in the ensuing years.

In 1926 the Gibson Nick Lucas Special guitar was placed on the market; it remained a solid seller well into the 1940s. It was one of the first flat-top guitars manufactured by Gibson and was manufactured from the specifications Nick Lucas required for the custom guitar Gibson made for him. Regarding the model, Tom and Mary Anne Gans wrote in *Guitars* (1977),

The guitar has a spruce top, strutted with Martin-type X bracing, rosewood sides and back with white plastic binding, and a sunburst finish. The finger-board is made of rosewood, with narrow rectangular-section frets, and the neck-to-body junction occurs at the twelfth fret. The headstock is inlaid with "The Gibson" in mother-of-pearl.

They also commented on how it differed from other models:

The proportions of the Nick Lucas Special are noticeably different from those of most other guitars of the period. The body is unusually deep for its size and short for its width. It would seem that the aim of the design was to make a guitar with some added bass resonance for vocal accompaniment, without losing too much of the balance and clarity associated with smaller-bodied instruments.

In their book the authors noted that Nick Lucas "had an enormous effect on the sales of acoustic guitars."

In its 1937 catalog Gibson noted,

This guitar was designed by Nick Lucas, famous star of talkies, records, stage and radio, whose popularity is justly deserved, as will be enthusiastically verified by anyone who has been fortunate enough to see and hear him play and sing. It has extra depth of tone but with a certain rich brilliancy in its voicing. Nick has inspired many boys and girls to take up the guitar—some of them are well known artists today—and the guitar you hear him play is the Nick Lucas model, designed for his own personal use and now offered to all guitarists who need this type of instrument.

In an interview in *Frets Magazine* (April, 1980), Nick Lucas told Mark Humphrey, "You'd be surprised how this guitar carries. I suggested the depth of the guitar to give it more volume, and it did. This was just a supposition—I have no technical knowledge of how to build a guitar."

After his return to the United States, Nick and Leo Fitzgerald renegotiated his recording contract with Brunswick. After recording with the company for a little more than two years, he had a string of hit records, including "My Best Girl," "Looking at the World thru Rose-Colored Glasses," "Side by Side," and "Bye Bye Blackbird." His new contract called for him to make enough recordings for a release each month, and for this he would receive five cents a disk in royalties, plus a recording fee of $3,000 per record. In the next four years he would become one of the biggest record sellers in popular music. To this day only two singers, Bing Crosby and Gene Austin, are reputed to have sold more 78 rpm records than Nick Lucas.

The years 1927 to 1930 were top moneymaking ones for Nick Lucas. With the big increase in income from vaudeville and recordings, he and his wife purchased a large home in the Forrest Hills section of Newark and he was hailed as "Newark's Favorite Son." Nick then returned to vaudeville on the Keith-Orpheum Circuit and played many major cities, solidifying his success in the field. He also had the opportunity to work with some of the biggest names in show business. He later recalled,

Every show I would stand in the wings and watch the great performers to see how they worked. I learned how to take a bow and all the other tricks of the stage. The performers were very kind to me and made suggestions and were willing to help me. I owe my showmanship to those old vaudeville days when I played with those wonderful and great artists.[3]

Billboard reviewed several of Nick's dates at this time, noting of his appearance at the New Palace in Chicago on March 31, 1927, "Nick Lucas, crooning a generous selection of popular tunes, was given generous encores. His medley of guitar numbers hit home strongly." Of his August 28, 1927, show at the New Orpheum Theatre in Los Angeles the trade paper wrote, "Nick Lucas' appearance was the signal for spontaneous applause" and noting that he was held for the next week, the reviewer commented, "Nick Lucas duplicated the hit he made at all of the shows last week. He gave a repertoire of different numbers this week and for encores obliged with numbers requested by the audience." When he returned to the New Palace in Chicago on November 20, 1927, he was "greatly applauded and was forced to four encores."

Working from week to week in vaudeville, sometimes doing split weeks or playing cut houses, where performers did three shows a day, was hectic and somewhat tiring, but, overall, Nick Lucas greatly enjoyed the experience. All the travel was done by train, which provided top-notch service and the best in cuisine. The travel routes were planned long in advance of the actual tours, and few problems ever arose in traveling from one play date to another. Lucas recalled, "the hotels were beautiful to live in" and a suite of rooms cost about $5 a day. "The food was terrific and room service was an art and these hotels had special kitchens. It was a delight and a joy to travel during those days," he recalled.[4] Lucas said the theaters in which he played all had good house orchestras, the dressing rooms were clean, and the audiences more than receptive.

He continued to have hit records for Brunswick, such as "In a Little Spanish Town," "I'm Looking over a Four Leaf Clover," "Moonbeam! Kiss Her for Me," "(Here Am I) Brokenhearted," "The Song Is Ended," and "Together." Regarding some of Nick's current releases, *Variety* (September 12, 1928) opined,

Nick Lucas, "The Crooning Troubadour," is just too bad with a new Brunswick quartet of sentimental ballads. "When You Say Goodbye" and "You're a Real Sweetheart" as one couple, and "Just Like a Mel-

ody" and "For Old Times' Sake" another. Lucas' song interpretations
are ever distinctive; made more so by intelligent selection of numbers.

The next month's release was reviewed by the same trade paper
on October 31, 1928: "Crooning Troubadour, as Lucas is styled, has
a couple of pat numbers for his intimately sympathetic vocal delivery in 'Marcheta' and 'Waiting for Ships That Never Come In.' Both
are ballad revivals. Violin and guitar accompaniments add further
charm to the numbers." Another big record for Lucas in 1928 was
"It Must Be Love," the official song of that year's Republican National Convention.

Probably one of the main reasons for the success of Nick Lucas's
Brunswick recordings was their simplicity. Usually, he made the
disks with just his guitar and maybe a backup by a pianist such as
Sammy Stept or organists like William Wirges or Lew White. Occasionally, a guest like David Rubinoff (who played violin on "So
Blue" in 1927) would join Nick, but mostly he just sang and accompanied himself on the guitar with those songs. The recordings were
done in a pleasing and simple manner and were not like most of the
over-produced disks of later years. Nick recalled that it was sometimes difficult to get a full three minutes out of some of the tunes he
was asked to record and that he had to improvise in order to stretch
a few of them to their allotted time limit. He was amused by so
many of the impromptu solos he did with his guitar on those records, but the buying public loved them.

In the summer of 1928 Nick Lucas placed the following full-page
advertisement in *Variety* (June 12, 1928) in the form of a letter:

I am taking this medium to thank my fellow performers, theatre managers, musicians, stage hands and all concerned in making my four of
the Keith-Albee-Orpheum Circuits which I just completed so successful and pleasant. I am glad to announce that I have re-signed for the
above circuits and the Interstate for next season, and also at this time
wish to say I have renewed my contract to record exclusively for the
Brunswick Phonograph Company. Many thanks to the entire recording staff and officials, and last but not least, my manager, Leo Fitzgerald for making the above possible.

That his vaudeville popularity went unabated was noted in the
October 6, 1928, issue of *Billboard*, which said that Lucas "was a tremendous box-office success during his recent engagement at the

Majestic Theatre, Fort Worth." Just how popular Nick Lucas had become in vaudeville was revealed early in 1929, when the results of a voting contest taken among the patrons on the Keith circuit were announced. Nick placed eighth in the poll, just sixty-nine votes behind seventh-placed Ted Lewis. They were preceded by Belle Baker and Sophie Tucker (who tied for first place), Van & Schenck, Rudy Vallee, Waring's Pennsylvanians, and Ted Lewis.

As a result, Lucas appeared on two NBC radio one-hour broadcasts on April 2 and 9, 1929. On the first show he appeared with Sophie Tucker, Ted Lewis, Rudy Vallee, Belle Baker, Van & Schenck, and Ben Bernie, and on the second radio hour he was again with Tucker and Lewis, plus Kate Smith and Waring's Pennsylvanians. Toward the end of March, 1929, Nick Lucas was headlining the vaudeville show at the Orpheum Theatre in Los Angeles. *Variety* (March 20, 1929) commented, "The crooner with his guitar and in a frock suit instead of a tux at night makes 'em take it. That Nick greatly resembles Wolfie Gilbert doesn't appear to be a liability in this city." It was during this run that his show was seen by Darryl F. Zanuck, the head of production at Warner Bros., who offered him a part in the upcoming movie musical *The Gold Diggers of Broadway.* Next he moved to the New Palace in Chicago, where *Billboard* (June 15, 1929) reported, "Nick Lucas stirred up some real enthusiasm with his crooning melodies to guitar accompaniment. Put his stuff across big and had to respond to insistent demands for an encore."

Nick Lucas returned to Broadway in the summer 1929 in the Florenz Ziegfeld musical *Show Girl,* with music by George Gershwin and lyrics by Ira Gershwin and Gus Kahn. During the Boston tryout for the show, Nick learned that George Gershwin was unhappy with one of his compositions for the show, "Liza," and Lucas suggested to him that he increase the beat of the tune. The end result of this suggestion was the hit of the show, which, ironically, Brunswick Records let Al Jolson record instead of Lucas. *Show Girl* opened on Broadway on July 2, 1929, at the Ziegfeld Theatre to only mild reception by the critics, although it did well financially. Nick appeared in two spots, singing "Liza" and "Singin' in the Rain." Also headlining the cast was the comedy team of Jimmy Durante, Lou Clayton, and Eddie Jackson; Eddie Foy, Jr.; Frank McHugh; Duke Ellington's Band; and Ruby Keeler in the title role. As a gimmick, when Ruby Keeler made her stage appearance, her real-life husband, Al Jolson, sang "Liza" to her from the audience. Regarding Nick Lucas's work in the musical, *Billboard* (July 13, 1929) reported that he was "offering his crooning specialty so well known to phonograph and radio fans."

After seven performances Nick Lucas left the show to resume his tour on the Keith-Albee-Orpheum Circuit. When he appeared at the Palace Theatre in Gotham, the *New York Times* (September 2, 1929) wrote, "Another Palace songster is Nick Lucas, who was for a brief while in 'Show Girl,' and whose crooning of popular ditties is said to be familiar to phonograph owners. Lucas caresses vocally some of Tin Pan Alley's lesser output, including an inevitable mother song, and for so doing he was recalled several times yesterday."

The next night, September 3, he appeared on an NBC radio broadcast sponsored by the Runswick-Balke-Collender Company, the owners of Brunswick Records. Also reviewing his latest Palace stand was *Billboard* (September 14, 1929), which stated, "Vaude can use Lucas, and his phenomenal disc-recording activity makes him a great subject for special exploitation."

As noted earlier, Nick Lucas appeared in Warner Bros.' *The Gold Diggers of Broadway*, which debuted theatrically early in September 1929. Earlier, Nick had had a best-selling record with "My Tonia," the theme song of the 1929 Fox production *In Old Arizona*, in which Warner Baxter won an Academy Award for his performance as the Cisco Kid. Nick himself first appeared in movie theaters in the summer of 1929 in the one-reel Vitaphone short *A Nick Lucas Song* and was also in the ten-minute special trailer advertising *The Gold Diggers of Broadway*. In the latter film he chatted briefly with the film's star, Conway Tearle, and then sang truncated versions of three songs from the film, "Tiptoe thru the Tulips," "Painting the Clouds with Sunshine," and "In a Kitchenette."

Signing to work on *The Gold Diggers of Broadway* for two weeks at $5,000 per week, Nick Lucas ended up spending ten weeks filming his scenes for the movie. The reason for this was that the production was plagued with problems, owing to the newness of the sound medium and the use of the Technicolor process. The latter required lights that were so hot, they caused hairline cracks in Nick's guitar; the heat even put cracks in his patent leather shoes. Because of the excessive heat the Technicolor scenes had to be curtailed and filming could only take place for short periods, thus dragging out the time it took to shoot the picture. Also, there was no lip synchronization, as there would be in filmed musical sequences in just a few years, and many retakes were necessary on the vocals and production numbers, all of which had to be perfectly done on the set. A twenty-five piece band, with its members being paid $10 an hour, was on the set at all times during the shooting.

When Nick Lucas signed for the film, he was assigned to do the song "Painting the Clouds with Sunshine," the movie's theme. After Darryl F. Zanuck saw the rushes, however, he told songwriters Al Dubin and Joe Burke to compose another number for Nick and they came up with "Tiptoe thru the Tulips." Nick worked closely with Dubin and Burke in putting the song together, but he never got composer credit, although many have done less on songs and still been credited as composers. He also sang "In a Kitchenette," "What Will I Do without You?" and "Go to Bed." When he did "Tiptoe thru the Tulips," the chorines actually danced among red and yellow tulips, a part of the Technicolor aspect of the movie.

The Gold Diggers of Broadway proved to be a huge success. *Billboard* (September 7, 1929) called it "by far the best thing thus far produced in the talkie era." *Variety* reported, "Lots of color—Technicolor—lots of comedy, girls, songs, music, dancing, production and Winnie Lightner, with Nick Lucas the main warbler. . . . That's what's going to send the picture into the money class for the Warners. . . ." Regarding Nick, the reviewer said,

> there's no voice on the discs like Lucas' for the type of number sung by him. He's a paradox, as on the screen, great and can win with his voice, while on the stage Nick must get over on the strength of the canned rep he has piled so high. The two certain songs sung by him among the several others in *The Diggers* are "Tulips" and "Painting the Clouds."

The film proved to be a big success all across the country and played for three months at the Winter Garden in New York. While the movie was at that theater, Nick Lucas became the "only single act doubling on Broadway" (*Variety*) when he also headlined the RKO Palace Theatre. For Nick Lucas, the film was a double success, in that it not only gave him a good role in a major motion picture, but it also provided him with the two songs most associated with his career, "Tiptoe thru the Tulips" and "Painting the Clouds with Sunshine." He recorded the two numbers for Brunswick Records, and the disk quickly became the top-selling record in the country and stayed that way for nearly two months. Its initial pressing sold over one million copies, and the disk eventually surpassed the three million mark. In addition, the sheet music to the two songs, featuring Nick's picture on the cover with the film's other stars, also sold past the million mark for both tunes.

In an era that became overpopulated with all-singing, all-talking, all dancing movies, *The Gold Diggers of Broadway* was the most successful of the genre. It eventually made over $7.5 million, making it Warner's second most successful grosser (the first was Al Jolson's 1928 *The Singing Fool*) until the advent of *Sergeant York* in 1941. Unfortunately, several factors eventually worked against the preservation of the movie, which has been lost to the ages. First, it was done in the sound-on-disk process, which soon became antiquated. Second, musicals lost their appeal in the early 1930s and were soon considered passé. Finally, the film was neglected due to its remake, *The Gold Diggers of 1933* (1933). Shot on nitrate base, the movie was allowed to decompose and only the last twenty minutes survive, although the feature was playing theatrically in Australia as late as 1939.

Following the acclaim he received in *The Gold Diggers of Broadway*, Nick Lucas was asked by Darryl F. Zanuck to appear in another Warner Bros. musical extravaganza, *The Show of Shows*. Leo Fitzgerald negotiated a contract that called for Nick to be paid $10,000 a week for two weeks' work on the film, plus the studio also paid for Nick and his wife and daughter's train trip to Hollywood and their two-week stay at the Ambassador Hotel. Appearing in the Technicolor sequence "The Chinese Fantasy," Nick Lucas portrayed a Chinese prince who serenades his lady love (Myrna Loy) with the song "Li-Po-Li." He also traded comedy patter with the movie's host, Frank Fay, and sang "Lady Luck" and "The Only Song I Know." Seventy-seven stars appeared in *The Show of Shows* and, while it did good box office, many consider it one of the weaker early sound musicals. Fortunately, the movie has survived and is often revived on cable television, with the charming "Chinese Fantasy" sequence still intact in its lovely Technicolor.

As a result of his successes in *The Gold Diggers of Broadway* and *The Show of Shows*, Warners offered Nick Lucas a seven-year contract, but he and Leo Fitzgerald turned it down since it did not match the money he was being paid on vaudeville. At the time, he had eighty weeks' advance booking at $3,000 per week, and on

Thanksgiving Day in 1929 he broke an eighteen-year-old house record at Proctor's Theatre in his hometown of Newark.

Although the stock market collapsed in the fall of 1929 and the
country's financial situation was becoming unstable, things looked
very good for Nick Lucas. In the five years since he started recording
for Brunswick, his disks had sold in the millions and he was one of
the top record sellers in the country. He had been in two Broadway
musicals and two big Hollywood productions, along with being one
of the highest paid performers in vaudeville. His guitar books were
best-sellers, as was the line of guitars bearing his name. As he em-
barked on his 1930 vaudeville tour, Nick Lucas was at the apex of
his career.

The Depression, however, grew worse and would make big inroads into show business. Within two years vaudeville and the record industry would be reeling from its effects; those areas that Nick
Lucas had found so profitable would be in turmoil. Vaudeville
would eventually die out and the record industry would not recover
until the beginning of World War II. Over 100 million records were
sold in the United States in 1929, but that figure dropped over 50
percent by the end of 1931.

Nick Lucas's records for Brunswick, however, continued to sell
well, and he had hits with "Lady Play Your Mandolin" and the com-
binations of "Dancing with Tears in My Eyes"/"Telling It to the
Daisies" and "You're Driving Me Crazy"/"I Miss a Little Miss." Regarding his August 1930 release "Singing a Song to the Stars"/"My
Heart Belongs to the Girl Who Belongs to Somebody Else," *Variety*,
on August 27, 1930, reported, "Supreme among those who lull their
listeners into pleasurable reverie is this graduate of the early era of
symphonic jazz . . . [the songs] are characteristic Lucas charmers."

At the end of 1930 Brunswick listed its top-selling singers as Al
Jolson, Harry Richman, Nick Lucas, Libby Holman, Marion Harris,
and Belle Baker. Nick Lucas continued to get rave reviews in vaudeville, as evidenced by his appearance at the RKO Palace Theatre in
New York early in December 1930. *Variety* called him a "show stop-
per," while the *New York Sun* said, "Mr. Lucas, whose virtuosity
with the guitar surpasses even his crooning, stopped the show until
he had dished up many of his old favorites." The *New York Evening
Graphic* noted, "Lucas sings without effort, and the result is so pleasant that one wishes that there could be more crooners like him. His
style is certainly distinctive." The *New York Herald Tribune* stated,

"Nick Lucas can still pick the guitar to perfection and his singing is above reproach," while the *New York Daily News* called him, "The daddy of all crooners." *Billboard* wrote, "Nick Lucas . . . clicked easily on his own with his crooning and guitaristics. Lucas drew big applause in three numbers before taking the bows and almost wearing out his welcome with encores. . . . Lucas was in good voice, and the regulars sensed it." The *New York World* reported, ". . . Mr. Lucas was well received with tremendous enthusiasm, that he is a wow, that he was forced to give four encores."

The successful vaudeville tour continued into 1931 and when he appeared in Omaha, Nebraska, the *Omaha Bee-News* (April 13, 1931) raved, "Nick Lucas' crooning rates high, but the combination of his crooning and guitar accompaniment is irresistible." He had just come from an engagement in Boston, where the *Paramount-Publix* reported, "First time in Boston's history S.R.O. business on 'Good Friday' at the Metropolitan."

When he headlined in Denver, Colorado, the *Rocky Mountain News* (May 8, 1931) stated, "And the melody—such melody!—flows in bountiful quantities from the ingratiating vocal chorus and deft fingers of that prince of entertainers—Nick Lucas. A packed house yesterday gave the world to know that it regards Nick Lucas as one of the most popular persons who ever smiled across Denver."

He continued to make guest appearances on radio, such as *The RKO Hour* in February, 1931, where *Variety* (February 11, 1931) commented, "Nick Lucas and Dr. Rockwell . . . saved the hour. . . . Lucas strummed and crooned two pops in his familiar and sure-fire manner."

He also continued to record for Brunswick; "Walkin' My Baby Back Home," "You Didn't Have to Tell Me," "Hello Beautiful," and "I Surrender Dear" fared well, as did the combination of "When the Moon Comes over the Mountain"/"That's My Desire." Nick was the first to have a hit record with the latter tunes, although they are most associated with Kate Smith, who co-wrote the first one, and Frankie Laine, respectively. Following a vocal chorus with Victor Young on "Goodnight Sweetheart," Nick Lucas parted company with Brunswick.

A national poll taken in the fall of 1931 noted that 64 percent of those questioned knew who Nick Lucas was, the same percentage for Ted Lewis and Albert Einstein. Following an appearance in Cleveland, Ohio, in August 1931, Archie Bell wrote in the *Cleveland*

News, "He's the sort of fellow you'd like to drop in any time, day or night, and entertain you with a song, the best modern representative of the ancient troubadour."[21]

That fall Nick began singing weeknights on NBC radio in a fifteen-minute program that soon landed Campbell's Soup as a sponsor at a salary of $2,000 per week. The program ran until February 1932 and usually broadcast twice a week, on Wednesday and Saturday, for fifteen minutes. The show, however, had stiff competition from Bing Crosby, who was appearing at the same times over the Columbia network. At the end of 1931 Brunswick Records listed him, along with Bing Crosby, the Boswell Sisters, and the Mills Brothers, as one of its four best-selling vocalists, despite the fact that he had not recorded for the company in three months.

Early in 1932 Nick resumed recording, this time for the Durium Company on its fifteen-cent cardboard Hit-of-the-Week label. He cut two records, "An Evening in Caroline" and "All of Me," for the label, which had the songs on one side of the disk and the artist's picture on the other. Both records sold in excess of 250,000 copies each; this represented half of what the label had sold during the summer of 1930 when Hit-of-the-Week disks reached their peak sales. By the end of 1932, however, Nick and Brunswick had settled their differences over a salary dispute, and he would record for the label for another year.

When his NBC radio show ended early in 1932, Nick Lucas returned to vaudeville and on February 11 of that year he headlined the opening of the RKO-Orpheum Theatre in Denver, Colorado, which seated 2,600 patrons. Regarding the opening, *Variety* reported, "Thousands stood in line and many were turned away the first day." The next month he made two appearances on the NBC radio show *RKO Theatre of the Air.*

By now, Nick was traveling to his engagements by car and plane, in addition to trains. Air travel, however, had its drawbacks, as noted in the May 10, 1932, issue of *Variety,* "Nick Lucas ruined two guitars flying in a plane from St. Louis to Chicago. Atmosphere cracked sound boxes."

On November 16, 1932, Lucas was the last act to headline the Palace Theatre in New York City before it was converted to a movie house. The event is considered the official end of big-time vaudeville.

In 1933 Nick returned to movies, starring in two shorts made by

Master Art Products in their "Organlogue" series, featuring organist Lew White. They were *Organloguing the Hits* and *Home Again*.
Other popular singers making shorts in this series included Irving
Kaufman, Donald Novis, and Singin' Sam (Harry Frankel). Lucas
starred in the first of Universal's "Vaudeville on Film" Menotone
musical shorts, *On the Air and Off*, that year, and in the last quarter
of 1933 he toured the South with Ray Teal's orchestra. In 1934 Nick
also starred in the Warner Bros. musical short *What This Country
Needs*, in which he reprised "Tiptoe through the Tulips."

In March 1934, Nick Lucas returned to network radio, headlining
a fifteen-minute, twice-a-week series on the Columbia Broadcasting
System (CBS). The series had him backed by Freddie Rich's orchestra and was broadcast each Wednesday at 11 P.M. and Friday at 6:30
P.M. Publicity for the program noted that the star played three banjos at one time during his song recitals, and another source claimed
he was "probably the only crooner on the air who doesn't mind
being called one." *Variety* (March 27, 1934) reported,

> Essentially a mike performer, and no novice at that via talkers and re-
> cords (he's been [one] of Brunswick's best sellers for years), Lucas
> knows his audible delivery and evidences that handsomely on his
> quarter hour. . . . He manifests canny choice of numbers, warbling his
> pops in tip-top manner to self-guitar accompaniment.

The series debuted March 21, 1934, and ended June 16, 1935. In
1934 Nick also recorded six sides for the American Record Company; they were issued as three disks on a variety of labels, including Melotone, Banner, Rex, Oriole, and Perfect.

In the mid-1930s Leo Fitzgerald suggested to Nick Lucas that he
should front a band, as this business was quite popular and he
thought Nick would make a good bandleader, especially with his
experience as a band sideman in the days before he became a solo
performer. Lucas then set about putting together a unit that was
called Nick Lucas and His Troubadours. This group toured for
nearly two years, successfully playing dates mostly in the Eastern
states since it was headquartered in New York. Nick, however, did
not like fronting a band, as he found the musicians too temperamental, and he disliked the expense of having to hire an accountant and
a tour bus and drivers.

Although he never commercially recorded with his band, Lucas and the unit appeared in the 1936 Warner Bros. short *Nick Lucas and His Troubadours.* The same year he also appeared in another Warners short, *Vitaphone Headliners,* in which he sang "Broken Hearted Troubadour." This sequence was later used in the 1947 short *Big Time Revue.*

In 1937 Nick became a regular on the CBS radio show *Al Pearce and His Gang,* and he also began recording for various transcription companies that leased their records to radio stations. Although he recorded for a number of such outfits, the bulk of his transcriptions were done for the C. P. MacGregor Company in Hollywood.

He also continued to appear in what was left of vaudeville. *Billboard* (August 27, 1938) noted that he and Phil Harris broke the house record at the Lyric Theatre in Indianapolis, Indiana, previously set by Eddy Duchin. He followed this engagement with appearances in Des Moines, Iowa; Chicago; Dayton, Ohio; and Kansas City, Kansas, that year. Nick also began appearing in nightclubs and he would continue to do so into the mid-1960s.

Leo Fitzgerald retired in the late 1930s and Nick signed with the agency of Fanchon and Marco. In 1939 he began a two-year world tour. Australia was the first leg of the tour; he took a boat there and along the way stopped at Pago Pago. When the boat docked, he found hundreds of natives waiting for him, carrying his guitar and songbooks. He gave an impromptu performance for them and the same thing happened at the next stop in the Fiji Islands. After reaching Melbourne, Australia, Nick headlined the Tivoli Theatre there and was also signed to star in an early morning weekday radio show. Its theme song was "Good Morning," which was one of six tunes he recorded for the Regal Zonophone label in Australia. He also had engagements in Brisbane and Sydney, but after six months he was forced to return home due to the outbreak of World War II. The ship he took had to travel in a zigzag path in order to avoid being attacked by Japanese planes.

Back in the United States, Nick Lucas continued to make personal appearances and also starred in two more short films, *Yankee Doodle Home* (Columbia, 1939) and *Congamania* (Universal, 1940). In 1944 he made four shorts for the Soundies Corporation of America: *Tiptoe thru the Tulips, Side by Side, Goodnight Wherever You Are,* and *An Hour Never Passes.*

After the war Nick and his wife sold their home in Newark and purchased a ranch in Colorado Springs, Colorado. They soon relocated to Encino, California, although Nick kept the ranch. He then did a two-month tour of the Hawaiian Islands.

In 1947 Nick Lucas signed to appear in *Ken Murray's Blackouts* at the El Capitan Theatre in Hollywood. The show had been running for several years with Marie Wilson as its headliner. Nick was so successful that he remained with the production for two years. During this run, *Billboard* reported, "If you happen to be one of the fortunate public to get seats to 'Ken Murray's Blackouts' and you hear the screams of 'teenagers' you will know that Nick Lucas is center stage. He is better than ever."

Just prior to going into this show, Nick resumed his commercial recordings for the Diamond label, cutting eight sides that proved to be good sellers. In 1948 he recorded for Capitol Records, again resulting in good sales.

Nick Lucas returned to Broadway in 1949 with a new rendition of the Ken Murray show "Blackouts of 1949." After its opening, the musical comedy was lambasted by the critics and ran for only six weeks. Lucas, however, got good reviews for his work in the show, as noted by Brooks Atkinson in the *New York Times,* who commented, "Until Nick Lucas came on in the last end of the show, with some lucid songs, the only tunes your reviewer could sort out from the general pandemonium were 'Silver Threads among the Gold' and 'Put on Your Old Grey Bonnet.' " After the show's closing, Nick remained in New York and was the guest star on the premiere program of *The Ken Murray Show* in 1950 on CBS-TV; for the same network he also was a guest on Ed Sullivan's *Toast of the Town.*

Following a cross-country club tour in 1951, he returned to Hollywood to star in seven short musicals made for television by Snader Transcriptions: *Bela Bimba, The Sunshine of Your Smile, Get Out Those Old Records, Looking at the World thru Rose Colored Glasses, Marie Ah Marie, Mexicali Rose,* and *Walking My Baby Back Home.* That year he also returned to network radio, headlining the ABC series *Saturday Night at the Shamrock,* which was broadcast from the Shamrock Hotel in Houston, Texas. The year 1951 also found Nick Lucas back on the big screen, appearing as himself, singing, "Let's Meander through the Meadow" in the Allied Artists musical *Disc Jockey.*

As the 1950s progressed, Nick Lucas continued to make guest appearances on national television on Kate Smith's and Art Linkletter's programs, among others, but he spent most of his time appearing in top night spots around the country. Throughout the decade, he appeared in cocktail lounges in Reno and Las Vegas with a backup trio, at a salary of $3,000 per week. He also continued to record. In 1953 he cut eight sides for Cavalier Records, which were issued as singles, as well as a ten-inch LP entitled *Tiptoe thru the Tulips with Nick Lucas.* In 1955 he began a twenty-five-year association with Accent Records; the previous year he cut a single for the Crown label. In 1956 he cut more sides for Cavalier and the next year did an album for Decca Records called *Painting the Clouds with Sunshine,* which was such a good seller that it remained in the company's catalog for fifteen years. In 1958 he guest starred on Patti Page's TV show *The Big Record* on CBS-TV and reprised his biggest record, "Tiptoe thru the Tulips"/"Painting the Clouds with Sunshine."

In the early 1960s Nick Lucas was a semiregular on Lawrence Welk's TV show, but after a half-dozen shows Welk refused to renew his contract because Lucas was "becoming too popular." He also appeared quite often on the West Coast show *Melody Ranch* with Johnny Bond. He continued his lucrative Reno, Las Vegas, and Lake Tahoe lounge dates and also played in other clubs throughout the country. During an engagement at the Cabana Club in Dallas, Texas, Nick and Bob Hope were having dinner when a man approached them and told Nick, "You are great and I have been a fan of yours for years." He also gave them passes to his own establishment, the Carousel Club, in Dallas. After 1963 when Nick was anywhere near Bob Hope, the comedian would tell anyone in earshot that it was Nick Lucas who introduced him to Jack Ruby.

By the mid-1960s Nick Lucas decided to curtail his constant work since his wife's health was not good and he was tired of the grind of the cocktail lounge circuit. Although he continued doing some club dates, he preferred working state and county fairs and home shows; he also continued to record for Accent Records. In the summer of 1966 he headlined the stage revue "The Blackouts of 1966" at the Cal-Neva in Lake Tahoe. Appearing at the same time in the club's lounge was his old friend Gene Austin.

Nick Lucas's career path took a major turn in the late 1960s with the arrival of Tiny Tim on the music scene. The long-haired singer became popular on the NBC-TV show *Laugh-In,* where he would often credit Nick as having introduced the songs he sang, including "Tiptoe thru the Tulips." Tim recorded "Tiptoe" for Reprise Records and it sold a half million copies. As a result, Lucas was swamped with work offers, and he and Tiny Tim met, became friends, and occasionally worked together. Nick appeared on *The To-night Show* on NBC-TV in the spring of 1969 when Tiny Tim announced his engagement to Victoria Pudinger. When the two were married on the program on December 17, 1969, Nick sang "Tiptoe thru the Tulips" and "Looking at the World thru Rose Colored Glasses" to the biggest viewing audience in the show's history. Lucas also continued to record for Accent Records and in the late 1960s made two albums for the company, *The Nick Lucas Souvenir Album* and *Rose Colored Glasses*.

Nick's wife of fifty-two years, Catherine, died in 1970. When he returned to work, it was on a part-time basis, mainly for service, charity, and fraternal organizations. In 1972 he was a guest on Merv Griffin's syndicated TV show, singing, "Tiptoe thru the Tulips" in a segment about the Roaring Twenties. For the next several years he would also make numerous appearances on Mayor Sam Yorty's radio and TV shows in Los Angeles.

Accepting a request from Nelson Riddle, Nick Lucas returned to films in 1974, singing on the soundtrack of the Paramount production *The Great Gatsby*. He was also featured on three numbers on the film's soundtrack issued on Paramount Records. He made some television commercials and became associated with the Mayfair Music Hall in Santa Monica, California, where he would continue to headline for the rest of the decade. In reviewing a 1974 show, the *Los Angeles Times* wrote, ". . . the silver throated (and haired) Nick Lucas suits the Mayfair beautifully. Most notably associated with 'Tip-Toe through the Tulips' he sang the old songs with appropriate sentiment—but not a trace of camp. A glowing star for a very pleasant show." In the fall of 1974 he returned to Paramount to sing "I Wished on the Moon" on the soundtrack of the film *Day of the Locust*.

In 1975 Nick made two appearances on the syndicated TV show *Vaudeville*, and *Daily Variety* (January 17, 1975) reported, "Nick Lucas, sounding as he did almost a half century ago, demonstrates how to sing authentic 'Tip-Toe thru the Tulips,' 'Painting the Clouds with Sunshine' and 'Has Anybody Seen My Gal' and audience reaction is solid as ever." Later in the year, an appearance at the Mayfair Music Hall was taped by the BBC, and he also was heard on the British radio show *Star Sound*. In the movie *Hearts of the West* (United Artists, 1975) Nick Lucas sang six songs, including the film's theme, "I'll See You in My Dreams."

Throughout the late 1970s and early 1980s Nick Lucas continued to make personal appearances, usually in the Southern California area. In 1977 he was one of a select group of entertainers to appear in the "Vaudeville Lives" series at the Variety Arts Theatre in Los Angeles, and the same year he did a special for Irish television. He opened 1980 by appearing in the Rose Bowl Parade on the "Tiptoe thru the Tulips" float and was also widely seen on the West Coast in numerous guest appearances on Wally George's television show. Late in 1980 he had his final recording session for Accent Records, waxing "Are You Lonesome Tonight?" and "How Did You Have the Heart to Break My Heart?" Vernon Scott wrote in a widely published United Press International story, "Nick was the Sinatra and Presley of his day and can honestly lay claim to being the progenitor of every minstrel and troubadour in this country who accompanies himself on the guitar. . . . Today Nick is a charming geezer in fine fettle, excellent voice and still an unabashed romantic. . . . He credits his longevity and good health to moderation."

The early 1980s found Nick Lucas still making personal appearances, along with guest shots on the Merv Griffin and Nelson Riddle shows. Health problems, however, began to develop in 1982, mainly with his back. After several months he suffered a stroke and his family moved him to Colorado Springs, Colorado, where he died from pneumonia on July 28, 1982. He was buried in Colorado Springs, survived by his daughter and three grandsons.

Nick Lucas had a twofold success in show business. He was one of the first crooners and had the longest-lived career performing in this style. He was also one of the most successful, having been a major name in vaudeville, records, movies, and radio. Second, he is remembered as the person most responsible for popularizing the guitar in American culture. His best-selling line of guitar songbooks, guitar picks, and the Gibson instrument that carried his name helped solidify the guitar as the most popular musical instrument of this century. Together, these factors, his singing and guitar playing, combined to make Nick Lucas one of the major entertainment figures of his time.

NOTES

1. Interview with Michael Pitts, July 1973.
2. Press booklet, 1975.

3. Interview with Michael Pitts, July 1973.
4. Interview with Michael Pitts, July 1973.
5. *Radio Dial* (April 5, 1934).
6. Undated press booklet.
7. Interview with Michael Pitts, 1973.
8. Taped comments sent to Michael Pitts, 1978.

5

Johnny Marvin

In his heyday in the late 1920s and early 1930s, Johnny Marvin was one of the most popular singers in the country. By mid-1928 his records had sold over ten million copies and within a year he was regarded as one of the three top record sellers in the country, along with Nick Lucas and Gene Austin. After several years of struggle, Marvin's rise to fame was meteoric; he was able to sustain his popularity until the inroads of the Depression killed his major sources of income, vaudeville and records. Marvin's pleasing and smooth singing voice, along with his ukulele strumming, made him a central figure in the musical world of the Roaring Twenties; his abilities catapulted him to the forefront among crooners. Today Johnny Marvin is largely forgotten. Except for a clique of collectors who seek and save his old 78 rpm disks, the crooner is a faded name from the past whose recordings have largely not been reissued. He is perhaps the least known of all the major crooners. One reason for this is that he died at the relatively early age of forty-seven in 1944, and during the last years of his life he had mainly forsaken entertaining for song writing. Although he had numerous best-selling records between 1927 and 1931, Johnny Marvin is not associated with any one particular song, such as Nick Lucas with "Tiptoe thru the Tulips" or Gene Austin with "My Blue Heaven." He also recorded on the same label, Victor Records, with Gene Austin, which kept him from becoming the company's major artist. Finally, Johnny Marvin, like the Jazz Age that spawned his success, simply was unable to sustain major popularity with the coming of the Depression. Gloomy economic times cast a pall on the type of music Johnny Marvin performed, and although he continued to have moderate success on the radio into the mid-1930s, his vogue had passed by 1932. When Johnny Marvin died late in 1944, his brief *Variety* obituary emphasized his recording of Western music and failed to mention his immense popularity as a suit-and-tie crooner in the Roaring Twenties.

John Senator Marvin was born in a covered wagon near Butler, Oklahoma, on July 11, 1897, the son of John Harvey and Mary Ellen "Molly" (Wallance) Marvin. The family had come from Missouri to settle on a tract of land provided by the U.S. government in Custer County, Oklahoma. The trip had taken nearly two years, and baby Johnny was born just before the family arrived at its homestead. His older siblings were Ethel (born 1893) and Charley (born 1984), and he was followed by Thelma (born 1901), Frank James "Frankie" (born 1904), and Fay (born 1907). John Harvey Marvin farmed for several years before going into the real estate business and opening an office in Butler in 1910, also offering farm loans and insurance. The next year the senior Marvin built a home in Butler and moved his family there from the farm.

Johnny Marvin came from a musical family. His father played the fiddle and guitar, while his mother played accordion and sang in church. The youngster, who was called Senator during his youth to avoid being confused with his father, inherited these traits and by the time he was a teenager, he and his father were entertaining at social gatherings and dances and earning $2.50 for their work. The elder Marvin, however, refused to share these proceeds with his son and this became the cause of conflict between the two, with Senator running away from home several times. In the summer of 1911 he went to Texas, where he broke his arm before returning home in the fall. In 1912 John H. Marvin moved his family to Arkansas and later Kansas City, but by the end of 1914 they had returned to Butler. In 1912, however, Senator briefly joined a circus.

By this time Senator Marvin played the ukulele and steel guitar, and in 1914 he left home to join a Hawaiian troupe. Replacing a member of the group who had died, he bleached his hair and colored his skin with walnut bleach. A mainstay of the act had Senator singing "Go to Sleep My Baby" to an infant who belonged to another member of the troupe. The act took Marvin to New York, where he remained until the spring of 1916, when he returned to live with his family in Butler. That summer he purchased a barber shop in Butler and began barbering, eventually adding a bathtub to his establishment. The show business bug bit him again, however, and during most of 1917 he toured in vaudeville before reopening the Marvin Barber Shop in Butler late that year. In the spring of 1918 he enlisted in the Navy and was sent to Oklahoma City; from there, he went to the San Diego Naval Station, where he spent the duration of World War I as a Navy barber. He continued that trade in San Francisco when the war ended, but he also dabbled in show business and worked in a beauty parlor.

By 1919 the young man was touring the country with a vaudeville act called Sargent, Marvin, and the Four Camerons. He toured with the group for two years, and when he returned to Butler to visit his family in the summer of 1921 the local newspaper, *The Butler Herald,* on June 30, 1921, noted that he was "connected with a renowned vaudeville troupe" and that he "plays some high-class music." The Sargent in the group was Charles Sargent.

During his tours, Marvin met Edna May, a stand-by singer from New York, and on March 7, 1923, they were married in that city and then took a honeymoon trip to California. Besides singing, Marvin played a variety of instruments, including guitar, ukulele, steel and Hawaiian guitar, fiddle, harmonica, mouth harp, and the musical saw, which he dubbed "the Arkansas fiddle." He and Edna used their savings to put together a touring band that included a tent, car, and bus. They toured in the West, playing engagements at theaters, dances, and private parties before losing the bus to torrential rain in Colorado. Edna then went back to her family in New York City to await the birth of their child, who was stillborn. Johnny, who had sold their car to pay for her fare east, worked his way to New York by performing, often as a street singer.

During the early 1920s Johnny Marvin, as he now called himself professionally, worked again with the baritone Charles Sargent. The two re-teamed as an act in 1924 and played various vaudeville engagements, with lukewarm reception, but the two did begin making records. Billed under the vaudeville act name of Sargent & Marvin, the duo waxed a dozen tunes for the Okeh and Pathé Actuelle labels. Johnny also sang solo on "Mrs. Murphy's Chowder" for Okeh, and in June, 1924, he had his initial session on his own, accompanying himself on the ukulele, singing, "You Know Me, Alabam' " for the Radiex label.

With the team of Sargent & Marvin going nowhere in vaudeville, Johnny decided to go solo and recorded two records for the Hollywood label, including "Just a Little Drink," which proved to be a good seller on the West Coast. When he appeared at Proctor's 125th Street Theatre in New York City in the fall of 1925, *Billboard* (October 17, 1925) compared him to Cliff "Ukulele Ike" Edwards and noted, "Although Marvin put his songs over well enough, his strong forte is playing the uke, which he picks in a mean manner. Among his other accomplishments is yodeling, though this, like the singing, is not of an unusual sort." The comparison to Cliff Edwards is a fitting one, in that Johnny Marvin was able to springboard to stardom due to the fact that he was able to successfully emulate Ukulele Ike.

By the mid-1920s Cliff Edwards had sold millions of records on the Pathé Actuelle and Perfect labels. Not only could Johnny Marvin sing as well as Edwards, he could also equal him on the ukulele. Furthermore, Marvin was able to master the difficult effect Edwards had created called "eefin'." This involved the ability to create the sound of a kazoo by using the mouth and vocal chords without actually playing the small instrument. As a result, Marvin quickly became popular with record producers, particularly those with small labels, who wanted to make records that would appeal to fans of Edwards' style of singing.

Now calling himself "The Ukulele Ace," Johnny Marvin signed to record with Columbia Records, and the disks he did for that label and its subsidiary, Okeh, were issued under his own name. The contract, however, was not exclusive, and Marvin found his services sought by the dimestore labels. From October to the end of 1925 he recorded two dozen songs for various labels, including Grey Gull, Edison, and Gennett. In order to avoid conflicts with his Columbia-Okeh contract, Marvin used a number of pseudonyms. Among them were Jimmy May and His Uke on Gennett and Bell and Honey Duke and His Uke on Grey Gull. It should also be noted that his Grey Gull disks were also issued on other dimestore labels, including Globe, Radiex, and Dandy.

In 1926 Johnny Marvin hit his stride as a recording artist, waxing some one hundred songs that year, about ninety of which were released. He also increased his use of recording pseudonyms. His Dandy release of "Toodle-Do" billed him as George Thorne, while on Madison's "Down Ole Virginia Way" he was called Billy Hancock, and the flip side, "Hard-Boiled Mama," listed him as Elton

Spence and His Ukulele. On Gennett records he was billed as Duke and His Uke, but on that label's subsidiary Champion he was dubbed Jack Lane and His Uke. In addition, on Adelphi's "I Can't Get over a Girl Like You Loving a Boy Like Me," he was listed as Ken Wallace. As Honey Duke and His Uke, Marvin became very popular on the low-priced Harmony label, even doing a disk of ukulele solos with vocal effects, "Twelfth Street Rag"/"Memphis Blues." Harmony was a subsidiary of Columbia, and songs he would record at various sessions were issued on both labels; the Columbia disks sold for one dollar, while the Harmony 78s were three for one dollar.

Between 1925 and 1927 Johnny Marvin did eight recording sessions for the Edison label, which issued its disks under his own name. As a freelance artist for Edison he was paid $100 for the first session and $125 for each of the remaining seven sessions. He often recorded the same song for different labels. For example, in April 1926 he waxed "So Is Your Old Lady" for the Harmony, Edison, and Okeh labels, although the Edison disk was not issued. Marvin's records were becoming good sellers, and in the summer of 1926 he had his first hit disk with "Breezin' Along with the Breeze" on Columbia (699-D), a song he also recorded for Edison (51793).

Contemporary reviews show that Johnny Marvin's disks possessed widespread appeal, as revealed by three *Variety* reviews. On April 7, 1926, that trade paper reviewed his record "So Does Your Old Mandarin"/"Sleepy Time" (Okeh 40575), saying, he "is a pop song recorder of the popular order. He zips his stuff over smartly, the uke stuff combining excellently with his idea of vocal rendition." On April 21, 1926, that paper's Abel Green reported, "Johnny Marvin proves he's a 'ukulele ace,' as is his picture house billing, with 'I Ain't in Love No More' and 'Hooray for the Irish!' It's Edison No. 51707." On September 1, 1926, the reviewer said, "Johnny Marvin is a uke specialist who should go in for the picture houses. He suggests exceptional possibilities in that field, judging by his instrumental and vocal delivery of 'Hello Aloha' and 'Tonight's My Night.' Marvin possess a resonant lyric voice for uke warbling and clicks on all six."

In addition to recording as a solo vocalist, Marvin also began singing the vocal refrain with various orchestras on disks, such as the Metropolitan Dance Orchestra and the Eight Devils on Grey Gull and Mike Marvel's Orchestra on Okeh. Johnny took a major step on the road to stardom when he signed to appear in the Broadway musical *Honeymoon Lane,* presented by A. L. Erlanger. Eddie Dowling headlined the production and also wrote the book, lyrics, and music with James Hanley. Marvin appeared in the show, playing the role of Honey Duke, his record pseudonym. Basically, he portrayed himself, appearing in a cabaret sequence performing three songs, "Half a Moon," "The Little White House," and "Jersey Walk." The production also launched the career of Kate Smith, who at the age of nineteen sang and danced in the show and garnered the lion's share of rave reviews.

Honeymoon Lane began rehearsals in New York City early in August 1926, and on August 23, 1926, Johnny Marvin recorded two of the show's tunes, "Half a Moon" and "Jersey Walk," for Columbia Records. The musical debuted in Atlantic City, New Jersey, August 29, 1926, at Nixon's Apollo Theatre and proved to be a big success. George R. Weintraub wrote in one of the local newspapers, "There is also 'Duke Uke' (Johnny Marvin) yelping with his ukulele and being held by a captivated house who refused to leave him go until he gave an encore." After a week's run the musical comedy moved to Philadelphia's Garrick Theatre, where it played for two weeks to rave reviews. During this pre-Broadway tryout, Johnny Marvin was billed as John Marvin in the play's cast list, but when *Honeymoon Lane* debuted on Broadway at the Knickerbocker Theatre on September 20, 1926, he was listed as Johnny Marvin. Again the production garnered rave reviews, as noted by Gordon M. Leland's comments in *Billboard* (October 2, 1926): "Clean and merry, *Honeymoon Lane* is a tonic for both children and adults." Regarding Marvin, he said, "Johnny Marvin proves himself another Cliff Edwards with his trusty ukulele and his untrusty vocal chords." The cast of the show was caricatured in "Le Messurier Sees 'Honeymoon Lane'" in the *New York Evening Journal* (October 10, 1926) and Johnny Marvin, pictured as resembling Cliff Edwards, is listed as "Another of These 'Uke' Kings."

The success of *Honeymoon Lane* quickly increased the demand for Johnny Marvin's professional services. He waxed songs from the show for the Edison, Okeh, Gennett, and Victor labels. For the latter he was paid $75 to do the vocal chorus and play the ukulele with Nat Shilkret and the Victor Orchestra on "Half a Moon" (Victor 20231). Shilkret was impressed with Marvin's singing and playing and requested him for further record work for Victor. On their second session together Johnny sang and played the uke on "All Alone Monday" (Victor 20259). This was followed by his first double-sided solo effort for the label, "I'd Love to Call You My Sweetheart"/ "Hum Your Troubles Away" (Victor 20288). In England, Marvin's records were issued on the HMV (His Master's Voice) label, and he soon gained a following in that country. Johnny also waxed "Half a Moon" with the Knickerbockers, a dance band led by Ben Selvin, on the Columbia label; with Nat Shilkret and the Victor Light Opera Company he was the soloist on "Jersey Walk," which was part of the disk "Honeymoon Lane—Vocal Gems" (Victor 35811).

Regarding all his "Honeymoon Lane" records, *Variety* (November 3, 1926) noted,

> Johnny Marvin, the uke strummer in "Honeymoon Lane," was kept busy recently "canning" his show's tunes for the various companies. For some he officiated as vocal soloist, but on Columbia No. 750 and Edison's No. 51841 Marvin is the soloist. "Half a Moon" and "Jersey Walk" are the selections from the musical comedy, recorded for both companies in identical manner, to self-uke accompaniment. Columbia goes it one better by featuring Marvin as being of the "Honeymoon Lane" Co.

In addition to rigorous recording work, Johnny Marvin also began appearing on radio as a regular weekly feature on Thursday afternoons on station WMCA. For that station he also appeared with the *Honeymoon Lane* cast for a midnight show on November 10, 1926, with Ernie Golden's Orchestra. In December 1926, Johnny Marvin signed with Fox Phonofilm to make a short subject, thus making him the first crooner to appear in a sound movie. He filmed *Strumming the Blues Away* for Fox Movietone early in 1927. This was the same song he had waxed for Victor as "Hum Your Troubles Away"; thus Marvin had the first sound film tie-in to a popular song.

At this time record companies were also playing up Marvin in their advertising. "Edison Recent Record Releases" brochure, showing disks issued between August and October 1926, carried a picture of Marvin with the listing for "Jersey Walk"/"Half a Moon" (Edison 51841) and noted, "Johnny Marvin and his 'Uke' delight the young folks and the old ones don't leave the room, either." He was billed as "The Ukulele Ace." An ad for Okeh Records in *The Talking Machine World* (November 15, 1926) prominently pictured Marvin with such best-sellers as Vernon Dalhart, Alma Rotter, and the Okeh-Kut-Ups.

Up to this point Johnny's career success was mainly based on his work in the recording field, as noted by *Variety* in its December 8, 1926, issue. The trade paper stated,

> The records and radio have done wonders for some pop song purvey-ors, particularly the uke specialists as witness Cliff Edwards and oth-ers, and particularly Johnny Marvin who a couple of seasons ago got nowhere when of Sargent and Marvin. Stepping out alone, Marvin is recording for Victor, Columbia, Okeh and Edison under his own name; as Honey Duke and His Uke for Harmony, Grey Gull, Gennett, Emerson and Bell; as Ukulele Luke for Cameo. Whether personality or whatever it is, Marvin has taken advantage of his opportunity to the fullest. . . . Marvin's activity of 25 to 30 recordings a month, practically one a day, is indicative of the personality uke and banjo songsters of the day who have made excellent progress on the strength of a current vogue.

Of the dimestore labels Marvin recorded for, Harmony was the best known since it was a subsidiary of Columbia and sold for three for one dollar, one-third the cost of the parent label. Both Bell and Grey Gull mainly drew their masters from Emerson, thus many of Marvin's records under pseudonyms appeared on these labels. Often the same song would be issued on several of them, but some-times with different takes. To complicate matters, Grey Gull also is-sued its records on cheap brands it produced, like Globe, Madison, Radiex, and Supreme. Another low-priced label, Dandy, used his Emerson masters as well. For Gennett Records, which had reduced its price to fifty cents by 1925, he mainly recorded as Duke and His Uke.

Record reviewers were also taking notice of Johnny Marvin, as noted by the December 27, 1926, issue of *Variety*: "Johnny Marvin has been making uke vocal numbers for the lesser companies. . . . Marvin strums his uke engagingly as regards pop ditties, 'I'd Love to Call You My Sweetheart' and 'Hum Your Troubles Away' are good examples of his style." The same source noted in its January 5, 1927, issue, "Marvin is again present with 'I'm on My Way Home' and 'Little White House,' his uke-singing impressing as ever." Ap-parently, the reviewer did not know that Johnny Marvin and Honey Duke were one, because in the same article he noted of the release

"Baby Face"/"Just a Little Longer" (Harmony 284-H), "Duke is a snappy strummer and vocalizer, and the melody ditties are made to order for his style of 'canned' entertainment."

Johnny Marvin spent the first half of 1927 in *Honeymoon Lane,* singing on radio and making records. He had around seventy disk releases that year, roughly half for Columbia, Okeh, Edison, Gennett, and the dime-store labels and the rest on Victor. Although he sold well on all labels, it was with Victor that he began drawing a major disk following. By this time Victor was controlled by J. W. Seligman & Co., New York bankers, who weeded their roster of veterans like Billy Murray and Henry Burr, reducing them mainly to occasional vocal refrains, in favor of new talent like Gene Austin and Marvin. For example, Billy Murray had a long and successful partnership with Aileen Stanley on Victor, but in 1927 it was Johnny who was paired with the popular songstress on a trio of releases: "Side by Side"/"Red Lips, Kiss My Blues Away" (Victor 20714); "Under the Moon" (Victor 20787); and "I Walked Back from the Buggy Ride" (Victor 20822). Regarding the last disk, Jim Walsh later wrote in *Hobbies* magazine (December 1963), "Aileen and Johnny give an excellent impersonation of a wise-cracking rustic couple, with the girl a bit suspicious of the boy's intentions."

Marvin and Aileen Stanley did not record again together until January 1929, when they dueted on "Won't You Tell Me, Hon (When We're Gonna Be One?)" and "Ev'rybody Loves You." Only the latter was issued (on Victor 21848), in March 1929, but apparently, it did not do well because it was deleted from the company catalog before the end of the year.

Record-wise, 1927 was Johnny Marvin's most prolific year. He made the first of several duets with Ed Smalle on "Don't Sing Aloha" (Columbia 891-D), and he also supplied vocal refrains on records for a number of groups like Jack Stillman's Orchestra, Bert Kaplan's Collegians, Fred Rich and His Hotel Astor Orchestra, the Knickerbockers, Paul Ash and His Orchestra, the Columbians, Jacques Renard and His Orchestra, Roger Wolfe Kahn and His Orchestra, Charlie Fry and His Million Dollar Orchestra, Arden-Ochman Orchestra, Edwin J. McEnelly's Orchestra, the Troubadours, and Jan Garber and His Orchestra.

With Nat Shilkret and the Victor Orchestra, however, Marvin got the most notice, as the company not only featured him on vocals but also released a number of solo disks with Marvin and his ukulele, including "Magnolia"/"Ain't That a Grand and Glorious Feeling?" (Victor 20731), "It's a Million to One You're in Love"/"I'm Afraid You Sing That Song to Somebody Else" (Victor 20832), and "Give Me a Night in June"/"After I've Called You My Sweetheart" (Victor 20984). He also had good selling duets with Ed Smalle on "Blue Skies" (Victor 20457) and "Just Another Day Wasted Away (Victor 20758). The latter was Victor's best-selling record for four months and was the biggest individual seller Johnny Marvin had for the label.

After appearing in *Honeymoon Lane* for one year, Marvin left the show in August 1927, to embark on a vaudeville tour of the Eastern states on the Keith-Albee circuit. Under the direction of Paul Dempsey in association with Frank Evans, Marvin made his big-time vaudeville debut August 29, 1927, in Pittsburgh, followed by engagements in Cleveland, Buffalo, and New York.

By this time Marvin had signed as an exclusive Victor Records performer, and *The Talking Machine World* (September 1927) noted, "The appearance of Mr. Marvin in a local theatre afforded Victor dealers a wonderful opportunity for effecting tie-ups, for in addition to having won a lasting popularity with radio audiences and record fans, he will confine his songs in his act to those of which he has made records, so whatever tie-up is used will be doubly effective." It was also announced in the article that Johnny "is under contract to make several releases for Vitaphone presentations." *Billboard* (September 3, 1927) said that Marvin "will begin a series of tie-ups concerned with his disc-recording activities."

The year 1928 found Johnny Marvin continuing the success that first began for him in 1925. His main avenues of activity continued to be records and vaudeville. In the latter, his act was reviewed by *Billboard* (January 14, 1928) when he appeared at Keith's Theatre in Cincinnati, Ohio. The reviewer noted, "Johnny Marvin, late of *Honeymoon Lane,* ingratiated himself into the warm affections of the audience through skillful use of his pleasing voice and likable personality. His applause continued long after his final bow."

By 1928 Johnny was solely recording for Victor Records and had some twenty releases that year, a mixture of solo disks and vocal refrains with established orchestras. In the latter vein he sang on "'S Wonderful"/"Funny Face" (Victor 21114) with Victor Arden and Phil Ohman and Their Orchestra. *Variety* (January 25, 1928) said,

"Johnny Marvin also contributes vocally for a tip-top dance disk." While most of his Victor work continued to be with Nat Shilkret, Marvin also did the vocals on "What D'Ya Say?" (Victor 21632) with Johnny Hamp and His Kentucky Serenaders, "Crazy Rhythm"/ "Heartbroken" (Victor 21650), and "Water Melon Smilin' on the Vine" (Victor 21653), both disks with Roger Wolfe Kahn and His Orchestra, and "She Didn't Say Yes, She Didn't Say No" (Victor 21667) with the All-Star Orchestra.

Victor often issued an artist on only one side of a record, with backing by another performer or orchestra. By now Marvin's popularity often was the main selling factor in such pairings, as noted by his solo appearances on "From Midnight til Dawn" (Victor 21230), "Without You, Sweetheart" (Victor 21259), "Get Out and Get under the Moon" (Victor 21432), "Oh! You Have No Idea" (Victor 21509), and "I'd Rather Be Blue" (Victor 21814). The year also provided him with a number of solo hits like "Think of Me, Thinking of You"/ "Golden Gate" (Victor 21427), "My Pet"/"I Still Love You" (Victor 21435), "Old Man Sunshine"/"If You Don't Love Me" (Victor 21609), "Happy Days and Lonely Nights"/"There's a Rainbow 'round My Shoulder" (Victor 21780), and "Sweethearts on Parade"/ "Where the Shy Little Violets Grow" (Victor 21820). He had a hit dueting with Ed Smalle on "Rain"/"After My Laughter Came Tears" (Victor 21172). Also selling well was another duet with Ed Smalle, "Mary Ann" backed by Marvin's self-penned "Old Fashioned Locket" on Victor 21299.

A major event in Johnny Marvin's career took place in February 1928, when he signed for a ten-week engagement at the Kit Kat Club in London, where Nick Lucas and Gene Austin previously had had great success. Around the same time he signed an agreement with the Harmony Company of Chicago, which would market a ukulele and ukulele banjo bearing Marvin's name. The uke was to be sold as the Johnny Marvin Ukulele.

On May 5, 1928, Johnny Marvin sailed for England with Frank Burke, former press agent for the Hennepin-Orpheum circuit, who became his personal manager. Immediately prior to setting sail on the *Leviathan*, Johnny recorded eight numbers for Victor in order to keep him on current releases. As a publicity stunt the Harmony Company made a special gold-engraved ukulele to be presented to the Prince of Wales, with his coat-of-arms and seal embossed on it. Marvin also took along 10,000 miniature ukuleles made by Harmony for throwaways during his London stay.

Johnny Marvin opened his London engagement at the Kit Kat Club on May 14, 1928, beginning a planned ten-week stand, including a music hall tour. In its May 19, 1928, issue the British correspondent for *Billboard* stated that Johnny was "already popular in England through the gramophone records." In addition to the Kit Kat Club, he also appeared at the London Coliseum and Astoria Cinema. *Billboard* (June 9, 1928) noted later in the tour, "Johnny Marvin is the big pull at the Cafe de Paris this week." The same trade paper stated on June 16, 1928, that Marvin "is credited with having brought the Prince of Wales twice in one evening to the Kit Kat Club, London, to hear his warbling and uke playing."

The London success accorded Johnny Marvin came to a sudden halt in mid-June 1928, when he began to develop throat problems, the same ailment that caused Nick Lucas to cut short his London run at the end of 1926. Johnny was forced to cancel the remainder of his British bookings and enter a London nursing home, where he underwent a tonsillectomy. Following his recovery from the surgery, he set sail to return to the United States on July 13, 1928. Although it was announced that he would return to London either in the fall or early in 1929, he never again appeared in the British Isles.

Upon returning to the United States, Johnny Marvin, now under the management of C. C. Cairns of the Victor Company, signed to appear in several short films for Metro-Goldwyn-Mayer. He also signed a vaudeville contract with Loew's Theatres for sixteen weeks at $1,000 per week. When he opened at Loew's State Theatre in New York in August 1928, *Variety* (August 15, 1928) opined, "Johnny Marvin, recording artist, lived up to billing in next to shut with his crooning repertoire which went over in pleasing style." In the same issue another reviewer noted,

> Good singing voice and personality should carry the boy far. For vaudeville Marvin has lined up a routine of four numbers, carrying his own accompaniment with either uke, musical saw or guitar. He attempts some comedy talk that matters little, but more than offsets this when crooning a tune. All numbers are enthusiastically received, with Marvin doing choruses of former recorded numbers for encore, with audience incited for requests.

During the same engagement, *Billboard* (August 18, 1928) reported,

Johnny Marvin, with his winning, wailing voice and ukulele. His sighing guitar and musical saw proved that he has lost none of his audience appeal by his recent trip abroad. His own song, "Think of Me, Thinking of You," was one of his best. The audience joined in his singing and his reception was cordial.

When Marvin appeared at Loew's State Theatre in New Orleans in October, 1928, his friend and fellow label mate Gene Austin joined him on stage. In the spring of 1927 Marvin had played guitar on Austin's Victor recording of "Cindy."

By the summer of 1928 it was reported that over ten million homes throughout the country owned Johnny Marvin records. When Victor 21509 was issued at that time, *Variety* (July 25, 1928) commented, "Two contrasting vocalists on a Victor record doing a novelty and a ballad. (Johnny) Marvin, recently returned from abroad, waxes rollicking with 'Oh! You Have No Idea.' It is coupled with (Harold) Yates's 'I'm Tired of Making Believe,' a sob number." Victor's August 1928 list of ten best-selling disks included Marvin's "Sweetheart o' Mine"/"Angel" (Victor 21376) and "Think of Me, Thinking of You"/"Golden Gate" (Victor 21427). Also on the list were two records by Paul Whiteman and one each by Gene Austin, George Olsen, Jimmie Rodgers, Frank Crumit, and Waring's Pennsylvanians.

On September 12, 1928, *Variety* reviewed Marvin's newest disk, "This comedian whips across a couple of Tin Pan Alley home-runs in 'Old Man Sunshine (Little Boy Bluebird)', coupled with a powerful fox-trot ballad, 'If You Don't Love Me.' Some trick jazzique accompaniment is in evidence for the musical background on Victor No. 21609." On October 17, 1928, the same trade paper reviewed another Marvin disk, "Here's a good couplet by one of Victor's most popular sellers. It's a smooth fox-trot ballad mating with a torrid ditty. The songs are titled 'Brokenhearted and Lonely' and 'Crazy Rhythm,' the latter hot survival of the flop show, *Here's How*." *Billboard* (December 22, 1928) reviewed Victor 21780, "Another selection from the score of *The Singing Fool* which promises to be almost as popular as 'Sonny Boy' is 'There's a Rainbow 'round My Shoulder.' Johnny Marvin sings it for the new Victor list in his usual genial fashion. With it he offers 'Happy Days and Lonely Nights.' "

Besides his continued success in vaudeville and records, important events took place in Johnny Marvin's life that would greatly impact his career. On a visit home to Butler, Oklahoma, he brought his younger brother Frank back with him to New York. Musically inclined like his sibling, Frank played guitar and steel guitar, sang, and yodeled. In New York City, Johnny got him a job as a delivery boy for Shapiro-Bernstein Music Company. Due to his musical ability, he began recording for dimestore labels, and because he was able to yodel he became much in demand as a recording artist. In 1928 Johnny also made him a part of his vaudeville appearances, and the two developed a new act that included singer Gloria Price. The trio would continue to appear on stage together until 1933.

Also in 1928, Johnny and Frankie Marvin befriended a young Oklahoma entertainer named Gene Autry who had come to New York in an effort to record. Influenced by the guitar playing of Nick Lucas and the singing of Jimmie Rodgers, whom he sounded like, Autry was finally placed at the American Record Corporation (ARC), which sold its product at discount through chain stores and mail-order catalogs. When Autry cut his first record in October 1929 for ARC, it was "My Dreaming of You," a song written by Johnny Marvin, and Johnny and Frankie played back-up guitars on the session. The brothers composed two other songs that Autry waxed for ARC late in 1929, "Stay Away from My Chicken House" and "Dust Pan Blues." Frankie Marvin also played steel guitar on several of Autry's record sessions, and Gene played guitar on Frankie Marvin's ARC recording of "I'm a Truthful Fellow."

Toward the end of 1928, two of the short films in which Marvin appeared were released, one from MGM and the other from Warner Bros., both entitled *Johnny Marvin*. Regarding the MGM short, *Variety* (November 7, 1928) said, "He (Marvin) shows a pleasant singing voice and a personality that should bring him return engagements on the vocal screen." The reviewer added, "Marvin uses two pop numbers crooning his tunes in snappy style, and supplying his own accompaniment with a uke. He attempts no comedy talk and tops his final ballad vocalizing off with an extra chorus played on a musical saw." Regarding the film's box office possibilities, the trade paper stated, "Short will prove acceptable on any talking program, spotted early, and in those localities where Marvin is a favorite on the records, will register solidly." *Billboard* (November 17, 1928) also reviewed the seven-minute MGM short, reporting that it was "One of the first of the M-G-M canned acts to be released," adding,

Marvin's act is one of the best of the singing type to come out of a can. The popular songster and Victor recording artiste sings two numbers current on the music counters, playing a uke accompaniment for the first and a guitar for the second. Both the singing and the music come from the amplifiers with clarity and impressiveness. Marvin's voice seems particularly suited to Movietone and his personality well adapted to the camera. Book this one.

Regarding Vitaphone Number 492, also called simply *Johnny Marvin, Variety* (November 21, 1928) noted that it may have been made prior to the M-G-M short because of the "Identification number and songs used. . . ." In this outing Johnny appeared on a draped set and was backed by a pianist, violinist, and guitarist as he performed four songs. Marvin also played guitar, ukulele, and musical saw in the short. The trade paper summed up the effort by saying, "Short while fair enough entertainment for an opening spot on a talking bill does not measure up to Marvin's M-G-M effort in which he appeared alone." In the Vitaphone short Johnny Marvin sang "Strumming My Blues Away," "A Little Music in the Moonlight," "Moonlight and Roses," and "'Deed I Do."

As 1929 opened, Johnny Marvin was at the pinnacle of his success. He ranked with Gene Austin, Whispering Jack Smith, and Frank Crumit as one of Victor Records' best-selling singers. He was a popular vaudeville attraction and the Johnny Marvin Ukulele was a good seller. He was also very popular in England, where his records were released by HMV (His Master's Voice), Victor's British label. For most of the year Marvin would ride the crest of this popularity, and it would be his most successful one to date.

By the end of 1929, however, several factors came into play that would eventually bring about a change in his career status. In 1929 vaudeville was beginning to feel the effects of radio and sound films, and with the coming of the Depression at year's end the medium began to fade in popularity. The recording industry was very successful in 1929 but began to go into a major slump with the coming of the 1930s.

Johnny Marvin kicked off 1929 by making a guest appearance on *The La Palina Club Smoker*, on the Columbia network. He made a second appearance on the program on March 13, 1929. The singer also starred in two more M-G-M Movietone shorts, both called *Johnny Marvin*. Released early in 1929, the first short had Marvin singing,

"You Lied, I Cried" and "Thinking of You." *Billboard* (February 2, 1929) said, "The act is on par with Marvin's first, with the singing and music reproduced clearly. It is adequate for better class houses." The short ran six minutes and the second *Johnny Marvin* M-G-M Movietone (and the third in the series), issued in the summer of 1929, was a minute longer. Here he performed "Heartbroken and Lonely" and "Old Man Sunshine." *Variety* (July 17, 1929) noted that "the recording artist whams out two pop vocals with neatness to his own accompaniment on the uke and steel guitar. . . . as done by Marvin without chatter or stalling, plus the singer's likable personality, it doesn't matter what he sings."

Johnny also appeared in two more Metro-Goldwyn-Mayer shorts in 1929. In *A Movietone Divertissment*, he was billed with Tom Waring of Waring's Pennsylvanians, Yvette Rogel, and the Happiness Boys (Billy Jones & Ernie Hare), and he sang "I Love You, I Still Love You," also playing the ukulele and musical saw. At the end of the year he was in the two-reel short *Metro Movietone Revue* #12, in which he sang "If You Don't Love Me" and "Sunshine." Also in the twenty-minute outing were the Locust Sisters, Miss Rose Marie Sinnott, George Dewey Washington, and Harry Rose. *Variety* (December 11, 1929) noted, "Nicely balanced layout makes this one okay for neighborhood grinds. All the songs used are a year or more old, thus automatically barring this revue from the better class houses."

In the summer of 1929, *Variety* (July 31, 1929) ran a two-page advertisement picturing Johnny Marvin as one of Warner Bros.-Vitaphone's short subject stars, although he only made one Vitaphone short and it had been released theatrically in 1928. At the time there was also an effort to pitch Johnny for feature films, but unlike Nick Lucas and Rudy Vallee he did not appear in features.

In 1929 Johnny Marvin had another twenty disk releases on Victor Records, and while he did a duet with Aileen Stanley on "Ev'rybody Loves You" (Victor 21848), his rendition of "You Wanted Someone to Play With," revived by Frankie Laine in 1967, was the seller side of Victor 21839 (backed by Miss Stanley doing "I'll Get By"). Marvin also dueted with Ed Smalle on "The Sun Is at My Window" (Victor 21866) and "Why Did You Leave Me?" (Victor 21990). On Victor 21959 Marvin and Smalle dueted on "I Get the Blues When It Rains," which *Variety* (May 15, 1929) called "a pip double," and Johnny went solo on "Down among the Sugar Cane." He waxed the latter song with Bennie Kruger and His Orchestra on Victor

21903, backed by "That's the Good Old Sunny South." Johnny and Ed Smalle also had a big hit as a duet on "A Precious Little Thing Called Love"/"Caressing You" (Victor 21892).

While Marvin did the vocal refrains with Nat Shilkret on "You Wouldn't Fool Me, Would You?" (Victor 21859) and "Georgia Pines" (Victor 22915), most of his 1929 Victor disks were solo two-sided releases, befitting his status as one of the biggest record sellers of the day. The buying public and the critics liked Johnny Marvin records. *Variety* (September 4, 1929) declared, "Johnny Marvin vocalizes 'Every Day Away from You' and 'Little by Little' (inevitable theme song) in zippy style" and noted on March 6, 1929, that "Johnny Marvin has turned out a classic couplet on No. 21851 with 'All by Myself in the Moonlight' and 'Sweetheart of All My Dreams.' "

On July 24, 1929, the same reviewer stated, "Johnny Marvin clicks with Al Jolson's hits from the forthcoming *Say It with Songs* (Warners), doing 'I'm in Seventh Heaven' and 'Used to You.' " In the October 16, 1929, issue of the same source, the reviewer said, " 'True Blue Lou,' from Paramount's *Dance of Life,* is being given lots of prominence by all the mechanicals. Here it's mated with 'Same Old Moon,' balladized by the indefatigable Johnny Marvin."

Victor Records gave Marvin, one of its biggest sellers, a great deal of hype in its monthly pamphlets. In the September 1929 *Victor Monthly Pamphlet*, No. 22039, "Baby! Oh Where Can You Be?"/"I'd Fall in Love with Me (If I Were You)" was given a write-up that included the hardships of the singer's early years. The pamphlet noted,

> Sledding was pretty rough for the first few years of his artistic career, but for Johnny success was bound to come. He had something buoyant and genuine to offer an eager public. Some thirty years or more have passed and Marvin has won his way into thousands of hearts by singing just such songs as these on his latest record. Both are light-hearted and sentimental. They have lively rhythm that inspires dancing, and their accompaniments are particularly fascinating. Steel guitar, banjo, violin, sax, and muted trumpet—each has its moment of attractive prominence. But, of course, Johnny's clear, sweet voice is the most important of this record's many charming features. You'll agree to that.

The same pamphlet hyped Victor's various couplings of the songs from the Warner Bros. feature *Say It with Songs* by organist Jesse Crawford, Nat Shilkret and the Victor Orchestra, George Olsen and

His Orchestra, Gene Austin, and Johnny Marvin. Regarding John-ny's renditions of "I'm in Seventh Heaven"/"Used to You" (Victor 21955), it read, "Johnny Marvin is splendid in his two songs—one lively, one dreamy and sentimental."

In the October pamphlet Marvin's disk of "Every Day Away from You"/"Little by Little" (Victor 22076) was featured. The blurb noted that Marvin played steel guitar on the disk and added, "Here is Johnny Marvin's appealing voice reinforced by the most attractive accompaniments you've ever heard. . . . a record you're certain to enjoy! The instrumental effects are numerous and melodious."

So popular was Johnny Marvin in 1929 that he was even able to have best-selling records with songs associated with other singers. Cliff Edwards (Ukulele Ike) had a major hit record on Columbia with the songs "Singin' in the Rain" and "Orange Blossom Time," which he sang in the Metro-Goldwyn-Mayer feature *Hollywood Revue of 1929*. Johnny also waxed the songs on Victor 22057, accom-panied by the Frohme Sisters on "Singin' in the Rain," and had a best-seller. The same thing also happened with "Tiptoe thru the Tu-lips" and "Painting the Clouds with Sunshine," which Nick Lucas introduced in *The Gold Diggers of Broadway*. Lucas's Brunswick re-cording of the two songs was the biggest record seller of 1929, but Marvin also managed to have a hit with the two numbers on Victor 22113. *Variety* (October 2, 1929) said that Johnny's record of the two numbers "interpreted without ornamentation." The same trade paper in its December 11, 1929, issue showed that Marvin's record was Victor's number-one seller in New York and number five in Chi-cago, behind Jean Goldkette and His Orchestra's rendition of the two tunes, which was at number two.

Despite the stock market crash in October 1929, things still looked good for Johnny Marvin's career at the start of 1930. During the week of February 1, 1930, he made the first of two appearances that year at the RKO Palace Theatre in New York. Appearing with him was his brother Frankie. *Variety* (February 5, 1930) noted that Johnny did "a song and instrumental routine in a likable way and regis-tered. Halfway down Marvin brought on a chap in misfit garb whom he introduced as his brother, with both going into a harmony double for a strong finish."

Billboard (February 8, 1930) wrote,

> Johnny Marvin, a Nick Lucas and Cliff Edwards rolled into one, is back
> after an appreciable absence in his guitarized singing. Johnny has an

unsensational but positive style; a great personality, too. His brother, Frank Marvin, is pulled on for yodeling, rube comedy that strikingly resembles the type cornered by Cicero Weaver, and duo melody. Johnny almost wore out his welcome with so-called requests, but their finish warble set things right.

Marvin opened the act singing, "Happy Days Are Here Again" and playing the guitar. He then sang "Have a Little Faith in Me" and did a tune on the musical saw, followed by comedy patter and the song "I'm a Dreamer, Aren't We All?." Following some comedy with Frankie Marvin, the latter sang "I'm Blue When It Rains," with Johnny accompanying him on the guitar. After two request numbers sung by Johnny, the duo closed the act with "The Yodel Song My Mammy Sang to Me."

Billboard (February 22, 1930) stated,

> Johnny Marvin belongs to the species of entertainers who are not so forte on warbling, but lean on their strumming accompaniment to tone down the melodic effects. Maybe Marvin is a big guy in disc recording—and that might apply just as well to broadcasting—but as a vaudeville single he lacks plenty. Fortunately, in this appearance at the Palace, the personable but pep-deficient artiste does not attempt to go it alone. He has with him a lad who is introduced as his brother, Frank Marvin. In sickly green shoes, ill-fitting suit and typical backwoods haircut, Frank sells himself pretty well as a rustic natural. Too often, however, he appears to have perhaps unconsciously adopted some of Cicero Weaver's favorite tricks. . . . Frank has more appealing pipes than his better-known brother—and he knows his yodels. About 10 minutes sliced off, and with both working together throughout, this act will be up to par. Even for the Palace.

Prior to the Palace engagement, in January 1930, Johnny and Frankie Marvin recorded together on "Mother's Song of Love"/ "The Girl I Left Behind" (Victor 40233), with Frankie doing the singing and Johnny playing steel guitar. Frank was also gaining recognition on his own, as noted in the April 1930 issue of *Talking Machine World:* "Frankie specializes in folk ballads, sometimes sentimental, more often comedy. He plays a brilliant guitar and likewise yodels. He tends to drawl a bit, and his humor is droll, completely natural, and of the people. His recent record of 'Slue Foot Lou' has been a best seller over a wide territory."

Following their Palace engagement Johnny and Frankie Marvin went on a limited vaudeville tour on the Keith-Albee circuit, and in March Johnny took over as master of ceremonies at the Keith-Albee Theatre in White Plains, New York. The effects of the Depression on the record industry can be noted by the fact that Johnny Marvin had only a dozen disk releases on Victor Records in 1930, and one of those was merely a vocal refrain with Don Azdiazu and His Havana Club Orchestra on "Be Careful with Those Eyes" (Victor 22441). More surprising was the fact that his record "Underneath Those Weeping Willow Trees"/"I'm Looking for a Gal" (Victor 23531) was issued on the label's "race" records series and he was listed as Honey Duke and His Uke, the only time he used that billing for Victor. He also vocalized with the High Hatters on "Red Hot and Blue Rhythm" (Victor 22314).

Still, Johnny's record popularity continued in 1930, despite plunging sales figures for the industry in general. Among his popular platters were "Lazy Lou'siana Moon"/"The One I Love Just Can't Be Bothered with Me" (Victor 22348), "Ro-Ro-Rollin' Along"/ "Down the River of Golden Dreams" (Victor 22418), "Go Home and Tell Your Mother"/"Little White Lies" (Victor 22502), and "Overnight"/"Cheerful Little Earfull" (Victor 22566).

Reviews also continued to be good, as noted by several appearing in *Variety* in early 1930. In the January 8 issue, the trade paper wrote, "(Victor 22186) Johnny Marvin is well sustained by 'Happy Days Are Here Again' (appropriate after Black November) and 'Lucky Me, Lovable You.' " The November 5, 1930, issue noted, " 'I Still Get a Thrill' and 'Bye Bye Blues,' freshly reestablishes Johnny Marvin (Victor 22534) as one of the most melodious, charming and agreeable male harmony dispensers among the mecanicals." A December 10, 1930, review by Bob Landry stated, "(Victor 22555) Another explanation of the prominence enjoyed in the mechanical field by this artist. 'I'm Yours' and 'You Darling' constitute a peach of a pair, laden with melody."

By the end of 1930 the sale of record players had declined 90 percent and the number of Victor Records sold that year totaled 17.7 million, almost one-half of what had been sold the previous year. Still, Johnny Marvin was listed as one of the company's disk leaders of the year, along with Rudy Vallee, Maurice Chevalier, Gene Austin, Helen Morgan, Helen Kane, and Buddy Rogers. Also selling well were the orchestras of Leo Reisman, Wayne King, Nat Shilkret, Duke

Ellington, King Oliver, Waring's Pennsylvanians, and the High Hatters, the latter led by Leonard Joy, and organist Jesse Crawford.

By 1931 the entertainment industry had been badly shaken by the Depression. Vaudeville was fading and the record industry was in serious trouble. Only films and radio managed to continue successfully. Since Johnny Marvin had been unable to parlay a film contract, he began working in network radio, as well as continuing in the remnants of records and vaudeville.

Only around seven million records were sold by the Victor Company in 1931 and few of those appear to have been by Marvin. He only had four releases for the company, one of them being with his brother Frankie. *Variety* (May 13, 1931) commented, "Johnny and Frankie (Victor 22649). Meaning Johnny and Frankie Marvin who merge for 'Little Sweetheart of the Mountains.' Bigger subject than 'Little Sweetheart of the Prairie' which Johnny Marvin accomplishes unaided on the reverse. Prairie or mountain, it's oh-hum and forgettable." Marvin's final Victor release of the year was the two-sided disk "Dr. Cheer" (Victor 22741). On it, he appeared as the title character who responds in song to a series of gags. On side one he crooned "Runnin' Wild" and "The Lonesome Road," while on the flip side he did "Slow and Easy," "When Your Hair Has Turned to Silver," and "I Walked Back from the Buggy Ride."

Johnny Marvin first starred on NBC radio in 1931 with a fifteen-minute program, which also featured brother Frankie, from New York's WJZ. This program of songs was broadcast each Tuesday night at 10:45 P.M. from February 3 to March 24. He also did two Friday broadcasts on February 5 and 13 at 8:30 P.M.

Marvin next appeared on NBC radio in 1931 as "Dr. Cheer," a fifteen-minute weekday program sponsored by Columbia Cleaners. This was a home dry-cleaning product developed by the Columbia Phonograph Company and it was guaranteed "non-explosive." The program said that Dr. Cheer "doesn't prescribe pink pills for your daily ills but solves your worries and problems with music." The show noted that Dr. Cheer was none other than Johnny Marvin, "who is known in twenty million homes through his phonograph records." The program consisted of Marvin singing songs prescribed to aid personal problems sent in by listeners.

In October 1931, Marvin returned to recording but this time for the American Record Company (ARC) rather than Victor. Two disks were issued from the session, "A Faded Summer Love"/"Lucille," which was billed as being by Johnny Marvin and His Orchestra, and "Guilty"/"Now That You're Gone." The disks were released on various ARC dimestore labels like Perfect, Oriole, Conqueror, Melotone, and Apex. It was also reported at the end of 1931 that Johnny had secured a financial interest in the Consolidated Record Company and would record and represent the label that produced radio transcriptions. This report, however, was inaccurate, as Marvin had no connection with the label.

When Victor Records released the names of its 1931 top sellers, the list did not include Johnny Marvin. Victor's top sellers for the year were Rudy Vallee, Russ Columbo, Maurice Chevalier, Frank Crumit, Helen Morgan, and Gene Austin. In March 1932, Johnny Marvin was back recording, this time for the Columbia label, waxing two disks. "Seven Come Eleven"/"Yodelin' My Way to Heaven" (Columbia 15750-D) alternate takes were issued on Okeh 41559 under the billing of the Marvin Trio. *Variety* (April 5, 1932) reviewed the Okeh release: "Novelty trio mixes up its vocalization and instrumentation in the Mills Bros. manner, only 'dirtier.' 'Yodelin' My Way to Heaven' permits some extra Swiss [Alpine] fol-de-rol, while 'Seven Come Eleven,' by its title alone, suggests its manner of sing-play treatment."

The second Columbia disk, "Dr. Brokenshire and Dr. Marvin" (Columbia 2655-D), was in the same vein as his earlier Victor "Dr. Cheer" platter. A two-part record, it teamed Johnny with radio announcer Norman Brokenshire, who did the comedy while Johnny vocalized on "Bend Down, Sister," "Take Your Girlie to the Movies," "Take It Slow and Easy," and "The Old Grey Mare" on side one, followed by "They're Wearing 'Em Higher in Hawaii," "So Is Your Old Lady," "Etiquette Blues," and "Seven Come Eleven" on side two. *Variety* (June 21, 1932) called it a "novelty Columbia disk, which medleys a flock of old numbers. . . . Not especially brilliant, but oke parlor vaude and suggests that the record would make a satisfactory one-to-fill on an unimportant radio hour, either in person by 'Broke' and Marvin, or right off the disk."

On August 22, 1932, the singer headlined a new radio series on NBC, broadcast Monday through Saturday at noon for fifteen minutes from station WEAF in New York City. Simply called *Johnny Marvin, Tenor,* the series ran until May 17, 1935, but during certain periods it was off the air as Marvin pursued brief vaudeville tours.

It was during this period that Johnny Marvin purchased one of the Thousand Islands in the St. Lawrence River, paying $35,000 for the property. He built a summer home on the island, had two boats, and installed an outdoor speaker on which he played his records for passing river traffic. It was also at this time that he divorced his wife, Edna, and married stage partner Gloria Price. They had two children, John and Glorianna.

In 1932 Marvin put together a book of yodel songs that the Southern Music Company published as *The Frankie and Johnny Marvin Folio of Down Home Songs, with Guitar Chords.* He remained active that year as a recording artist. For Crown Records he did "Home on the Range"/"Ma and Pa (Send Their Sweetest Love)" (Crown 3310) with guitarist Johnny Amendt. An unissued Crown master he did at the time, "When You Kiss That Girl Goodbye," was finally issued on the Continental label in 1944, causing some sources to claim he was recording at that late date. He also had a final session with Victor Records on May 31, 1932, which produced three disks: "When You Hear Me Call"/"I'm Gonna Yodel My Way to Heaven" (Victor 23691), "The Man with the Big Black Mustache"/"Seven Come Eleven" (Victor 23708), and "Jack and Jill"/"Go Along Bum and Keep Bumming Along" (Victor 23728). Victor only sold 3.1 million records that year, and Marvin's sales on the three disks were minimal. More successful, however, was a self-penned two-part platter called "I'm the Man That's Been Forgotten" (Melotone M-12610) for ARC. Roy Smeck played steel guitar on the disk, which was similar to "My Forgotten Man" from Warner Bros.' *The Gold Diggers of 1933,* in that both dealt with World War I veterans being pushed aside by hard economic times. Johnny and his brother Frankie also teamed for "Beech Fork Special"/"Red Wing" (Melotone 12521), billed as Frankie and Johnny.

Due to his NBC radio work, Johnny Marvin was also cast in his final theatrical short subject, *Rambling 'round Radio Row #3,* a 1932 Warner Bros. release. Jerry Wald starred in this series as himself, meeting various denizens of the radio world, including Johnny, Jay C. Flippen, Guy Lombardo and His Royal Canadians (including brothers Carmen, Victor, and Liebert Lombardo), Baby Rose Marie, Aunt Jemima (Tess Gardella), and William Hall. *Variety* (October 25, 1932) judged it, "Just a so-so double-reeler." Early in 1933 Johnny Marvin had another session with ARC Records, waxing "Rock-a-Bye Moon"/"I'm Playing with Fire," which was issued on such labels as Melotone, Banner, Oriole, and Panchord, the latter a British company.

Following a successful engagement at the Roxy Theatre in New York, he and brother Frankie broke up their act, although Johnny continued to work with Ruth Cleary, a Janet Gaynor lookalike. During the years the brothers were together, 1928 to 1933, they played the Keith-Orpheum vaudeville circuit all over the country and Canada and twice broke box office records in Providence, Rhode Island. By now, Johnny was getting guarantees and a percentage on his theater dates.

Late in 1934 Johnny and Frankie reteamed to record "Lazy Texas Longhorns" on the Decca label, with Johnny doing a solo on the flip side, "I Want My Boots on When I Die" (Decca 5056). The disk was released in England on Panachord, as were two songs from a 1935 record session, "The Last Mile"/"Beneath a Bed of Daisies" (Panachord 25973). Two other songs, "Grandma's Rockin' Chair" and "By Big Swiss Cheese," were also done at that session but were rejected. This was to be Johnny Marvin's final commercial record session of the 1930s.

When Johnny Marvin's daytime NBC radio show ended in the spring of 1935, he moved to Oklahoma City, where he did a program on station WKY, sponsored by Kane's Coffee. He was billed as "The Lonesome Singer of the Air." The WKY radio show lasted until 1937 and, at that time, Johnny Marvin relocated with his family to Los Angeles, at 410 South San Vicente Boulevard.

By this time he was financially secure, and, except for occasional appearances, he pretty much gave up stage work. Instead, he began to work primarily behind the microphone and cameras as a radio producer and composer. Over the years Johnny Marvin had written several popular songs, most of which he recorded. He and Charles Sargent composed "Mrs. Murphy's Chowder," which Johnny sang solo on Columbia Records in 1924 at one of his first sessions. During his Victor years he composed "An Old Fashioned Locket," "Don't Leave Me Now," "Underneath Those Weeping Willow Trees," and what was probably his most popular work, "Think of Me, Thinking of You." Ernest Tubb revived the number on Decca Records in 1964. As noted, Johnny also composed "I'm the Man That's Been Forgotten," which he recorded for ARC in 1932.

After settling in Los Angeles, Johnny went into partnership with Gene Autry and the two formed Western Music Publishing Company. Frankie Marvin had been working for Gene Autry since 1934 in films, radio, and personal appearances. In the next eight years

Johnny Marvin composed some seventy published songs, many of which were used in Gene Autry's Republic Westerns. Some sources claim that Johnny can be spotted playing guitar with musical groups in some of the Autry movies. Although Autry's name is on many of the Marvin compositions, this was mainly for business purposes and the songs were mostly done by Johnny, although he occasionally worked with others like Fred Rose.

Among the songs Johnny Marvin wrote in the late 1930s and early 1940s were "Eyes to the Skies," "I Just Want You," "It Was Only a Hobo's Dream," "The Old Geezer," "A Gold Mine in Your Heart," "Poor Little Dogie," "Knights of the Open Road," "As Long as I Have My Horse," "I'm Beginning to Care," "Old November Moon," "Goodbye, Little Darlin', Goodbye," "Keep Rollin' Lazy Longhorns," "There's a Little Deserted Town," "I've Learned a Lot about Women," "Goodbye, Pinto," "Rhythm of the Hoofbeats," "Dude Ranch Cow Hands," and "At the Close of a Long Long Day."

In 1938 Johnny composed several songs for a Republic Western to star Gene Autry, called *Under Western Skies.* Among them were "Listen to the Rhythm of the Range" and "Dust." Autry, however, had a salary dispute with Republic and refused to do the film; newcomer Roy Rogers got the assignment, which included singing Marvin's songs. Not only was Rogers a huge success in his starring debut, but "Dust" was nominated for an Academy Award as Best Song.

In addition to composing, Johnny Marvin also worked at radio station KFI and in 1940 he became a producer on the CBS radio show *Melody Ranch,* starring Gene Autry. That year he also joined the American Society of Composers, Authors, and Publishers (ASCAP).

In the late 1930s Johnny returned to recording but not commercially. He did a series of disks for the Hollywood-based C. P. MacGregor Company, which made radio transcriptions. In the fall of 1940 he cut four songs for the Decca label, which were issued on two records, "We Like It"/"Me and My Shadow" (Decca 5891) and "No One to Kiss Goodnight"/"As Long as I Live" (Decca 5904). This was his last disk session.

In the early 1940s Gene Autry left radio and the screen for World War II service, and Johnny Marvin somewhat cut back his composing activities, working for other studios besides Republic. As the war progressed, he began entertaining with various USO troupes and in 1944 went with Joe E. Brown on a tour of military bases in the South Pacific. There he contracted dengue fever, a form of malaria, which plagued him upon his return home.

While working with the Autry organization, Marvin had converted to the Christian Science faith under the auspices of Ina Mae Autry, Gene's wife. Thus Johnny refused medical treatment for his ailment and suffered with it for over six months, although he continued to entertain at California military bases. His health grew worse and on December 20, 1944, he suffered a fatal heart attack at his home at 6647 Radford Avenue in North Hollywood.

During the mid- and late 1920s and early 1930s, Marvin was one of the country's most popular crooners. His rise to fame was quick, after years of struggle, but his popularity seemed to fade almost as fast. More than any of the crooners, Johnny Marvin was a product of the Roaring Twenties. His smooth singing and ukulele playing mirrored the times that spawned his popularity, and when the Depression came, Marvin became a relic of the past. Although he was a multifaceted entertainer and one of the best ukulele players of his day, Johnny Marvin will always be remembered for his crooning. Unfortunately, in some ways, he was a label mate of fellow crooner Gene Austin and this tended to dilute his reputation, as did the fact that he virtually abandoned the stage in the mid-1930s to concentrate mainly on composing. Certainly, Marvin was one of the most successful and talented of the crooners, yet he remains one of the least remembered. With the hundreds of songs he recorded between 1924 and 1940, Johnny Marvin is a crooner waiting rediscovery.

6

Rudy Vallee

Rudy Vallee was a show business legend whose career spanned the 1920s into the 1980s. He was considered the personification of the romantic crooner who sang love songs through a megaphone and made feminine hearts flutter. While this image stayed with Vallee throughout his career, he was much more than just a singer of love songs. An extremely talented musician, he helped popularize the saxophone, was a composer, led a successful band, and was the nation's first singing idol. In addition, he was the king of radio variety show hosts, a leading nightclub entertainer, the star of film musicals who developed into a top-notch character actor, a major record seller, and an international favorite. He later starred on Broadway (developing into a first-rate character actor) and television. He continued working well into the mid-1980s, long after his contemporaries had passed from the scene. While the image of the romantic crooner will also be associated with Rudy Vallee, the core of his success and longevity was his ability to change with the times and adapt to various show business mediums. Of all the crooners he was in many ways the most versatile and, as a result, he remained in the public eye for six decades.

Hubert Prior Vallée was born July 28, 1901, in Island Pond, Vermont, the son of Charles Alphonse and Katherine Agnes (Lynch) Vallée. His paternal ancestry went back to 1645, when Pierre La Vallée came to Quebec, Canada, from Normandy. His mother's family was Irish, from County Cork. Hubert Vallée's paternal grandfather was the first of the family to live in the United States. Hubert was one of five children, but two died in infancy. He had a sister Kathleen and a younger brother, William, who became a well-known illustrator. Charles Vallée was a druggist, and when Hubert was four years old the family moved to Westbrook, Maine, where the elder Vallée became the town pharmacist.

Young Hubert exhibited an early love of music but had little interest in school. (Nevertheless, he once told his mother to save a report card because he knew that someday he would be famous.) At sixteen, he lied about his age and enlisted in the Navy but was soon discharged. Returning home, he became infatuated with the saxophone and developed into a disciple of the master of the instrument, Rudy Wiedoeft. Wiedoeft became his mentor and it was because of his admiration for the musician that Vallee was dubbed "Rudy" by his friends.

In 1920 Vallee entered the University of Maine but after one year transferred to Yale University in order to get more music courses and to major in Spanish. He earned money by playing the saxophone at various functions and also played accompaniment to silent films. He even worked with a band that appeared with Rudolph Valentino and his wife, Natascha Rambova, when they toured New England in 1923, sponsored by Mineralava.

After two years at Yale he received an offer and took time off to go to London, where he played saxophone with the Havana Band at the Savoy Hotel. Besides being heard over British radio with the band, he gave saxophone lessons. Rudy worked with the Savoy Havana Band from September 1924 to July 1925, and during that period he made a number of records with the group for the English Columbia and HMV (His Master's Voice) labels. These were his first commercial disks, although in 1921 and 1922 he had cut a trio of private records on which he did saxophone solos. He played alto and tenor sax, along with the clarinet, with the British band, and in the spring of 1925 he was the saxophonist on an HMV recording session with Beatrice Lillie and Gertrude Lawrence. In July 1925, Rudy began making electrical recordings with the Savoy Havana Band; all his disks prior to that date had been acoustic.

Vallee returned to Yale University in the fall of 1925 and continued his musical activities, which included making a series of personal recordings. During his last two years in college, he was very active musically and became a member of a band called the Yale

Collegians, under the direction of Lester Laden. With that group he was part of a vocal trio on "You'll Do It Someday" on the Edison label, and for the same company he also sang in a trio with Joe Herlihy's orchestra on "Bye-Bye, Pretty Baby."

He graduated in June 1927, planning to go to South America and become a prosperous cattle rancher. Lacking funds, however, he rejoined the Yale Collegians and after a tour appeared in several well-known New York City groups before taking over the Yale Collegians as its leader. In the summer of 1928 he also supplied the vocals on a disk by Franchini's Serenaders on the Vocalion label.

Billed as Rudy Vallee and His Yale Collegians, the group became a popular dance band attraction in the New York area. Taking note of their success, Don Dickerman hired them to appear at his new Heigh-Ho Club on East 53rd Street. It was here that Rudy used a small megaphone to project his voice, and when the band started broadcasting over radio station WABC he introduced the greeting "Heigh-Ho Everybody" into the English language.

The band began recording for the dimestore label Harmony Records, and while the first couple of disks featured vocals by band members Sleepy Ward and George Morrow, Rudy soon took over the singing chores. A series of best-sellers followed, including "The Song I Love," "Let's Do It," "Doin' the Raccoon," "Makin' Whoopee"/ "If I Had You," "Marie"/"Caressing You," and "Outside." The disks were also issued on the Velvet Tone and Diva labels, and on the latter the band was billed as Frank Mater and His Collegians.

The Yale Collegians were an immediate success at the Heigh-Ho Club, and, thanks to the WABC broadcasts, Rudy Vallee was the talk of the town. Soon radio station WOR had the group doing a show, and on it, Rudy used a microphone for the first time, with great success since the instrument nicely carried his rather high, nasal crooning voice. As fan mail began pouring in, Rudy decided to change the name of the band to the Connecticut Yankees to give it a broader appeal.

Soon Rudy and his band were appearing on radio stations WJZ and WMCA, as well as playing tea dances at the Hotel Lombardy and broadcasting a dance program from the New Venice. As a result, Rudy was signed to appear in vaudeville on the Keith-Orpheum circuit, in addition to inking a recording contract with Victor Records. As *Variety* (February 13, 1929) noted, "Etherizing thus extensively and intensively, Vallee risked overdoing himself, but somehow sidestepped that and, instead, cinched himself with dial fans."

In 1929 Rudy married tea heiress Leonie Cauchois, but both immediately realized they had made a mistake and the marriage was annulled. Rudy Vallee always claimed that his initial success was based on the fact that he and the Connecticut Yankees were different from other singers and bands. Following a successful run, the group moved from the Heigh-Ho Club to the Versailles on East 60th Street. After a few weeks the latter venue became the Villa Vallee; Rudy operated the club for a year before closing it in 1930.

Early in 1929 Rudy began recording with Victor Records; his first disk for the company was "Weary River," backed by "Deep Night," a song he wrote with pianist Charles Henderson. The record was an immediate success and was followed by more best-sellers, including "Honey"; "Coquette"; "The One That I Love Loves Me"; "Huggable, Kissable You"; "Sposin' "; "Miss You"; "Baby, Oh Where Can You Be?"; "Where Are You Dream Girl?"; and the self-penned "I'm Just a Vagabond Lover," a song that became so closely associated with Rudy that he was dubbed "The Vagabond Lover." Sheet music that carried Rudy's picture on the cover also sold well. In fact, Vallee established himself as the nation's top record and sheet music seller in 1929.

Vallee's debut in big-time vaudeville was just as successful as his radio and recording work. The band opened at $1,500 per week at the Palace Theatre in New York and stayed for a month, going up to $2,000 the last two weeks. Regarding its February 1929 opening at the Palace, Elias E. Sugarman wrote in *Billboard* (March 2, 1929) that Vallee and the group were "broadcasting 'names' of unsurpassing local drawing power," adding, "Just eight melodically gifted youths, but carrying a Dempsey punch and other things. Vallee is the guiding spirit rather than a band leader. Plays the sax and clarinet and whispers songs in show-stopping delivery. Pleasing comedy bits interstice ensemble numbers. They had to beg off." The next week (March 9, 1929) Sugarman reported, "Rudy was handed a loud ovation and the matinee ladies ate up every note that issued from his inseparable megaphone."

As a result of his Palace success, Rudy Vallee was signed at $4,000 per week to appear at the Paramount Theatre in New York, with a minimum stay of ten weeks. So popular had Rudy become that in March 1929, he was voted the fourth most popular star on the Keith-Orpheum vaudeville circuit, coming in behind only long-time favorites Belle Baker, Sophie Tucker, and Van & Schenck, the latter top-ping Rudy by only forty-five votes. His high standing is even more phenomenal since he and his band had only been in vaudeville a few weeks.

During this time, Rudy and his group made their movie debuts in the Vitaphone short *Rudy Vallee and His Connecticut Yankees*, in which he sang two songs, including "Deep Night." That summer they journeyed to Hollywood to appear in their first feature film, *The Vagabond Lover*, for Radio Pictures. It told of the rise of a young singer, played by Rudy, and his quest for romance. Veteran Marshall Neilan directed the film, but Rudy later claimed he was gone most of the time and that the assistant director handled the chore.

A laboratory fire almost destroyed the film negative; it debuted in November 1929 to bad reviews and big box office receipts. Richard B. Jewell and Vernon Harbin wrote in *The RKO Story* (1982) that it was "one of the studio's solid box-office successes." They added, "Vallee was as stiff as a frozen mackerel throughout, and the rest of the acting faltered considerably, but audiences, who flocked to see Rudy perform with his Connecticut Yankees band, didn't seem to mind." *Photoplay* (May 1930) stated, "Rudy goes through the whole gamut of emotions without moving a muscle. But when he sings—sh, that's another story. (A better one, too.) Vallee fans will be pleased."

While Rudy Vallee's emoting left much to be desired, *The Vagabond Lover* does present the crooner and his band as they neared the apex of their popularity. The highlight of the movie is the crooner's rendition of "A Little Kiss Each Morning," "If You Were the Only Girl in the World," "I'll Be Reminded of You" and "I Love You, Believe Me, I Love You," all of which he waxed successfully for Victor Records. In later years, the star claimed that the film "nearly killed us with the public." He used it as a part of his nightclub act, claiming that the movie was shown only to captive audiences in prisons and comfort stations and that all the theaters that showed it had to be fumigated.

The high point of Rudy Vallee's popularity came with his appearances at the Paramount theaters in New York and Brooklyn, beginning in May of 1929 and continuing well into the next year. Attendance was so great that it was likened to the mob scenes in *Ben Hur* (1926). These appearances established Rudy Vallee as this country's first singing idol, predating Frank Sinatra, Elvis Presley, and other heartthrobs.

Vallee and his band were signed for twenty weeks at the theaters at $4,500 per week. After six record-breaking weeks at the New York Paramount, the band equaled that success with a month's stay at the Brooklyn Paramount. This continued for over a year, except for the hiatus to make *The Vagabond Lover*. He also did two more movie shorts in 1929, *Rudy Vallee* and *Radio Rhythm*, both for Paramount. Regarding the former, *Billboard* (June 29, 1929) reported that it was "only a little better than the poorest canned nets yet done. The Vallee 'personality,' which fails to be found, and his 'whispering' voice, combined with the efforts of a second-rate orchestra, render this short considerably below par." Regarding *Radio Rhythm*, the same publication (August 10, 1929) noted, "A pretty fair musical short. . . . The band is good but Vallee as a screen personality is a total loss. His appearance on the screen gives one the idea that he is simply going through his musical paces to get his check at the end of the week."

Solidifying Rudy's popularity was his debut on network radio on August 1, 1929, on NBC. Each Thursday evening he and the Connecticut Yankees broadcast a half-hour series of dance music via a coast-to-coast system broadcast from WEAF. On the initial show, the group played ten of its recent Victor recordings. On September 24, 1929, the program became one hour in length and was called *The Fleischmann Hour*, sponsored by Fleischmann Yeast. Rudy would be a Thursday night staple on NBC radio for the next decade.

Just how successful Rudy Vallee had become was noted in the September 7, 1929, issue of *Billboard*. The publication reported that when the crooner and his band played the Ritz Ballroom in Bridgeport, Connecticut, the year before, they took home $167.55. Making a return engagement a year later they were assured either a cash guarantee of $2,800 or 60 percent of the admissions. Around the same time, November 29, 1929, an Associated Press story stated that Rudy said he was not the idol of flappers but that he was "a hard-working man." In the article Vallee claimed that of the thousands of letters he received, two-thirds were from wives and mothers, with one-third from flappers. He also noted about 25 percent of his correspondence came from men. Realizing his debt to radio, Vallee said, "I hope that the day will never come when I am not a source of pleasure and interest on the air. I know that I always will want to broadcast, as I am never so happy as when before the microphone. I realize that ours is a radio band. We owe our success to the radio fan."

Like the singing idols who followed him, Rudy Vallee was far more beloved by fans than by critics. Noting an appearance at the Paramount Theatre in New York, a critic for *Billboard* (November 23, 1929) complained, "The more one sees of Rudy the more he realizes that this boy should stick to the radio and leave the stage alone. His numbers at the Paramount are not received with any marked enthusiasm and fall considerably flatter than is to be expected." On the other hand, *Variety* (June 11, 1930) analyzed his success,

> Quite a lot of space to devote to Rudy but worth it especially considering of all freak sensations Vallee certainly is holding up so well. Quite surprising to show people too, but Vallee apparently is progressing with the trend of things, maintaining pace and tempo with contemporaneous ether standards and yet remaining distinctive.

Rudy Vallee had become such a box office draw that the producers of the Paramount feature *Glorifying the American Girl* (1929) tried to save an otherwise lost cause by including the crooner in its cast, singing, "I'm Just a Vagabond Lover." Despite coming hard times, the singer's records continued to sell, and *Variety* (December 25, 1929) noted that the pairing of "A Little Kiss Each Morning"/"I'll Be Reminded of You" from *The Vagabond Lover* were "both well-established via radio . . . indicating enormous sales for this disc." When Rudy's picture was offered to those who requested it, fifty thousand copies had to be ordered to meet the demand. Even the singer's writing was bought, as he penned an article for the NEA Service called "Women Are More Romantic Than Men" (March 26, 1930). In 1930 he also wrote the first of his three autobiographies, *Vagabond Dreams Come True*, published by Grosset and Dunlap.

During the summer of 1930, Rudy and the Connecticut Yankees toured the country, and his weekly radio broadcasts originated in whatever city the group happened to be in each Thursday. The tour did not include big cities, and Vallee was guaranteed a weekly salary of $18,000 to $20,000 against 60 to 65 percent of the net gross. This set a record for salaries paid to any orchestra or band on tour. In September the band returned to the Brooklyn Paramount Theatre and another salary hike. NBC also renewed Vallee's contract, paying him $175,000 for seventy weekly broadcasts. With his new contracts, Vallee had an earning power of $650,000 in the last half of 1930, giving him "an income tax target in the millionaire's division" (*Variety*, June 25, 1930).

In July 1930, Rudy Vallee returned to his hometown of Westbrook, Maine, where he was "tendered the greatest reception ever by the city of Westbrook to one of its sons" (*Variety*, July 23, 1930). Over 10,000 people crowded into the small community for a large parade, banquet, and ball. Rudy was given the keys to the city, and among those present were Maine's governor W. Tudor Gardiner and local congressman Carroll L. Beedy. Some five hundred young women applied for job of waiting tables at the banquet and fifty were chosen. One local woman even wrote a song for the occasion, called "We're Proud of You, Rudy Vallee."

That summer Vallee's agency, NBC Artists' Service, and his manager, Edwin W. Scheuing, announced that the star and his band had been booked for another 70 weeks on *The Fleischmann Hour*, 130 weeks in Paramount Publix Theatres, 81 more weeks at the Villa Vallee, and 72 more weeks with RCA Victor Records. Only the Villa Vallee engagements failed to meet these dates. By now Rudy was fodder for the tabloid journals, and the phrase "Women Love Him; Men Hate Him" had been coined for the singer.

While Victor and Brunswick records tried to instigate a feud between Rudy and Nick Lucas as to who was the first crooner, neither took part since they were good friends. However, rival band leader Will Osborne did feud with Vallee over the first crooner title, even going so far as to sing a song called "I'd Like to Break the Neck of the Man Who Wrote the Stein Song." Will Osborne's tune was a poke at Rudy Vallee's most popular recording, "The Stein Song," which he recorded for Victor in February 1930. The disk had sold over one million copies in a year when Victor sold 17.7 million records (down due to the effects of the Depression), one-half of its 1929 stateside sales. The song was also the best-seller for sheet music in 1930. Rudy had first heard it at the University of Maine, it having been based on the march "Opie" by U.S. Army bandmaster Emil Fenstad. The song was translated into many languages and became a worldwide favorite; it also caused an increase in enrollment at the University of Maine.

Although 1930 was not a banner year for record sales, Rudy still managed several good sellers besides "The Stein Song" and these included "Beside an Open Fireplace," "Kitty from Kansas City," "Betty Coed," and "You're Driving Me Crazy." In later years Rudy complained that he had tried to help many small publishers during the Depression by recording their songs, some of which were not good, thus further lessening a record market badly hurt by the Depression and radio.

For Paramount, Rudy and his Connecticut Yankees also sang, but did not appear, in a trio of Betty Boop cartoons, *The Stein Song* (1930), *Betty Coed,* and *Kitty from Kansas City* (the latter two in 1931). These three cartoons, all directed by Dave Fleischer, had Rudy and the band performing their Victor best-sellers. Mae Questel provided the voice of Betty Boop in all three cartoons. She also appeared with Rudy and the band in the 1931 short *Musical Justice,* and as a live-action Betty Boop she was with Rudy in the 1932 one-reeler *Musical Director,* in which the singer crooned "Keep a Little Song Handy." Rudy also performed that number in another 1932 Paramount short, *Rudy Vallee Melodies.* Vallee played a singing school teacher in the 1932 short *Knowmore College,* for Paramount. This one stuck him with a song called "You Can Find a Rhyme for Everything but an Orange."

While most people were feeling the effects of the Depression in the early 1930s, this was a time when Rudy Vallee was at the peak of his popularity and earning power. At the end of 1930 Victor Records named him its top seller, both as a singer and as a bandleader. Other sellers that year on the label among the bands were Leo Reisman, Waring's Pennsylvanians, Wayne King, Nat Shilkret, the High Hatters, Duke Ellington, and King Oliver. Among the vocalists who did well on Victor were Maurice Chevalier (whom Rudy could mimic beautifully), Gene Austin, Johnny Marvin, Helen Morgan, Helen Kane, and Buddy Rogers.

Vallee also continued to be a major attraction, as noted when his band grossed $60,000 at the Chicago Theatre (Chicago), in what *Billboard* (March 7, 1931) termed "a phenomenal run." By the summer of 1931 Rudy was earning $12,000 per week, between personal appearances, his NBC radio show, and a starring part in the Broadway musical *George White's Scandals of 1931.* In the latter he appeared as a solo at $2,500 per week, singing the songs "This Is the Missus" and "Life Is Just a Bowl of Cherries." Also headlining the musical were Willie and Eugene Howard, Ray Bolger, Ethel Merman, and Joan Abbott. The show opened in Atlantic City in August 1931 and the next month came to Broadway, where it had a successful run into the following February. After that, an abbreviated version of the show went on tour, also to good success. When the touring company reached Chicago in June 1932, *Variety* noted, "Rudy Vallee, getting top billing, maintained his popularity with the strongest reception."

Rudy Vallee married for the second time in July 1931, in New Jersey to Fay Webb, the daughter of the chief of police in Santa Monica, California. They had dated for nearly two years before the nuptials. The marriage, however, was a rocky one and eventually Rudy sued his wife for divorce, charging her with infidelity with an adagio dancer. The 1934 divorce case drew headlines around the world, with Mrs. Vallee trying to implicate Alice Faye, who first worked with Rudy in *George White's Scandals of 1931*, as his lover. The accusations proved to be false, and the trial judge ruled in Rudy's favor, granting him a divorce. Fay Webb Vallee appealed the decision to the Appellate Court in New York and a year later lost the appeal. She died in 1934.

Even though he was married, Rudy Vallee seemed to lose none of his appeal to women and his career continued in high gear. When *The Fleischmann Hour* was broadcast from station KFI in Los Angeles in the summer of 1931, *Variety* (June 30, 1931) appraised,

> the Rudy Vallee program was like a breath of civilization as it percolated out here on a coast-to-coast hookup. New tunes and big league air are a relief compared to the local banalities which clog the ether. Heard 3,000 miles away from the home plate, Vallee's style was decidedly refreshing. For one thing, it impresses anew that the auditor gets a decent idea of the lyrics and melody from the crooner's megaphone and baton, which certainly can't be said for most out there.

When he and the Connecticut Yankees closed their stand at the Paramount theaters in New York and Brooklyn in the summer of 1931, after two and one-half years, it was the longest personal appearance of a performer with one organization in film stage show history.

However, one aspect of Rudy's career—recordings—began to slide in 1931. Although he continued to keep up the recording pace he set for 1929 and 1930 with Victor, his sales fell off with decent sellers only with "Life Is Just a Bowl of Cherries"/"This Is the Missus" and "My Song"/"The Thrill Is Gone." Ironically, some critics felt that his vocal style was improving, as noted by Bob Landry in *Variety* (August 18, 1931) in a review of "When Yuba Plays the Rumba on the Tuba":

It is almost a thrill to hear the great, crooner-lover develop the volubil-ity of a Latin. The words tumble over one another in the rush. This contrasts vividly with the usual stately progress of melting syllables that the world instantly knows as the Prince Charming from Maine. That Vallee has improved a great deal in the passage of the last few years has been evident.

One of the songs Vallee waxed for Victor in 1931 was "As Time Goes By," but it was only a moderate seller. Ironically, Rudy had a big hit with the record in 1942 when Victor reissued his recording to take advantage of the popularity of the song in the motion picture *Casablanca*.

Victor Records and Rudy Vallee came to a parting of the ways in the fall of 1931, after the company let Ray Noble record "Goodnight Sweetheart," a song Rudy popularized on radio. He signed with Du-rium Products to record on their Hit-of-the-Week label. These disks were one-sided, with a playing time of nearly five minutes. The flexible disks, which usually had the artist's picture on the flip side, sold at newsstands for fifteen cents and had reached a sales peak of 500,000 copies per disk in the summer of 1930. By the time Rudy signed with the label, sales had dipped to about 300,000 per record, still far better than those with the major labels. He worked for Du-rium from November 1931, to March 1932, and had a half-dozen disks released by the label, including "A Faded Summer Love"/ "You Try Somebody Else," "Home," "By the Sycamore Tree," and "By the Fireside/Lovable."

By 1932 Rudy Vallee felt that a change in format was needed for *The Fleischmann Hour*. Prior to this, the program had basically been Rudy and the Connecticut Yankees with an occasional guest, such as Kate Smith, who received her first national attention due to three appearances on the program in 1931, just before launching her own series. Under Vallee's direction the program took on new dimen-sions, with additional guests and dramatic and musical produc-tions. Most of the biggest names in show business appeared on the program during its run, including George Gershwin. Rudy launched many stars' careers, including Alice Faye, Edgar Bergen and Charlie McCarthy, George Burns and Gracie Allen, Bob Hope, Red Skelton, Ezra Stone, Joe Penner, and Ed Gardner. *The Fleisch-mann Hour* was considered the Palace Theatre of the air, and it has often been called the finest variety program in the history of radio.

According to the ratings of the day, Rudy's weekly program reached between 30 and 40 percent of the listening audience during its time period for most of the decade it was on the air.

Following his brief stay with the Hit-of-the-Week label, Rudy and his band signed with Columbia Records; he remained with the company for nearly a year. Many of the disks he made for Columbia were called "radio records" because on them Rudy introduced songs in the same manner that he did on his NBC program. Several of these records were pressed in blue shellac and contain a drawing and facsimile signature on the label.

Among the records Rudy did for Columbia were "I Guess I'll Have to Change My Plans," "Same Old Moon," "Say It Isn't So," "Let's Put Out the Lights and Go to Sleep"/"Me Minus You," "Please"/"How Deep Is the Ocean," "Brother, Can You Spare a Dime?," "Till Tomorrow," "The Language of Love," "Linger a Little Longer in the Twilight," "The Whisper Waltz," "Old Man Harlem," and "I've Got to Sing a Torch Song"/"The Shadow Waltz." Due to the Depression, these records were only moderate sellers and by the summer of 1933 Rudy was again with Victor, but this time his disks were released on the thirty-five cent Bluebird label.

In 1933 Vallee returned to films, appearing as himself in the all-star Paramount comedy *International House.* He appeared via a futuristic television device, singing, "Thank Heaven for You," and when W. C. Fields makes some derogatory comments about his crooning, Rudy admonishes him from the screen. The next year the singer had his second starring role in a feature film in Fox's *George White's Scandals,* which featured Rudy's discovery, Alice Faye, as the co-star. Alice had been singing with Rudy's band since he noticed her in the chorus of *George White's Scandals of 1931.* In 1933 she did the vocals on three of his Bluebird disks, "Honeymoon Hotel," "Shame on You," and "Happy Boy, Happy Girl." When Lillian Harvey walked out on the leading role in the musical, Alice Faye tested for the part and it launched her successful movie career. A fairly pleasant affair, *George White's Scandals* gave Vallee four tunes, but only one of them, "Hold My Hand," was memorable. Alice Faye had the film's best song, "Oh You Nasty Man."

Rudy Vallee's best role in a musical came at Warner Bros. in 1935 when he starred in *Sweet Music,* in which he played a bandleader who romances a dancer (Ann Dvorak). Rudy and the Connecticut Yankees were in top form on several songs in the movie: the title song, "There's a Different You," plus "Ev'ry Day" and "There Is a Tavern in the Town." The film also featured Helen Morgan, who sang "I See Two Lovers." Vallee appeared in the short *The Great Megaphone Mystery* (1935), made to promote *Sweet Music*.

By the end of 1933 Rudy Vallee and the Connecticut Yankees were again recording on the Victor label. In 1934 he had a best-selling record, "The Drunkard Song," his revised version of "There Is a Tavern in the Town," which he sang the following year in *Sweet Music*. The released take had Rudy cracking up on the lyrics throughout the song, and it is sometimes referred to as "The Rudy Vallee Laughing Song."

He remained with Victor until the spring of 1936, when he signed with the American Record Company, owned by Warner-Brunswick Corporation. The company's records, which were issued on the Melotone, Perfect, and Conqueror labels, sold for thirty-five cents and Vallee stayed with them for one year.

Upon the request of George White and against Rudy Vallee's better judgment, he took over the lead in *George White's Scandals of 1936*, which opened on Broadway with co-stars Willie and Eugene Howard, Bert Lahr, and Cliff Edwards. Thanks mainly to Rudy's presence the show survived, but it was critically lambasted. Vallee, however, left the show after an altercation with producer George White. Cliff Edwards returned to the leading part, but the production folded the following week.

On August 6, 1936, Rudy Vallee's NBC Thursday night radio show became *The Royal Gelatin Hour*, sponsored by Royal Gelatin. The series continued its variety show format, with ratings near the 30 percent mark the first season, but by 1937 they had dropped to 15.7 and increased slightly to 16.4 in 1939. During the 1937 to 1939 seasons, the program had tough competition in its time period from *The Kate Smith Hour*.

In the spring of 1937 Rudy returned to England and appeared with his band during the coronation of King George VI. The group appeared at Ciro's, the Finsbury Park, and the Holborn Empires, and *The Royal Gelatin Hour* was broadcast from London on May 6 and 13, 1937. While in London, Rudy also recorded with Carroll Gibbons and His Orchestra on the English Columbia label, doing his initial waxings of "The Whiffenpoof Song" and "Vieni, Vieni."

Both "Vieni, Vieni" and "The Whiffenpoof Song" were 1937 record successes for Vallee, but only after he recorded them again in the United States for Victor. "Vieni, Vieni" reached the number one spot on the Hit Parade in the summer of 1937, and "The Whiffen-poof Song" not only was a big record seller but was also Rudy's favorite of his recordings. The singer first heard "The Whiffenpoof Song" when he was at Yale, and he revised the number and wrote a new piano arrangement for it. However, Yale University was unhappy about his recording the song and refused his offer of donating the royalties from the work to the school.

Vallee recorded for Victor Records from 1937 to 1938, with his disks being again released on the Bluebird label. In 1938 he was back at Warner Bros. to star in the musical *Gold Diggers in Paris*, with direction by Ray Enright and the musical numbers staged by Busby Berkeley. This light farce offered Rudy four songs, including "The Latin Quarter" and "A Stranger in Paree."

Late in 1938 he began recording for the Decca label; one of his most successful platters for them was a duet with Frances Langford on "This Can't Be Love." He also cut two Victor Herbert songs for Decca, "Toyland" and "Moonbeams." Another good seller Rudy had for Decca was the combination of the comedy number "Lydia, the Tattooed Lady" and "You Took Me out of This World." The latter was co-written by Rudy with Milton Berle and remained one of the singer's favorite songs. Over the years Rudy Vallee got composer credit for a number of popular songs, including "Deep Night"; "I'm Still Caring"; "I'm Just a Vagabond Lover"; "I Love the Moon"; "The Stein Song"; "Kitty from Kansas City"; "Forgive Me"; "Magic of the Moonlight"; "Vagabond Dreams Come True"; "The Golden West, a Silvery Nest, and You"; "She Loves Me Just the Same"; "To the Legion"; "Song of the Navy"; "My Cigarette Lady"; "Two Little Blue Eyes"; "Old Man Harlem"; "Somewhere in Your Heart"; "Just an Old Banjo"; "The Drunkard Song"; "Betty Coed"; "All Right, All Right, All Right"; "Vieni, Vieni"; "The Whiffenpoof Song"; "Don't Play with Fire"; "Oh! Ma Ma! (The Butcher Boy)"; "Phil the Fluter's Ball"; "It's Way Past My Dreaming Time"; "You Took Me out of This World"; "Where To?"; "That Woman of Mine"; "Snowflakes"; "Goodnight Sweetheart"; "Sweet Lorraine"; and "Talk to Me."

The star's final film of the 1930s was *Second Fiddle* (1939), also known as *Irving Berlin's Second Fiddle* since the composer wrote the half-dozen songs used in this show business musical. Rudy played an actor who is asked to romance his skater co-star (Sonja Henie) for publicity purposes, much to the chagrin of his girlfriend (Mary

Healy). A publicist (Tryone Power) actually loves the leading lady, and all kinds of romantic contrivances ensue before the happy ending. Vallee sang four songs in the film and waxed them for Decca. The mediocre Irving Berlin tunes were "When Winter Comes," "An Old Fashioned Tune Is Always New," "I'm Sorry for Myself," and "I Poured My Heart into a Song."

Late in 1939 Vallee left Decca Records and recorded for Eli Oberstein's United States Record Corporation, which released his disks on the Varsity label. That year saw the end of *The Royal Gelatin Hour*, which had its final broadcast on September 28, 1939. Rudy also dismantled the Connecticut Yankees and for the rest of his career would work as a solo act.

Following the demise of his network radio show, Rudy returned to California where he had a residence. He planned a long vacation, but a survey showed that radio listeners wanted him back on the air. On March 7, 1940, he returned to network radio, headlining *The Sealtest Show Presents Rudy Vallee*, a thirty-minute variety program sponsored by Sealtest on NBC. The program featured regulars John Barrymore (until he died in 1942) and Joan Davis and weekly guest stars. While Rudy usually sang two songs each broadcast, the emphasis of the show was on comedy and it became an immediate ratings success. Sometimes called *Vallee Varieties*, the show ran until July 1, 1943, when the star left to join the armed forces. After that, the program was known as the *Sealtest Village Store*.

In 1941 Vallee purchased a mansion in the Hollywood Hills that he dubbed Silvertip. The home had been built by film star Ann Harding in 1930 and was made-to-order for Vallee's heavy schedule as a party host. He resided there until his death in 1986.

Early in 1942 Vallee resumed recording for Victor Records and did new versions of his earlier hits "I'm Just a Vagabond Lover" and "The Drunkard Song" and his radio theme, "My Time Is Your Time." Another activity for the star was becoming part-owner of a Hollywood night spot called the Pirate's Den in 1941. He and Don Dickerman, the original owner of the Villa Vallee (later the Copacabana) in New York, went into partnership on the venture and enlisted other backers, including Errol Flynn, Tony Martin, Bob Hope, Bing Crosby, Fred MacMurray, Ken Murray, Jimmy Fidler, and Vic Irwin. At first the club enjoyed great success, but after a couple of years business began to fall off. Due to other commitments on the part of the investors (including Rudy), the ownership group sold out to Fred MacMurray, who operated the night spot for another year before its closing.

In Hollywood Rudy Vallee also resumed his movie career in 1941, starring in two features, *Too Many Blondes* for Universal and *Time Out for Rhythm,* a Columbia Release. In *Too Many Blondes* Vallee played a radio star whose new wife and co-star (Helen Parrish) is being pursued by a rival (Jerome Cowan). To make his wife jealous, the star pretends to romance a waitress (Iris Adrian) whose trucker boyfriend (Lon Chaney) aspires to culture. The silly comedy did give Rudy the opportunity to sing "Let's Love Again" and "The Man on the Flying Trapeze," a song that he often did in personal appearances.

Time Out for Rhythm had Rudy as a promoter who starts a talent agency and pushes dancer Ann Miller for the lead in a television production. As a result, he nearly loses his friendship with partners Richard Lane and Allen Jenkins. The film also featured singer Joan Merrill, the Three Stooges, and Glen Gray and His Cama Loma Band. *Variety* (May 28, 1941) noted, "Rudy Vallee demonstrates he's better on the radio than for pictures and his script part and direction [don't] help any." The low budget musical afforded Vallee only one song, "Obviously the Gentleman Prefers to Dance."

One reward of the Columbia dual-biller, however, was that it was seen by producer-director Preston Sturges, who promptly cast Vallee in the new Paramount comedy *The Palm Beach Story* (1942). That movie forever changed Rudy Vallee's screen image. Considered one of the screwball comedy classics, *The Palm Beach Story* told of a married couple (Claudette Colbert, Joel McCrea) who split, with the woman attracting the attentions of rich John B. Hackensacker III (Rudy) and her husband being romanced by the man's sister (Mary Astor). The movie gave Vallee a chance to show his ability at underplaying a part, and he stole the show as the wealthy stuffed-shirt. He would be typecast in such movie roles for the next decade. So good was Vallee's performance in the film that he was named one of the best actors of the year by the National Film Board of Review. *The Palm Beach Story* also gave Vallee a chance to sing, doing a few bars of "Isn't It Romantic" and then crooning "Goodnight Sweetheart," as he attempts to woo Claudette Colbert.

Next, Rudy starred with Dick Powell, Mary Martin, Betty Hutton, and Eddie Bracken in another big-budget Paramount comedy, *Happy Go Lucky,* in 1943. Here he was cast as a highbrow millionaire being pursued by gold digger Mary Martin on a Caribbean cruise, despite the fact she loves poverty-ridden Dick Powell. While Vallee did not sing in this feature, its best-remembered song was Betty Hutton's exuberant "Murder He Says."

No doubt Rudy Vallee could have continued his acting in films, but World War II brought a hiatus to his movie career for two years. With the United States' involvement in World War II, Rudy Vallee wanted to serve his country and in August 1942, he accepted the position of bandmaster of the United States Coast Guard Marching Band. The brainchild of Lieutenant Maxwell A. Sturges, assistant personnel officer of the Eleventh Naval District, the band was made up of the finest musicians in the country, including harpist Robert Maxwell, the composer of "Shangri-La." Rudy not only served as bandmaster, but he also played saxophone and clarinet in the band, provided the vocals, and worked (along with Jimmie Grier and David Rubinoff) as an arranger.

The marching band supplied entertainment for those at its Coast Guard base and throughout the Eleventh Naval District, which ranged from San Diego to Point Arguello. It also worked with other branches of the armed forces, service groups and hospitals, and various benefit organizations. The band appeared regularly at the Long Beach Auditorium and broadcast on *The Fitch Bandwagon* on NBC radio. In addition, the Coast Guard Marching Band recorded many fifteen-minute programs for the Armed Forces Radio Service (AFRS), as well as numerous recordings for the United States Coast Guard. These recordings were made especially for Coast Guard personnel and were not available commercially until the mid-1970s, when some of them were released on a long-playing album by Mark 56 Records. A few of the records were also issued on V-Disc for armed forces personnel. Rudy Vallee always considered the two years he spent as bandmaster of the United States Coast Guard Marching Band some of the most rewarding of his long career.

While serving in this capacity, Vallee married for the third time, to actress Bettejane Greer in 1943. He also served as her manager, as he did for others, including Victor Borge and Maxie Rosenbloom. The marriage, unfortunately, was not successful and lasted only one year. Rudy blamed himself for the breakup, saying he spent too much time away from home to be a good husband. He and his third wife remained friends, however, and he continued to promote her career. As Jane Greer, she became a popular leading lady in movies during the 1940s and 1950s.

In the fall of 1944 Vallee returned to network radio with *The Drene Show* for Proctor and Gamble, broadcast for a half hour each Saturday night on NBC, beginning September 9. Two months later the show was moved to Thursday nights; it remained there for two seasons, leaving the air on June 27, 1946. The show featured a number of guest acts its first season, with musical interludes by Rudy, the Les Paul Trio, and a vocal group lead by Mel Torme. The second season leaned more toward comedy, with series regulars Monty Woolley, Billie Burke, and Pinky Lee. Music was provided by Xavier Cugat and His Orchestra. *The Drene Show* was a ratings success and a triumphant return to network radio for Rudy Vallee.

Movies also wanted Rudy back and, beginning in 1945, he would be featured in fourteen motion pictures through 1950. He marked his return to films with a guest appearance in the Fred Allen comedy *It's in the Bag!* for United Artists in 1945. Allen played the owner of a flea circus after an inheritance, and in one comedy sequence Rudy appeared as a waiter. *Man Alive* (1945) brought him another stuffed-shirt role, this time as the romancer of a woman (Ellen Drew) who thinks her husband (Pat O'Brien) is dead after being in a car crash. The man pretends to be a ghost to scare off the unwanted suitor. *People Are Funny* (1946) cast Vallee as a hard-to-please radio show sponsor who is convinced by an agent (Philip Reed) to hire an announcer (Jack Haley) and back his new show. The film gave him the opportunity to sing "Alouetta," which he recorded at the time for Enterprise Records. Next, Rudy was a business executive in the comedy *The Fabulous Suzanne*, released by Republic late in 1946. His character gets involved with a waitress (Barbara Britton) who can pick horse-race winners and decides to use her gift on the stock market.

The Sin of Harold Diddlebock (1947) brought Harold Lloyd back to the screen and reunited Vallee with producer-director Preston Sturges. Opening with a segment from *The Freshman* (the 1925 vehicle starring Harold Lloyd), the comedy showed what happened to Diddlebock (Lloyd), who had stumbled along life's path and had not become a success. Rudy was cast as a grasping capitalist banker. In 1950 the movie was re-edited and reissued as *Mad Wednesday*, with Vallee's part deleted.

One of Rudy Vallee's best postwar movie parts was in *The Bachelor and the Bobby Soxer* in 1947 for RKO. He played the stuck-up boyfriend of a judge (Myrna Loy) who sentences a playboy (Cary Grant) to be the constant companion of her younger sister (Shirley Temple), who has a crush on him. The playboy and the boyfriend are soon at odds when the former falls for the judge. The entertaining comedy grossed over $5.5 million and was called *Bachelor Knight* in Great Britain. Rudy also had a small but very good role for RKO as a kindly physician in the family drama *I Remember Mama* (1948), the story of a Norwegian immigrant couple (Irene Dunne, Oscar Homolka) as seen through the eyes of their oldest daughter (Barbara Bel Geddes).

Ring Lardner's book *The Big Town* was the basis for the independent production *So This Is New York* (1948), which starred Henry Morgan as a rube who inherits money and comes to the big city, where he is fleeced by a variety of characters, including Vallee's race track denizen. In 1954 the feature was reissued by Favorite Attractions as *Broadway Guys,* with Rudy given top billing.

Vallee worked again for Preston Sturges in *Unfaithfully Yours* (1948), the first of four features he was do to for 20th Century-Fox. Here he was the supposed romantic rival of a symphony orchestra leader (Rex Harrison) who plans three ways to do away with his unfaithful wife (Linda Darnell) as he conducts a concert. Although the film proved to be only mildly amusing, it was remade in 1984 with Armand Assante essaying Vallee's role. The actor was cast again as a blueblood, who romances the estranged wife (Laraine Day) of a writer (Kirk Douglas), in *My Dear Secretary* (1948), an alleged comedy that almost wrecked Kirk Douglas's career. Next, Rudy was a straitlaced lawyer in the comedy *Mother Is a Freshman* (1949), in which Loretta Young played a pretty widow who gets a family scholarship and attends the same school as her daughter (Betty Lynn), with both of them falling for a professor (Van Johnson).

The Beautiful Blonde from Bashful Bend (1949), his last film with Preston Sturges, cast Rudy as the naive owner of a goldmine who is romanced by a saloon gal (Betty Grable) on the lam after trying to kill her two-timing gambler boyfriend (Cesar Romero). Vallee and Betty Grable dueted on ''In the Gloaming,'' but overall the Technicolor production was flat and unfunny. Much better was *Father Was a Fullback* (1949), the last of his four 20th Century-Fox features. Again he was typecast as a prissy type, this time as the bothersome head of a college alumni association forever threatening the school's harried football coach (Fred MacMurray), who has the support of a faithful wife (Maureen O'Hara) as the two try to deal with their daughters (Betty Lynn, Natalie Wood).

Rudy ended his spate of postwar movie roles with *The Admiral Is a Lady*, a 1950 United Artists release. This time he is a jukebox manufacturer whose wife (Hillary Brooke) has been romancing the boyfriend of a WAVE (Wanda Hendrix). When the boyfriend turns up missing, four ex-GIs (Edmond O'Brien, Johnny Sands, Steve Brodie, Richard Erdman) try to locate him and one of them (O'Brien) falls for the WAVE.

After two seasons as the star, producer, and director of *The Drene Show*, Vallee opted not to continue the program for a third year. Instead he signed with a tobacco company and headlined *The Philip Morris Show* on NBC, a half-hour Tuesday program that featured music and comedy, plus guest stars. The show was broadcast from September 10, 1946, to March 4, 1947. Vallee, however, was not happy with the show, mainly due to a cut budget and trouble with the advertiser and network executives. After two broadcasts from the then emerging Las Vegas, Rudy was glad to say farewell to network radio for awhile.

In the postwar period Rudy Vallee also returned to making records. In 1945 he cut a disk for Freddy Martin's Maestro Music label. The songs were "Waiting" and "That Woman of Mine"; the record featured a picture of Rudy on the label with a facsimile signature. The next year he cut some sides for Enterprise Records and returned to the singles charts with the coupling of "The Whiffenpoof Song" and "Alouetta." Eight of the Enterprise songs were combined into a 78 rpm album, simply titled *Rudy Vallee*. In the spring of 1950 Rudy did a single for Victor Records, "Sentimental Me"/"Niccolo and His Piccolo."

Another activity in which the star invested a great deal of time, energy, and money was his company, Vallee-Video. Seeing a big future in television, Rudy envisioned making 16mm films for TV and was one of the first to use canned laughter and announced title credits in his productions. He brought songs to life through performances, sketches, and animation, and he himself appeared in such shorts as *These Foolish Things* and *Under a Campus Moon*. Among the performers to work for Vallee-Video were Ed Wynn, Pinky Lee, Buddy Lester, and Cyril Smith. Also planned was a series of half-hour TV dramas to star Ralph Byrd in his famed "Dick Tracy" role, but Byrd, a close friend of Vallee's, died in 1952 before the deal could be consummated with NBC-TV. Production delays and costs and the lack of a lucrative deal with a national sponsor eventually spelled the demise of Vallee-Video.

On September 3, 1949, Vallee married for the fourth and final time. His bride was Eleanor Norris, a twenty-one-year-old beauty he had first met at King's Beach on Lake Tahoe five years before. The two had dated over the years and, after Eleanor graduated from college, they were wed. The marriage proved to be a permanent and happy one; the couple was together for thirty-seven years until Rudy's death in 1986.

Eleanor and Rudy not only traveled together, but she often appeared in his nightclub act and did advance publicity for his appearances. In the 1960s she did occasional television commercials and was a spokesperson for Metropolitan Insurance. After Rudy's death, she hosted a cable television program in Los Angeles.

From the late 1940s into the early 1960s Vallee's major source of income came from yearly tours of night spots around the country and abroad. He first began appearing solo in nightclubs, supper clubs, and hotels in the early 1940s, but he did not get into touring until the demise of his network radio programs. Over the years Rudy honed his act into one of the top-notch one-man shows in the country. Running nearly two hours, the act featured Rudy doing songs and comedy patter, the latter sometimes including ventriloquism and imitations. He balanced the nostalgia of his crooner image with a natural ability to tell amusing stories and jokes, and over the years he developed into a very fine humorist. The nightclub circuit caused the Vallees to travel constantly, mostly by car and train, and they criss-crossed the country many times over the next dozen years, as Rudy was still a major club attraction.

Although Rudy Vallee felt that there was a big future in television production, he did not like the way he came across on the small screen. Early in 1949 he made his network television debut on the CBS-TV series *Toast of the Town,* hosted by Ed Sullivan. He was so successful that the sponsor, Emerson Radio, offered him Sullivan's job, which he declined. He received several offers to do a TV series, including those from the American Tobacco Company and the William Morris agency. In the mid-1950s he was one of the major contenders for the job of emcee of the CBS-TV series *The $64,000 Question,* but the nod went to Hal March. Considering the quiz show scandals in 1958, it was probably fortuitous that Vallee did not get the job.

As the 1950s progressed, the actor did begin to make occasional appearances on television, such as "The Playboy" segment of *Eddie*

Cantor Comedy Theatre on ABC-TV in 1955 and *The Shower of Stars* and *December Bride,* both on CBS-TV. One of his most satisfying TV outings was on the NBC-TV program *Matinee Theatre* in 1956, when he recreated his stage role from Jean Kerr's play *Jenny Kissed Me.* He first appeared in the role of the Catholic priest in the play in summer stock in 1954 (Rudy initially did stock in 1939 in the play *The Man in Possession*), and in 1956 he did a revival of the production at the Pasadena Playhouse with Lee Remick.

Rudy was back on network radio in 1950 with *The Rudy Vallee Show,* a weekday disk jockey program from New York station WOR, broadcast nationally by the Mutual Network. The series ran from February 20, 1950, to April 27, 1951.

In the mid-1950s Vallee returned to films in Universal's *Ricochet Romance* (1954), an unsuccessful attempt to make a screen team of Marjorie Main and Chill Wills. Rudy appeared to good effect as snooty Worthington Higgenmacher, a guest at a Western dude ranch plagued by a nosy cook (Main) and a daffy owner (Wills). Even better for the actor was his role (as himself) in the Paris-lensed United Artists' musical *Gentlemen Prefer Brunettes* (1955), the sequel to *Gentlemen Prefer Blondes* (1953). The story had two showgirls (Jane Russell, Jeanne Crain) coming to Paris and becoming a success while being romanced by two Americans (Scott Brady, Alan Young). Vallee's role poked fun at his singing idol image and allowed him to perform two songs, "Have You Met Miss Jones?" and "I Wanna Be Loved by You." The movie's soundtrack was issued on Coral Records. His final 1950s film appearance was in *The Helen Morgan Story* for Warner Brothers in 1957. In it he appeared as himself, singing "My Time Is Your Time."

The singer also continued to record in the 1950s. In 1952 he cut a single, "Bubbles in My Beer"/"The Beer That I Left on the Bar," for MGM Records, and for Victor he waxed "The Whiffenpoof Song"/ "Taps" the following year. Both records were issued on 78 rpm and 45 rpm formats.

In the summer of 1954 Rudy recorded his first long-playing album, a ten-inch disk called *Rudy Vallee's Drinking Songs,* issued on the Storyville label. The next year he recorded another ten-inch LP, *Songs of a Vagabond Lover,* for Capitol. On it, he sang eight of his past hits, and the album was also released as a two-disk, 45 rpm extended-play album. In 1956 Rudy recorded his favorite LP, *The Kid from Maine,* for Unique Records, a division of RKO. Here he sang a dozen of his former best-sellers, backed by Joseph J. Leahy's orchestra direction. In the late 1950s Vallee also cut another album, *Rudy Vallee Reads Fairy Tales*, a children's album issued on the Treasure label. On it, he recited "Seven at a Blow," "The Frog Prince," "Rumpelstiltskin," and "The Golden Goose," all noted Grimm fairy tales.

In 1955 Vallee was back on network radio, hosting *The Kraft Music Hall* on CBS from February 27 to June 1, 1955. He also began to be more active on television. One of his best-remembered roles came in 1957 with the CBS special *Lucy Takes a Cruise to Havana*, starring Lucille Ball and Desi Arnaz with Vivian Vance and William Frawley. He guest starred along with Ann Sothern and Cesar Romero. He also had a good dramatic role in Robert Von Scoyk's "The Battle for Wednesday" on *Kraft Theatre* on NBC, telecast January 1, 1958. That spring he guest starred on the NBC special *Hansel and Gretel*, in which he sang "Men Rule the Evening." The soundtrack was released on MGM Records. Rudy also appeared on numerous television musical and variety programs, such as *Ruth Lyons 50-50 Club* and *The Garry Moore Show*.

By the late 1950s Rudy Vallee was still in the public eye, but many regarded him as a star of yesteryear. Columnist John Crosby wrote, "Rudy Vallee as a bigtime radio entertainer disappeared long ago." Vallee became unhappy about the fading nightlife in America and his too often having to play one-night stands in sometimes seedy locales. When he appeared on interview programs, like Mike Wallace's syndicated talk show or Jackie Gleason's 1961 CBS-TV program, he was presented as a figure from the past.

Not really caring for nostalgia, Rudy Vallee tried to remain in the mainstream of entertainment, shifting his image from that of a singer to a funny man and raconteur. In that vein, an appearance by Rudy at the Anaheim Bowl in Anaheim, California, was released on an LP by Crown Records as *Is This Your Rudy Vallee?* in 1960. Except for special parody lyrics, songs were deleted in favor of talk and comedy on the album.

Fortune took a major step in the entertainer's favor when in 1961 he was asked to essay the role of J. B. Biggley in the upcoming Broadway musical *How to Succeed in Business without Really Trying*, based on the book by Shepherd Mead. Robert Morse played the role of a young man who uses various devious methods to climb the career ladder at World Wide Wickets Inc., in Gotham. Biggley is the president of the organization, who is carrying on an affair with his feather-headed secretary (Virginia Martin), as Morse, who has fallen for another secretary (Bonnie Scott), tries to get his job. Frank Loesser wrote the music and lyrics for the show, which was directed by Abe Burrows, who co-wrote the play, with musical staging by Bob Fosse.

During the show's rehearsals, Vallee was told he did not project well and would have to be replaced. He proved to producers that he would have no trouble being heard by audiences, and when the show opened on Broadway on October 14, 1961, it was a huge success and Rudy garnered great reviews. The production went on to win the Pulitzer Prize, New York Drama Critics Award, and seven Tony Awards. Vallee's role of the crusty but amorous company president fitted the image he had created in films in the 1940s and was an offshoot of the type of roles he had in movies like *The Palm Beach Story* and *The Bachelor and the Bobby Soxer*. The show also gave him two songs, a duet with Robert Morse on "Grand Old Ivy" and a love song with Virginia Martin, "Love from a Heart of Gold." Although Robert Morse left the show after two years and was replaced by Darryl Hickman, Rudy remained for the entire three-year run of the musical, never once missing any of its 1,144 performances.

Vallee's triumphant return to the stage also made him the toast of Broadway. He was constantly being interviewed, and, indefatigable as ever, he was soon giving Sunday concerts at Brighton Beach in Brooklyn, as well as doing a vaudeville show at the Atlantic City Steel Pier. He also kept up a schedule that included radio and television appearances, charity shows, and club engagements. He was in demand for appearances at opening nights, various dinners and tributes, and parties.

He also returned to recording. Besides waxing his two numbers from "How to Succeed" for the RCA Victor original cast album, he also made an album for the Decca label called *Stein Songs,* sponsored by the beer industry. Two cuts from the LP, "The Whiffenpoof Song" and "The Stein Song," were issued as a 45 rpm single. In the summer of 1963 Rudy made a personal appearance at the NCO Club at Kindley Field in Bermuda, doing his one-man show. The performance was recorded and, with songs deleted, it was released on the Jubilee record album *The Funny Side of Rudy Vallee.* The LP proved to be Rudy's biggest seller, eventually selling over 400,000 copies.

The star was also in demand for endorsements. He appeared in national advertisements for Heublein Whiskey and New England Life Insurance, among others.

In 1962 the entertainer's second volume of memoirs, *My Time Is Your Time*, written with Gil McKean, was published by Ivan Obolensky. It was in this period that the Vallees became close friends with Richard and Pat Nixon, who were living in New York City. During the remaining years of his life, Rudy remained a Nixon ally, even defending him during the Watergate era.

In the late 1950s there was a movement for Rudy to run for the post of mayor of Los Angeles, and during the 1960s and early 1970s he campaigned actively for that city's mayor, Sam Yorty. Rudy also gave some consideration to running for the Senate from California in the 1960s, although the only political job he held was as a member of the Los Angeles Board of Traffic Commissioners, a post that Yorty appointed him to in 1970. Always outspoken on a variety of issues, Vallee, on *The Joe Pyne Show* in 1968, suggested that the Vietnam War could be ended with the use of nuclear weapons.

During his third year on Broadway, Rudy Vallee starred in the one-hour CBS-TV summer replacement series *On Broadway Tonight*. The theme of the show was the introduction of new talent, and with Rudy's reputation of being a star maker he fit well into this format. Each week he would interview unknown performers and they would do their act. Among those introduced on the series were George Carlin, Rodney Dangerfield, Rich Little, Marilyn Michaels, Richard Pryor, Renee Taylor, and Jo Anne Worley. Each week Rudy would also feature a well-known guest star, such as Tony Martin and Jack E. Leonard, and occasionally he would also perform. The series debuted July 8, 1964, and ran until September of that year. A ratings success, it returned in January 1965 and ran through March of that year.

Following a three-year run on Broadway, Rudy and Eleanor Vallee returned to Silvertip for a brief rest before Vallee began another tour in *Jennie Kissed Me* in 1965. When the play was staged in Aurora, Illinois, Robert Barclay wrote in the *Aurora Beacon-News*, "Rudy Vallee, a very funny man . . . Everybody there was having a wonderful time." When the show appeared at the Avondale Playhouse in Indianapolis, Indiana, Corbin Patrick said in *The Indianapolis Star*, "Vallee has the part down pat and plays it with authority. . . . The comedy's greatest virtues are that it furnishes him with a vehicle that he can use and that it comes under the heading of good, clean family entertainment."

Vallee then appeared in a road tour of *How to Succeed in Business without Really Trying*. He also kept doing his one-man show and guest starring on television, usually on variety, quiz, and talk programs.

In the fall of 1966 a British group called the New Vaudeville Band had a hit record with "Winchester Cathedral." Since the song was done in the style of Vallee's old recordings, he became associated with the tune; as a result, he did an album for the Viva label called *Hi-Ho Everybody*, on which he performed the song. In its first three weeks of release the LP sold over 35,000 copies. In reviewing the album, *Variety* noted, "Vallee is still singing well. . . . He's especially good on a material piece, 'Who Likes Good Pop Music?' "

Early in 1967 Vallee was back in Hollywood, doing the film version of *How to Succeed in Business without Really Trying*, which was released by United Artists. Although Bing Crosby, Mickey Rooney, and Milton Berle were all considered for the part, Rudy was signed to repeat his Broadway success and again received critical acclaim. The musical translated well to the big screen and proved to be a box office success, although for the film Rudy had only one song, a duet with Robert Morse on "Grand Old Ivy," which was on the film's United Artists Records soundtrack.

In 1968 Vallee did two more movies. He was featured in the Elvis Presley musical comedy *Live a Little, Love a Little*, released by Metro-Goldwyn-Mayer, and he was the narrator of the United Artists comedy *The Night They Raided Minsky's*. In the latter, he performed the title song and "Take Ten Terrific Girls."

In 1969 it was announced that he would appear in the feature *The Silent Treatment*, but it was never filmed. He did do a cameo in the little-seen *The Phynx* in 1970, and in 1971 he sang "I Can't Give You Anything but Love" on the soundtrack of *The Grissom Gang*. Other work in 1969 included narrating a portion of the long-playing album *MacArthur's Legacy*, on Key Records, a documentary on General Douglas MacArthur. Vallee also did his final radio series that year, narrating episodes of *The Dizzy Decade* for Westinghouse Broadcasting.

As the 1960s began to close, the entertainer occasionally talked of retirement, but it never came to pass. He told Gene Hansaker of the Associated Press, "I live in the present and the future." One of his ventures was to form a dinner club in Southern California that sold memberships to over two dozen restaurants.

He also continued his one-man show. Of an appearance in Dallas, Texas, *Variety* commented, "Vallee, a handsome, imposing figure who doesn't move from his tracks during the 55-minute outing, still gets good mileage from low key comedy material, in machine-gun delivery. . . . His pipes are still good."

Opinionated as ever, however, the entertainer was not happy with the current music scene. He told an interviewer for the *Muncie (Indiana) Star* (May 6, 1969),

> I'm very frankly dumbfounded and flabbergasted about a lot of the rock-and-roll groups today. I don't understand why they are a success. . . . Some of the music is so banal, so repetitious, so uninspired melodically and lyrically. I can't comprehend why so many records are sold today.

He added, "I guess I'm a little old fashioned and conservative. I don't understand the very fast pace in films and on stage today."

In the late 1960s and early 1970s Vallee was involved in quite a bit of television activity. Besides making numerous appearances on talk and variety shows like those of Johnny Carson, Mike Douglas, and Merv Griffin, he also did several dramatic and comedy TV guest spots. In 1967 he made three appearances as the gout-ridden arch villain Phineas Fogg on the ABC series *Batman,* and he had good dramatic roles in the syndicated series *Death Valley Days* in 1968 and on NBC's *The Name of the Game* in 1970. Particularly memorable was the November 30, 1970, episode of *Here's Lucy* on CBS, starring Lucille Ball. On it, he portrayed himself, singing, "I'm Just a Vagabond Lover" and "The Whiffenpoof Song." The plot had Rudy being down-and-out, with scatterbrained Lucy trying to help him revive his career. He guested as himself on the CBS show *The Chicago Teddy Bears* in 1971, and later that year he and Robert Morse were reunited for the "Marmalade Wine" segment of NBC's *Night Gallery.* He also had good roles in two guest appearances on the ABC series *Alias Smith and Jones* in 1971 and 1972.

As the decade of the 1970s dawned, Vallee remained active on a professional basis. He appeared in Las Vegas in the revue *The Newcomers of 1928* with Harry Richman and Billy Gilbert, and he toured in *The Big Show of 1928* with Sally Rand, Louis Jordan, and the Ink Spots. He and Nick Lucas did a nostalgia revue in Chicago, and Rudy continued to hone his one-man show. By this time he was doing two hours, operating his own sound system, spotlight, and colorwheel and showing 200 slides. He summed up the show by saying, "I control everything by myself. I 'mime' some of the songs. . . . don't sing them 'live.' And one solid hour of humor: sex, anatomy, religion, politics, drinking, hair, and topics of the day."

Around 1974 his show was recorded and released on a two-LP set called *An Evening with Rudy Vallee* on Mark 56 Records. During that period, the same label also issued an album made up of material from Rudy's 1930s radio program called *The Fleischmann's Hour Presents Rudy Vallee* and another from 1940s disks, *Rudy Vallee and His Famous World War II U.S. Coast Guard Band.*

From 1971 to 1985 Rudy made several appearances on Frank Breesee's *Golden Days of Radio* shows. From 1981 to 1983 the program provided weekly repeats of Rudy's radio shows of the past.

In the mid-1970s Rudy and Robert Morse were reunited for a revival of *How to Succeed in Business without Really Trying* at the Los Angeles and San Francisco Civic Light Opera. The production ran for a total of fourteen weeks, with Rudy again getting rave reviews.

Prior to the revival, he had mimed the role of King Septimus in a stock production of *Once upon a Mattress,* and following the Civic Light Opera production he toured in another nostalgia revue, *The Big Broadcast of 1976.* In 1976 he also had the role of a nasty music publisher who becomes a murder victim in "The Adventure of the Tyrant of Tin Pan Alley," an episode of the NBC series *Ellery Queen.*

Vallee's third volume of memoirs, *Let the Chips Fall,* was published by Stackpole Books in 1975. This time out, Rudy recounted various episodes from his life and career, including several romances, a chapter on his father, and his feuds with the likes of Victor Borge, George White, and Milton Berle. The picture-laden volume also updated Rudy's career from the early 1960s and included a chapter on his various trials and tribulations with *How to Succeed in Business without Really Trying.* A slightly updated version of the book was published in paperback the next year as *Rudy Vallee Kisses and Tells.*

As the 1970s came to a close, Rudy Vallee remained active, still doing his one-man show and appearing on TV talk shows, but the demand for his services began to decline. On January 20, 1979, he guest starred on the NBC series *CHiPS* in an episode called "Pressure Point," in which he portrayed a wealthy businessman, who, along with his granddaughter (Mary Frances Crosby), is being forced to pay for protection by gangsters. The program's ratings were noticeably up for Rudy's appearance, but no further dramatic offerings came along. He did guest star on the NBC special *Men Who Rate a "10,"* hosted by Gloria Swanson, on October 7, 1980. He sang "As Time Goes By."

On July 28, 1981, Rudy Vallee celebrated his eightieth birthday. The event was publicized by the media around the world, and Rudy was featured in several magazine articles and television interviews. He received gifts and congratulations from hundreds of people, and Los Angeles Mayor Sam Yorty even suggested changing the name of the street where the Vallees lived to Rue De La Vallee. A city councilman, however, objected, and the ensuing foray over the matter ended in Rudy not getting the name change but gaining a modicum of sympathetic publicity. One letter writer even suggested changing the name of the entire area to the San Fernando Vallee.

From 1980 to 1985 Rudy was heard weekly on PBS-TV, singing the title song to the nostalgia series *Matinee at the Bijou*. In addition to enacting his one-man show a couple of times each month, Vallee involved himself in several projects. These included plans for doing his act on Broadway, compiling a record album of his many bestsellers, writing another book, and developing a TV program on which commentators and political figures would debate important issues, with Rudy as the chief judge. Of these, only the record album came to fruition, albeit not in the format Vallee envisioned.

By 1985 he had finished the record album project, which had twenty-seven songs with commentary by Rudy. He called the album, a two-record set, *Songs to Make Love By*, and planned to market it via television, which had proven so successful for such singers as Slim Whitman, Jim Nabors, and Christy Lane. No distributor was found during Vallee's lifetime; however, the album was released in 1991 on CD and cassette by the Good Music Company as *My Time Is Your Time*. Rudy's commentary was not used and the songs he had chosen were augmented by additional selections from his Victor 78s, the Unique album, and radio broadcasts.

Rudy Vallee's final movies were *Sunburst* (1975); *Won Ton Ton, the Dog Who Saved Hollywood* (1976); and *The Perfect Woman* (1981). *Sunburst* cast Rudy as a rural character, but following scattered release in the mid-1970s this stalker melodrama remained obscure until it was issued on video in the 1990s as *Slashed Dreams*. In *Won Ton Ton, the Dog Who Saved Hollywood*, Rudy was one of many guest stars, but he was memorable in his brief role as an autograph hound. In *The*

Perfect Woman he was cast, along with Cameron Mitchell and Marie Windsor, as one of the three rulers of a planet who decree that their king must marry an Earth woman, and they send an emissary (Fred Willard) to find the mate.

Although the Broadway appearance and the TV series Rudy planned never got off the ground, he did spend much of the mid-1980s working on his fourth book, which dealt with the various women in his life. The nickname "The Vagabond Lover" fit Rudy, as he was known to have romanced dozens of women before his marriage to Eleanor. Among those he discussed were Ginger Rogers, Hedy Lamarr, Yvonne De Carlo, Linda Darnell, Marie Windsor, Alice Faye, Mary McBride, June Knight, Joan Crawford, Judy Canova, Sheila Ryan, Ann Sothern, Adrienne Ames, Mary Brian, and Wendy Barrie. The project never reached completion during his lifetime.

In the meantime Vallee enjoyed considerable recognition from many quarters. In the early 1980s Rudy was voted Man of the Year by the state of Maine, and in 1984 he received the Great American Award from the city of New Orleans and led the Mardi Gras Parade. The following year he was named Irishman of the Year at the Los Angeles St. Patrick's Day Parade, and in Washington, D.C., he was honored with "Rudy Vallee Day" as the American Film Institute inducted him into its Hall of Fame at Washington, D.C.'s Kennedy Center. In 1985 he also appeared with Linda Nardini in the well-received music video "Girls Talk." As the year drew to a close, *Daily Variety* (December 10, 1985) carried an advertisement with a picture of Vallee, along with the name and address of his talent representative. The ad read "The voice, the magic, the legend continues. . . ."

Early in 1986 Rudy Vallee recorded for the last time, the unreleased song "Junior Movie Star." Not long afterward he suffered a minor fall in his home, and a week later his doctor suggested that he have a throat x-ray since his voice sounded raspy. The x-ray showed a malignancy of the esophagus, but Rudy was advised not to have surgery since the tumor might take years to spread. The entertainer, however, opted for the operation and, after making a will leaving his entire estate to his wife, he underwent a thirteen-hour operation at Cedars-Sinai Hospital in Los Angeles. He came through the operation successfully, but a week later he had a reaction to medication, which resulted in a stroke.

He spent six months in the hospital receiving therapy and was finally able to return home. He died there on July 3, 1986, while watching the unveiling of the newly restored Statue of Liberty in New York harbor on television.

Following his death, tributes to Rudy Vallee came from across the country from his many friends and colleagues, including Richard Nixon. President Ronald Reagan said, "He was a dedicated patriot who interrupted his career to serve in the U.S. Coast Guard, and it was appropriate that Rudy's last moments were spent watching the illumination of the Statue of Liberty. The music of Rudy Vallee will be part of American culture for generations to come." In his memory, civic offices all over California closed and the California Senate adjourned its session in tribute to him.

After a memorial service, Rudy's ashes were taken to Maine, where he was buried beside his parents. Rudy's home was eventually sold to Arsenio Hall. His immense memorabilia collection, which included more than 550 scrapbooks, was sold to the Thousand Oaks Public Library in California, where it took more than a decade to catalog the mass of material Rudy Vallee had saved in his lifetime.

In retrospect, Rudy Vallee was one of the giants of the entertainment industry in the twentieth century. One of the true pioneers of radio, he was also the nation's first singing idol. A starmaker of the first magnitude, he helped scores of other performers along the way to stardom. A first-class musician, singer, and entertainer, he successfully conquered nearly all available areas of the entertainment industry in his more than sixty years as an active performer. Not just a personality of his time, Vallee proved himself to be one of the most enduring and remembered entertainers of all time.

Discography

Singles: 78s and 45s

1924

Edison

51422-L Arkansas Traveler (credited to the Blue Ridge Duo). Also Blue Amberol Cylinder 4936.

51422-R Little Brown Jug (credited to the Blue Ridge Duo). Also Blue Amberol Cylinder 4973.

51498-L Life's Railway to Heaven (credited to the Blue Ridge Duo). Also Blue Amberol Cylinder 4968.

51498-R You Will Never Miss Your Mother until She Is Gone (credited to the Blue Ridge Duo). Also Blue Amberol Cylinder 4961.

51502-L Susie Ann (credited to the Blue Ridge Duo). Also Blue Amberol Cylinder 4978.

51502-R Turkey in the Straw (credited to the Blue Ridge Duo). Also Blue Amberol Cylinder 4977.

51515-L (matrix 9728) Blue Ridge Blues

217

(credited to the Blue Ridge Duo). Also Blue Amberol Cylinder 4976.

51515-R (matrix 9727) Lonesome Road Blues (credited to the Blue Ridge Duo). Also Blue Amberol Cylinder 4975.

51611-L Got the Railroad Blues. Also Blue Amberol Cylinder 5058.

Vocalion

A 14809 The Wreck on the Southern 97 (credited to George Reneau). Also Vocalion A 5029.

B 14809 Lonesome Road Blues (credited to George Reneau). Also Vocalion B 5029.

A 14811 You Will Never Miss Your Mother until She Is Gone (credited to George Reneau). Also Vocalion A 5030.

B 14811 Life's Railway to Heaven (credited to George Reneau). Also Vocalion B 5030.

A 14812 Turkey in the Straw (credited to George Reneau). Also Vocalion A 5031.

B 14812 Little Brown Jug (credited to George Reneau). Also Vocalion B 5031.

A 14813 Casey Jones (credited to George Reneau). Also Vocalion A 5032.

B 14813 Arkansaw Traveler (instrumental; credited to George Reneau). Also Vocalion B 5032.

A 14814 Here, Rattler, Here (Calling the Dog) (credited to George Reneau, who takes the vocal). Also Vocalion A 5033.

B 14814 When You and I Were Young, Maggie (credited to George Reneau). Also Vocalion B 5033.

A 14815 Blue Ridge Blues (credited to George Reneau). Also Vocalion A 5034.

B 14815 Susie Ann (credited to George Reneau). Also Vocalion B 5034.

A 14821 A Thousand Miles from Here (w. Roy Bergere). Also Guardsman 7004.

B 14821 All Day Long (w. Roy Bergere). Also Guardsman 7004.

A 14841 Sally Gooden (w. Uncle "Am" Stuart). Also Brunswick 1002, Vocalion A 5037.

A 14846 Old Liza Jane (w. Uncle "Am" Stuart). Also Brunswick 1004.

A 14896 Smoky Mountain Blues (credited to George Reneau). Also Vocalion A. 5049

B 14896 Red Wing (credited to George Reneau). Also Vocalion B 5049.

A 14897 The C & O Wreck (credited to George Reneau). Also Vocalion A 5050.

B 14897 Jesse James (credited to George Reneau). Also Vocalion B 5050.

B 14916 Choo Choo (I Gotta Hurry Home) (w. the Ambassadors). Also Vocalion X 9523.

A 14918 The Baggage Coach Ahead (credited to George Reneau; vocal by Reneau). Also Vocalion A 5052 and Silvertone 3047 (credited to George Hobson).

B 14918 Softly and Tenderly (credited to George Reneau). Also Vocalion B 5052 and Silvertone 3047 (credited to George Hobson).

A 14930 The New Market Wreck (credited to George Reneau). Also Vocalion B 5054 and Silvertone 3052 (credited to George Hobson).

B 14930 The Bald-Headed End of the Broom (credited to George Reneau). Also Vocalion B 5054 and Silvertone 3052 (credited to George Hobson).

A 14946 I've Got the Railroad Blues (credited to George Reneau). Also Vocalion A 5055.

B 14946 Birmingham (credited to George Reneau). Also Vocalion B 5055.

A 15046 My Redeemer (credited to George Reneau; vocal by Reneau). Also Vocalion A 5064.

B 15046 We're Floating Down the Stream of Time (credited to George Reneau; vocal by Reneau). Also Vocalion B 5064.

1925

Victor

19585-A When My Sugar Walks Down the Street (w. Aileen Stanley and Nat Shilkret & His Orchestra).

19599-A The Only, Only One for Me (w. Nat Shilkret & His Orchestra).

19599-B I Never Knew How Much I Love You (w. Nat Shilkret & His Orchestra).

19625-A Yearning (Just for You). Also Zonophone 3880.

19625-B No Wonder (That I Love You). Also Zonophone 3880.

19637-A Way Down Home (w. Carson Robison).

19638-A The Flapper Wife (w. Nat Shilkret & His Orchestra a.k.a. International Novelty Orchestra).

19649-A Joanna (w. International Novelty Orchestra).

19649-B Nora Lee (w. International Novelty Orchestra).

19656-A Everything Is Hotsy Totsy Now (w. Billy "Yuke" Carpenter).

19656-B Yes Sir, That's My Baby (w. Billy "Yuke" Carpenter).

19677-A Let It Rain, Let It Pour. Also Zonophone 3901.

19677-B What a Life (When No One Loves You). Also Zonophone 3901.

19857-A Save Your Sorrow (w. Nat Shilkret).

19864-B I Never Knew.

19899-A Sleepy Time Gal (w. Dave Franklin and May Singhi Breen). Also His Master's Voice EA 32.

19899-B Five Foot Two, Eyes of Blue (Has Anybody Seen My Girl?) (w. Dave Franklin and May Singhi Breen). Also His Master's Voice EA 32.

19928-B Sweet Child (I'm Wild about You) (w. Dave Franklin). Also His Master's Voice B 2293 and EA 30.

19950-B How I Love Her and She Loves Me Is Nobody's Business (w. Dave Franklin). Also Canadian Victor 19953-B and His Master's Voice B 2350.

20030-B My Bundle of Love. Also His Master's Voice B 2359.

Vocalion

A 14991 The Prisoner's Song (credited to George Reneau; vocal by Reneau). Also Vocalion A 5056 and Silvertone 3045 (credited to George Hobson).

B 14991 The Lightning Express (credited to George Reneau). Also Vocalion B 5056 and Silvertone 3045 (credited to George Hobson).

A 14997 Rock All Our Babies to Sleep (credited to George Reneau). Also Vocalion A 5057 and Silvertone 3044 (credited to George Hobson).

B 14997 Little Rosewood Casket (credited to George Reneau). Also Vocalion B 5057 and Silvertone 3044 (credited to George Hobson).

A 14998 Wild Bill Jones (credited to George Reneau; vocal by Reneau). Also Vocalion A 5058 and Silvertone 3046 A (credited to George Hobson).

B 14998 The Letter Edged in Black (credited to George Reneau; vocal by Reneau). Also Vocalion B 5058 and Silvertone 3046 B (credited to George Hobson).

A 14999 Wild and Reckless Hoboes (credited to George Reneau; vocal by Reneau). Also Vocalion A 5059.

B 14999 Woman's Suffrage (credited to George Reneau; vocal by Reneau). Also Vocalion B 5059.

1926

Victor

19968-B Behind the Clouds. Also His Master's Voice B 2345.

20044-A Ya Gotta Know How to Love. Also His Master's Voice B 2350.

20044-B Bye Bye, Blackbird. Also His Master's Voice B 2345 and Sunbeam P-507 (LP).

20084-A Tamiami Trail (w. Frank Banta). Also His Master's Voice B 2349.

20084-B But I Do—You Know I Do (w.

Frank Banta). Also His Master's Voice B
2349.

20107-B Here I Am (w. Frank Banta). Also
His Master's Voice EA 142.

20143-A For My Sweetheart. Also His Master's Voice EA 127.

20143-B Me Too. Also His Master's Voice B
2359.

20336-B Some Day (w. Nat Shilkret and the
Victor Orchestra).

20371-A To-night You Belong to Me. Also
His Master's Voice B 2442 and EA 142.

20371-B It Made You Happy When You
Made Me Cry. Also His Master's Voice B
2442.

20397-A I've Got the Girl (w. Abel Baer).
Also His Master's Voice B 2422.

20411-A (I've Grown So Lonesome) Thinking of You (w. Abel Baer). Also His Master's Voice AM 743 and B 2441.

20411-B Sunday (W. Abel Baer). Also His
Master's Voice B 2432.

20478-A Everything's Made for Love (w. Art
Fowler). Also His Master's Voice B 2455.

20673-A When the Moon Shines Down
upon the Mountain (credited to pseudonym Bill Collins).

1927

Bluebird

B-6815-B Yesterday.

B-7751-A Ain't She Sweet (w. Nat Shilkret & His Orchestra). Also Montgomery
Ward M-7061-B.

Victor

20561-A Forgive Me (w. Nat Shilkret & His
Orchestra). Also His Master's Voice EA
208.

20561-B Someday Sweetheart (w. Abel Baer).
Also His Master's Voice EA 208 and Sunbeam P-507 (LP).

20568-A Ain't She Sweet? (w. Nat Shilkret & His Orchestra). Also His Master's
Voice B 2488 and EA 185.

20568-B What Do I Care What Somebody Said? Also His Master's Voice B 2488 and EA 275.

20569-A Muddy Water. Also His Master's Voice B 2529.

20569-B My Idea of Heaven (Is to Be in Love with You). Also His Master's Voice B 2515 and EA 185.

20673-B Cindy (credited to pseudonym Bill Collins).

20716-A C'est Vous (It's You) (w. Jacques Renard and His Orchestra). Also His Master's Voice B 5349.

20730-A One Sweet Letter from You (w. Abel Baer).

20730-B Yesterday. Also Bluebird B-7751-A, Electrola E.G. 723, His Master's Voice B 2564, and AM 919.

20964-A My Blue Heaven (w. Herb Borodkin, Milton Rettenberg, and Bob McGimsey). Also Electrola E.G. 753, Victor 24573-A, His Master's Voice B 2644 and EA 262, and RCA Victor 47-1510 (45 rpm).

20964-B Are You Thinking of Me To-night? Also His Master's Voice B 2644 and EA 262.

20977-A Are You Happy? (w. Nat Shilkret & His Orchestra). Also His Master's Voice B 2642 and EA 261.

20977-B The Sweetheart of Sigma Chi. Also Bluebird B-6815-A, Montgomery Ward M-7061-A, and His Master's Voice B 2642 and EA 261.

21015-A There's a Cradle in Carolina (w. Nat Shilkret & His Orchestra). Also His Master's Voice EA 275.

21015-B My Melancholy Baby (w. Nat Shilkret & His Orchestra). Also Victor 24640-B.

21080-B Nothin' (w. Nat Shilkret and the Victor Orchestra). Also His Master's Voice B 5429 and EA 344.

21098-A The Lonesome Road. Also His Master's Voice B 3018 and EA 550.

1928

Bluebird

B-7751-B The Dream Girl of Pi K.A. (w. orchestra) Victor 21329-A Tomorrow. Also His Master's Voice EA 350.

21329-B So Tired. Also His Master's Voice EA 350.

21334-A Ramona (w. Viola Klaiss and orchestra). Also Victor 24573-B, RCA Victor WPT-6, 599-9114, and EPA 5132 (all RCA releases are 45 rpm; the latter two are promotional).

21334-B Girl of My Dreams (w. Bob Mc-Gimsey, Nat Shilkret & His Orchestra). Also His Master's Voice B 2852 and EA 341.

21374-A Without You, Sweetheart. Also His Master's Voice EA 360.

21374-B In My Bouquet of Memories (w. Nat Shilkret & His Orchestra). Also His Master's Voice B 2789 and EA 360.

21454-A Just Like a Melody Out of the Sky (w. Nat Shilkret & His Orchestra). Also His Master's Voice B 2803 and EA 394.

21454-B I Can't Do without You (w. Nat Shilkret and band). Also His Master's Voice B 2803.

21545-A Memories of France (w. Nat Shilkret and His Orchestra). Also His Master's Voice EA 413.

21545-B Old Pals Are the Best Pals after All (w. Nat Shilkret & His Orchestra). Also His Master's Voice EA 413.

21564-A Jeannine (I Dream of Lilac Time) (w. Nat Shilkret & His Orchestra). Also His Master's Voice B 2854 and EA 400.

21564-B Then Came the Dawn (w. orchestra). Also His Master's Voice B 2854 and EA 427.

21714-A St. Louis Blues (w. orchestra, including Glenn Miller, Benny Goodman, and Del Staigers). Also Bluebird B-6863-A.

21714-B The Voice of the Southland. Also Electrola E.G. 1149, His Master's Voice B 2904 and EA 482.

21779-A Sonny Boy (w. orchestra). Also His Master's Voice EA 451.

21779-B (I Got a Woman, Crazy for Me) She's Funny That Way (w. orchestra). Also His Master's Voice EA 451.

21798-A I Can't Give You Anything but Love (w. Nat Shilkret & His Orchestra). Also His Master's Voice EA 470.

21798-B I Wonder If You Miss Me Tonight (w. Nat Shilkret & His Orchestra). Also His Master's Voice B 2953 and EA 470.

21827-A Sentimental Baby (w. Ben Pollack and His Park Central Orchestra). Also La Voce del Padrone R 14070 and Zonophone EE 144.

21833-A Carolina Moon (w. Andy Sannella and orchestra). Also His Master's Voice B 2995, RCA Victor WPT-6 and 27-0015 (45 rpm).

21833-B I Wish I Had Died in My Cradle (before I Grew Up to Love You). Also His Master's Voice B 3294.

21916-A The Dream Girl of Pi K.A. (w. orchestra).

21916-B My Sorority Sweetheart (w. orchestra).

1929

Bluebird

B-7557-A A Garden in the Rain (w. Nat Shilkret & His Orchestra).

Victor

21856-A Weary River (w. Nat Shilkret & His Orchestra). Also Special Exploitation Record, His Master's Voice B 2995 and EA 512.

21856-B The Song I Love (w. Nat Shilkret &

His Orchestra). Also His Master's Voice EA 512.

21893-A Wedding Bells Are Breaking Up That Old Gang of Mine (w. Smalle, Dick Robertson, and Leonard Joy & His Orchestra). Also His Master's Voice B 3063 and EA 527.

21893-B That's What I Call Heaven (w. Leonard Joy & His Orchestra). Also His Master's Voice B 3063.

21915-A Dream Mother (w. Nat Shilkret & His Orchestra). Also His Master's Voice B 3077 and EA 547.

21915-B A Garden in the Rain (w. Nat Shilkret & His Orchestra). Also His Master's Voice EA 547.

21952-A Little Pal (w. Nat Shilkret & His Orchestra). Also His Master's Voice B 3113 and EA 590.

21952-B Why Can't You? (w. Nat Shilkret & His Orchestra). Also His Master's Voice B 3113 and EA 590.

22033-A Maybe!—Who Knows? (w. Leonard Joy & His Orchestra). Also His Master's Voice B 3117 and EA 593.

22033-B I've Got a Feeling I'm Falling (w. Leonard Joy & His Orchestra). Also His Master's Voice B 3117 and EA 593.

22068-A Ain't Misbehavin' (w. Leonard Joy & His Orchestra). Also His Master's Voice B 3185.

22068-B Peace of Mind (w. Leonard Joy & His Orchestra). Also His Master's Voice B 3201.

22128-A How Am I to Know? (w. Nat Shilkret & His Orchestra). Also His Master's Voice B 3255 and EA 698.

22128-B Please Come Back to Me (w. Nat Shilkret & His Orchestra). Also His Master's Voice B 3255 and EA 645.

22223-A My Fate Is in Your Hands (w. Fats Waller and Leonard Joy & His Orchestra). Also His Master's Voice B 3297.

22223-B All That I'm Asking Is Sympathy (w. Leonard Joy & His Orchestra). Also His Master's Voice B 3297 and EA 698.

1930

Victor

22299-A St. James' Infirmary (w. Leonard Joy & His Orchestra). Also Bluebird B-6863-B.

22299-B After You've Gone (w. Leonard Joy & His Orchestra). Also Alberti Special Record L.24635, His Master's Voice EA 1376, and Victor 24640-A.

22341-A To My Mammy (w. Leonard Joy & His Orchestra). Also His Master's Voice B 3502 and EA 804.

22341-B Let Me Sing and I'm Happy (w. Leonard Joy & His Orchestra). Also His Master's Voice B 3502 and EA 803.

22416-A Under a Texas Moon (w. Leonard Joy & His Orchestra). Also His Master's Voice EA 764.

22416-B Telling It to the Daisies (w. Leonard Joy & His Orchestra).

22451-A Absence Makes the Heart Grow Fonder for Somebody Else (w. Leonard Joy & His Orchestra).

22451-B Rollin' Down the River (w. Leonard Joy & His Orchestra). Also His Master's Voice B 3572.

22490-A When They Changed My Name to a Number (w. Leonard Joy & His Orchestra).

22490-B For Sweethearts Only (w. Leonard Joy & His Orchestra).

22518-A Nobody Cares If I'm Blue (w. Leonard Joy & His Orchestra). Also His Master's Voice B 3690.

22527-A If I Could Be with You (One Hour To-Night) (w. Nat Shilkret & His Orchestra).

22527-B This Side of Paradise (w. Nat Shilkret & His Orchestra).

22539-A A Vision of Virginia (w. Andy Sannella). Also His Master's Voice EA 832.

22539-B Alabama Lullaby (w. Andy Sannella). Also His Master's Voice EA 832.

22601-A You're Driving Me Crazy (What
Did I Do?) (w. Leonard Joy & His Orchestra). Also His Master's Voice B 3762.

22601-B Crying Myself to Sleep (w. Leonard
Joy & His Orchestra). Also His Master's
Voice B 3762.

1931

Bluebird

B-7557-B Please Don't Talk about Me When
I'm Gone.

Hit of the Week

L3 Now That You're Gone (Ahora que ya te
fuiste) (w. Hit of the Week Orchestra).

Perfect

2760 A Faded Summer Love/Goodnight
Sweetheart (w. orchestra). Also Banner
32291, Conqueror 7903, Oriole 2355, and
Romeo 1729; a different version of each
song was released on Apex 41441, Royal
91227, Sterling 91227, Domino 51017, and
Ace 51017.

12790 The Lonesome Road (w. orchestra).
Also Banner 32385, Oriole 2418, Romeo
1805.

15513 What Is It?/Who Am I? (w. orchestra). Also Banner 32259, Conqueror 7820,
Oriole 2333, Romeo 1703, Apex 41399,
Crown 91197, Sterling 291197, Domino
51001, Ace 351001, Decca F-2619/F-2686,
and Imperial 2627 ("Who Am I?" only).

15514 Maybe It's the Moon/How's Your
Uncle? (w. orchestra). Also Banner 32256,
Conqueror 7853, Oriole 2335, Apex
41400, Crown 91198, Sterling 291198,
Royal 391198, Domino 51001, Ace 351001,
and Decca F-2686/F-2619.

15521 If I Didn't Have You/In a Dream (w.
orchestra). Also Banner 32281, Oriole
2345, Romeo 1716, Apex 41419, Sterling

291205, Domino 51012, Ace 351012, and Imperial ("If I Didn't Have You" only).

15526 Guilty/Blue Kentucky Moon (w. orchestra; actually Ed Kirkeby's orchestra). Also Banner 32285, Oriole 2352, Romeo 1721, Apex 41425, Crown 91211, Sterling 291211, Royal 391211, Domino 51014, Sun 251014, and Ace 351014; "Guilty" coupled with releases by other artists on Imperial 2617 and Melotone 12245 (Canadian).

15542 Lies/I'm Sorry Dear (w. orchestra). Also on Banner 32325, Oriole 2380, Rome 1752, Sterling 91235, Royal 91235, Domino 51024, and Ace 51024.

Victor

22635-A When Your Lover Has Gone (w. Leonard Joy & His Orchestra). Also His Master's Voice B 3903.

22635-B Please Don't Talk about Me When I'm Gone. Also His Master's Voice B 3936.

22687-A Now You're in My Arms (w. Leonard Joy & His Orchestra).

22687-B If You Should Ever Need Me (w. Leonard Joy & His Orchestra).

22739-A Without That Gal (w. Nat Shilkret & His Orchestra). Also His Master's Voice B 3922.

22739-B I'm Thru with Love (w. Nat Shilkret & His Orchestra). Also His Master's Voice B 3922.

22806-A Blue Kentucky Moon. Also HMV EA 969.

22806-B Love Letters in the Sand. Also HMV B 3997 and EA 969.

22891-B Mood Indigo (w. Nat Shilkret & His Orchestra). Also His Master's Voice N 4251.

1932

Perfect

12862 Just a Little Home for the Old Folks (A Token from Me)/A Little Street

Where Old Friends Meet (w. members of Dorsey Brothers Orchestra). Also Banner 32614, Conqueror 8081, Melotone M 12529, Oriole 2595, Melotone 91450, Crown 91450, and Decca F-3332/F-3392.

12901 A Ghost of a Chance/When I Was a Boy from the Mountains (and You Were a Girl from the Hills) (w. members of Dorsey Brothers Orchestra). Also Banner 32729, Melotone M 12658, Oriole 2673, Romeo 2046, and Decca F-3332/F-3392.

1933

Perfect

12963 Did You Ever See a Dream Walking?/ Build a Little Home (w. Candy Candido and Otto "Coco" Heimel). Also Banner 32920, Conqueror 8260, Melotone M 12864, Oriole 2808, Romeo 2181, Melotone 91687, and F-3861/F-3933.

12968 Easter Parade/Everything I Have Is Yours (w. orchestra, including Jimmy Dorsey, Joe Venuti, Candy and Coco). Also Banner 32935, Oriole 2816, Romeo 2189, Melotone M 12878 and 91685; "Everything I Have Is Yours" also available on Conqueror 8263, Rex 8110, and Decca F-3861.

13044 Dear Old Southland/Jam House Blues (w. Candy and Coco). Also Banner 33172, Melotone M 13139, Oriole 2974, Romeo 2384, and Melotone 91845; "Dear Old Southland" also available on Decca F-3933.

1934

Victor

24663-A Ridin' around in the Rain (w. Candy Candido and Otto "Coco" Heimel). Also His Master's Voice N 4337.

24663-B All I Do Is Dream of You (w. Otto "Coco" Heimel and Arthur "Monk" Hazel). Also His Master's Voice EA 1376.

24725-A Blue Sky Avenue (w. Otto "Coco" Heimel and Leo Dunham).

24725-B When the Roll Is Called by the Fireside (w. Otto "Coco" Heimel and Leo Dunham).

Vocalion

2833 Kingfish Blues/New Orleans (w. Candy and Coco; Austin plays piano only). Also Brunswick 500506 ("New Orleans" coupled with "Bugle Call Rag"); "Candy" is Leo Dunham.

2849 China Boy/Bugle Call Rag (w. Candy and Coco; Austin plays piano only). Also Brunswick 500506 ("Bugle Call Rag" coupled with "New Orleans"); "Candy" is Leo Dunham.

1936

Decca

904 A Until Today (w. Victor Young and His Orchestra).

904 B When I'm with You (w. Victor Young and His Orchestra). Also Decca F-6091.

926 A If I Had My Way (w. Victor Young and His Orchestra).

926 B I Cried for You (w. Victor Young and His Orchestra). Also Decca F-6091.

1937

Decca

1578 A Thrill of a Lifetime (w. Bob Mitchell). Also Panachord 26031.

1578 B Marie (w. Bob Mitchell). Also Panachord 25997.

1656 A Dear Old Southland (w. Candy and Coco). Also Panachord 26027.

1656 B China Boy (w. Candy and Coco). Takes A and C both issued under this number.

3102 A Paradise Isle (w. Sam Koki and His Islanders). Also Decca 3102 (Canadian).

3102 B Down Where the Trade Winds Blow (w. Sam Koki and His Islanders). Also Decca 3102 (Canadian).

Panachord	26027 China Boy (w. Candy and Coco). Take C only.

1938

Bluebird	B-7557-A A Garden in the Rain; remastering of March 13, 1929, recording.
	B-7557-B Please Don't Talk about Me; remastering of February 5, 1931, recording.
Decca	1832 A Music, Maestro, Please! (w. orchestra). Also Panachord 25997.
	1832 B I'm in a Mellow Mood (w. orchestra). Also Panachord 26031.

1941

Decca	3939 A Tonight You Belong to Me (w. instrumental accompaniment).
	4175 A If I Could Be with You (One Hour Tonight) (w. instrumental accompaniment). Also Coral 60050 A.
	4175 B Forgive Me (w. instrumental accompaniment).

1942

Decca	3939 B Carolina Moon (w. instrumental accompaniment).
	4333 A My Blue Heaven (w. instrumental accompaniment).
	4333 B Yesterday (w. instrumental accompaniment).
	4354 A Ramona (w. instrumental accompaniment). Also Coral 60050 B.
	4354 B Jeannine (I Dream of Lilac Time) (w. instrumental accompaniment).

1945

4 Star	1010 Frankie and Johnny/Gene Austin Blues.
	1011 My Blue Heaven/But I'm Alright.
	1057 Melancholy Baby/Wrong Kind of Man.

1058 Someday Sweetheart/Here It Is Springtime.

1947

Austin

GA 501/GA 502 Keep a Knocking/Sweetheart of Sigma Chi (w. Otto Heimel and Red Wootten).

GA 503/GA 504 You're Gonna Cause Me Trouble/My Blue Heaven (w. Otto Heimel and Red Wootten). A copy has never been located; its existence is purely speculative.

GA 505/GA 506 Melancholy Baby/Lonesome Road (w. Otto Heimel and Red Wootten).

GA 507/GA 508 Under the Spell of the Voodoo Drum/Ain't Misbehavin' (w. Otto Heimel and Red Wootten).

GA 501/GA 505 Keep a Knocking/My Melancholy Baby (w. Les Paul). "Keep a Knocking" also on Universal U-100 and Musicana 7012.

GA 502/GA 504 Sweetheart of Sigma Chi/My Blue Heaven (w. Les Paul). "My Blue Heaven" also on Universal U-100 and Musicana 7012.

GA 503/GA 506 You're Gonna Cause Me Trouble/Lonesome Road (w. Les Paul).

GA 509/GA 510 Broken Dreams/Ace in the Hole (w. Les Paul). "Ace in the Hole" (edited version) also on Universal DF-1007, London 567 and L567.

London

566 Hush Little Darling/Git Along (w. the Meadowlarks).

London

567 Ace in the Hole/I'm Crying Just for You (w. Les Paul Trio). Also London L567 "Ace in the Hole," an edited version of GA 510.

Universal

U-100 My Blue Heaven/Keep a Knockin' (w. Les Paul and rhythm accompaniment). Also Musicana 7012, Austin GA 504 ("My Blue Heaven"), and GA 501

("Keep a Knockin' "). All issues other than Austin label have electronic reverberation added.

U-122 Cala-California/Yearning (w. Les Paul and the Honeydreamers). Also Musicana 7016.

U-130 T-E-X-A-S Spells Texas/Dream on Little Plowboy (w. rhythm accompaniment). Also Universal Double Feature DF 2009.

U-131 Give Me a Home in Oklahoma/I'm Coming Home (w. rhythm accompaniment).

U-141 Don't Hang Around/Dream on Little Plowboy (B-side same as U-130).

Universal Double Feature

DF 1006 My Blue Heaven/Lonesome Road (w. Sammy Porfirio's Orchestra). Also Fraternity F-779 (45 rpm release).

DF 1007 Ace in the Hole/Frankie and Johnnie (w. Les Paul). "Ace in the Hole" an edited version of Austin GA 510.

DF 2008 Sunflower/Careless Hands (w. Sammy Porfirio's Orchestra).

1953

RCA

EPA-4057 Ramona/She's Funny That Way/I'm in the Mood for Love/The Sweetheart of Sigma Chi/Sleepy Time Gal/My Blue Heaven (EP) (w. George Barnes and Frank Carroll). Also RCA EPB-3200, RCA RCX-113, RCA 547-0346 (selections 1–3), and RCA 547-0347 (selections 4–6).

EPB-3200 Lonesome Road/Someday Sweetheart/Who/How Come You Do Me Like You Do?/One Sweet Letter from You/I Can't Give You Anything but Love (EP) (w. George Barnes and Frank Carroll). Also RCA 547-0346 (selections 4–6) and RCA 547-0347 (selections 1–3).

1957

RCA

20-6880 Too Late/That's Love (w. orchestra directed by Charles Grean). Also RCA 47-6880 (45 rpm release).

20-6969 A Porter's Love Song to a Chamber Maid/I Could Write a Book (orchestra directed by Charles Grean). Also RCA 47-6969 (45 rpm release).

20-7117 Wonder/I'm Not the Braggin' Kind (w. orchestra directed by Charles Grean). Also RCA 47-7117 (45 rpm release); "I'm Not the Braggin' Kind" also on RCA EPA-1-1547 (45 rpm).

EPA-1-1547 Memories of You/Where the Shy Little Violets Grow/Take Your Shoes Off Baby (45 rpm release).

1958

RCA

20-7237 Sweetheart of De Molay/The Sunshine of Your Smile (w. orchestra and chorus directed by Charles Grean). Also RCA 47-7237 (45 rpm release).

1960

Dot

160 My Blue Heaven/Ramona (w. Billy Vaughn Orchestra). Also Goldies P-2699 (45 rpm releases).

1967

Professional recording session producing stereo master tape; not issued on disk (w. vocal and instrumental accompaniment).

St. Louis Blues (3:04 min.).

Evergreen Lady of Spring (1:43 min.).

You're Gonna Cause Me Trouble (2:33 min.); duet with Mona Clark.

Lazy Lou'siana Moon (2:10 min.).

Chopsticks (2:08 min.).

Moanin' Low (2:31 min.).

Can't Help Lovin' That Man of Mine (1:44 min.); vocal by Mona Clark.

How Come You Do Me Like You Do? (2:23 min.); duet with Mona Clark.

See You When Your Troubles Get Like Mine (2:45 min.).

Nobody's Sweetheart Now (1:30 min.).

After You've Gone (1:47 min.).

Long-Playing Records

Decca	DL 8433 *My Blue Heaven* (195?). Reissue of Decca material.
Dot	DLP-3300 *Gene Austin's Great Hits* (w. orchestra directed by Billy Vaughn). Also Dot DLP-25300 (stereo).
Fraternity	F-1006 *Gene Austin and His Lonesome Road* (1957. Reissue of Universal material.
RCA	LPM-1547 *Restless Heart* (w. orchestra directed by Charles Grean) (1957).
	LPM-2490 *My Blue Heaven* (1962). Reissue of Victor material.
	LPM-3200 *My Blue Heaven* (w. George Barnes and Frank Carroll) (1953); 10-inch disk.
	VPM-6056 *This Is Gene Austin* (1972). Recorded May 9, 1961, at Western Recorders, Hollywood.
Sunbeam	P-507 *Old Pals Are the Best Pals* (1978). Reissue of Victor material.
Vik	LVA-1007 *All-Time Favorites by Gene Austin* (1955?). Same as "X" LVA-1007.
	LX-998 *All-Time Favorites by Gene Austin* (1957). Same as "X" LVA-1007.
"X"	LVA-1007 *Gene Austin Sings All-Time Favorites* (1955). Reissue of Victor material.

Radio Transcriptions

Standard Program Library R109 (w. Candy and Coco). Recorded August 1935.

A 498 Why Do I Love You? ("Show Boat")
A 499 Stormy Weather ("Cotton Club Parade")
A 500 Sometimes I'm Happy ("Hit the Deck")
A 501 Sally ("Sally")
A 502 Lonesome Road
A 503 Solitude
A 504 Old Rocking Chair
A 505 Don't Leave Me Daddy

Standard Program Library R110 (w. Candy and Coco). Recorded July 1935, nos. 1–4; August 1935, nos. 5–9.

A-476 Honeysuckle Rose
A-477 I Kiss Your Hand Madame
A-478 I'm Coming Virginia
A 479 My Blue Heaven
A 506 Riverside Drive
A 507 Yearning
A 508 Remember

A 509 New Orleans

A 510 You're More Than Love

Standard Program Library R111 (w. Candy and Coco). Recorded October 1935.

A 543 Smoke Rings

A-544 Fair Weather Mama

A 545 Who ("Sunny")

A-546 The Two of Us

A-551 Smoke Gets in Your Eyes ("Roberta")

A 552 Someday Sweetheart

A 553 Pretty Is as Pretty Does

A 554 Git Along

Standard Program Library R112 (w. Candy and Coco). Recorded October 1935.

A-555 Sleepy Time Gal

A-556 Voodoo Drums

A-557 Sweetheart of Sigma Chi

A-558 Some of These Days

Thesaurus Record 377 (Nathaniel Shilkret Orchestra/vocals by Felix Knight and Gene Austin); recorded c. May 1937.

Red Mill Valley Medley (vocal by Knight)

Spanish Serenade

I'm a Rockin' in the Saddle (vocal by Austin)

Indian Summer

Thesaurus Record 408 (Nathaniel Shilkret Orchestra/vocals by Yvonne Doran, Gene Austin and Felix Knight); recorded c. May 1937.

Sweet Adeline Medley (vocals by Doran and Austin)

Blue Danube

Then You'll Remember Me (vocal by Knight)

Zigeuner

Thesaurus Record 414 (Nathaniel Shilkret Orchestra/vocals by Gene Austin and Felix Knight); recorded c. May 1937; reissued as Thesaurus Record 414-775.

Somebody Loves Me (vocal by Austin)

If I Should Send a Rose (vocal by Knight)

Fleurette

Cuban Serenade

Standard Program Library R121 (w. Candy and Coco). Recorded August 11, 1938.

I'm Coming Home

I Fell Down and Broke My Heart

Rootin' Tootin' Shootin' Man from Texas

Song of the Saddle

Why Can't I Be Yours Tonight? (nos. 1–5 from "Songs and Saddles")
I'm in a Mellow Mood
One Sweet Letter from You
Forgive Me
Standard Program Library R-122 (w. Candy and Coco). Recorded August 11, 1938.
Dear Old Southland
Stardust
I Cried for You
Tomorrow
Muddy Water
If I Had My Way
The Meanest Gal in Town
The Last Round Up (from "Ziegfeld Follies")
Thesaurus Record 636 (w. Candy and Coco). Allegedly recorded February 27, 1939.
Sleepytime Gal
I Wonder Who's Kissing Her Now
I'm Getting Sentimental over You
Blue Sky Avenue
Thesaurus Record 651 (w. Candy and Coco). Allegedly recorded February 27, 1939.
I'm Coming Home
I Fell Down and Broke My Heart
Why Can't I Be Your Sweetheart Tonight?
Song of the Saddle
Thesaurus Record 683 (w. Candy and Coco). Allegedly recorded February 27, 1939.
Smoke Rings
Sweetheart of Sigma Chi
Tomorrow
I Cried for You
Thesaurus Record 704 (w. Candy and Coco). Allegedly recorded February 27, 1939.
My Blue Heaven
Melancholy Baby
Girl of My Dreams
Then Came the Dawn
Thesaurus Record 709 (w. Candy and Coco). Allegedly recorded February 27, 1939.
Marie
Old Fashioned Love
Lonesome Road
Yearning

Naval Air Reserve Show #19 (w. George Barnes and His Octet), c. 1948.
  I Can't Give You Anything but Love (vocal by the Five Singing
    Honeydreamers)
  My Blue Heaven (vocal by Austin)
  I Surrender Dear (vocal by the Five Singing Honeydreamers)
  Goose Pimples (instrumental)
  Treasury Department "Guest Star" No. 563 (w. Del Sharbutt and Harry
    Sosnik and His Orchestra), c. 1957
  Exactly Like You (w. Harry Sosnik and His Orchestra)
  Medley: I Thought about You/How Come You Do Me Like You Do?/
    Bye Bye Blackbird (w. guitar, string bass, and drums
    accompaniment)
  Medley: I'm Not the Braggin' Kind/Lonesome Road/My Blue Heaven
    (w. guitar, string bass and drums accompaniment)
  Lullaby of Broadway (w. Harry Sosnik and His Orchestra)

Compact Discs

Living Era   CD AJA5217 *Gene Austin: The Voice of the Southland* (1996).
              Recordings date from the 1925–1936 period.
Take Two   TT 414CD *Gene Austin: A Time to Relax* (1995); 20 of Austin's
              best-known hits recorded between 1925 and 1936; in-
              cludes "Album Notes" by Randy Skretvedt.

CHAPTER 2—RUSS COLUMBO

78 RPM Recordings

1930

Victor   22546 A Peach of a Pair (credited to Gus Arnheim and His
              Orchestra). Also His Master's Voice B 5953.

1931

Victor   22801 Guilty/I Don't Know Why (I Just Do) (w. orchestra).
              Also His Master's Voice B 3997/B 4042.
              22802 You Call It Madness (but I Call It Love) (w. orches-
              tra)/Sweet and Lovely (w. Nat Shilkret and His Orches-
              tra). Also Bluebird B 6503 and His Master's Voice B
              3984/His Master's Voice B 3984 and Victor 27635.

22826 Good Night, Sweetheart/Time on My Hands (w. Nat Shilkret & His Orchestra). Also Victor 27636/Bluebird B 6503.

22861 You Try Somebody Else/Call Me Darling (Call Me Sweetheart, Call Me Dear) (w. Leonard Joy and His Orchestra). Also Victor 27634.

22867 Where the Blue of the Night (Meets the Gold of the Day) (w. Leonard Joy and His Orchestra)/Prisoner of Love (w. Nat Shilkret and His Orchestra). Also His Master's Voice B 4079 and Victor 27637/His Master's Voice B 4079 and Victor 27635.

22903 Save the Last Dance for Me/All of Me (w. Leonard Joy and His Orchestra). Also Victor 27634 (Save the Last Dance for Me).

1932

Victor

22909 You're My Everything/Just Friends (w. Leonard Joy and His Orchestra).

22976 Paradise/Auf Wiedersehen, My Dear (w. Leonard Joy and His Orchestra). Also Victor 27636/Victor 27637.

24045 Just Another Dream of You/Living in Dreams (w. orchestra).

24076 As You Desire Me/The Lady I Love (w. orchestra). Also His Master's Voice B 6265 (As You Desire Me).

24077 My Love/Lonesome Me (w. orchestra).

24194 Street of Dreams/Lost in a Crowd (w. orchestra).

24195 Make Love the Thing/I Called to Say Goodnight (w. orchestra).

1934

Brunswick

6972 When You're in Love/Let's Pretend There's a Moon (w. Jimmie Grier and His Orchestra). Also Decca F-5405/ Decca F-5596.

Decca

F-5405 When You're in Love/Too Beautiful for Words (w. Jimmie Grier and His Orchestra).

5001S Too Beautiful for Words/I See Two Lovers (w. Jimmie Grier and His Orchestra). Also released on Special Editions label.

1941

RCA

Songs Made Famous by the Golden Voice of Russ Columbo (78-album set, culled from the October 1931–April 1932 sessions).

45 RPM Recordings

RCA/Collector's Record #3 You Call It Madness/My Time Is Your Time (Rudy Vallee) (a mail-in promotion with the purchase of Halo Shampoo, dating from the late 1950s/early 1960s).

Long-Playing Albums/Cassettes

Bluebird	CPL1-1756(e) *Russ Columbo—A Legendary Performer* (1977). Includes: Just Friends; Where the Blue of the Night; All of Me; Time on My Hands; Save the Last Dance for Me; Auf Wiedersehen, My Dear; Paradise; I Don't Know Why; You Call It Madness; Prisoner of Love; Just Another Dream of You; My Love.
Bronco Gegund	[Russ Columbo air checks] (variation of Totem 1031 LP).
Golden Legends	2000/1 *The Films of Russ Columbo* (consists of songs from Columbo's last three films, as well as the complete transcription of his short *That Goes Double.*
Pelican LP	141 *Russ Columbo—Prisoner of Love* (from the June–November 1932 Victor sessions).
RCA	LPL1-1798 *Russ Columbo: A Legendary Performer* (1976).
	LPT-5 *Columbo, Crosby and Sinatra* (196?).
	LSA 3066 *Love Songs by Russ Columbo* (1972). Includes: Call Me Darling; Sweet and Lovely; Just Friends; Where the Blue of the Night; You Try Somebody Else; You're My Everything; All of Me; Time on My Hands; Save the Last Dance for Me; Auf Wiedersehen, My Dear; Paradise.
	LVA-1002 *Love Songs by Russ Columbo* (195?). Also released in the 1950s (with different cover artwork) as LX-996 and LPM-2072.
Russ Columbo Archives	*Gone but Not Forgotten: 51 Great Songs by the Romantic Voice of Russ Columbo* (4-album set).
Sandy Hook	2006 *Russ Columbo* (1978). Includes: Peach of a Pair; Street of Dreams; The Lady I Love; I Call to Say Goodnight; I Don't

Know Why; I See Two Lovers; You Call It Madness; Lonesome Me; My Love; Lost in a Crowd; Make Love the King; Guilty; Prisoner of Love; Goodnight Sweetheart.

2038 *Russ Columbo on the Air*—1933–34 (1980) Air checks similar to Totem 1031 LP; includes: More Than You Know; Time on My Hands; You're My Past, My Present and My Future; Coffee in the Morning; Lover; You Call It Madness; The House Is Haunted; Time on My Hands; Easy Come, Easy Go; With My Eyes Wide Open I'm Dreaming; Stardust; True; Rolling in Love; I've Had My Moments; I'm Not Lazy, I'm Dreaming.

Totem   1031 *Russ Columbo on the Air* (consists of air checks from Columbo's 1934 radio program).

Zodiac   ZR3003 *Russ Columbo—Broadcasts & Movies, 1932–34* (cassette) (1980). Broadcasts: You Call It Madness; Who; Time on My Hands; I've Got to Pass Your House; You're My Past, My Present and My Future; Coffee in the Morning; Lover; Poor Folks; I've Had My Moments; I'm Not Lazy, I'm Dreaming. Movies: Broadway thru a Keyhole; Wake Up and Dream (excerpts).

Compact Discs

Living Era (Great Britain)   *Prisoner of Love* (1997).
Take Two   *Russ Columbo: Save the Last Dance for Me* (1994).

CHAPTER 3—BING CROSBY

According to Crosby's leading discographer, J. Roger Osterholm, the singer recorded more than 2,200 songs (many as duplicates; over 1,600 individual songs in all), spanning a period of 52 years. In contrast, Elvis Presley—Crosby's closest rival in total record sales (both were reputed to have about 500 million disks as of 1994) and one of his many stylistic imitators (31 Crosby songs were reinterpreted by the King of rock 'n' roll)—cut 500-odd songs through 24 years.

Countless anthologies including one or more Crosby tracks have been issued in every disk format. Only those releases with contents substantially given over to Crosby material have been considered for inclusion in this listing.

45 RPM and 78 RPM Recordings

1926

Columbia   142785 I've Got the Girl (w. Don Clarke Biltmore Hotel Orchestra).

Victor   37285 Wistful and Blue (w. Paul Whiteman & His Orchestra).

1927

Victor   20418 Lonely Eyes (w. Paul Whiteman Chorus)/Wistful and Blue (featuring Paul Whiteman & His Orchestra; w. Al Rinker).

20508 Muddy Water (featuring Paul Whiteman & His Orchestra).

20513 That Saxophone Waltz (featuring Paul Whiteman & His Orchestra; w. Al Rinker, Charles Gaylord, Jack Fulton, and Austin Young).

20627 Side by Side (featuring Paul Whiteman & His Orchestra; w. the Rhythm Boys)/Pretty Lips (featuring Paul Whiteman & His Orchestra; w. Al Rinker).

20646 I'm in Love Again (featuring Paul Whiteman & His Orchestra; w. Al Rinker, Charles Gaylord, Jack Fulton, and Austin Young).

20679 Magnolia (w. The Rhythm Boys).

20683 Shanghai Dream Man (featuring Paul Whiteman & His Orchestra; w. Al Rinker, Charles Gaylord, Jack Fulton, and Austin Young).

20751 I'm Coming, Virginia (featuring Paul Whiteman & His Orchestra; w. the Rhythm Boys).

20783 Ain't She Sweet—Sweet Lil/I Left My Sugar Standing in the Rain—Mississippi Mud (w. the Rhythm Boys). Also Victor 24240.

20828 My Blue Heaven (featuring Paul Whiteman & His Orchestra; w. Jack Fulton, Charles Gaylord, Austin Young, and Al Rinker).

20882 The Calinda (Boo-Joom, Boo-Joom, Boo!) (featuring Paul Whiteman & His Orchestra; w. Jack Fulton, Charles Gaylord, and Austin Young).
20883 Five Step/It Won't Be Long Now (w. The Rhythm Boys).
20973 Missouri Waltz (featuring Paul Whiteman & His Orchestra: w. Al Rinker, Charles Gaylord, Jack Fulton, and Austin Young).

1928

Columbia　1401 Evening Star (featuring Paul Whiteman & His Orchestra).
1402 Constantinople/Get Out and Get under the Moon (w. Paul Whiteman Chorus).
1441 Because My Baby Don't Mean Maybe Now (featuring Paul Whiteman & His Orchestra).
1444 'Tain't So, Honey, 'Tain't So (featuring Paul Whiteman & His Orchestra)/That's My Weakness Now (w. the Rhythm Boys).
1448 Chiquita/Lonesome in the Moonlight (w. Paul Whiteman Chorus).
1455 That's Grandma/Wa Da Da (w. The Rhythm Boys).
1465 I'm on the Crest of a Wave (featuring Paul Whiteman & His Orchestra; w. Jack Fulton, Charles Gaylord, and Austin Young).
1492 Georgie Porgie (w. Paul Whiteman Chorus).
1496 I'd Rather Cry over You (featuring Paul Whiteman & His Orchestra).
1505 Out of Town Gal (featuring Paul Whiteman & His Orchestra; w. the Rhythm Boys).
50070 La Paloma (w. Paul Whiteman Chorus).
50098 Silent Night, Holy Night/Christmas Melodies (featuring Paul Whiteman & His Orchestra).
Okeh　40979 Mississippi Mud (w. Frank Trumbauer).
Victor　21103-A Changes (featuring Paul Whiteman & His Orchestra; w. Al Rinker, Harry Barris, Jack Fulton, Charles Gaylord, and Austin Young). Also Victor 25370.
21103-B Mary (featuring Paul Whiteman & His Orchestra). Also Victor 26415.
21104 Miss Annabelle Lee (w. the Rhythm Boys).
21218 Ol' Man River/Make Believe (featuring Paul Whiteman & His Orchestra). Also Victor 25249.

21240 Sunshine (featuring Paul Whiteman & His Orchestra; w. Al Rinker, Jack Fulton, Charles Gaylord, and Austin Young).

21274 Mississippi Mud/From Monday On (featuring Paul Whiteman & His Orchestra; w. Al Rinker, Jack Fulton, Charles Gaylord, and Austin Young; Irene Taylor and Harry Barris also on "Mississippi Mud"). Also Victor 25366 (Mississippi Mud), 25368 and 27688 (From Monday On).

21302 What Price Lyrics? (w. the Rhythm Boys). Also Victor 24349.

21315 March of the Musketeers (featuring Paul Whiteman & His Orchestra; w. Al Rinker, Charles Gaylord, Jack Fulton, Austin Young, and Cullen).

21365 I'm Wingin' Home (featuring Paul Whiteman & His Orchestra; w. Al Rinker, Charles Gaylord, Jack Fulton, and Austin Young).

21389-A I'm Afraid of You (featuring Paul Whiteman & His Orchestra). Also Victor 27685.

21389-B My Pet (featuring Paul Whiteman & His Orchestra; w. Al Rinker, Charles Gaylord, and Jack Fulton).

21398 You Took Advantage of Me (featuring Paul Whiteman & His Orchestra; w. Jack Fulton, Charles Gaylord, and Austin Young)/Do I Hear You Saying? (featuring Paul Whiteman & His Orchestra; w. Al Rinker and Charles Gaylord). Also Victor 25369 (You Took Advantage of Me).

21431 Dancing Shadows (featuring Paul Whiteman & His Orchestra; w. Al Rinker, Charles Gaylord, and Jack Fulton).

21438 Louisiana (featuring Paul Whiteman & His Orchestra; w. Jack Fulton, Charles Gaylord, and Austin Young). Also Victor 25369.

21453 It Was the Dawn of Love (featuring Paul Whiteman & His Orchestra; w. Al Rinker, Charles Gaylord, and Austin Young).

21464 There Ain't No Sweet Man (featuring Paul Whiteman & His Orchestra). Also Victor 25675.

21678 Grieving (featuring Paul Whiteman & His Orchestra; w. Al Rinker, Charles Gaylord, and Jack Fulton).

35934 Metropolis, Part Three (w. Paul Whiteman Chorus).

35992 High Water (featuring Paul Whiteman & His Orchestra). Also Victor 36186.

36199 Mississippi Mud (featuring Paul Whiteman & His Orchestra; w. the Rhythm Boys). Also Victor 39000 and
67200.

39003 Let 'Em Eat Cake (w. Paul Whiteman Chorus).

1929

Columbia   1629 My Suppressed Desire/Rhythm King (featuring Paul
Whiteman & His Orchestra; w. the Rhythm Boys).

1683 Makin' Whoopee (featuring Paul Whiteman & His Orchestra; w. Jack Fulton, Charles Gaylord, and Austin
Young).

1694 I'll Get By/Rose of Mandalay (w. Ipana Troubadours).

1755 Coquette/My Angeline (w. Paul Whiteman & His Orchestra).

1771 Louise (featuring Paul Whiteman & His Orchestra).

1773 Till We Meet Again/My Kinda Love.

1819 Louise/So the Bluebirds and the Blackbirds Got Together (w. the Rhythm Boys).

1822 Reaching for Someone (featuring Paul Whiteman & His
Orchestra).

1844 Your Mother and Mine (featuring Paul Whiteman &
His Orchestra; w. Al Rinker and Harry Barris).

1845 Orange Blossom Time/Your Mother and Mine (featuring Paul Whiteman & His Orchestra).

1851 Baby, Oh Where Can You Be?/I Kiss Your Hand, Madame.

1862 S'posin' (featuring Paul Whiteman & His Orchestra).

1877 Little Pal/I'm in Seventh Heaven (featuring Paul Whiteman & His Orchestra).

1945 Oh Miss Hannah (featuring Paul Whiteman & His Orchestra).

1974 Waiting at the End of the Road (featuring Paul Whiteman & His Orchestra).

1993 At Twilight (featuring Paul Whiteman & His Orchestra).

2001-A Gay Love. Also Velvetone 2536, Clarion 5476, Harmony 1428, and Diva 3428.

2001-B Can't We Be Friends?

2010 (I'm a Dreamer) Aren't We All?/If I Had a Talking Pic-
ture of You (featuring Paul Whiteman & His Orchestra;
Jack Fulton, Al Rinker, and Harry Barris also on ''[I'm a
Dreamer] Aren't We All?'').

2023 Great Day (featuring Paul Whiteman & His Orchestra).

2023 Great Day/Without a Song (featuring Paul Whiteman & His Orchestra).

Okeh   41181 Let's Do It/The Spell of the Blues (w. Dorsey Brothers).

41188 If I Had You (w. Sam Lanin's Orchestra)/My Kinda Love (w. Dorsey Brothers).

41228 I'm Crazy over You/Susanna (w. Sam Lanin's Orchestra).

1930

Columbia   2047 A Bundle of Old Love Letters (featuring Paul Whiteman & His Orchestra).

2098 After You've Gone (featuring Paul Whiteman & His Orchestra).

2163 Song of the Dawn.

2164 A Bench in the Park/Happy Feet (featuring Paul Whiteman & His Orchestra).

2170 I Like to Do Things for You (featuring Paul Whiteman & His Orchestra; w. the Rhythm Boys).

2171 You Brought a New Kind of Love to Me/Living in the Sunlight, Loving in the Moonlight (featuring Paul Whiteman & His Orchestra).

2223 A Bench in the Park (w. The Rhythm Boys).

2224 Sittin' on a Rainbow (w. Paul Whiteman Chorus).

50070 La Golondrina (w. Paul Whiteman Chorus).

Victor   22528 Three Little Words (w. Duke Ellington and the Rhythm Boys). Also Victor 25076.

22561 It Must Be True/Fool Me Some More (featuring Gus Arnheim and His Orchestra). Also Victor 25280 (It Must Be True).

22580 Them There Eyes/The Little Things in Life (featuring Gus Arnheim & His Orchestra; w. the Rhythm Boys). Also Bluebird 7102 (The Little Things in Life).

1931

Brunswick   6090 Out of Nowhere/If You Should Ever Need Me. Also Brunswick 80043.

6120 Just One More Chance/Were You Sincere? (w. Victor Young's Orchestra). Also Brunswick 80044 (Just One More Chance).

6140 I'm Through with Love/I Found a Million-Dollar Baby. Also Brunswick 80045.

6145 At Your Command/Many Happy Returns of the Day. Also Brunswick 80058.

6159 Star Dust/Dancing in the Dark.

6169 Dancing in the Dark/Star Dust. Also Brunswick 80056.

6179 I Apologize/Sweet and Lovely. Also Brunswick 80057 (1944).

6200-A Now That You're Gone. Also Brunswick 80044.

6200-B A Faded Summer Love. Also Brunswick 80055.

6203 Too Late/Good Night, Sweetheart (w. Victor Young's Orchestra). Also Brunswick 80046.

20102 Gems from "George White's Scandals" (w. Mills Brothers, Boswell Sisters, and the Victor Young Orchestra).

20105 St. Louis Blues (w. Duke Ellington). Also Columbia 55003).

20106 Face the Music Medley, Part One.

20109 Lawd, You Made the Night Too Long (w. Don Redman).

Victor   22618 I Surrender, Dear (featuring Gus Arnheim & His Orchestra). Also Victor 25280.

22691 Ho Hum!/I'm Gonna Get You (featuring Gus Arnheim & His Orchestra; w. Loyce Whiteman).

22700 One More Time/Thanks to You (featuring Gus Arnheim & His Orchestra).

22701-A Just a Gigolo (w. Harry Barris and members of Gus Arnheim's Orchestra). Also Bluebird 7118.

22701-B Wrap Your Troubles in Dreams (w. Harry Barris and members of Gus Arnheim's Orchestra). Also Bluebird 7102.

24078 Poor Butterfly (featuring Paul Whiteman & His Orchestra; w. Al Rinker, Charles Gaylord, Jack Fulton, and Austin Young).

1932

Brunswick   6226 Where the Blue of the Night (Meets the Gold of the Day)/I'm Sotty, Dear.

6240 Dinah/Can't We Talk It Over? (w. Mills Brothers). Also Brunswick 6485.

6248 Snuggled on Your Shoulder (Cuddled in Your Arms)/I Found You.

6259 Starlight/How Long Will It Last?

6268 Love, You Funny Thing!/My Woman.

6276 Shadows in the Window/Shine (w. Mills Brothers). Also Brunswick 6485 and Columbia 4305-M (Shine).

6285 Paradise/You're Still in My Heart.

6306 Happy-Go-Lucky You and Broken Hearted Me/Lazy Day (w. Isham Jones's Orchestra).

6320-A Sweet Georgia Brown (w. Isham Jones's Orchestra). Also Brunswick 6635, Vocalion 2867, Melotone 13127, Romeo 2336, Conqueror 8363 and 9551, Okeh 2867, Banner 33160, Perfect 13034, Oriole 2962, and Lucky 60010.

6320-B Let's Try Again (w. Isham Jones's Orchestra).

6329 Cabin in the Cotton/With Summer Coming On (w. Lennie Hayton's Orchestra).

6351-A Love Me Tonight.

6351-B Some of These Days (w. Lennie Hayton's Orchestra). Also Vocalion 2869, Melotone 13130, Okeh 2869, Conqueror 8366 and 9551, Brunswick 635, Lucky 60010, Banner 33163, Perfect 13037, Oriole 2965, Columbia 4305-M, and Romeo 2339.

6394 Please/Waltzing in a Dream (w. Anson Weeks's Orchestra).

6406 How Deep Is the Ocean/Here Lies Love. Also Columbia 4301 (How Deep Is the Ocean).

6414 Brother, Can You Spare a Dime?/Let's Put Out the Lights (w. Lennie Hayton's Orchestra).

6427 I'll Follow You/Some Day We'll Meet Again.

1933

Brunswick 6454 Just an Echo in the Valley/ (I Don't Stand) A Ghost of a Chance with You.

6464 Street of Dreams/It's within Your Power.

6472 You're Getting to Be a Habit with Me/Young and Healthy (w. Guy Lombardo & His Royal Canadians).

6477 You're Beautiful Tonight, My Dear (w. Guy Lombardo & His Royal Canadians).

6480-B Try a Little Tenderness.

6491 I've Got the World on a String/Linger a Little Longer in the Twilight. Also Columbia 4301-M (I've Got the World on a String).

6515 You've Got Me Crying Again/What Do I Care, It's Home.

6525-B My Honey's Lovin' Arms (w. Mills Brothers). Also Columbia 4304-M.

6533-A Someone Stole Gabriel's Horn (w. Dorsey Brothers). Also Melotone 13170, Perfect 13055, Banner 33203, Vocalion 2879 and 4522, Oriole 2998, Okeh 2879 and 4522, Conqueror 8417, and Romeo 2372.

6533-B Stay on the Right Side of the Road (w. Dorsey Brothers). Also Melotone 13169, Banner 33202, Vocalion 4522, Romeo 2371, Conqueror 8416 and 9557, Perfect 13054, Oriole 2997, and Okeh 4522.

6594 Learn to Croon/Moonstruck (w. Jimmie Grier's Orchestra).

6599-A I've Got to Sing a Torch Song (w. Jimmie Grier's Orchestra).

6599-B Shadow Waltz (w. Jimmie Grier's Orchestra). Also Melotone 13136, Conqueror 8372 and 9553, Okeh 2877, Banner 33169, Romeo 2345, Vocalion 2877, Perfect 13043, and Oriole 2971.

6601-A Down the Old Ox Road (w. Jimmie Grier's Orchestra). Also Melotone 13135, Columbia 4303, Romeo 2344, Conqueror 8371, Banner 33168, Perfect 13042, and Oriole 2970.

6601-B Blue Prelude (w. Jimmie Grier's Orchestra). Also Vocalion 2868, Melotone 13128, Conqueror 8364 and 9553, Romeo 2337, Okeh 2868, Banner 33161, Perfect 13035, and Oriole 2963.

6610 There's a Cabin in the Pines/I've Got to Pass Your House to Get to My House.

6623 My Love/I Would If I Could, but I Can't (w. Jimmie Grier's Orchestra).

6643-A Thanks (w. Jimmie Grier's Orchestra). Also Columbia 4303-M, Vocalion 2870, Melotone 13131, Okeh 2870 and 33164, Conqueror 8367, Perfect 13038, Oriole 2966, Banner 33164, Romeo 2340, and Silvertone 8367.

6643-B Black Moonlight (w. Jimmie Grier's Orchestra). Also Melotone 13127, Vocalion 2867, Conqueror 8364 and 9553, Romeo 2336, Okeh 2867, Banner 33160, Perfect 13034, and Oriole 2962.

6644-A The Day You Came Along (w. Jimmie Grier's Orchestra). Also Vocalion 2830, Melotone 13132, Columbia 8368, Romeo 2341, Okeh 2830, Banner 33165, Perfect 13039, and Oriole 2967.

6644-B I Guess It Had to Be That Way. Also Melotone

13165, Banner 33198, Perfect 13050, Oriole 2993, Okeh 2878, Conqueror 8412, and Romeo 2367.

6663-A The Last Round-Up (w. Lennie Hayton's Orchestra). Also Columbia 4302-M, Vocalion 2879, Okeh 2879, Banner 33203, Perfect 13055, Oriole 2998 Melotone 13170, Conqueror 8417, and Romeo 2372.

6663-B Home on the Range (w. Lennie Hayton's Orchestra). Also Columbia 4302-M, Melotone 13131, Vocalion 2870, Lucky 60003, Romeo 2340, Okeh 2870, Conqueror 8367, Banner 33164, Perfect 13038, and Oriole 2966.

6694-A Beautiful Girl (w. Lennie Hayton's Orchestra). Also Melotone 3132, Conqueror 8368, Romeo 2341, Okeh 2830, Banner 33165, Perfect 13039, Oriole 2967, and Vocalion 2830.

6694-B After Sundown. Also Melotone 13135, Conqueror 8371, Romeo 2344, Banner 33168, Perfect 13042, and Oriole 2970.

6695-A Temptation (w. Lennie Hayton's Orchestra). Also Melotone 13136, Okeh 2877, Banner 33169, Romeo 2345, Perfect 13043, Oriole 2971, Conqueror 8372, and Vocalion 2877.

6695-B We'll Make Hay while the Sun Shines (w. Lennie Hayton's Orchestra). Also Vocalion 2868, Melotone 13128, Romeo 2337, Conqueror 9557 and 8364, Okeh 2868, Banner 33161, Perfect 13035, and Oriole 2963.

6696-A Our Big Love Scene. Also Melotone 13133, Banner 33166, Romeo 2342, Conqueror 8369, Perfect 13040, and Oriole 2968.

6696-B We're a Couple of Soldiers My Baby And Me. Also Melotone 13129, Banner 33162, Romeo 2338, Conqueror 8365, Perfect 13036, and Oriole 2964.

6724-A Did You Ever See a Dream Walking? (w. the King's Men).

6724-B Let's Spend an Evening at Home. Also Vocalion 2869, Melotone 13130, Conqueror 8366, Okeh 2869, Banner 33163, Perfect 13037, Oriole 2965 and Romeo 2339.

1934

Brunswick 6794-A Little Dutch Mill (w. Jimmie Grier's Orchestra). Also Melotone 13133, Conqueror 8369, Romeo 2342, Banner 33166, Perfect 13040, and Oriole 2968.

6794-B Shadows of Love. Also Melotone 13134, Conqueror

8370, Okeh 2834, Banner 33167, Romeo 2343, Perfect 13041, Oriole 2969, and Vocalion 2834.

6852-A Love Thy Neighbor (w. Nat Finston's Orchestra). Also Okeh 2845, Banner 33201, Perfect 13053, Oriole 2996, Melotone 13168, Vocalion 2845, Conqueror 8415, and Romeo 2370.

6852-B Ridin' around in the Rain (w. Jimmie Grier's Orchestra). Also Melotone 13167, Okeh 2835, Banner 33200, Romeo 2369, Perfect 13052, Oriole 2995, Vocalion 2835, and Conqueror 8414.

6853-A May I? (w. Nat Finston's Orchestra). Also Melotone 13167, Okeh 2835, Banner 33200, Perfect 13052, Conqueror 8414, Romeo 2369, Oriole 2995, and Vocalion 2835.

6853-B She Reminds Me of You (w. Jimmie Grier's Orchestra). Also Melotone 13168, Okeh 2845, Banner 33201, Romeo 2370, Perfect 13053, Oriole 299, Vocalion 2845, and Conqueror 8415.

6854-A Good Night, Lovely Little Lady. Also Melotone 13134, Okeh 2834, Romeo 2343, Banner 33167, Perfect 13041, Oriole 2969, Vocalion 2834, and Conqueror 8370.

6854-B Once in a Blue Moon (w. Nat Finston's Orchestra). Also Melotone 13129, Conqueror 8365, Banner 33162, Perfect 13036, Romeo 2338, and Oriole 2964.

6936-A Love in Bloom (w. Irving Aaronson's Orchestra). Also Melotone 13165, Romeo 2367, Okeh 2878, Vocalion 2878, Banner 33198, Perfect 13050, Conqueror 8412, and Oriole 2993.

6936-B Straight from the Shoulder (w. Irving Aaronson's Orchestra). Also Melotone 13169, Banner 33202, Perfect 13054, Oriole 2997, Conqueror 8416, and Romeo 2371.

6953 I'm Hummin'—I'm Whistlin'—I'm Singin'/Give Me a Heart to Sing To (w. Irving Aaronson's Orchestra). Also Melotone 13166, Banner 33199, Perfect 13051, Oriole 2994, and Romeo 2368.

Decca 100 I Love You Truly/Just a Wearyin' for You.

101 Let Me Call You Sweetheart/Someday Sweetheart.

179 The Moon Was Yellow (and the Night Was Young)/The Very Thought of You (w. George Stoll Orchestra).

245 Two Cigarettes in the Dark/The Sweetheart Waltz.

309 With Every Breath I Take/Maybe I'm Wrong Again (w. George Stoll Orchestra).

310 June in January/Love Is Just Around the Corner (w. George Stoll Orchestra).

1935

Decca 391-A (Swanee River) Old Folks at Home. Also Decca 18804.

391-B It's Easy to Remember (w. the Rhythmettes & Three Shades of Blue/George Stoll Orchestra). Also Decca 3731-B.

392 Soon/Down by the River (w. George Stoll Orchestra).

543 I Wished on the Moon/Two for Tonight (w. Dorsey Brothers Orchestra).

547 I Wish I Were Aladdin/From the Top of Your Head (w. Dorsey Brothers Orchestra).

548 Without a Word of Warning/Takes Two to Make a Bargain (w. Dorsey Brothers Orchestra).

616 Red Sails in the Sunset/Boots and Saddle (w. Victor Young's Orchestra). Also Decca 2677-A (Boots and Saddle).

617 On Treasure Island/Moonburn (w. Joe Sullivan and Victor Young's Orchestra).

621 Silent Night, Holy Night (w. Guardsmen Quartet and Victor Young's Orchestra).

631 My Heart and I/Sailor Beware.

1936

Decca 756 Lovely Lady/Would You? (w. Victor Young's Orchestra).

757 The Touch of Your Lips/Twilight on the Trail (w. Victor Young's Orchestra). Also Decca 2677-B.

791 We'll Rest at the End of the Trail/Robins and Roses (w. Victor Young's Orchestra). Also Decca 2678-A.

806 It Ain't Necessarily So/I Got Plenty of Nuttin' (w. Victor Young's Orchestra).

870 Empty Saddles/Roundup Lullaby (w. the Guardsmen and Victor Young's Orchestra).

871 I'm an Old Cowhand/I Can't Escape from You (w. Jimmy Dorsey & His Orchestra). Also Decca 2679 (I'm an Old Cowhand).

880 Song of the Islands/Aloha Oe (Farewell to Thee) (w. Dick McIntyre & His Harmony Hawaiians)

886 Hawaiian Paradise/South Sea Island Magic (w. Dick McIntyre & His Harmony Hawaiians).

905 Shoe Shine Boy/The House Jack Built for Jill. Also Decca 3601-A (Shoe Shine Boy).

907 A Fine Romance/The Way You Look Tonight (w. Dixie Lee Crosby). Also Decca 23681.

912 Me and the Moon/Beyond Compare (w. Victor Young & His Orchestra).

947 Pennies from Heaven/Let's Call a Heart a Heart (w. George Stolle & His Orchestra). Also Decca 25230.

948 So Do I/One, Two, Button Your Shoe (w. George Stoll & His Orchestra). Also Decca 25232.

1044 Just One Word of Consolation/Dear Old Girl (w. the Three Cheers).

1937

Decca

175 Sweet Leilani/Blue Hawaii (w. Lani McIntyre & His Hawaiians).

1184 Sweet Is the Word for You/I Have So Little to Give You (for Love Alone) (w. Victor Young's Orchestra).

1185 Too Marvelous for Words/What Will I Tell My Heart? (w. Jimmy Dorsey & His Orchestra). Also Decca 25193 (Too Marvelous for Words).

1186 Moonlight and Shadows/I Never Realized (w. Victor Young's Orchestra).

1201 The One Rose (That's Left in My Heart)/Sentimental and Melancholy (w. Victor Young's Orchestra). Also Decca 3541-A (The One Rose).

1210 Never in a Million Years/In a Little Hula Heaven (w. Jimmy Dorsey & His Orchestra).

1234 My Little Buckaroo/What Is Love? (w. Victor Young's Orchestra). Also Decca 2679-B (My Little Buckaroo).

1301-A Peckin' (w. Jimmy Dorsey & His Orchestra).

1375 The Moon Got in My Eyes/(You Know It All) Smarty (w. John Scott Trotter's Orchestra).

1376 It's the Natural Thing to Do/All You Want to Do Is Dance (w. John Scott Trotter's Orchestra).

1451 Remember Me?/I Still Love to Kiss You Goodnight (w. John Scott Trotter's Orchestra). Also Decca 18866 (Remember Me?).

1462 Can I Forget You?/The Folks Who Live on the Hill (w. John Scott Trotter's Orchestra).

1483-B Bob White (Whatcha Gonna Swing Tonight?)/Basin Street Blues (w. Connee Boswell and John Scott Trotter's Orchestra).

1518 Sail Along, Silvery Moon/When You Dream about Hawaii (w. Lani McIntyre & His Hawaiians).

1938

Decca   554 When the Organ Played "Oh Promise Me"/Let's Waltz for Old Time's Sake (w. Eddie Dunstedter).

1565 There's a Gold Mine in the Sky/In the Mission by the Sea (w. Eddie Dunstedter). Also Decca 2678-B (There's a Gold Mine in the Sky).

1616 Dancing under the Stars/Palace in Paradise.

1648 On the Sentimental Side/My Heart Is Taking Lessons (w. John Scott Trotter's Orchestra). Also Decca 25233.

1649 Moon of Manakoora/This Is My Night to Dream (w. John Scott Trotter's Orchestra).

1794 Don't Be That Way/Little Lady Make-Believe. Also Decca 3603-B.

1819 Let Me Whisper I Love You (w. John Scott Trotter's Orchestra)/Sing Low, Sweet Chariot (w. Paul Taylor Choristers). Also Decca 3540-A.

1845 Sweet Hawaiian Chimes/Little Angel.

1874 When Mother Nature Sings Her Lullaby (w. Eddie Dunstedter)/Darling Nellie Gray (w. Paul Taylor Choristers). Also Decca 3540-B (Darling Nellie Gray).

1887-A Alexander's Ragtime Band (w. Connee Boswell, Eddie Cantor, and John Scott Trotter's Orchestra).

1887-B Home on the Range—True Confession (w. Connee Boswell and John Scott Trotter's Orchestra).

1888 Now It Can Be Told/It's the Dreamer in Me (w. John Scott Trotter's Orchestra).

1933 I've Got a Pocketful of Dreams/A Blues Serenade (w. John Scott Trotter's Orchestra). Also Decca 3543-A (A Blues Serenade).

1934 Don't Let That Moon Get Away/Laugh and Call It Love (w. John Scott Trotter's Orchestra).

1960 Mr. Crosby and Mr. Mercer/Small Fry (w. Johnny Mercer and Victor Young's Small Fryers). Also Decca 3600-A (Small Fry).

2001 Mexicali Rose/Silver on the Sage (w. John Scott Trotter's Orchestra).

2023 Without a Song (w. Paul Whiteman).

2123 My Reverie/Old Folks (w. Bob Crosby's Orchestra).

2147 You Must Have Been a Beautiful Baby/Summertime (w. Bob Crosby's Orchestra).

1939

Brunswick   6533 Someone Stole Gabriel's Horn (recorded March 14, 1933; w. Dorsey Brothers Orchestra).

Decca   2200 You're a Sweet Little Headache/Joobalai (w. John Scott Trotter's Orchestra).

2201 I Have Eyes/The Funny Old Hills (w. John Scott Trotter's Orchestra).

2237 It's a Lonely Trail (When You're Travelin' All Alone)/ When the Bloom Is on the Sage (w. John Scott Trotter's Orchestra).

2257-A Just a Kid Named Joe (w. John Scott Trotter's Orchestra). Also Decca 3601-B.

2257-B The Lonesome Road (w. John Scott Trotter's Orchestra). Also Decca 3541-B.

2273 I Cried for You/Let's Tie the Old For-Get-Me-Nots (w. John Scott Trotter's Orchestra). Also Decca 3542-A (I Cried for You).

2289 My Melancholy Baby/Between a Kiss and a Sigh (w. John Scott Trotter's Orchestra). Also Decca 3542-B.

2315 Ah! Sweet Mystery of Life/Sweethearts (w. Victor Young's Orchestra).

2316 I'm Falling in Love with Someone/Gypsy Love Song (w. Frances Langford).

2359 East Side of Heaven/Sing a Song of Sunbeams (w. John Scott Trotter's Orchestra).

2360 That Sly Old Gentleman (from Featherbed Lane)/Hang Your Heart on a Hickory Limb. Also Decca 3600-B (That Sly Old Gentleman).

2374 Deep Purple/Star Dust (w. Matty Malneck & His Orchestra). Also Decca 25285.

2385 Poor Old Rover (w. the Foursome)/Little Sir Echo (w. the Music Maids).

2400 God Bless America/The Star-Spangled Banner (w. Max Terr's Mixed Chorus and John Scott Trotter's Orchestra). Also Decca 23579.

2413 And the Angels Sing/S'posin' (w. the Music Maids and John Scott Trotter's Orchestra). Also Decca 3543.

2447 I'm Building a Sailboat of Dreams/Down by the Old Mill Stream.

2448 Whistling in the Wildwood (w. John Scott Trotter's Orchestra).

2494 Alla En El Rancho Grande/Ida, Sweet as Apple Cider (w. the Foursome and John Scott Trotter's Orchestra)

2535 I Surrender, Dear/It Must Be True. Also Decca 25229.

2626 (Ho-Die-Ay) Start the Day Right/Neighbors in the Sky (w. Connee Boswell and John Scott Trotter's Orchestra).

2640 An Apple for the Teacher (w. Connee Boswell and John Scott Trotter's Orchestra)/Still the Bluebird Sings. Also Decca 3602-A (An Apple for the Teacher).

2641 Go Fly a Kite/A Man and His Dream (w. John Scott Trotter's Orchestra).

2671 What's New?/Girl of My Dreams (w. John Scott Trotter's Orchestra). Also Victor 18866 (Girl of My Dreams).

2676 Home on the Range/Missouri Waltz.

2680 When You're Away/Thine Alone.

2700 Gus Edwards Medley/In My Merry Oldsmobile (w. the Music Maids). Also Decca 3602 (Gus Edwards Medley).

2775 My Isle of Golden Dreams/To You Sweetheart, Aloha (w. Dick McIntyre & His Harmony Hawaiians).

2800 Ciribiribin (They're So in Love)/Yodelin' Jive (w. Andrews Sisters and Joe Ventuti's Orchestra).

2874 Somebody Loves Me/Maybe.

1940

Decca

948-A Wrap Your Troubles in Dreams (w. Jimmy Dorsey and His Orchestra). Also Decca 25193.

2948-B Between 18th & 19th on Chestnut Street (w. Connee Boswell and John Scott Trotter's Orchestra).

2998 I'm Too Romantic/The Moon and the Willow Tree (w. John Scott Trotter's Orchestra).

2999 Sweet Potato Piper (w. the Foursome and John Scott Trotter's Orchestra)/Just One More Chance (w. John Scott Trotter's Orchestra).

3024 Tumbling Tumbleweeds/If I Knew Then (What I Know Now) (w. John Scott Trotter's Orchestra). Also Decca 4200-B.

3064 The Singing Hills/Devil May Care (w. John Scott Trotter's Orchestra). Also Decca 4200-A.

3098-A I Dream of Jeanie with the Light Brown Hair. Also Decca 18801.

3098-B The Girl with the Pigtails in Her Hair. Also Decca 3603.

3118-A Yours Is My Heart Alone. Also Decca 23716.

3118-B Beautiful Dreamer. Also Decca 18802.

3133 Sierra Sue/Marcheta (w. John Scott Trotter's Orchestra).

3161 I Haven't Time to Be a Millionaire/April Played the Fiddle (w. John Scott Trotter's Orchestra).

3162 The Pessimistic Character/Meet the Sun Half-Way (w. John Scott Trotter's Orchestra).

3182 On Behalf of the Visiting Firemen/Mister Meadowlark (w. Johnny Mercer and Victor Young's Orchestra).

3257 I'm Waiting for Ships That Never Come In/Cynthia.

3297/3298 Ballad for Americans (Four Parts). Also Decca DA 3554/3555.

3299 A Song of Old Hawaii/Trade Winds (w. Dick McIntyre's Orchestra).

3300 Only Forever/When the Moon Comes over Madison Square.

3309 That's for Me/Rhythm on the River.

3321 Can't Get Indiana Off My Mind/I Found a Million-Dollar Baby.

3354 Where the Blue of the Night (Meets the Gold of the Day) (w. ParadiseIsland Trio)/The Waltz You Saved for Me.

3388 Legend of Old California/Prairieland Lullaby.

3423 Do You Ever Think of Me?/You Made Me Love You (w. Merry Macs and Victor Young's Orchestra).

1941

Decca

3450 Please/You Are the One (w. John Scott Trotter's Orchestra).

3477 When I Lost You/When You're a Long Long Way from Home.

3565 Along the Santa Fe Trail/I'd Know You Anywhere (w. John Scott Trotter's Orchestra). Also Decca 4201 (Along the Santa Fe Trail).

3584 A Nightingale Sang in Berkeley Square/Lone Star Trail (w. John Scott Trotter's Orchestra). Also Decca 4201-B.

3590 New San Antonio Rose/It Makes No Difference Now (w. Bob Crosby's Orchestra). Also Decca 18766.

3609 Did Your Mother Come from Ireland?/Where the River Shannon Flows (w. the King's Men and Victor Young's Orchestra).

3614 Chapel in the Valley/When Day Is Done.

3636 It's Always You/You Lucky People You.

3637 You're Dangerous/Birds of a Feather.

3644 Dolores (w. Merry Macs and Bob Crosby's Bob Cats)/ De Camptown Races (w. the King's Men).

3689-B Yes Indeed/Tea for Two (w. Connee Boswell).

3731 With Every Breath I Take (w. the Rhythmettes and Three Shades of Blue).

3736 My Buddy/I Only Want a Buddy—Not a Sweetheart.

3797 Paradise Isle/Aloha Kuu Ipo Aloha (w. Paradise Island Trio).

3840 You and I/Brahms' Lullaby (Cradle Song) (w. John Scott Trotter's Orchestra).

3856 Be Honest with Me/Goodbye, Little Darlin', Goodbye (w. John Scott Trotter's Orchestra). Also Decca 18767 and 25231.

3886 'Til Reveille/My Old Kentucky Home (w. John Scott Trotter's Orchestra). Also Decca 18803.

3887 Pale Moon (w. Merry Macs)/Who Calls?.

3952 You Are My Sunshine/Ridin' Down the Canyon (w. Victor Young's Orchestra). Also Decca 18768.

3965 You're the Moment of a Lifetime (w. Floras Negras)/ No Te Importe Saber (Let Me Love You Tonight).

3970 The Waiter and the Porter and the Upstairs Maid/Birth of the Blues (w. Mary Martin and Jack Teagarden's Orchestra).

3971 The Whistler's Mother-In-Law/I Ain't Got Nobody (w. Muriel Lane and Woody Herman's Woodchoppers).

4000 Sweetheart of Sigma Chi/Dream Girl of Pi Kappa Alpha. Also Decca.

4033 Day Dreaming/Clementine (w. the Music Maids and Hal Hopper).

4064 Do You Care?/Humpty Dumpty Heart.

4065 Shepherd Serenade (w. W. Harry Sosnik's Orchestra)/ The Anniversary Waltz (w. Victor Young's Orchestra). Also Decca 23716 (Anniversary Waltz).

1942

Decca

4152 Oh! How I Miss You Tonight/Dear Little Boy of Mine.

4162 Deep in the Heart of Texas (w. Woody Herman's Woodchoppers)/Let's All Meet at My House (w. Muriel Lane and Woody Herman's Woodchoppers).)

4163-B Blue Shadows and White Gardenias.

4173 Sing Me a Song of the Islands/Remember Hawaii (w. Dick McIntyre & His Harmony Hawaiians).

4183 Blues in the Night/Miss You (w. John Scott Trotter's Orchestra).

4184 I Don't Want to Walk without You/Moonlight Cocktail (w. John Scott Trotter's Orchestra).

4193-A Skylark (w. John Scott Trotter's Orchestra).

4249 The Lamplighter's Serenade/Mandy Is Two (w. Victor Young's Orchestra).

4339 The Singing Sands of Alamosa/I'm Drifting Back to Dreamland.

4343 Conchita, Marquita, Lolita, Pepita, Rosita, Juanita Lopez/The Old Oaken Bucket.

4367 Hello, Mom/A Boy in Khaki—A Girl in Love.

18278 Lily of Laguna (w. Mary Martin)/Wait Till the Sun Shines, Nellie (w. Mary Martin, Jack Teagarden, and Bob Crosby's Bob Cats).

18316 I'm Thinking Tonight of My Blue Eyes/I Want My Mama. Also Decca 18769 (I'm Thinking Tonight of My Blue Eyes).

18354 Just Plain Lonesome/Got the Moon in My Pocket.

18360 Mary's a Grand Old Name/The Waltz of Memory (w. John Scott Trotter's Orchestra).

18371 When My Dreamboat Comes Home (w. John Scott Trotter's Orchestra).

18391 When the White Azaleas Start Blooming/Nobody's Darlin' but Mine (w. Victor Young's Orchestra). Also Decca 18770.

18424 Happy Holiday (w. the Music Maids)/Be Careful, It's My Heart (w. John Scott Trotter's Orchestra).

18425 Abraham/Easter Parade (w. Ken Darby Singers).

18426 I've Got Plenty to Be Thankful For/Song of Freedom (w. Ken Darby Singers).

18427 I'll Capture Your Heart (w. Fred Astaire and Margaret Lenhart)/Lazy.

18429 White Christmas (w. the Ken Darby Singers and John Scott Trotter's Orchestra)/Let's Start the New Year Right (w. Bob Crosby's Orchestra).

18432-A My Great, Great Grandfather.

18510-A Silent Night, Holy Night (w. Max Terr's Mixed Chorus).

18513-A Moonlight Becomes You.

18531-B Darling, Je Vous Aime Beaucoup.

18432-B The Bombadier Song (w. the Music Maids and Hal Hopper).

18510 Silent Night (w. Max Terr's Chorus and John Scott Trotter's Orchestra; reissued as #23777 in 1946).

18511 Faith of Our Fathers/God Rest Ye Merry Gentlemen (w. Max Terr's Mixed Chorus).

18513 Moonlight Becomes You/Constantly (w. John Scott Trotter's Orchestra).

18514 The Road to Morocco/Ain't Got a Dime to My Name.

18531-A I Wonder What's Become of Sally.

1943

Decca 8561 Sunday, Monday, or Always/If You Please (w. Ken Darby Singers).

18564 People Will Say We're in Love/Oh, What a Beautiful Mornin' (w. Trudy Erwin and the Sportsmen Glee Club).

18570 I'll Be Home for Christmas/Danny Boy (w. John Scott Trotter's Orchestra).

18580-A The Day after Forever. Also Decca 18704-B.

18580-B It Could Happen to You. Also Decca 23686.

23277 Pistol Packin' Mama/Victory Polka (w. Andrews Sisters and Vic Schoen & His Orchestra).

23281 Jingle Bells/Santa Claus Is Comin' to Town (w. Andrews Sisters and Vic Schoen's Orchestra).

1944

Decca 18586 Poinciana (Song of the Tree)/San Fernando Valley (w. John Scott Trotter's Orchestra).

18595 I Love You/I'll Be Seeing You (w. John Scott Trotter's Orchestra).

18597 Swinging on a Star/Going My Way (w. Williams Brothers Quartet and John Scott Trotter's Orchestra).

18608 Amor/Long Ago (and Far Away) (w. John Scott Trotter's Orchestra). Also Decca 23680.

18621 Too-Ra-Loo-Ra-Loo-Ra/I'll Remember April (w. John Scott Trotter's Orchestra). Also Decca 18704 (Too-Ra-Loo-Ra-Loo-Ra).

23350 Is You Is or Is You Ain't (Ma' Baby)/A Hot Time in the Town of Berlin (w. Andrews Sisters and Vic Schoen & His Orchestra).

23364 Don't Fence Me In/The Three Caballeros (w. Andrews Sisters and Vic Schoen & His Orchestra). Also Decca 23484 (Don't Fence Me In).

Victor 27685 Lovable (featuring Paul Whiteman and His Orchestra).

27688 That's Grandma (w. the Rhythm Boys).

1945

Decca   18635 Evelina/The Eagle and Me (w. Camerata's Orchestra).

18640 Sleigh Ride in July/Like Someone in Love (w. John Scott Trotter's Orchestra).

18644 Let's Take the Long Way Home/I Promise You.

18649 More and More/Strange Music.

18658 All of My Life/A Friend of Yours (w. John Scott Trotter's Orchestra).

18675 June Comes around Every Year/Out of This World.

18686 If I Loved You/Close as Pages in a Book (w. John Scott Trotter's Orchestra).

18690 On the Atchison, Topeka, and the Santa Fe/I'd Rather Be Me (w. Six Hits & a Miss and John Scott Trotter's Orchestra).

18705 Ave Maria/Home Sweet Home (w. Victor Young Choir).

18708 It's Been a Long, Long Time (w. the Les Paul Trio)/ Whose Dream Are You?

18720 Aren't You Glad You're You?/In the Land of Beginning Again (w. John Scott Trotter's Orchestra).

18721 The Bells of St. Mary's/I'll Take You Home Again, Kathleen.

18731-A Walking the Floor over You. Also Decca 18770.

18735 Symphony.

18743 It's Anybody's Spring/Welcome to My Dream.

18746 Day by Day/Prove It by the Things You Do (w. Mel Torme and His Mel-Tones).

18790 Personality/Would You?

18801 Nell and I.

18802 Sweetly She Sleeps, My Alice Fair.

18804 Old Black Joe.

18829 These Foolish Things/They Say It's Wonderful.

18860 You May Not Love Me.

18887 Just One of Those Things.

18898 Begin the Beguine/September Song. Also Decca 23754 (September Song).

23379 Ac-Cent-Tchu-Ate the Positive/There's a Fellow Waiting in Poughkeepsie (w. Andrews Sisters and Vic Schoen & His Orchestra).

23392 Just a Prayer Away/My Mother's Waltz (w. Ken Darby Singers and Victor Young's Orchestra).

23410 Yah-Ta-Ta, Yah-Ta-Ta (Talk, Talk, Talk)/You've Got Me

Where You Want Me (w. Judy Garland and Joseph Lilley's Orchestra).

23413 You Belong to My Heart/Baia (w. Xavier Cugat's Orchestra).

23417 My Baby Said Yes/Your Socks Don't Match (w. Louis Jordan & His Tympany Five).

23437 Good, Good, Good/Along the Navajo Trail (w. Andrews Sisters and Vic Schoen & His Orchestra).

23457 I Can't Begin to Tell You/I Can't Believe That You're in Love with Me (w. Carmen Cavallaro's Orchestra).

40000 Put It There, Pal/The Road to Morocco (w. Bob Hope).

1946

Decca

18735 Symphony/Beautiful Love (w. Victor Young's Orchestra).

18746 Day by Day (w. Mel Torme & His Mel-Tones and instrumental trio; recorded 1945).

18790 Personality (w. Eddie Condon's Orchestra).

18860 Just My Luck.

18829 They Say It's Wonderful (w. Jay Blackton's Orchestra).

18887 Night and Day.

18912 Early American/Iowa.

23469 Give Me the Simple Life/It's the Talk of the Town (w. Jimmy Dorsey's Orchestra).

23482 Mighty Lak' a Rose/The Sweetest Story Ever Told (w. the Song Spinners).

23495 McNamara's Band/Dear Ol Donegal (w. the Jesters and Bob Haggart & His Orchestra).

23508 Sioux City Sue/You Sang My Love Song to Somebody Else (w. the Jesters and Bob Haggart & His Orchestra).

23510 I'll Be Yours (J'Attendrai)/We'll Gather Lilacs.

23530 I've Found a New Baby/Who's Sorry Now.

23547 Haste Manana/Siboney.

23569 South America, Take It Away/Get Your Kicks on Route 66 (w. Andrews Sisters and Vic Schoen & His Orchestra).

23636 Baby, Won't You Please Come Home?/That Little Dream Got Nowhere.

23646 Cuba (w. Trudy Erwin).

23647 You Keep Coming Back Like a Song/Getting Nowhere (w. John Scott Trotter's Orchestra).

23648 Everybody Step/Serenade to an Old-Fashioned Girl.

23649 All by Myself/I've Got My Captain Working for Me Now.

23650 A Couple of Song and Dance Men (w. Fred Astaire).

23655 Sweet Lorraine/The Things We Did Last Summer.

23661 Gotta Get Me Somebody to Love/Pretending.

23678 Till the Clouds Roll By.

23679 Dearly Beloved/I've Told Every Little Star.

23680 All Through the Day.

23686 When You Make Love to Me.

1947

Decca

23739 A Gal in Calico/Oh but I Do (w. the Calico Kids).

23745 Among My Souvenirs/Does Your Heart Beat for Me?

23754 Temptation.

23784 So Would I.

23804 Connecticut/Mine (w. Judy Garland).

23819 Easter Parade (w. Victor Young's Orchestra).

23840 That's How Much I Love You/Rose of Santa Rosa (w. Bob Crosby's Orchestra).

23843 On the Sunny Side of the Street (w. Lionel Hampton).

23848 As Long as I'm Dreaming/Smile Right Back at the Sun.

23849 Country Style/My Heart Is a Hobo.

23850 Gotta Get Me Somebody to Love/What Am I Gonna Do about You? (w. Les Paul Trio)

23885 Tallahassee/Go West Young Man (w. Andrews Sisters and Vic Schoen & His Orchestra).

23954 I Do, Do, Do Like You/The Old Chaperone (w. the Skylarks).

23975 Feudin' and Fightin' (w. Bob Haggart & His Orchestra).

23990 Whiffenpoof Song/Kentucky Babe (w. Fred Waring's Glee Club).

23999 The Freedom Train (w. Andrews Sisters and Vic Schoen & His Orchestra)/The Star Spangled Banner (recitation).

24100 It Still Suits Me (w. Lee Wiley)/Kokomo, Indiana (w. the Skylarks).

24101 You Do/How Soon (Will I Be Seeing You?) (w. Carmen Cavallaro's Orchestra).

24114 After You've Gone/Blue (w. Eddie Condon).

24170 I Kiss Your Hand, Madame.

40012 Lullaby (from "Jocelyn")/Where My Caravan Has Rested (w. Jascha Heifetz).

40038 Alexander's Ragtime Band (EP; w. Al Jolson and Morris Stoloff's Orchestra).

40039 There's No Business Like Show Business (EP; w. Andrews Sisters, Dick Haymes, and Vic Schoen & His Orchestra). Includes "Anything You Can Do."

1948

Decca

24269 Pass the Peace Pipe/Suspense.

24273 Happy Birthday—Auld Lang Syne (w. Ken Darby Singers).

24278 Ballerina/Golden Earrings (w. John Scott Trotter's Orchestra).

24279 Now Is the Hour/Silver Threads among the Gold (w. Ken Darby Choir).

24282 You Don't Have to Know the Language/Apalachicola, Fla. (w. Andrews Sisters and Vic Schoen & His Orchestra).

24283 But Beautiful/The One I Love

24295 Galway Bay/My Girl's an Irish Girl (w. Victor Young's Orchestra).

24433 Blue Shadows on the Trail (w. Ken Darby Choir and Victor Young's Orchestra)/A Fella with an Umbrella.

24481 160 Acres (w. Andrews Sisters and Vic Schoen & His Orchestra).

1949

Decca

24524 If You Stub Your Toe on the Moon (w. the Rhythmaires).

24532 Far Away Places (w. Ken Darby Choir).

24609 Some Enchanted Evening/Bali Ha'i.

24616 Careless Hands (w. Ken Darby Singers and Perry Botkin's Orchestra).

24618 Riders in the Sky (w. Ken Darby Singers and Perry Botkin's Orchestra).

24798 Dear Hearts and Gentle People (w. Jud Conlon's Rhythmaires and Perry Botkin's Orchestra)/Mule Train (w. Perry Botkin's Orchestra).

24800 Way Back Home (w. Fred Waring's Pennsylvanians).

1950

Decca   24820 Have I Told You Lately That I Love You? (w. Andrews Sisters and Vic Schoen & His Orchestra).

24827 Quicksilver (w. Andrews Sisters and Vic Schoen & His Orchestra).

24863 Chattanoogie Shoe Shine Boy (w. Vic Schoen's Orchestra).

27018 I Didn't Slip—I Wasn't Pushed—I Fell (w. Sy Oliver's Orchestra & Aristokats).

27111 La Vie En Rose/I Cross My Fingers (w. Axel Stordahl's Orchestra).

27112 Play a Simply Melody/Sam's Song (credited to "Gary Crosby & Friend"; w. Matty Matlock's Orchestra).

27117 All My Love (w. Victor Young & His Orchestra).

27159 Rudolph, the Red-Nosed Reindeer (w. John Scott Trotter's Orchestra).

27219 Beyond the Reef/Harbor Lights (w. Lynn Murray's Orchestra).

27229 Silver Bells (w. Carol Richards).

40181 A Crosby Christmas (EP; w. Gary, Phillip, Dennis, and Lindsay Crosby).

1951

Decca   27239 A Marshmallow World (w. Sonny Burke's Orchestra).

27477 Sparrow in the Tree Top (w. Andrews Sisters and Vic Schoen & His Orchestra).

27577 When You and I Were Young, Maggie; Blues/Moonlight Bay (w. Gary Crosby).

27623 Gone Fishin' (w. Louis Armstrong).

27653 Shanghai.

27830 Domino (w. John Scott Trotter's Orchestra).

40839 There's No Business Like Show Business (w. Dick Haymes and Andrews Sisters).

1952

Decca   28255 Zing a Little Zong (w. Jane Wyman).

28265 Till the End of the World (w. Grady Martin & His Slew Foot Five).

28419 Cool Water/South Rampart St. Parade.

28470 You Don't Know What Lonesome Is/Open up Your Heart.

28511 Keep It a Secret/Sleighbell Serenade (w. Jud Conlon's Rhythmaires).

1953

Decca   28581 Hush-a-Bye/Mother Darlin'.
28733 Tenderfoot/Walk Me by the River.
28743 Granada/It Had to Be You.
28814 Mademoiselle De Paree/Embrasse Moi Ben-De.

1954

Decca   28955 Down by the Riverside (w. Gary Crosby)/What a Little Moonlight Can Do.
28969 Changing Partners (w. Jud Conlon's Rhythmaires)/ Y'All Come.
29024 Secret Love/My Love, My Love.
29054 Young at Heart/I Get So Lonely (w. Guy Lombardo & His Royal Canadians).
29147 Call of the South/Cornbelt Symphony (w. Gary Crosby).
29251 Count Your Blessings (Instead Of Sheep)/What Can You Do with a General (w. Joseph Lilley's Orchestra).
29357 Song from Desire/Who Gave You the Rose? (w. Alfred Newman & His Orchestra).

1955

Decca   29410 The Search Is Through/The Land around Us
29483 Farewell/Jim, Johnny & Jonas.
29568 All She Said Was "Unh Huh"/She's the Sunshine of Virginia.
29636 Angel Bells/Let's Harmonize.

1956

Capitol   3506 Now You Has Jazz (w. Louis Armstrong).
3507 True Love (w. Grace Kelly)/Well Dad You Evah? (w. Frank Sinatra).
Decca   29817 When You're in Love/John Barleycorn.
29850 In a Little Spanish Town (w. the Buddy Cole Trio).
29981 Swanee/Honeysuckle Rose (w. the Buddy Cole Trio).

1957

Decca   30262 Around the World (in Eighty Days).
Kapp   196 How Lovely Is Christmas.

1969

Amos   111 Hey Jude/Lonely Street.
               116 It's All in the Game/More & More.

1970

Daybreak   1001 And the Bells Rang/Time to Be Jolly.

78 RPM Album Sets

Brunswick   B-1012 *Bing Crosby, Volume 1.*
               B-1015 *Bing Crosby, Volume 2.*
Columbia   M-555 *Crosby Classics.*
Decca   A-10 *Music of Hawaii.* Crosby heard on two sides: "Song of
               the Islands" and "Aloha Oe."
               A-50 *Patriotic Songs for Children.* Crosby heard on two sides:
               "God Bless America" and "The Star-Spangle Banner."
               A-69 *Cowboy Songs.*
               A-96 *George Gershwin Popular Songs.* Crosby heard on two
               sides: "Maybe" and "Somebody Loves Me."
               A-134 *Ballad for Americans: In Four Parts.*
               A-140 *Favorite Hawaiian Songs.*
               A-159 *Christmas Music.* Crosby heard on two sides: "Silent
               Night, Holy Night" and "Adeste Fideles."
               A-181 *Star Dust.*
               A-193 *Hawaii Calls.* Crosby heard on two sides: "A Song of
               Old Hawaii" and "Trade Winds."
               A-202 *Small Fry.*
               A-221 *Crosbyana.*
               Under Western Skies.
               A-396 *Holiday Inn.*
               Merry Christmas.
               A-405 *Going My Way.* Includes a song not in the picture,
               "Home Sweet Home."
               A-410 Bells of St. Mary's. Includes a song not in the picture,
               "I'll Take You Home Again, Kathleen."

A-417 *Don't Fence Me In.* Also Decca A-559.

A-420 *The Happy Prince* (plays the Prince in Oscar Wilde's fairy tale).

A-423 *Road to Utopia.*

A-440 *Stephen Foster Songs.* Also Decca A-482.

A-453 *What So Proudly We Hail* (4 sides).

A-460 *Favorite Hawaiian Songs, Volume 1.*

A-461 *Favorite Hawaiian Songs, Volume 2.*

A-481 *Blue Skies.*

A-485 *Bing Crosby—Jerome Kern.*

A-505 *Victor Herbert Melodies.*

A-547 *El Bingo.*

A-553 *The Small One* (narrates Charles Tazewell's Christmas story).

A-578 *Bing Crosby—Drifting and Dreaming.*

A-621 *St. Valentine's Day—Bing Crosby.*

The Man without a Country (narrates the Edward Everett Hale story).

Victor P-4 Bix Beiderbecke Memorial Album (w. Paul Whiteman & His Orchestra; Crosby heard on ten of twelve sides).

P-100 *A Souvenir Program* (w. Paul Whiteman & His Orchestra; Crosby heard on nine of ten sides).

Long-Playing Albums

Amos	7001 *Hey Jude/Hey Bing!* (1969).
Brunswick	BL-54005 *Bing in the 1930s.*
	BL-58000-1 *Bing Crosby.*
Columbia	CL-2502 *Der Bingle.*
	CL-6027 *Crosby Classics, Vol. 1.*
	CL-6105 *Crosby Classics, Vol. 2.*
Decca	DL-4086 *My Golden Favorites.*
	DL-4250 *Easy to Remember.*
	DL-4251 *Pennies from Heaven.*
	DL-4252 *Pocket Full of Dreams.*
	DL-4253 *East Side of Heaven.*
	DL-4254 *The Road Begins.*
	DL-4255 *Only Forever.*
	DL-4256 *Holiday Inn.*
	DL-4257 *Swinging on a Star.*
	DL-4258 *Accentuate the Positive.*
	DL-4259 *Blue Skies.*
	DL-4260 *But Beautiful.*

DL-4261 *Sunshine Cake.*
DL-4262 *Cool of the Evening.*
DL-4263 *Zing a Little Zong.*
DL-4264 *Anything Goes.*
DL-5010 *Foster.*
DL-5011 *El Bingo.*
DL-5020 *Christmas Greetings* (w. Andrews Sisters).
DL-5037 *St. Patrick's Day.*
DL-5039 *St. Valentine's Day.*
DL-5052 *Bells of St. Mary's.*
DL-5063 *Don't Fence Me In.*
DL-5064 *Porter.*
DL-5081 *Gershwin.*
DL-5092 *Holiday Inn Selections.*
DL-5105 *Blue of the Night.*
DL-5107 *Cowboy Songs, Vol. 1.*
DL-5119 *Drifting & Dreaming.*
DL-5122 *Hawaiian Favorites, Vol. 1.*
DL-5126 *Stardust.*
DL-5129 *Cowboy Songs, Vol. 2.*
DL-5272 *Emperor Waltz.*
DL-5284 *Mr. Music.*
DL-5298 *Hits from Broadway Songs.*
DL-5299 *Favorite Hawaiian Songs.*
DL-5302 *Go West Young Man.*
DL-5310 *Way Back Home.*
DL-5323 *Bing with Dixieland Bands.*
DL-5326 *Yours Is My Heart Alone.*
DL-5331 *Country Style.*
DL-5340 *Down Memory Lane.*
DL-5343 *Down Memory Lane, Vol. 2.*
DL-5403 *When Irish Eyes Are Smiling.*
DL-5499 *Song Hits of Paris.*
DL-5508 *Some Fine Old Chestnuts.*
DL-5520 *Bing Sings Hits.*
DL-5556 *Country Girl* (w. Andrews Sisters).
DL-6000 *Small One.*
DL-8083 *White Christmas.*
DL-8110 *Lullaby Time.*
DL-8128 *Merry Christmas* (1955).
DL-8207 *Shillelaghs and Shamrocks* (1958).
DL-8210 *Home on the Range.*
DL-8365 *Twilight on the Trail.*

DL-8419 *A Christmas Sing with Bing around the World* (1956).

DL-8687 *Around the World with Bing Crosby*.

DL-8780 *Bing in Paris*.

DL-8781 *That Christmas Feeling*.

DL-9054 *Bing—Musical Autobiography, 1927–1934*.

DLP-5001 *Jerry Kern Songs*.

DLP-6001 *Ichabod Crane*.

Golden Age   5023 *Crosby's Radio Shows* (1978) (w. original radio cast).

MCA   3031 *Bing Crosby's Greatest Hits* (1977; 1939–1947 recordings).

Reprise   2020 *America, I Hear You Singing* (1964) (w. Frank Sinatra and Fred Waring).

United Artists/K-Tel NE-951 *Bing Crosby on Broadway* (Bing Crosby at the London Palladium) (1976) (w. Rosemary Clooney and the Crosby Family).

Compact Discs

Affinity   CD AFS 1021-2 *The Jazzin' Bing Crosby, 1927–1940*. 2-CD set with 24-page booklet; 48 cuts (EEC release).

Ariola Express   295040 *Bing Crosby—Dream a Little Dream of Me*. Includes material originally cut by Brunswick and Okeh (U.K. release).

Ariola Express   295040-201 *Bing Crosby*. 16 tracks; 14 with Gus Arnheim's Orchestra, 1 with Paul Whiteman, 1 with Duke Ellington (German release; also released by RCA as BPCD-5092 in Australia.)

ASV AJA-5043   *Here Lies Love*. 18 songs. (U.K. release.)

AJA-5072   *On the Sentimental Side*. 20 tracks. (U.K. release.)

Axis CDAX-701592 *The Stars in Song*. Crosby duets with several other stars (Australian release).

BBC   CD-648 *Bing Crosby: 1927–1934*. Culled from the LP *The Golden Years in Digital Stereo* (U.K. release); also issued as ABC 836172-2 in Australia.

BBC   CD-766 *Classic Crosby 1931–1938*. 18 tracks (U.K. release; also issued in Australia as ABC-838985.)

Bar One	BC-012 *Bing's Hollywood—Alternate Takes.*
	BC-013 *Bing—Beyond Compare.*
	BCT-001 *Bing Crosby's Treasury.*
Bella Musica	BMCD-89921 *Bing Crosby.* 18 tracks; monaural mix.
Bluebird	CD-6845-2 *Bix Beiderbecke—Bix Lives.* Includes 8 Crosby songs.
BNR	CD 211 *The Quintessential Bing Crosby.* 2-CD set; 50 tracks culled from *The Complete Bing Crosby.*
Castle Communications	CCSCD-275 *The Collection.* 24 songs accompanied by Buddy Cole; augmented by Pete Moore's Orchestra (U.K. release).
CBS Special Products	A2-201 *The Bing Crosby Story.* 2-CD set; 16 songs per disk.
Collection OR-0084	*Bing Crosby* [Classics]. 18 tracks (U.K. release).
Columbia	C3K-44229 *Bing Crosby the Crooner: The Columbia Years 1928–1934.* 3-CD set; released in the U.K. as CBS 465596.
Columbia	CK 48974 *16 Most Requested Songs.*
Companion	6187152 *Twenty Golden Memories* (Danish release).
Conifer	CDHD-123 *Remembering 1927–1934* (U.K. release).
Conquistador	CONQ-004) *Bing Crosby—Eleven Historic Recordings.* 11 tracks.
Curb	D2-77340 *All-Time Best of Bing Crosby.*
	D2-77617 *Best of Bing Crosby and Fred Astaire.*
Daybreak	824705-2 *Bing and Basie.*
Decca Jazz	GRD 603 *Bing Crosby and Some Jazz Friends.* Early recordings; many are duets; also released as MCA GRP-16032.
Dejavu	DVCD-2078 *Bing Crosby Christmas Collection.* 12 tracks.
	DVLP-2124 *The Bob Hope Collection.* Includes 9 Crosby songs (U.K. release).
	DVRECD-16) *The Bing Crosby Story* (U.K. release).
	Double Play GRF-016 *Everything I Have Is Yours.* 29 tracks.
Echo Jazz	EJCD-12 *Bing Crosby.* 16 tracks (U.K. release); alternate title: *Big Band Days.*

EMI	72438575472 *50th Anniversary Concert—Palladium.*
Entertainers	CD-0248 *The Best of Bing Crosby.* 23 tracks; volume 2 of 3-part set entitled *The Crooners* (with Frank Sinatra and Dean Martin).
Evasound	EMD-002 *Bing Crosby—Please* (Australian release).
Flapper Past	CD-9739 *Bing Crosby—That's Jazz* (U.K. release).
	CD-9784 *The Movie Hits.* 22 songs culled from Crosby's early films.
GNP Crescendo	GNPD-9044 *The Radio Years, Vol. 1.* 12 tracks; includes solos and duets with Judy Garland, Connee Boswell, and George Burns.
	GNPD-9046 *The Radio Years, Vol. 2.* 12 solos and duets.
	GNPD-9051 *The Radio Years—1931–1943.*
	GNPD-9052 *The Radio Years—1944–1953.*
Golden Olden	GOR CD101 *A Little Bit of Irish: Bing Crosby.*
Hallmark	306722 *Bing Sings Country.*
Harmony	HARCD-120 *Portrait of a Song Stylist.* 14 tracks accompanied by Buddy Cole; augmented by Pete Moore's Orchestra (U.K. release).
Intertape	500-027 *Bing Crosby* (U.K. release).
JSD	JSPCE-701 *Bing Crosby and Jimmy Durante—Start Off Each Day with a Song* (U.K. release).
	JSPCE-702 *Bing Crosby and Judy Garland* (U.K. release).
Laserlight	5411 *A Visit to the Movies.*
	12732 *American Legends.*
	15-411 *A Visit to the Movies.* A reissue of the February 1968 LP *Thoroughly Modern Bing,* minus 1 track.
	15-444 *White Christmas.* 17 tracks; source appears to have been the *Kraft Music Hall* radio programs. (U.K. release).
Lasertech	944D *The Bing Crosby Collection.*
Living Era	AJA 5005-R *Bix 'n' Bing* (U.K. release).
	AJA 5147 *Bing Crosby and Friends.*

London	820-552-2 *Where the Blue of the Night* (U.K. release).
	820-553-2 *Out of Nowhere* (U.K. release).
	820 586-2 *Bing: Feels Good, Feels Right* (U.K. release).
MCA	33XD-511 *Merry Christmas*. 14 tracks. (Japanese release.)
	255-199-2 *White Christmas*. 4-track EP.
	256 137-2 *Sixteen Original World Hits—Golden Gate Collection* (Australian release).
	D2-11503 *B.C. and the Andrews Sisters*.
	DMCAT-111 *Bing Crosby—White Christmas*. 3 songs (U.K. release).
	DMCL-1607 *The Best of Bing Crosby* (U.K. release).
	DMCL-1777 *White Christmas*. Film soundtrack; 10 songs, 9 with Crosby (U.K. release).
	DMCTV 3 *Twenty Golden Greats* (U.K. release).
	JVC-499 *Bing Crosby Sings Again*.
	JVC-500 *Bing Crosby Sings Christmas Songs*.
	MCAD-1620 *Bing Crosby's Greatest Hits*.
	MCAD-5764 *Bing Crosby Sings Again*. Also released as JVC-499.
	MCAD-5765 *Bing Crosby Sings Christmas Songs*. Also released as JVC-500.
	MCAD-11719 *Bing's Gold Records*.
	MCAD-25205 *Bing Crosby—Holiday Inn*.
	MCAD-25989 *Bing Crosby—Blue Skies*.
	MCAD-31367 *Swinging on a Star*. 12 tracks.
	MCD 18348 *My Greatest Songs—Bing Crosby*. 14 tracks. (Australian release.)
	MSD-35082 *Bing Crosby's Hawaii*.
	MSD3-37079 *36 All-Time Greatest Hits*.
Magic Dawe	3 *Bing Crosby and Friends*. 15 radio duets with Ethel Merman, Judy Garland, the Andrews Sisters, Bob Crosby, Patti Page, Al Jolson, etc. (U.K. release).
Magic Dawe	48 *Bing Swings*. 19 songs, featuring many accompanists and duets from the Philco and Chesterfield radio shows (U.K. release).

Parade	PAR 2021 *Bing Crosby—The Most Welcome Groaner* (U.K. release; also issued as part of a 3-CD set entitled *We Must Never Say Goodbye*. Parade PAK-904).
Parrot	PARCD-001 *Peggy Lee with Bing Crosby.* Features duets with Peggy Lee and Fred Astaire (U.K. release).
Pickwick	PWK-065 *Bing Crosby Sings the Great Songs* (U.K. release).
	PWK-088 *Bing Crosby Sings More Great Songs* (U.K. release).
	PWKS-561 *Christmas with Bing* (U.K. release).
Pilz	CD 44-5445-2 *Crosby Family Christmas.* 10 cuts, with 5 including his sons; they appear to be taken from radio programs.
Pilz	CD 44-5446-2 *Christmas with Bing and Frank.* Culled from a 1957 Sinatra TV program.
Pro-Arte	CDD-432 *Pennies from Heaven.*
	CDD-437 *Paper Moon—Paul Whiteman.* Includes 9 tracks with Crosby as a vocalist.
	CDD-457 *Pocketful of Dreams.* 18 tracks.
RCA	9678-2-R *Paul Whiteman and His Orchestra: The Victor Masters.* Includes 8 cuts with Crosby as a vocalist.
	BVCJ-2029 *Bing with a Beat* (Japanese release).
	R25J-1003 *Fancy Meeting You Here.* 13 duets with Rosemary Clooney (Japanese release).
Readers Digest	RDCD-121-6 *The Bing Crosby Years.* 6-CD set; 112 tracks, 45 featuring Crosby (U.K. release).
Regal	1572742 *Classic Performances.* Includes 16 standards (Australian release).
Sandy Hook	SH-2095 *Blues Skies Soundtrack.*
Saville	CDSVL 219 *Sing a Song of Sunbeams.* 18 cuts (U.K. release).
Silver Eagle	SED-10633, *Disc 1, Bing Sings: All about Love* (part of a 3-CD set entitled *The Complete Bing Crosby*).
Silver Eagle	SED-10633, *Disc 2, Bing Swings: Straight Down the Middle* (part of a 3-CD set entitled *The Complete Bing Crosby*).

	SED-10633. *Disc 3, From Broadway to Hollywood* (part of a 3-CD set entitled *The Complete Bing Crosby*).
Sony/Collectors Series	*The Bing Crosby Story.*
Spectrum	U-4016) *Bing and Louis Live* (U.K. release).
Stagedoor	SDC-8087 *Bing Crosby* (U.K. release).
Starlite	CDS-51058 *Bing Crosby with Gary Crosby and the Andrews Sisters.*
Telstar	TCD-2469 *Christmas with Bing Crosby.* 20 songs; 2 are duets with David Bowie (U.K. release).
Timeless Jazz Nostalgia	CBC 1-004 *Bing Crosby: 1926–1932.* 24 tracks (U.K. release).
Verve	UDCD 670 *Bing Sings whilst Bregman Swings.*
Warwick	1005 *10th Anniversary Collection.* U.K. release of the 3-CD set *The Complete Bing Crosby.*
World Star	WSC-99055 *White Christmas* (Australian release; also issued in Italy by Lotus with number CD-5001).
	WSC-99056 *High Society* (Australian release; also issued in Japan as CAP TOCP-6587).

CHAPTER 4—NICK LUCAS

Note: This discography lists only solo commercial recordings and does not include the scores of records Nick Lucas made between 1918 and 1924 as a band sideman, test pressings, radio transcriptions, or unissued material. He began his recording career in 1912 doing guitar test pressings for Thomas A. Edison, and his last unissued session was in November, 1980, for Accent Records. Altogether, he recorded steadily for some seventy years.

Pathé	020794 Pickin' the Guitar/Teasin' the Frets (guitar solos)
Brunswick	2536 Pickin' the Guitar/Teasin' the Frets
	2768 My Best Girl/Dreamer of Dreams
	2827 If I Can't Have You/I've Named My Pillow after You
	2846 When I Think of You/The Only, Only One
	2906 By the Light of the Stars/Isn't She the Sweetest Thing?
	2940 I Might Have Known/I'm Tired of Everything but You

2961 Brown Eyes, Why Are You Blue?/If You Hadn't Gone Away

2990 Sleepy Time Gal/I Found Somebody to Love

3021 Forever and Ever with You/Smile a Little Bit

3052 A Cup of Coffee, a Sandwich and You/Whose Who Are You?

3088 Always/I Don't Believe It—But Say It Again

3141 My Bundle of Love/No Foolin'

3184 Bye Bye Blackbird/Adorable

3185 I'm Glad I Found a Girl Like You

3229 Sleepy Head/How Many Times?

3283 Looking at the World thru Rose Colored Glasses/Let Me Live and Love You Just for Tonight

3367 Because I Love You/When You're Lonely

3369 I'd Love to Call You My Sweetheart/Precious

3370 Hello, Bluebird/I've Got the Girl

3433 In a Little Spanish Town/Put Your Arms Where They Belong

3439 I'm Looking over a Four Leaf Clover/High, High, High Up in the Hills

3466 I'm Looking for a Girl Named Mary/Underneath the Weeping Willow

3492 Moonbeam! Kiss Her for Me/So Blue

3512 Side by Side/Why Should I Say I'm Sorry?

3518 Rosy Cheeks/Underneath the Stars with You

3602 (Here Am I) Brokenhearted/Sing Me a Baby Song

3614 I Can't Believe That You're in Love with Me/Sweet Someone

3684 Among My Souvenirs/(My) Blue Heaven

3736 The Song Is Ended/Kiss and Make Up

3749 Together/Keep Sweeping the Cobwebs off the Moon

3773 My Ohio Home/Without You, Sweetheart

3850 I Still Love You/Sunshine

3853 I'm Waiting for Ships That Never Come In/Marcheta

3965 Just Like a Melody from out of the Sky/For Old Times' Sake

3966 You're a Real Sweetheart/When You Said Goodnight (Did You Really Mean Goodbye?)

4016 Chiquita/Someday, Somewhere

4141 My Tonia/The Song I Love
4156 I'll Get By/How about Me?
4171 When the World Is at Rest/I'll Never Ask for
    More
4214 Some Rainy Day/I'm Telling You
4215 Old Timer/Heart o' Mine
4302 Coquette/I've Got a Feeling I'm Falling
4378 Singin' in the Rain/Your Mother and Mine
4390 When My Dreams Come True/Just Another
    Kiss
4418 Tiptoe thru the Tulips/Painting the Clouds with
    Sunshine
4464 My Song of the Nile/Ich Liebe Dich (I Love
    You)
4468 Sweethearts' Holiday/Where Are You Dream
    Girl?
4547 I Don't Want Your Kisses/Until the End
4860 Singing a Song to the Stars/My Heart Belongs
    to the Girl Who Belongs to Somebody Else
4896 Just a Little Closer/Don't Tell Her What's Hap-
    pened to Me
4900 The Kiss Waltz/Go Home and Tell Your Mother
4959 Three Little Words/Wasting My Love on You
4960 Maybe It's Love/I'm Yours
4987 You're Driving Me Crazy/I Miss a Little Miss
6013 Lady Play Your Mandolin/Say "Hello" to the
    Folks Back Home
6045 You Didn't Have to Tell Me/When You Were
    the Blossom of Buttercup Lane and I Was Your
    Little Boy Blue
6048 Walking My Baby Back Home/Falling in Love
    Again
6049 Hello Beautiful/Running between the Raindrops
6089 Wabash Moon/I Surrender Dear
6098 Let's Get Friendly/Boy! Oh! Boy! Oh! Boy! I've
    Got It Bad
6104 Now You're in My Arms/Can't You Read be-
    tween the Lines?
6147 That's My Desire/When the Moon Comes over
    the Mountain
6195 Goodnight Sweetheart

Hit-of-the-Week   A-4-8-1 All of Me
                   B-3-4 An Evening in Caroline

Brunswick	6508 Pickin' the Guitar/Teasin' the Frets
	6459 More Beautiful Than Ever/I'm Sure of Everything but You
	6462 I Called to Say Goodnight/Till Tomorrow
Melotone	33061 Love Thy Neighbor/A Thousand Goodnights
	33062 Goin' Home/Carry Me Back to the Lone Prairie
	33124 For All We Know/Moonglow
Regal Zonophone	G-23898 A Man and His Dream/An Apple for the Teacher
	G-23899 Over the Rainbow/The Man with the Mandolin
	G-23900 Good Morning/Go Fly a Kite
Diamond	2018 If I Had My Way/Coax Me a Little Bit
	2019 Painting the Clouds with Sunshine/What Ya Gonna Do?
	2021 Seems Like Old Times/Give My Heart a Break
	2022 My Blue Heaven/Everyone Is Looking for the Rainbow
Capitol	15242 Tiptoe thru the Tulips/Side by Side
	15353 Don't Gamble with Romance/Tea Time on the Thames
	57-607 Bye Bye Blackbird/Don't Call Me Sweetheart Anymore
Cavalier	823 Tiptoe thru the Tulips/Painting the Clouds with Sunshine
	824 My Blue Heaven/Francine
	825 Coquette/Teardrops
	826 Lady Be Good/Till the End of Forever
Crown	141 Looking at the World thru Rose Colored Glasses/Did You Ever See a Dream Walking?
Accent	AC-1026 Paper Roses/Bella Nonna (Little Grandmother)
	AC-1030 Soldier's Guitar/Kind and Considerate
	AC-1033 Pasta Cheech/Not Guilty
Cavalier	873 Got Out Those Old Records/Francine
Accent	AC-1117 Hello, Dolly/Tiptoe thru the Tulips
	AC-1206 It's Been a Good Life/Darling, I Love You
	AC-1237 Brown Eyes, Why Are You Blue?/Worryin'
	AC-1239 Our San Diego/I'm Blue for You
	AC-1273 Looking at the World thru Rose Colored Glasses/I'm Sitting on Top of the World

AC-1274 A Cup of Coffee, a Sandwich and You/I
Want to Hold You in My Arms
AC-1322 Silver Sails/Tiptoe thru the Tulips

Long-Playing Albums

An Evening with Nick Lucas (Take Two TT-1001-S) (1982)
The Nick Lucas Souvenir Album (Accent ACS-5027) (1968)
Painting the Clouds with Sunshine (Decca DL-8653) (1957)
Rose Colored Glasses (Accent ACS-5043) (1969)
The Singing Troubadour (ASV AJA-5022) (1983)
Tiptoe thru the Tulips with Nick Lucas (Cavalier LP-50033) (1953)
Tiptoe thru the Tulips with Nick Lucas (Cavalier CVLP-6007) (1956)
Nick Lucas—The Singing Troubadour (ASV AJA-5022)

CHAPTER 5—JOHNNY MARVIN

Johnny Marvin had many recording pseudonyms. The following is a list
of them, with the record companies on which they were issued: Dr.
Cheer (Victor), Dr. Marvin (Columbia), Duke & His Uke (Gennett),
Frankie & Johnny (w. Frankie Marvin; Melotone), Henry Duke & His Uke
(National Music Lovers), Honey Duke (Grey Gull, Harmony), Honey
Duke & His Uke (Bell, Emerson, Globe, Grey Gull, Harmony, Supreme,
Victor), Billy Hancock (Madison), Jack Lane & His Uke (Champion), Mac-
Donald & Broones (Champion), Marvin Trio (Okeh), Jimmy May & His
Uke (Bell, Emerson, Gennett), Robbins & Uke (Challenge, Champion),
Elton Spence & His Uke (Madison), George Thorne (Dandy), Ukulele
Luke (Cameo), and Ken Wallace (Adelphi).
The following discography contains single recordings. Not included is
Johnny Marvin's work as a sideman or radio transcriptions. In case of
multiple issuance on various labels, the parent company only is listed.

Okeh	40139 Farewell Blues/Go 'Long Mule (w. Charles Sargent)
	40178 St. Louis Blues/You Know Me, Alabam' (w. Charles Sargent)
	40205 Pete the Greek (w. Charles Sargent)/Mrs. Murphy's Chowder
	40241 Thousand Mile Blues (w. Charles Sargent)/Minnie the Mermaid
Pathé	Actuelle 032051 I'm All Broken Out with the Blues/Tell Me with Smiles (w. Charles Sargent)
Pathé	Actuelle 032057 There's Yes! Yes! In Your Eyes/Big Boy (w. Charles Sargent)

	032097 Sunshine (w. Charles Sargent)
Oriole	216 You Know Me, Alabam'
Radiex	2156 You Know Me, Alabam'
Hollywood	860 Thousand Mile Blues/Go 'Long Mule
	1076 Just a Little Drink/I Wonder Why
Grey Gull	1309 Show Me the Way to Go Home*
	2208 Bam Bam Bamy Shore (as Jimmy May & His Uke)
	2209 Show Me the Way to Go Home (as Jimmy May & His Uke)
	2213 Roll 'Em Girls* (w. Arthur Fields)
	2213 Roll 'Em Girls* (w. Joe Sargent)
	2218 She's Gonna Be a Big Help to Me/Five Foot Two, Eyes of Blue*
	2219 Sleepy Time Gal/Lovin' You, That's All*
Columbia	511-D Down by the Winegar Wolks/I Love My Baby
	547-D I Ain't in Love No More/In My Gondola
Edison	51709 12th Street Rag (ukulele solo)
Okeh	40508 Show Me the Way to Go Home/Wait 'til Tomorrow Night
Gennett	3188 Wait 'til Tomorrow Night/Tweedle-Dee Tweedle-Doo (as Jimmy May & His Uke)
Grey Gull	1320 I'm Sitting on Top of the World* (w. Metropolitan Dance Orchestra)
	1380 Animal Crackers* (w. the Eight Devils)
	2221 Clap Hands! Here Comes Charlie/I'm Having Lots of Fun
	2223 I Love My Baby/Toodle-Do*
	2230 Oh, What a Shame*
	2256 Chinky Charleston*
	2261 I Expect John Henry Tonight* (w. Joe Sargent)
	2265 Hard-Boiled Mama (as Elton Spence & His Uke)
Harmony	94-H Hot Coffee/That Certain Party*
	115-H 12th Street Rag/Memphis Blues* (ukulele solos)
	145-H Hooray for the Irish/I'm Gonna Let the Bumble Bee
	152-H Sleepy Town/I'd Rather Be Alone* (w. Billy Carr)
	169-H So Is Your Old Lady/Hello, Aloha! How Are You?*
	199-H I'm Full of Love for Her/Oh Boy! How It Was Raining*
	221-H Calling Me Home/Precious*
	259-H Mary Lou/Pretty Cinderella*
	284-H Baby Face/Just a Little Longer*
	306-H It Made You Happy When You Made Me Cry/Thinking of You*

	326-H Angel Eyes/Since I Found You*
Okeh	40558 Clap Hands! Here Comes Charlie/In Your Green Hat
	40575 So Does Your Old Mandarin/Sleepy Time
	40604 So Is Your Old Lady/Could I? I Certainly Could
	40634 Tonight's My Night with Baby/Hello, Aloha! How Are You
	40657 No Foolin'/Who Wouldn't?
	40668 Precious (w. Mike Marvel's Orchestra)
	40683 Pretty Cinderella/Trudy
	40704 I'm on My Way Home/The Little White House
Globe	2222 Talking in My Sleep*
	2224 Aunt Lucy*
Edison	51707 Hooray for the Irish!/I Ain't in Love No More
	51709 Memphis Blues (ukulele solo)
	51793 Breezin' Along with the Breeze/Who Wouldn't?
	51841 Jersey Walk/Half a Moon
	51881 I Can't Get Over a Girl Like You Loving a Boy Like Me/I'd Love to Call You My Sweetheart
Columbia	606-D Thanks for the Buggy Ride/Under the Ukulele Tree
	648-D Somebody's Lonely/(There's a Blue Ridge in My Heart) Virginia
	699-D Breezin' Along with the Breeze/Hello, Baby
	750-D Half a Moon/Jersey Walk
	798-D You Will, Won't You? (w. the Ipana Troubadours)
	831-D A Little Music in the Moonlight/My Lady
	832-D Half a Moon (w. The Knickerbockers)
Emerson	3016 Sleepy Time Gal (as Jimmy May & His Uke)
	3039 Under the Ukulele Tree (as Jimmy May & His Uke)
Madison	18004 Down Ole Virginia Way (as Billy Hancock)/Hard Boiled Mama (as Elton Spence & His Uke)
Gennett	6011 Jersey Walk/I Can't Get over a Girl Like You Loving a Boy Like Me (as Duke & His Uke)
	6023 Hello, Swanee, Hello (as Duke & His Uke)
Victor	20231 Half a Moon (w. Nat Shilkret & The Victor Orchestra)
	20259 All Alone Monday (w. Nat Shilkret & The Victor Orchestra
	20288 I'd Love to Call You My Sweetheart/Hum Your Troubles Away
	20338 We'll Have a Kingdom (w. Roger Wolfe Kahn & His Orchestra)
	20352 Sweet Thing (w. Nat Shilkret & the Victor Orchestra)
	20386 12th Street Rag/Memphis Blues (w. William Carola; instrumentals)

20397 'Deed I Do

35811 Honeymoon Lane—Vocal Gems (Jersey Walk) (w. Victor Light Opera Company

Emerson 3098 I Need Lovin'/Thinking of You*

3106 My Little Bunch of Happiness* (w. Jack Stillman's Orchestra)

3108 I Never See Maggie Alone*

3109 She Keeps Me in the Dark*

3120 Ain't She Sweet?/Crazy Words, Crazy Tune*

3135 Mine* (w. Bert Kaplan's Collegians)

Edison 51928 Strumming/'Deed I Do

51992 Ain't She Sweet?/I Can't Believe That You're in Love with Me

Columbia 871-D Crazy Words, Crazy Tune/High, High, High Up in the Hills (w. Fred Rich & His Hotel Astor Orchestra)

885-D 'Deed I Do/Coronado Nights (w. the Radiolites)

891-D Don't Sing Aloha (w. Ed Smalle)/Proud (of a Baby Like You)

893-D The Kinkajou (w. the Knickerbockers)

944-D Beedle-Um-Bo (w. Ed Smalle and Paul Ash & His Orchestra)

961-D A Lane in Spain (w. the Columbians)

982-D Nesting Time/Calling (w. the Knickerbockers)

1015-D Rosa Lee/Twilight Rose (w. the Columbians)

1020-D Me and My Shadow/Roamin' in the Sunset

Bell 479 I Never See Maggie Alone/She Keeps Me in the Dark*

491 Ain't She Sweet?/Crazy Words, Crazy Tune*

516 One O'Clock Baby/You'll Never Be Missed a Hundred Years from Now*

Okeh 40769 Ain't She Sweet?/Since I Found You

40802 At Sundown/Wherever You Go—Whatever You Do

Grey Gull 2321 I'm Looking over a Four Leaf Clover*

2323 Get Away, Old Man, Get Away*

4119 Hand Me Down My Walking Cane*

4124 Tenting Tonight on the Old Camp Ground*

8101 Roll 'Em Girls* (w. Jack Kaufman)

Harmony 368-H At Sundown/If You See Sally*

409-H Red Lips, Kiss My Blues Away/Just the Same*

Gennett 6085 You'll Never Be Missed a Hundred Years from Now/I'll Just Go Along (as Duke & His Uke)

Supreme 1314 That Certain Party*

Victor 20457 Blue Skies (w. Ed Smalle)

20478 Oh! How She Could Play the Ukulele (w. Jacques Renard & His Orchestra)

20487 You Went Away Too Far and Stayed Away Too Long

20493 A Little Birdie Told Me So (w. Roger Wolfe Kahn &
His Orchestra)

20497 I Can't Believe That You're in Love with Me

20596 Honolulu Moon (w. Hilo Orchestra)

20601 Judy Medley—Wear Your Sunday Smile (w. Nat Shilkret & the Victor Orchestra)

20603 There's Everything Nice about You (w. Ed Smalle)

20612 There's Everything Nice about You

20675 Me and My Shadow

20682 Stop Go/Something to Tell

20714 Side by Side/Red Lips, Kiss My Blues Away (w. Aileen Stanley)

20726 My Wife's in Europe Today (w. Charlie Fry & His
Million Dollar Orchestra)

20727 Whoo-Do? You-oo, That's Who!

20729 I Could Waltz Forever (w. Nat Shilkret & the Victor
Orchestra)

20731 Magnolia/Ain't That a Grand and Glorious Feeling?

20732 Just Like a Butterfly (w. Nat Shilkret & His Victor Orchestra)

20741 In a Shady Nook by a Babbling Brook

20758 Just Another Day Wasted Away (w. Ed Smalle)

20759 There's a Trick in Pickin' a Chick-Chick-Chicken
Today (w. Nat Shilkret & the Victor Orchestra)

20787 Under the Moon (w. Aileen Stanley)

20819 What Do We Do on a Dew-Dew-Dewy Day? (w. Nat
Shilkret & the Victor Orchestra)

20822 I Walked Back from the Buggy Ride (w. Aileen
Stanley)

20832 It's a Million to One You're in Love/I'm Afraid You
Sing That Song to Somebody Else

20833 Sweet Marie/Bye Bye, Pretty Baby (w. Jan Garber &
His Orchestra)

20848 Sixty Seconds Every Minute (w. Jan Garber & His Orchestra)/Tired Hands (w. the Troubadours)

20882 Baby's Blue (w. Nat Shilkret & the Victor Orchestra)

20893 Marvelous/It All Belongs to Me

20899 Are You Thinking of Me Tonight? (w. Franklyn Baur,
Elliott Shaw, and Nat Shilkret & the Victor Orchestra)

20902 Pull Yourself Together

20981 When the Morning Glories Wake Up in the Morning
(w. Jacques Renard & His Orchestra)

20984 Give Me a Night in June/After I've Called You Sweetheart

21040 There's a Cradle in Caroline (w. Ed Smalle and Nat Shilkret & the Victor Orchestra)

21042 Kiss and Make Up (w. Ed Smalle)

21114 Funny Face/'S Wonderful (w. Arden-Ohman Orchestra)

21153 Is She My Girl Friend?/Keep Sweeping the Cobwebs off the Moon

21154 What Are You Waiting For? (w. Edwin J. McEnelly's Orchestra)

21172 Rain/After My Laughter Came Tears (w. Ed Smalle)

21230 From Midnight till Dawn

21259 Without You, Sweetheart (w. Nat Shilkret & the Victor Orchestra)

21299 Mary Ann (w. Ed Smalle)/An Old Fashioned Locket

21376 Angel/Sweetheart o' Mine

21427 Think of Me, Thinking of You/Golden Gate

21432 Get Out and Get under the Moon (w. Nat Shilkret & His Orchestra)

21435 My Pet/I Still Love You

21463 I'd Rather Cry over You (w. Nat Shilkret & the Victor Orchestra)

21509 Oh! You Have No Idea

21609 Old Man Sunshine/If You Don't Love Me

21632 What D'Ya Say? (w. Johnny Hamp & His Kentucky Serenaders)

21650 Crazy Rhythm/Heartbroken and Lonely (w. Roger Wolfe Kahn & His Orchestra)

21653 Water Melon Smilin' on the Vine (w. Roger Wolfe Kahn & His Orchestra)

21667 She Didn't Say Yes, She Didn't Say No (w. the All-Star Orchestra)

21780 Happy Days and Lonely Nights/There's a Rainbow 'round My Shoulder

21814 I'd Rather Be Blue (w. Nat Shilkret & the Victor Orchestra)

21820 Sweethearts on Parade/Where the Sky Little Violets Grow

21839 You Wanted Someone to Play With

21848 Ev'rybody Loves You (w. Aileen Stanley)

21851 All by Yourself in the Moonlight/Sweetheart of All My Dreams

21859 You Wouldn't Fool Me, Would You? (w. Nat Shilkret & the Victor Orchestra)

21866 The Sun Is at My Window (w. Ed Smalle)

21892 A Precious Little Thing Called Love/Caressing You (w. Ed Smalle)

21903 Down among the Sugar Cane/That's the Good Old Sunny South (w. Benny Kruger & His Orchestra)

21955 I'm in Seventh Heaven/Used to You

21959 I Get the Blues When It Rains (w. Ed Smalle)/Down among the Sugar Cane

21990 Why Did You Leave Me? (w. Ed Smalle)/Some Sweet Day

22022 Your Mother and Mine/Finding the Long Way Home

22039 Baby, Oh Where Can You Be?/(If I Were You) I'd Fall in Love with Me

22055 Wouldn't It Be Wonderful?/I'm the Medicine Man for the Blues

22057 Singin' in the Rain (w. the Frohme Sisters)/Orange Blossom Time

22076 Little by Little/Ev'ry Day Away from You

22113 Tip Toe thru the Tulips/Painting the Clouds with Sunshine

22125 True Blue Lou/Same Old Moon

22148 If I Had a Talking Picture of You/I'm a Dreamer, Aren't We All?

22180 Melancholy/Satisfied

22186 Lucky Me, Lovable You/Happy Days Are Here Again

22195 Georgia Pines (w. Nat Shilkret & the Victor Orchestra)

22273 With You/Have a Little Faith in Me

22302 Cryin' for the Carolines/Blue Eyes

22314 Red Hot and Blue Rhythm (w. the High Hatters)

22348 Lazy Lou'siana Moon/The One I Love Just Can't Be Bothered with Me

22418 Ro-Ro-Rollin' Along/Down the River of Golden Dreams

22440 Dancing with Tears in My Eyes/I'm in the Market for

22441 Be Careful with Those Eyes (w. Don Azpiazu & His Havana Club Orchestra)

22502 Go Home and Tell Your Mother/Little White Lies

22534 I Still Get a Thrill/Bye Bye Blues

22555 You Darlin'/I'm Yours

22566 Overnight/Cheerful Little Earfull

23531 Underneath Those Weeping Willow Trees/I'm Looking for a Gal*

	22604 To Whom It May Concern/Yours and Mine
	22649 Little Sweetheart of the Mountains (w. Frankie Marvin)/Little Sweetheart of the Prairie
	22666 Would You Take Me Back Again?/Rocky Mountain Rose
	22741 Dr. Cheer—Parts 1 & 2
Perfect	12758 Guilty/Now That You're Gone
	15536 A Faded Summer Love/Lucille (as Johnny Marvin & His Orchestra)
Columbia	2655-D Dr. Brokenshire and Dr. Marvin—Parts 1 & 2 (w. Norman Brokenshire)
	15750-D Seven Come Eleven/Yodelin' My Way to Heaven
Okeh	41559 Seven Come Eleven/Yodelin' My Way to Heaven (as the Marvin Trio)
Crown	3310 Home on the Range/Ma and Pa (Send Their Sweetest Love) (w. Johnny Amendt)
Victor	23691 When You Hear Me Call/I'm Gonna Yodel My Way to Heaven
	23708 The Man with the Big Black Mustache/Seven Come Eleven
	23728 Jack and Jill/Go Along Bum and Keep Bumming Along
Melotone	M-12460 I'm the Man That's Been Forgotten—Parts 1 & 2 (w. Roy Smeck)
	M-12521 Beech Fork Special/Red Wing (w. Frankie Marvin; as Frankie & Johnny)
	M-12610 Rock-a-Bye Moon/I'm Playing with Fire
Decca	5056 Lazy Texas Longhorns (w. Frankie Marvin)/I Want My Boots on When I Die
Panachord	25973 The Last Mile/Beneath a Bed of Daisies
Decca	5891 Me and My Shadow/We Like It
	5904 No One to Kiss Me Goodnight/As Long as I Live
Continental	C-3011 When You Kiss That Girl Goodbye

Long-Playing Record Albums

Johnny Marvin—A Voice of the Twenties (Take Two TT-232) (1987)
Johnny Marvin—Radio Favorite (Vocalists Showcase #8) (1998) *as Honey Duke and His Uke

CHAPTER 6—RUDY VALLEE

Note: The discography contains only recordings made by Rudy Vallee as a vocalist or with his band. Not included are his records as a band sideman, private pressings, radio transcriptions, or unissued material. Only single releases are listed.

Vocalion	15706 Isle of Moonlit Sky/Iona Lu (w. Franchini's Serenaders)
Harmony	724-H Lady Whippoorwill (v. George Morrow)/Right Out of Heaven (v. Sleepy Ward)
	728-H Dream Sweetheart (v. Sleepy Ward)/Salaming the Rajah (v. George Morrow)
	759-H Doin' the Raccoon/Bye and Bye Sweetheart
	808-H Let's Do It/Come West, Little Girl, Come West
	811-H The Song I Love/Sweetheart of All My Dreams
	825-H Makin' Whoopee/If I Had You
	832-H When the World Is at Rest/In a Great Big Way (v. Annette Hanshaw)
	834-H Marie/Caressing You
	857-H Outside
	881-H Lover, Come Back to Me
	1087-H Land of Going to Be
	1247-H You'll Do It Someday
Victor	21868 Weary River/Deep Night
	21869 Honey/Sweet Suzanne
	21880 Coquette/Lover, Come Back to Me
	21924 Bye and Bye Sweetheart/My Time Is Your Time
	21963 The One That I Love Loves Me/Underneath the Russian Moon
	29167 I'm Just a Vagabond Lover/I'm Still Caring
	21983 Every Moon's a Honeymoon/Huggable, Kissable You
	21998 Sposin'/The One in the World
	22029 Miss You/Heigh-Ho, Everybody, Heigh-Ho
	22034 Baby, Oh Where Can You Be?/You're Just Another Memory
	22062 Pretending/Where Are You Dream Girl?
	22084 Me Queres?/On the Alamo
	22090 That's When I Learned to Love You/A Kiss to Remember
	22136 You Want Lovin'/Lonely Troubadour
	22193 A Little Kiss Each Morning/I'll Be Reminded of You
	22196 Believe It or Not/I Love the Moon

22118 Perhaps/The Album of My Dreams

22227 If You Were the Only Girl in the World/I Love You, Believe Me, I Love You

22261 M-A-R-Y I Love Y-O-U/Gypsy Dream Rose

22284 Love Made a Gypsy Out of Me/Beside an Open Fireplace

22321 The Stein Song/St. Louis Blues

22361 I Still Remember/I Never Dreamt

22412 Reminiscing/The Verdict Is Life with You

22419 Kitty from Kansas City/If I Had a Girl Like You

22435 The Song without a Name/My Heart Belongs to The Girl Who Belongs to Somebody Else

22445 Old New England Moon/How Come You Do Me Like You Do?

22473 Betty Coed/Violets/Friends

22489 Good Evenin'/Just a Little Closer

22506 I'm Confessin'/My Bluebird Got Caught in the Rain

22545 Goodnight Poor Harvard/Down the Field/The Triple Cheer/Princeton Cannon March Song

22560 Sweetheart of My Student Days/Stolen Moments

22572 You're Driving Me Crazy/Thinking of You Dear

22574 She Loves Me Just the Same/Washington and Lee Swing

22585 Tears/Don't Forget Me in Your Dreams

22595 My Temptation/When Your Hair Has Turned to Silver

22611 Would You Like to Take a Walk?/Ninety-Nine Out of a Hundred

22615 When You Fall in Love, Fall in Love with Me/The Wind in the Willows

22672 Whistling in the Dark/My Cigarette Lady

22679 You're Just a Lover/Two Little Blue Eyes

22742 When Yuba Plays the Rhumba/I'm Keepin' Company

22751 Hikin' Down the Highway/Makin' Faces at the Man in the Moon

22752 Many Happy Returns of the Day/Pardon Me Pretty Baby

22773 As Time Goes By/Begging for Love

22774 Why Dance?

22783 This Is the Missus/Life Is Just a Bowl of Cherries

22784 The Thrill Is Gone/My Song

Hit-of-the-Week   M-4-5 A Faded Summer Love/You Try Somebody Else

A-3-4 Home

B-1-2 By the Sycamore Tree

C-1-2 Was That the Human Thing to Do?

C-3-4 The Wooden Soldier and the China Doll

D-2-3 By the Fireside/Lovable

Columbia   2700 I Guess I'll Have to Change My Plans/Maori

2702 Same Old Moon/Strange Interlude

2714 Say It Isn't So/Three's a Crowd

Victor   24075 Song of the Navy/To the Legion

Columbia   2715 Let's Put Out the Lights and Go to Sleep/Me Minus You

2724 How Deep Is the Ocean?/Please

2725 Brother, Can You Spare a Dime?/I'll Never Have to Dream Again

2730 Till Tomorrow/Here It Is Monday and I've Still Got a Dollar

2733 Just an Echo in the Valley/The Language of Love

2737 I'm Playing with Fire/A Bedtime Story

2738 Linger a Little Longer in the Twilight/A Jug of Wine, a Loaf of Bread and Thou

2744 The Girl in the Little Green Hat/Hey! Young Fella

2746 The Whisper Waltz/Pretending You Care

2756 Meet Me in the Gloaming/Maybe I Love You Too Much

2764 Here Is My Heart/Old Man Harlem

2771 I Can't Remember/I Lay Me Down to Sleep

2773 I've Got to Sing a Torch Song/The Shadow Waltz

Bluebird   B-5097 My Moonlight Madonna/On the Air

B-5098 When the Sweet Magnolias Bloom Again/Thank Heaven for You

B-5114 A Heart of Stone/Lazybones

B-5115 Don't Blame Me/Stringin' Along on a Shoe String

B-5118 Moonlight Down in Lover's Lane/To Be or Not to Be in Love

B-5132 Free/Three Wishes

B-5171 Honeymoon Hotel (v. Alice Faye)/By a Waterfall

B-5172 The Last Roundup/Shanghai Lil

B-5175 Shame on You (v. Alice Faye)/Love Is the Sweetest Thing

B-5177 Savage Serenade/Nagasaki

B-5182 Happy Boy, Happy Girl (v. Alice Faye)/Empty Days

Victor

24458 Everything I Have Is Yours/My Dancing Lady

24459 Orchids in the Moonlight/Flying Down to Rio

24475 I Raised My Hat/Puddin' Head Jones

24476 Suddenly/What Is There to Say?

24554 Goin' to Heaven on a Mule/Don't Say Goodnight

24558 Carolina/Dancing in the Moonlight

24580 You Oughta Be in Pictures/Without That Certain Thing

24581 Hold My Hand/Nasty Man

24642 Sleepy Head/The Sweetest Music This Side of Heaven

24646 Spellbound/So Help Me

24697 I'm Hummin', I'm Whistlin', I'm Singin'/Panama

24702 Somewhere in My Heart/Just an Old Banjo

24721 The Drunkard Song/Lost in a Fog

24722 Out in the Cold Again/Ha-Cha-Cha

24723 P.S. I Love You/Strange

24739 The Drunkard Song/The Tattooed Lady

24740 An Earful of Music/When My Ship Comes In

24827 Ev'ry Day/Sweet Music

24833 Fare Thee Well Annabelle/There's a Different "You" in Your Heart

24838 On the Good Ship Lollipop (v. the Stewart Sisters)/A Pretty Girl Is Like a Melody

24895 Life Is a Song/Open Your Eyes

24899 Love Dropped in for Tea/Seein' Is Believin'

25089 I Couldn't Believe My Eyes/His Majesty, the Baby

25092 The Pig Got Up and Slowly Walked Away/The Gentleman Obviously Doesn't Believe in Love

25109 Page Miss Glory/Plain Old Me

36171 The Rudy Vallee Medley (Parts 1 & 2) (12" disk)

25231 Hypnotized

25233 Everything's in Rhythm in My Heart/Say the Word and It's Yours

25234 He Wooed Her and Wooed Her and Wooed Her/I Can Wiggle My Ears

25260 Knick Knacks on the Mantel/There's Always a Happy Ending

25267 There Isn't Any Limit to My Love/I Don't Want to Make History

25313 Is It True What They Say about Dixie?

Melotone   6-06-08 Would You?/Us on a Bus

6-06-09 The Glory of Love/She Shall Have Music

6-07-03 Call of the Prairie/I'm on a Wild Goose Chase

6-08-04 These Foolish Things/Dream Time

6-08-09 Empty Saddles/Rhythm of the Range

6-10-10 A Fine Romance/The Waltz in Swing Time

6-10-11 The Way You Look Tonight/Bojangles of Harlem

7-01-01 I Was Saying to the Moon/Who Loves You?

7-01-04 All's Fair in Love and War/Speaking of the Weather

7-05-26 Seventh Heaven/The Coronation Waltz

7-06-11 Turn Off the Moon/That's Southern Hospitality

English Columbia   DB.1697 Goodnight, My Love/The You and Me That Used to Be

DB.1703 The Whiffenpoof Song/Vieni, Vieni

Bluebird   7067 Harbor Lights/Heaven Help This Heart of Mine

7069 Vieni, Vieni/Don't Play with Fire

7078 The Old Sow Song/With His Head Tucked under His Arm (v. Cyril Smith)

7120 An Old Flame Never Dies/If You Were Someone Else

7135 The Whiffenpoof Song/Mad Dogs and Englishmen

7140 Kitty from Kansas City/Deep Night

7226 In the Mission by the Sea/When the Organ Played "O Promise Me"

7238 Have You Met Miss Jones?/I'd Rather Be Right

B-10069 Rudy Vallee Surprises (Parts 1 & 2) (v. Red Stanley & Cyril Smith)

Victor   36204 All Points West (Parts 1 & 2)

Bluebird	7331 I'll Take Romance/A Little White Schoolhouse

Bluebird   7331 I'll Take Romance/A Little White Schoolhouse
7342 The One I Love/Melody Farm
7368 Outside/Life Is Just a Bowl Of Cherries
7543 Oh! Ma-Ma! (The Butcher Boy) (v. Red Stanley)/Lonesome That's All
7645 Naturally/My Best Wishes
7649 Dream Dust/A Twinkle in Your Eye
7667 Hawaiian War Chant (v. the Gentlemen Singers)/Phil the Fluter's Ball

Victor   25835 A Stranger in Paree/The Latin Quarter
25836 Day Dreaming All Night Long/I Wanna Go Back to Bali

Decca   2246 Sing for Your Supper/Oh Diogenes
2248 This Can't Be Love (w. Frances Langford)/The Shortest Day of the Year
2318 Toyland
2551 I Poured My Heart into a Song/When Winter Comes
2552 I'm Sorry for Myself/An Old Fashioned Song Is Always New
2656 I Want My Mama/It's Way Past My Dreaming Time
2683 Moonbeams
2708 Lydia, The Tattooed Lady/You Took Me Out of This

Varsity   8203 Six Women/Plaza 3-4783
8211 The Whiffenpoof Song/Lazy Rolls the Rio Grande
8274 Kitty from Kansas City/When Yuba Plays the Rhumba on the Tuba
8295 Adios/Pourquoi?
8327 Let's Do It (Parts 1 & 2)

Victor   27823 A Letter from London/I Just Couldn't Say It Before
27844 I'm Just a Vagabond Lover/My Time Is Your Time

Maestro Music Enterprise   107 Waiting/That Woman of Mine
181/182 Alouetta/The Whiffenpoof Song
183/184 Amado Mio/The Gypsy
193/194 I'm Kinda Selfish That Way/Summer Sweetheart
195/196 The Stein Song/Alouetta
223/224 It's Time to Sing a Goodnight Song/The Stein Song

Victor	20-3793 Sentimental Me/Niccolo and His Piccolo
MGM	11267 Bubbles in My Beer/The Beer That I Left on the Bar
Victor	20/47-5441 The Whiffenpoof Song/Taps
Decca	25556 The Whiffenpoof Song/The Stein Song

Albums

The Best of Rudy Vallee (Camden CDN-170)
The Best of Rudy Vallee (RCA LSP-3816) (1967)
The Best of Rudy Vallee (RCA International 1343) (1971)
An Evening with Rudy Vallee (Mark56 681) (1974)
The Fleischmann's Hour (Mark 56 613) (1973)
The Funny Side of Rudy Vallee (Jubilee 2051) (1963)
The Greatest Vaudeo-Doe-R of All Time (Pickwick P/SP-3063) (1967)
Heigh Ho, Everybody (Olympic 7128) (1974)
Heigh Ho, Everybody, This Is Rudy Vallee (ASV 5009) (1982)
Hi Ho, Everybody (Viva V36005) (1966)
Is This Your Rudy Vallee? (Crown CLP-5204) (1960)
The Kid from Maine (Unique 116) (1956)
Rudy Vallee and His Connecticut Yankees (Halcyon 105) (1986)
Rudy Vallee and His Connecticut Yankees (Sunbeam 515) (1984)
Rudy Vallee and His Famous World War II Coast Guard Band (Mark 56 714) (1975)
Rudy Vallee on the Air (Totem 1027) (1977)
Rudy Vallee Reads Fairy Tales (Treasure 407) (1959)
Rudy Vallee's Drinking Songs (10″ Storyville 315) (1954)
Sing for Your Supper (Conifer CMS-005) (1989)
Songs of a Vagabond Lover (10″ Capitol H-550) (1955)
Stein Songs (Decca DL-4242/74242) (1962)
The Young Rudy Vallee (RCA LPM-2507) (1962)

Compact Discs

As Time Goes By (Varese Sarabande VSD-5827) (1998)
Dancing in the Moonlight (The Entertainers CD-349) (1996)
Heigh-Ho Everybody! (Flapper CD-7077) (1995)
I'm Just a Vagabond Lover (Laserlight 12-596) (1995)
My Time Is Your Time (The Good Music Company) (1991)
Sing for Your Supper (Conifer CMSCD-005)
Vagabond Lover (Pro-Arte/Fanfare CDD-459) (1989)
The Voice That Had Them Fainting 1928–1937 (Take Two TT-405CD) (1992)

Filmography

CHAPTER 1—GENE AUSTIN

Sadie McKee (Metro-Goldwyn-Mayer, 1934).
Ferry-Go-Round (RKO, 1934).
Gift of Gab (Universal, 1934).
Night Life (RKO, 1935).
Klondike Annie (Paramount, 1936).
Bad Medicine (RKO, 1936).
Trailing Along (RKO, 1937).
Songs and Saddles (Road Show Pictures, 1938).
My Little Chickadee (Universal, 1940).
One Dozen Roses (Soundies Distributing Corp. of America, 1942).
That Rootin' Tootin' Shootin' Man from Texas (Soundies Distributing Corp. of America, 1942).
I Hear Ya Knockin' but Ya Can't Come In (Soundies Distributing Corp. of America, 1942).
Take Your Shoes Off Daddy (Murray Hollywood Productions, 1943); Doris Sherrell sings, with Austin playing piano.
I Hear Ya Knockin' but Ya Can't Come In (Murray Hollywood Productions, 1943); Doris Sherrell sings, with Austin playing piano.
You're Marvelous (Martin Murray Productions, 1943).
Boogie Woogie Wedding (Martin Murray Productions, 1943); Doris Sherrell sings, with Austin playing piano.
(My) Melancholy Baby (Martin Murray Productions, 1943).
Keep a Knockin' (Martin Murray Productions, 1943); Doris Sherrell sings, with Austin playing piano.
My Blue Heaven (Martin Murray Productions, 1943).
I Want to Be Bad (Soundies Distributing Corp. of America, 1944).
I Want to Lead a Band (Soundies Distributing Corp. of America, 1944).
Moon over Las Vegas (Universal, 1944).

Imagine (Soundies Distributing Corp. of America, 1944).
Follow the Leader (Monogram, 1944).
Pagliacci Swings It (Universal, 1944).
My Blue Heaven (Soundies Distributing Corp. of America, 1945).
Fried Green Tomatoes (Universal and Act III Communications, 1991); Austin
  is heard singing "My Blue Heaven" approximately twelve minutes into
  the film; despite the reference to Victor, RCA, and BMG in the closing
  credits, the recording here was made for Decca in 1942.

CHAPTER 2—RUSS COLUMBO

Gus Arnheim and His Ambassadors (Warner Bros., 1929).
Wolf Song (Paramount, 1929).
The Street Girl (Radio Pictures, 1929).
Dynamite (Metro-Goldwyn-Mayer, 1929).
The Wonders of Women (Metro-Goldwyn-Mayer, 1929).
Hello, Sister (Sono Art-Worldwide, 1930).
The Texan (Paramount, 1930).
Hellbound (Tiffany, 1931).
That Goes Double (Warner Bros., 1933) (short).
Broadway thru a Keyhole (Twentieth Century/United Artists, 1933).
Moulin Rouge (Twentieth Century/United Artists, 1934).
Wake Up and Dream (Universal, 1934). British title: *Castles in the Air;* referred
  to in early press releases as *The Love Life of a Crooner.*

CHAPTER 3—BING CROSBY

King of Jazz (Universal, 1930).
Two Plus Fours (Pathé, 1930) (short).
Ripstitch the Tailor (Pathé, 1930) (unreleased short).
Check and Double Check (RKO, 1930).
Confessions of a Co-Ed (Paramount, 1931).
Reaching for the Moon (United Artists, 1931).
Billboard Girl (1931) (short).
Dream House (1931) (short).
Sing, Bing, Sing (1931) (short).
Bring on Bing (1931) (short).
The Big Broadcast of 1932 (Paramount, 1932).
Hollywood on Parade (1932) (short).
Just One More Chance (1932) (short).
College Humor (Paramount, 1933).

Going Hollywood (Cosmopolitan Pictures Production, 1933).
Too Much Harmony (Paramount, 1933).
Please (1933) (short).
Where the Blue of the Night (1933) (short).
We're Not Dressing (Paramount, 1934).
She Loves Me Not (Paramount, 1934).
Just an Echo (1934) (short).
I Surrender Dear (1934) (short).
Here Is My Heart (Paramount, 1934).
Mississippi (Paramount, 1935).
Two for Tonight (Paramount, 1935).
The Big Broadcast of 1936 (Paramount, 1935) (guest appearance).
Star Night at the Cocoanut Grove (1935) (short).
Rhythm on the Range (Paramount, 1936).
Pennies from Heaven (Paramount, 1936).
Waikiki Wedding (Paramount, 1937).
Double or Nothing (Paramount, 1937).
Swing with Bing (1937) (short).
Doctor Rhythm (Paramount, 1938).
Sing You Sinners (Paramount, 1938).
Don't Hook Now (1938) (short).
East Side of Heaven (Universal, 1939).
Paris Honeymoon (Paramount, 1939).
The Star Maker (Paramount, 1939).
If I Had My Way (Universal, 1940).
Rhythm on the River (Paramount, 1940).
Road to Singapore (Paramount, 1940).
Road to Zanzibar (Paramount, 1941).
Birth of the Blues (Paramount, 1941).
Angels of Mercy (1941) (short).
The Road to Victory (1941) (short).
Road to Morocco (Paramount, 1942).
Holiday Inn (Paramount, 1942).
My Favorite Blonde (1942) (Crosby unbilled).
Star Spangled Rhythm (Paramount, 1942).
Dixie (Paramount, 1943).
Going My Way (Paramount, 1944).
Princess and the Pirate (1944) (Crosby unbilled).
Here Comes the Waves (Paramount, 1944).
Out of This World (1945) (voice only).
The Bells of St. Mary's (RKO, 1945).
Duffy's Tavern (Paramount, 1945).
Road to Utopia (Paramount, 1945).

All-Star Bond Rally (Twentieth Century-Fox, 1945) (short).
Hollywood Victory Caravan (Twentieth Century-Fox, 1945) (short).
Blue Skies (Paramount, 1946).
Welcome Stranger (Paramount, 1947).
Road to Rio (Paramount, 1947).
Variety Girl (Paramount, 1947).
My Favorite Brunette (1947) (Crosby unbilled).
The Emperor Waltz (Paramount, 1948).
A Connecticut Yankee in King Arthur's Court (Paramount, 1948).
Top o' the Morning (Paramount, 1948).
The Adventures of Ichabod and Mr. Toad (Paramount, 1948) (voice only).
Mr. Music (Paramount, 1950).
Riding High (Paramount, 1950).
Here Comes the Groom (Paramount, 1951).
Just for You (Paramount, 1952).
Road to Bali (Paramount, 1952).
The Greatest Show on Earth (1952) (Crosby unbilled).
Son of Paleface (1952) (Crosby unbilled).
Little Boy Lost (Paramount, 1953).
Scared Stiff (1953) (Crosby unbilled).
White Christmas (Paramount, 1954).
The Country Girl (Paramount, 1954).
High Society (Metro-Goldwyn-Mayer, 1956).
Anything Goes (Paramount, 1956).
Bing Presents Oreste (1956) (short).
Man on Fire (Metro-Goldwyn-Mayer, 1957).
Showdown at Ulcer Gulch (1958) (short).
Alias Jesse James (1959) (Crosby unbilled).
Say One for Me (Twentieth Century Fox, 1959).
High Time (Twentieth Century-Fox, 1960).
Let's Make Love (1960).
Pepe (1960) (Crosby plays himself).
The Road to Hong Kong (United Artists, 1962).
The Sound of Laughter (1963) (documentary).
Robin and the Seven Hoods (Warner Bros., 1964).
Stagecoach (Twentieth Century-Fox, 1966).
Cinerama's Russian Adventure (1966) (Crosby provides narration).
Bing Crosby's Washington State (1968) (short).
That's Entertainment (Metro-Goldwyn-Mayer, 1974).

CHAPTER 4—NICK LUCAS

Nick Lucas Song (Warner Bros., 1929) (short).
Trailer to the Gold Diggers of Broadway (Warner Bros., 1929) (short).

The Gold Diggers of Broadway (Warner Bros., 1929).
The Show of Shows (Warner Bros., 1929).
Organloguing the Hits with Nick Lucas, the Crooning Troubadour (Master Art Products, 1933) (short).
Home Again (Master Art Products, 1933) (short).
On the Air and Off (Universal, 1933) (short).
What This Country Needs (Warner Bros.-Vitaphone, 1934) (short).
Nick Lucas and His Troubadours (Warner Bros.-Vitaphone, 1936) (short).
Vitaphone Headliners (Warner Bros.-Vitaphone, 1936) (short).
Yankee Doodle Home (Columbia, 1939) (short).
Congamania (Universal, 1940).
Big Time Revue (Warner Bros., 1947).
Disc Jockey (Allied Artists, 1951).
The Great Gatsby (Paramount, 1974).
Day of the Locust (Paramount, 1974).
Hearts of the West (United Artists, 1975).

CHAPTER 5—JOHNNY MARVIN

As Performer

Strumming the Blues Away (Fox Phonofilm, 1928) (short).
Johnny Marvin (Metro-Goldwyn-Mayer, 1928) (short).
Johnny Marvin (Warner Bros., 1928) (short).
A Movietone Divertissment (Metro-Goldwyn-Mayer, 1929) (short).
Johnny Marvin (Metro-Goldwyn-Mayer, 1929) (short).
Johnny Marvin (Metro-Goldwyn-Mayer, 1929) (short).
Metro Movietone Revue, #12 (Metro-Goldwyn-Mayer, 1929) (short).
Rambling 'round Radio Row #3 (Warner Bros., 1932) (short).

As Composer

Springtime in the Rockies (Republic, 1937).
The Old Barn Dance (Republic, 1938).
Under Western Skies (Republic, 1938).
Gold Mine in the Sky (Republic, 1938).
The Man from Music Mountain (Republic, 1938).
Prairie Moon (Republic, 1938).
Rhythm of the Saddle (Republic, 1938).
Come On, Ranger (Republic, 1938).
Western Jamboree (Republic, 1938).
Home on the Prairie (Republic, 1939).

Mountain Rhythm (Republic, 1939).
Rovin' Tumbleweeds (Republic, 1939).
South of the Border (Republic, 1939).
Shooting High (Republic, 1940).
Rancho Grande (Republic, 1940).
Gaucho Serenade (Republic, 1940).
Ride, Tenderfoot, Ride (Republic, 1940).
Barnyard Follies (Republic, 1940).
Heart of the Rio Grande (Republic, 1942).
Riders of the Northland (Columbia, 1942).
The Man from Music Mountain (Republic, 1943).
Boss of Boomtown (Universal, 1944).
Under California Skies (Republic, 1948).

CHAPTER 6—RUDY VALLEE

Rudy Vallee and His Connecticut Yankees (Warner Bros., 1929) (short).
Rudy Vallee (Paramount, 1929) (short).
Radio Rhythm (Paramount, 1929) (short).
The Vagabond Lover (Radio, 1929).
Glorifying the American Girl (Paramount, 1929).
Campus Sweethearts (Radio, 1930) (short).
The Stein Song (Paramount, 1930) (short; voice only).
Betty Coed (Paramount, 1931) (short; voice only).
Kitty from Kansas City (Paramount, 1931) (short; voice only).
Musical Justice (Paramount, 1931) (short).
Paramount Pictorial #7 (Paramount, 1931) (short).
Knowmore College (Paramount, 1932) (short).
Rudy Vallee Melodies (Paramount, 1932) (short).
Musical Doctor (Paramount, 1932) (short).
International House (Paramount, 1933).
George White's Scandals (Fox, 1934).
The Great Megaphone Mystery (Warner Bros., 1935) (short).
Sweet Music (Warner Bros., 1935).
A Trip thru a Hollywood Studio (Warner Bros., 1935) (short).
For Auld Lang Syne (Warner Bros., 1938) (short).
Gold Diggers in Paris (Warner Bros., 1938).
Second Fiddle (20th Century-Fox, 1939).
Picture People #3 (RKO, 1940) (short).
Picture People #4 (RKO, 1941) (short).
Picture People #5 (RKO, 1941) (short).
Screen Snapshots #9 (Columbia, 1941) (short).

Too Many Blondes (Universal, 1941).

Time Out for Rhythm (Columbia, 1941).

Hedda Hopper's Hollywood (Paramount, 1942) (short).

The Palm Beach Story (Paramount, 1942).

Happy Go Lucky (Paramount, 1943).

Rudy Vallee's Coast Guard Band (Warner Bros., 1944) (short).

U.S. Coast Guard Band (Warner Bros., 1944) (short).

It's in the Bag (United Artists, 1945).

Man Alive (RKO, 1945).

Screen Snapshots (Columbia, 1945) (short).

People Are Funny (Paramount, 1946).

The Fabulous Suzanne (Republic, 1946).

The Sin of Harold Diddlebock (United Artists, 1947) (reissued in 1950 as *Mad Wednesday* by RKO).

The Bachelor and the Bobby Soxer (RKO Radio, 1947).

I Remember Mama (RKO, 1948).

So This Is New York (United Artists, 1948) (reissued in 1954 as *Broadway Guys* by Favorite Attractions).

My Dear Secretary (United Artists, 1948).

Unfaithfully Yours (20th Century-Fox, 1948).

Mother Is a Freshman (20th Century-Fox, 1949).

The Beautiful Blonde from Bashful Bend (20th Century-Fox, 1949).

Father Was a Fullback (20th Century-Fox, 1949).

The Admiral Was a Lady (United Artists, 1950).

Ricochet Romance (Universal-International, 1954).

Gentlemen Marry Brunettes (United Artists, 1955).

The Helen Morgan Story (Warner Bros., 1957).

Jazz Ball (NTA, 1958).

How to Succeed in Business without Really Trying (United Artists, 1967).

Live a Little, Love a Little (Metro-Goldwyn-Mayer, 1968).

The Night They Raided Minsky's (United Artists, 1968) (narrator).

The Phynx (Warner Bros., 1970).

The Grissom Gang (Cinerama, 1971) (voice only).

Sunburst (Cinema Financial, 1975) (Video Title: *Slashed Dreams*).

Won Ton Ton, the Dog Who Saved Hollywood (Paramount, 1976).

The Perfect Woman (Gold Key, 1981).

Bibliography

CHAPTER 1—GENE AUSTIN

Agan, John A. "The Voice of the Southland: Louisiana's Gene Austin." *North Louisiana Historical Association Journal* 28, no. 4 (Fall 1997): 123–37.

Cohen, Norm, and Tor Magnusson. "George Reneau: A Discographical Survey." *JEMF Quarterly* 15, no. 56 (Winter 1979): 208–14. Covers the impact Austin had on Reneau's recording career.

Kay, George W. "Gene Austin—Balladeer from the Bayou." *The Second Line* 21 (January–February 1969): 149–53.

Lamparski, Richard. *Whatever Became of . . . ? Second Series.* New York: Crown, 1968. Also published in Canada by General Publishing Company Limited.

Magnusson, Tor. "Fats Waller: Some Considerations on Two Recording Dates." *Annual Review of Jazz Studies I* (1982): 79–84.

———. "Fats Waller with Gene Austin on the Record." *Journal of Jazz Studies* 4, no. 1 (Fall 1974) 75–83.

———. "The Gene Austin Recordings," *Matrix* (Hayes, Middlesex, Great Britain), no. 91 (February 1971): 1–2; no. 92 (April 1971): 1–4; no. 93 (July 1971): 5–6; no. 94 (no date): 7–8; no. 95 (December 1971): 9–10; no. 96 (April 1972): 11–12; no. 97 (September 1972): 13–16; no. 98 (November 1972): 17–18; no. 99/100 (April 1973): 19–22; no. 101 (August 1973): 23–24; no. 102/103 (May 1974): 25–28; no. 104 (August 1974): 1:I–2:I; no. 107/108 (December 1975): 29–32.

———. "The Gene Austin Recordings." *Skivsamlaren* (Goteborg, Sweden), no. 15 (February 1983): 1–82. Survey of Austin's sound recordings, films, radio and television appearances, sheet music, and song compositions (those written by Austin and those published by Gene Austin, Inc.).

Magnusson, Tor, and Don Peak. "Gene Austin's 'Candy and Coco': The Identity of the Second 'Candy' Disclosed." *Storyville* 145 (March 1991): 4–7.

McAndrew, John. "Star Studded Shellac." *The Record Changer* 14, no. 3 (1955): 16.

Pabst, Ralph M. *Gene Austin's Ol' Buddy*. Phoenix, Ariz.: Augury Press, 1984. Allegedly edited transcripts of tape recordings made by Austin; in effect, his autobiography.

Parish, James R., and Michael R. Pitts. "Gene Austin." In *Hollywood Songsters—A Biographical Dictionary*. New York: Garland, 1991, 47–51.

Peak, Don, and Tor Magnusson. "Les Paul with Gene Austin: The '40 Masters.' " *Record Research* 231/232 (October 1987): 1, 4–5.

Pitts, Michael R. "Pop Singers on the Screen." *Film Fan Monthly* 112 (October 1970): 15–18.

Scott, John L. "Gene Austin's Star Overcomes Eclipse," *Los Angeles Times*, March 8, 1959, 5:2.

Smith, H. Allen. "A Crooner Comes Back." *Saturday Evening Post* 230, no. 9 (August 31, 1957): 25, 66–68.

———. "A Friend in Las Vegas." In *A Short History of Fingers and Other State Papers*. Boston: Little, Brown and Company, 1964(?), 44–57. Also published in Canada by Little, Brown & Company Limited.

———. "Gene Austin's Phone Call." In *The Best of H. Allen Smith*. New York: Trident, 1972, 211ff.

Taylor, Erma. "Presenting Gene Austin—America's Favorite Recording Artist of Ten Years Ago Is Still a Big Seller, but Now He Has His Own Orchestra and Crashes the Movies." *The Metronome* (October 1934): 35–36, 41.

Walsh, Jim. "Favorite Recording Artists—Gene Austin." *Hobbies* (February 1957): 34–36, 55, 64; (March 1957): 30–32.

———. "Singer and Record 'Fiend' Find Much to Talk About." *Johnson City Press* (Tennessee), April 27, 1939, 10.

Williams, Ned E. "Gene Austin Began on a Calliope." *The Metronome* (September 1928): 51, 63.

CHAPTER 2—RUSS COLUMBO

Coslow, Sam. *Cocktails for Two: The Many Lives of Giant Songwriter Sam Coslow*. Bayside, NY: Arlington House, 1977.

Deal, Robert T. *The Story of Russ Columbo*. Middlesex, England: Hampton/Memory Lane, 1988.

Hall, Warren. "Kept Alive by Conspirators," *The American Weekly* (October 8, 1944): 19.

"He's Thrilling, Girls, This Russ Columbo!" *Anderson (Indiana) Bulletin* (November 28, 1931): 5.

Hemming, Roy, and David Hajdu. "Russ Columbo." In *Discovering Great Singers of Classic Pop*. New York: Newmarket Press, 1991, 54–58.

Lamparski, Richard. *Lamparski's Hidden Hollywood*. New York: Fireside Books, 1981.

Parish, James Robert. *The Hollywood Celebrity Death Book*. New York: Pioneer Books, 1993.

Parish, James Robert, and Michael R. Pitts. "Russ Columbo." In *Hollywood Songsters—A Biographical Dictionary*. New York: Garland, 1991.

Ramsey, Walter. "The Tragic Death of Russ Columbo." *Radio Stars* (December 1934): 34–36, 83, 85, 87, 89, 91.

"Russ Columbo Proves Latest Sensation of Broadway." *Anderson (Indiana) Daily Bulletin* (September 12, 1931): 5.

CHAPTER 3—BING CROSBY

Barnes, Ken. *The Crosby Years*. New York: St. Martin's, 1980. Includes chronological discography and filmography.

Bassett, John, et al. *The Bing Crosby LP-ography*. 1977. Rev. ed.; originally published in 1973.

Bauer, Barbara. *Bing Crosby*. New York: Pyramid, 1977. Focuses on Crosby's film career.

Bing Crosby: A Pictorial Tribute. New York: Dell, 1977.

Bing Crosby on Broadway [64-page Uris Theatre playbill]. New York: Dell, 1977.

Bishop, Bert, and John Bassett. *Bing: Just for the Record* [private publication]. 1980. Discography of Crosby's commercial recordings.

Bookbinder, Robert. *The Films of Bing Crosby*. Secaucus, N.J.: Citadel, 1977. Covers 55 feature film roles, 17 cameo appearances, 1 TV movie, 2 narrative contributions, and an anthology.

Carpozi, George, Jr. *The Fabulous Life of Bing Crosby*. New York: Manor, 1977. pap.

Crosby, Bing. *Bing Crosby*. 1991.

Crosby, Bing, and Pete Martin. *Call Me Lucky*. Introduction by Gary Giddins. New York: Da Capo Press, 1993. Reprint of Crosby's 1953 autobiography published by Simon & Schuster. Also serialized in *The Saturday Evening Post* (February 14, 21, 28, March 7, 14, 21, 28, and April 4, 1953) and a *Reader's Digest Condensed Book*.

Crosby, Gary, and Ross Firestone. *Going My Own Way*. Garden City, N.Y.: Doubleday, 1983. Centers on Crosby's harsh treatment of his eldest son.

Crosby, Kathryn. *Bing and Other Things*. New York: Meredith, 1967. Covers her life in general, with a particular emphasis on her marriage to Crosby.

———. *My Life with Bing*. Wheeling, Ill.: Collage, 1983. Covers the period up to 1965. While candid in tone, some stories vary from those in *Bing and Other Things*.

Crosby, Ted, and Larry Crosby. *Bing*. New York: World, 1937. Revised by Ted Crosby as *The Story of Bing Crosby* in 1946; includes a foreword by Bob Hope.

Friedland, Michael. *Bing Crosby: An Illustrated Biography*. North Palmfret, UT: Andre Deutsch, 1999.

A Guy Called Bing. Manchester, U.K.: World Distributors, 1977.

Koenig, Joseph L. *Bing*. New York: Dell, 1977. pap.

Martin, George V. *The Bells of St. Mary's*. New York: Grosset & Dunlap, 1946.

Mello, Edward J., and Tom McBride. *Bing Crosby Discography*. San Francisco, January 31, 1947.

Mielke, Randall G. *The Road to Box Office: The Seven Film Comedies of Bing Crosby, Bob Hope and Dorothy Lamour, 1940–1962*. Jefferson, N.C.: McFarland, 1997.

Mize, J. T. H. *Bing Crosby and the Bing Crosby Style: Crosbyana thru Biography-Photography-Discography*. Chicago: Who Is Who in Music, 1946. Revised in an alphabetized discography through 1947; includes listings of album sets and Brunswick masters released on other labels.

Morgereth, Timothy A. *Bing Crosby: A Discography, Radio Program List and Filmography*. Jefferson, N.C.: McFarland, 1987. A chronological listing of recordings to 1957, radio shows to 1954, and motion pictures.

Netland, Dwayne. *The Crosby: Greatest Show in Golf*. New York: Doubleday, 1975.

O'Connell, Sheldon, with Gordon Atkinson. *Bing: A Voice for All Seasons* [private publication], 1984.

Osterholm, J. Roger. *Bing Crosby: A Bio-Bibliography*. Westport, CT: Greenwood, 1994.

Paradissis, A. G. *The Bing Book of Verse*. Melbourne, Australia: Globe, 1983.

Pleasants, Henry. *The Great American Popular Singers*. New York: Simon & Schuster, 1974. Each chapter focuses on an important popular music vocalist; Crosby's significant legacy is discussed at length.

Pugh, Colin. *Alternate Bing Crosby*. (Privately issued): Bristol, U.K., 1988. A listing of alternate recording takes by Crosby.

Reynolds, Fred. *The Crosby Collection: Part One, 1926–34*. Gateshead, U.K.: John Joyce and Son, 1991.

———. *Road to Hollywood: The Bing Crosby Films*. Rev. ed. Gateshead, Tyne & Wear, U.K.: John Joyce and Son, 1986. The first edition includes a foreword by Crosby.

Rosenbaum, Linda. *Bing Crosby Album*. Sacramento, CA: Lorelei, 1977.

Shepherd, Donald, and Robert F. Slatzer. *Bing Crosby: The Hollow Man*. New York: St. Martin's, 1981. Reprinted by Pinnacle (New York, 1982).

Thomas, Bob. *The One and Only Bing*. New York: Grosset & Dunlap, 1977. Includes "A Special Tribute to Bing Crosby," by Bob Hope.

Thompson, Charles. *Bing: The Authorized Biography*. London: W. H. Allen, 1976. Also published by David McKay (New York, 1976). Revised as *The Complete Crosby*.

Ulanov, Barry. *The Incredible Crosby*. New York: Whittlesey House/McGraw-Hill, 1948.

Zwisohn, Laurence J. *Bing Crosby: A Lifetime of Music*. Los Angeles: Palm Tree Library, 1978. Includes a foreword by song composer James Van Heusen. The bulk of the work lists Crosby's recordings in alphabetical order.

CHAPTER 4—NICK LUCAS

Hoover, Will. *Picks!: The Colorful Saga of Vintage Celluloid Guitar Plectrums*. San Francisco: Miller Freeman Books, n.d.

Nick Lucas interviews with Michael R. Pitts (1974–1981).

Olbrecht, James. "Nick Lucas: The First Star of Recorded Guitar." *Guitar Player* (December 1980).

Parish, James Robert, and Michael R. Pitts. *Hollywood Songsters*. New York: Garland, 1991.

Pitts, Michael R. "Nick Lucas on Film, Stage, Radio and Records." *Classic Images* 103 (January 1984).

"Nick Lucas, the Crooning Troubadour." *Focus on Film* 20 (Spring 1975).

Rigler & Deutsch Index. Washington, D.C.: Library of Congress, n.d.

Rust, Brian, and Allen G. Debus. *The Complete Entertainment Discography from 1897 to 1942*. 2nd ed. New York: Da Capo Press, 1989.

Simross, Lynn. "Tiptoeing through a Comeback," *Los Angeles Times*, August 5, 1975.

Slide, Anthony. *The Vaudevillians: A Dictionary of Vaudeville Performers*. Westport, Conn.: Arlington House, 1981.

CHAPTER 5—JOHNNY MARVIN

The ASCAP Biographical Dictionary of Composers, Authors and Publishers. New York: American Society of Composers, Authors and Publishers, 1966.

Frankie Marvin interview with Jim Bedoian and Eugene Earle (June 5, 1983).

Jacobs, Mary. "Flopping Was a Habit with Him." *Radio Stars* (April 1934).

Rust, Brian, and Allen G. Debus. *The Complete Entertainment Discography from 1897 to 1942.* 2nd ed. New York: Da Capo Press, 1989.

CHAPTER 6—RUDY VALLEE

Kiner, Larry F. *The Rudy Vallee Discography.* Westport, Conn.: Greenwood Press, 1985.
Parish, James Robert, and Michael R. Pitts. *Hollywood Songsters.* New York: Garland, 1991.
Slide, Anthony. *The Vaudevillians: A Dictionary of Vaudeville Performers.* Westport, Conn.: Arlington House, 1981.
Vallee, Eleanor, with Jill Amadio. *My Vagabond Lover: An Intimate Biography of Rudy Vallee.* Dallas, Texas: Taylor Publishing Company, 1996.
Vallee, Rudy. *Let The Chips Fall.* Harrisburg, Pa.: Stackpole Books, 1975.
Vallee, Rudy, with Gil McKean. *My Time Is Your Time: The Rudy Vallee Story.* New York: Ivan Obolensky, 1962.

Index

Abbott, Joan, 193
acoustic era recording, 9–10, 26, 58, 134, 137–38
Acuff-Rose, 34
Adams, Rick, 78
Adrian, Iris, 200
African Americans. *See* minstrelsy; Negro
All-Star Orchestra, 169
Allen, Fred, 202
Amendt, Johnny, 181
American Ragtime Octette, 45
American Record Company (ARC), 58, 152, 172, 179–81, 197
American Society of Composers, Authors, and Publishers, 68, 183
American vernacular singing, 5–12
Amos and Andy, 109
Antelline, Agnes, 69–71, 73, 75, 78
Archerd, Amy, 120
Arden-Ochman Orchestra, 167–69
Armstrong, Louis, 127
Arnheim, Gus, 35–37, 86–87, 108–11
Arnold, Kathryn, 56, 58–61, 63, 67–68
Associated Press, 120–21, 190, 210
Astaire, Adele, 138
Astaire, Fred, 138

Atkins, Chet, 133
Atkinson, Brooks, 154
Austin, Gene, 29–30, 36, 43, 128, 142, 155, 159, 169, 171, 176, 178, 180, 193; bibliography, 295–96; biography, 51–84; daughters: Anne, 67; Charlotte, 70, 73, 75; death in Palm Springs, 78; discography, 217–39; English tour, 60–61; governor's race, 77; investment in stock market, 67–68; Las Vegas residency, 75–76; military service, 54–55; music and lyrics composed by Austin, 79–80; My Blue Heaven [nightclub], 71–72, 75–76; *My Blue Heaven* [yacht], 63–64; original name, 51; recordings, 2–3, 12, 39, 56–59, 61–62, 76–77; sheet music with Austin cover photo, 82; songs published by Gene Austin, Inc., 81; songwriting, 23, 42, 55–56, 71. *See also* Kathryn Arnold; Agnes Antelline; Doris Sherrell; LouCeil Hudson; Gigi Theodora
Austin, Jim, 52–53, 59–60
Autry, Gene, 133, 172, 182–83
Autry, Ina Mae, 184

Bacall, Betty, 122
Backer, Les, 33
Bailey, Mildred, 101
Bailey's Lucky Seven, 134
Baker, Belle, 145, 149, 188
Banta, Frank, 133
Barnes, George, 77
Barnes, Ken, 125
Barrios, Valentin, 126
Barris, Harry, 104–9. *See also* Rhythm Boys
Barrymore, John, 199
Baur, Franklyn, 28
Baxter, Warner, 146
Beedy, Carroll L., 192
Beiderbecke, Bix, 127
Bell, Archie, 150–51
Bell, Rex, 77
Bennett, Constance, 90
Bennie Kruger and His Orchestra, 174–75
Benny, Jack, 32, 118
Bergere, Roy, 55–56
Berkeley, Busby, 198
Berle, Milton, 198
Berlin, Irving, 7–8, 15, 113, 198–99
Bernie, Ben, 36, 145
Berry, Chuck, 23
Bert Ambrose Orchestra, 16
Bert Kaplan's Collegians, 167
Billboard, 56, 73–74, 77, 136–37, 139, 143–47, 150, 153–54, 162, 164, 168–74, 176–77, 188, 190–91, 193
Blane, Sally, 89, 93
Blau, George, 46
Bluebird [record company], 47, 196, 198
blues, 6, 17
Bogart, Humphrey, 35, 122
Boles, John, 107
Bolger, Ray, 193
Bolitho, William, 33
Boone, Pat, 23

Borge, Victor, 201
Boswell Sisters, 90, 151
Bow, Clara, 31
Bowie, David, 125
Bowlly, Al, 44, 49
Bracken, Eddie, 200
Brando, Marlon, 118
Brice, Fanny, 101
Brokenshire, Norman, 180
Brooklyn Paramount, 88, 110
Brown, Joe E., 183
Brown, Lansing V., Jr., 93
Browne, Ted, 17–18, 48
Bruno, Paul, 95
Brunswick [record company], 58, 87, 91, 151, 176, 192; Nick Lucas recordings, 133, 135–38, 141–52
Buchanan, Jack, 138
Buck, Gene, 68
Buddy Cole Trio, 119
Burkan, Nathan, 68
Burke, Frank, 169
Burke, Joe, 147
Burns, Haydon, 77
Burr, Henry, 9, 28–29, 167; recordings, 10
Burton, Beatrice, 59
Bushkin, Joe, 124–25
Butler, Ralph, 2

Cagney, James, 35
Cairns, C. C., 170
Callaway, Sheldon Keate, 94
Candido, Johnny. *See* Candy and Coco
Candy & Coco, 70–75
Cantor, Eddie, 101, 104, 116
Carmichael, Hoagy, 127, 197
Carpenter, Billy "Yuke," 58
Carpenter, Ken, 119
Carroll, Carroll, 115
Carroll, Frank, 77
Carroll Gibbons and His Orchestra

Carter, Jimmy, 126
Cassidy, Hartley, 78
Cavanaugh, James, 104
Chaney, Lon, 200
Chaplin, Charlie, 101
Charlie Fry and His Million Dollar
    Orchestra, 167
Chevalier, Maurice, 178, 180, 193
The Clan, 121–22
Clark, Don, 102
Clayton, Lou, 56, 145
Clayton-Jackson-Durante, 77
Cleary, Ruth, 182
Clooney, Rosemary, 122, 124, 126
Coco & Malt. *See* Candy & Coco
Coco-Malt, 72
Colombo, Julia, 85
Colombo, Nicholas, 85
Columbia [record company], 16, 19–
    20, 22–23, 25–31, 47, 135, 176,
    196; Bing Crosby recordings, 103,
    106, 111; English Columbia, 186,
    197; Johnny Marvin recordings,
    162–66, 179–80, 182; Nick Lucas
    recordings, 133
Columbo, Russ, 21, 35–39, 128, 180;
    bibliography, 296–97; biography,
    85–95; death, 93–94; discogra-
    phy, 239–42; family members,
    85, 94; films, 49, 90–92; original
    name, 85; rivalry with Crosby,
    87–88, 91–92, 94–95, 110
Como, Perry, 95, 114, 122
compact discs, 23–25
Connecticut Yankees, 187–89, 191,
    193–97, 199
Conqueror, 180, 197
Conrad, Con, 31, 87, 89
Coogan, Jackie, 101
Cook, Frederick Albert, 135
Cornell, Don, 95
Coslow, Sam, 34, 42–43, 48
Covey, Dave, 78

Cowan, Jerome, 200
Crawford, Jesse, 179
Crosby, Bing, 2, 4, 20–22, 30, 34–39,
    42, 85–88, 94–95, 140, 142, 151;
    attitude toward television,
    117–18; bibliography, 297–99; bi-
    ography, 97–129; birthdate con-
    troversy, 97; business interests,
    115; criticism of film industry,
    123; death, 126–27; discography,
    242–76; family members, 97–99,
    106, 127; films, 108–14, 116,
    118–23; jukeboxes, 49; legacy,
    127–128; lung operation, 124; ori-
    gin of nickname, "Bing," 98; ori-
    gin of nickname, "Der Bingle,"
    113; radio work, 107–8, 114–15,
    118, 122, 151; recordings, 1, 34,
    48, 102–6, 109, 111–12, 114, 119,
    121–24; rivalry with Sinatra,
    114–15; screen tests, 106–7; tele-
    vision work, 117–20, 122–24. *See
    also* Russ Columbo; Kathryn
    Grant; Dixie Lee; Musicaladers;
    Rhythm Boys; Al Rinker
Crosby, Everett, 109–10
Crosby, Gary, 117, 119–21
Crosby, Harry, Jr., 125–26
Crosby, Larry, 117
Crumit, Frank, 28–29, 39, 49, 171,
    180
Cummings, Constance, 90–91
Curtis, Tony, 95, 121

Dalhart, Vernon, 69, 166
Damerell, Stanley, 2
Davis, Benny, 63
Davis, Joan, 199
Davis, Meyer, 69
Davis, Sammy, Jr., 121–22
Deal, Robert, 91–92
Decca [record company], 91, 111–
    112, 119, 155, 182, 198–99, 208;
    British Decca, 124. *See also* MCA

Index

DeForest, Lee, 14, 21
De Leath, Vaught, 14
Dell, Dorothy, 89
Del Rio, Dolores, 41
Dempsey, Paul, 168
Desmond, Johnny, 95
Dickerman, Don, 187, 199
Dillinger, John, 69
Dixon, Mort, 92
Donaldson, Walter, 59, 61–63, 103
Don Azdiazu and His Havana Club
    Orchestra, 17
Dorsey, Jimmy, 11
Dowling, Eddie, 164
Downey, Morton, 32
Dr. Cheer [radio personality], 179
Dubin, Al, 90, 147
Duchin, Eddy, 153
Duke and His Uke, 163–64, 166
Dunagan, John, 77–78
Durante, Jimmy, 32, 34, 77, 145
Dvorak, Ann, 196

Earl Fuller's Jazz Band, 133
Edison [record company], 26–27, 42,
    57, 187; Diamond Discs, 27;
    Johnny Marvin recordings,
    162–67; test pressings, 132
Edison, Thomas, 26–28, 48
Edwards, Cliff, 28, 36, 43, 162, 164,
    166, 176, 197; eefing, 30, 45, 162;
    recordings, 3, 58 Edwin J. Mc-
    Enelly's Orchestra, 167
The Eight Devils, 163
electronic recordings, 25–31, 138.
    See also microphones
Ellington, Duke, 47, 145, 178–79, 193
Elton Spence and His Ukulele,
    162–63
Enright, Ray, 198
Erlanger, A. L., 164
Ernie Golden's Orchestra, 165
Esau, Uncle, 53–54, 59–61, 68, 73

Evans, Frank, 168
Ewen, David, 61–62

Fain, Sammy, 34
Fairbanks, Douglas, 109
Falk, Peter, 122
Faye, Alice, 194, 196
Fay, Frank, 32
Faylen, Carol, 122
Felix Mendelssohn and His Orches-
    tra, 44
Fenstad, Emil, 192
Fields, Benny, 34
Fields, W. C., 196
Fio Rito, Ted, 132, 134–35
Fisher, Alan, 126
Fitzgerald, Leo, 136, 138, 140, 142,
    144, 148, 152–53
Fleischer, Dave, 193
Fleischmann Yeast, 190
Flippen, Jay C., 181
Ford, John, 122
Foster, Stephen, 8, 29, 68
Fox [film studio], 146, 196. *See also*
    Twentieth Century-Fox
Foy, Eddie, Jr., 90, 145
France, 54–55
Francis, Connie, 23
Frank, Abe, 86, 107–9
Frankel, Harry (aka Singin' Sam),
    152
Frankie and Johnny [Marvin broth-
    ers performing duo], 181
Frank Mater and His Collegians,
    187
Fred Waring's Pennsylvanians, 145,
    171, 174, 179, 193
Freeman, Mona, 118
Frohme Sisters, 176

Gable, Clark, 35
Gans, Tom and Mary Anne, 141–42
Gardiner, W. Tudor, 192

Garland, Beverly, 122
Garland, Judy, 118
Garroway, Dave, 77
Gaylord, Chester, 33
Gellhorn, Martha, 32
Gennett [record company], 47, 134, 162–64, 166–67
George Olsen and His Orchestra, 106, 171, 175
George, Wally, 157
Gershwin, George and Ira, 29, 145
Gibson Guitar Company, 131, 141–42
Gilbert and Sullivan [composers], 99
Gilbert, John, 49
Gilbert, Joseph George, 44
Gilbert, Wolfie, 145
Gillespie, Jimmy, 102
Gillham, Art, 3–4, 16–29, 33, 36, 46–48
Gillham, Gertrude, 23
Gillham, Louisa Canada, 19
Goldstein, Leonard, 107
Gonzaga, 98–100
Goodman, Benny, 89
Gould, Jack, 118
Grable, Betty, 116
Grant, Cary, 202
Grant, Kathryn, 120, 124, 126–27; children, 120
Great Depression, 4, 25, 27, 32, 35, 37, 87, 131, 149, 159–60, 173, 176, 178–79, 192–93, 196
Green, Abel, 163
Greene, Gene, 45–46
Greer, Bettejane, 201
Grey Gull [record company], 162–63, 166
Grier, Jimmie, 86, 91, 201
Griffin, Merv, 78, 156–57
Grizzard, George, 77
Guest, Lionel, 25
Guinan, Texas, 90

Guthrie, Woody, 7
Guy Lombardo and His Royal Canadians, 181

Hadju, David, 88
Haley, Bill, 2
Hallet, Mel, 133
Hall, Russell, 72
Hall, Warren, 94
Hall, William, 181
Hammerstein, Oscar, II, 65, 91
Hancock, Billy, 162
Handy, W. C., 17, 47
Happiness Boys, 174
Harbin, Vernon, 189
Harding, Ann, 199
Harding, Warren G., 69
Harmony [record company], 163, 166–67, 187
Harney, Ben, 17
Harris, Marion, 11, 149
Harris, Phil, 153
Harvey, Lillian, 196
Haymes, Dick, 114
Hayton, Lennie, 111
Healy, Mary, 198–99
Heimel, Otto. *See* Candy and Coco
Hemming, Roy, 88
Henderson, Charles, 116, 188
Henie, Sonja, 198
Henley, James, 164
Hennepin-Orpheum circuit, 169
Herbert, Victor, 68, 198
Herlihy, Joe, 187
Herman, Woody, 86
High Hatters, 178–79, 193
Hill, Joe, 6–7
Hines, Earl, 86
His Majesty's Grenadier Guards, 25
His Master's Voice, 165, 173, 186
Hit-of-the-Week [record company], 151, 195–96
Hobart, Valentine, 98

Hoffman, Biff, 4
Holiday, Billie, 127
Hollywood Roosevelt, 86
Holman, Libby, 149
Honey Duke and His Uke, 162–64, 166–67, 178
Hoover, Herbert, 35
Hope, Bob, 111, 113, 117–18, 121
Hopper, Hedda, 92
Houston, David, 77
Howard, Eugene, 193, 197
Howard, Joe, 137
Howard, Willie, 193, 197
Hudson, LouCeil, 76–77
Humphrey, Mark, 142
Hutton, Betty, 200–201
Hyams, Joe, 120–21
Hylton, Jack, 139

Irwin, May, 9

Jackson, Eddie, 77, 145
Jackson, Mahalia, 120
Jacques Renard and His Orchestra, 167
Jan Garber and His Orchestra, 167
jazz, 2, 4, 6
Jean Goldkette and His Orchestra, 176
Jenkins, Allen 200
Jessel, George, 101
Jewell, Richard B., 189
Jimmy May and His Uke, 162
Johnny Hamp and His Kentucky Serenaders, 169
Jolson, Al, 8, 15, 38, 46, 48, 57–58, 90, 104, 116, 145, 148–49, 175
Jolson, Harry, 48
Joplin, Scott, 48
Joy, Leonard, 179
J. W. Seligman and Co., 167

Kahn, Gus, 59, 145
Kahn, Otto, 139

Kane, Helen, 178
Kapp, Jack, 111–12; *See also* Decca
Kaufman, Irving, 28, 152
Kay, Lambdin, 19
Keeler, Ruby, 90, 145
Keith-Albee-Orpheum circuit, 105, 138, 140, 142, 144–46, 168, 178, 181, 187–89
Kelly, Grace, 119
Kemp, Hal, 112
Kenton, Stan, 86
Kentucky Five, 132–33
Kern, Jerome, 65, 91
Kerr, Bob, 70, 73
Kerr, Jean, 206
King, Eddie, 16, 28
King, Wayne, 178, 193
King Oliver, 179, 193
Kirkeby, Ed, 66–67
Knapp, Lieutenant, 55
Knickerbockers, 165, 167
Knight, June, 91
Krupa, Gene, 89

Laden, Lester, 187
Laemmle, Carl, 93
Lahr, Bert, 197
Laine, Frankie, 150, 174
Lamour, Dorothy, 41, 113, 117
Landry, Bob, 178, 194
Lane, Richard, 200
Lang, Eddie, 111
Lang, Walter, 94
Langford, Frances, 198
Lanin, Sam, 133–34. *See also* Bailey's Lucky Seven
Lardner, Ring, 203
Lawford, Peter, 121
Lawrence, Gertrude, 186
Leahy, Joseph J., 207
Lee, Dixie, 109, 117–18; children, 120–21. *See also* Gary Crosby
Leland, Gordon M., 164

LeMaire, Rufus, 136
Leslie, Edgar, 31
Les Paul Trio, 202
Lewis, Gordon, 95
Lewis, Jerry, 118, 121
Lewis, Jerry Lee, 23
Lewis, Ted, 71, 116, 145, 150
Lillie, Beatrice, 186
Linkletter, Art, 154
Little, "Little" Jack, 3, 20–21, 27–28, 36, 48; recordings, 30–31
Little Richard, 23
Lloyd, Harold, 202
Locust Sisters, 174
Lombard, Carole, 92–94
Loy, Myrna, 148, 202
Lucas, Belle, 51–53, 59–60, 67–68, 71
Lucas, Frank, 132–33
Lucas, Lemuel Eugene. *See* Gene Austin
Lucas, Nick, 32–33, 41–43, 58, 78, 159, 169, 172, 174, 176, 192, 211; bibliography, 299; biography, 131–58; British tour, 138–40; daughter, Emily, 133; death, 157; discography, 276–80; family members, 131–32; films, 146–48, 151–56; guitar instruction books, 140–41; legacy, 131, 157; marriage to Catherine Cifrodella, 132, 142, 153–54, 156; original of nickname, "The Crooning Troubador," 136; original name, 131; radio work, 135, 138, 151–54, 156; recordings, 132–38, 141, 146–51, 153–55; songwriting, 141; television work, 155–57; vaudeville performing, 142–46, 151, 154; world tour [1939–1941], 153
Lucas, Nova, 51–53
Lucas Novelty Quartet, 133
Lucas Ukulele Trio, 133
Lyman, Abe, 86, 90

Lyman, Tommy, 62
Lynn, Betty, 203

MacDonald, Eugene, 135
MacDonough, Silvio, 68
MacMurray, Fred, 86, 200, 203
Malneck, Marty, 102, 104
Manning, T. D., 39
Manone, Wingy, 70
March, Hal, 205
Martin, Dean, 118, 120–22
Martin, Freddy, 204
Martin, Mary, 200–201
Martin, Tony, 95
Marvin, Frankie, 172, 176–79, 181–82
Marvin, Johnny, 24, 48, 58, 193; biography, 159–84; discography, 280–87; family members, 160–61, 181; films, 165, 172–74; legacy, 159–60, 184; London tour, 169–70; marriages, 181; pseudonyms, 162–63, 166, 178; radio work, 165, 173, 179–83; recordings, 162–69, 171, 173–83; vaudeville performing, 161–62, 168, 170–71, 178, 182
Marvin Sargent and the Four Camerons, 161
Marvin Trio, 180
Maxwell, George, 68
Maxwell, Robert, 201
McHugh, Frank, 122, 145
Melotone [record company], 152, 180–81, 197
Mercer, Johnny, 94–95, 110
Merman, Ethel, 193
Merriman, H. O., 25
Metro-Goldwyn-Mayer [film studio], 170, 172–74, 176
MGM [record company], 206–7, 210
microphones, 12–14, 20, 58, 116
Middleton, Scott, 47

Mike Marvel's Orchestra, 163
Miller, Ann, 200
Miller, Jack, 33
Mills Brothers, 151
Mills, Colonel, 53
Mills, Irving, 47
Mineralava, 186
Minnelli, Liza, 124
minstrelsy, 8
Miss Patricola, 10–11
Mitchell, Thomas, 122
Mize, J. T. H., 116
Molina, Carlos, 108
Moody, Phillip, 78
Morgan, Helen, 178, 180, 193, 197
Morrissey, Will, 101
Morrow, Bill, 117
Morrow, George, 187
Morse, Robert, 207–8, 210
motion pictures; talkies, 27
Murphy, Mary, 118
Murray, Billy, 9–10, 28–29, 48, 167
Murray, Ken, 75, 154
Musicaladers, 100. *See also* Bing
    Crosby; Al Rinker

Nat Shilkret and the Victor Orches-
    tra, 57–59, 62, 164, 167–69, 175,
    178, 193
NEA Service, 88, 191
Negri, Pola, 86, 101
Negro church singing, 5–6
Neilan, Marshall, 189
New Vaudeville Band, 210
New York, 5, 16, 19, 55–63; clubs, 12,
    61; 1964–65 World's Fair, 122;
    radio broadcasting, 14–15
New York Times, 11–12, 23, 35, 38, 61,
    118, 139, 146, 154
Nicholls, Horatio, 44
Noble, Ray, 195
North, Sheree, 118
Norvis, Donald, 152

Oberstein, Eli, 199
O'Brien, George, 31
O'Connell, Cardinal, 21
O'Grady, Ellen, 34
O'Hara, Maureen, 203
O'Keefe, Walter, 107
Okeh [record company], 19, 86,
    161–67
O'Melveny, John, 109
Original Dixieland Jazz Band, 17
Oriole [record company], 152,
    180–81
Oriole Terrace Orchestra, 134–36
Orkin, Earl, 127
Osborn, Bob, 103
Osborne, Will, 192
Osterholm, J. Roger, 116, 119, 124–
    25, 127–28
O'Sullivan, Denis, 99
Ott, Captain, 63–64
Overstreet, Tommy, 77

Page, Patti, 77, 120, 155
Paley, William, 110
Paramount [film studio], 43, 49, 91,
    109–13, 118–19, 156, 175, 190–91,
    193, 196, 200 Paramount Publix
    chain, 87–88, 90, 101–2, 192
Paramount Theatre [Brooklyn],
    189–91, 194
Paramount Theatre [New York],
    103, 110, 114, 188–91, 194
Parker, "Colonel" Tom, 2, 73–74
Parker, Don, 133
Parrish, Helen, 200
Paterson, George, 93
Pathe Actuelle [record company],
    133, 161–62
Pathe [film company], 108
Pathe [record company], 19, 45, 58,
    133
Paul Ash and His Orchestra, 167
Peak, Don, 61

Pepper, Jack, 78
Perfect [record company], 133, 152, 162, 180, 197
Peters, Stuart, 94
Pinero, Manuel, 126
Pleasants, Henry, 116
Porter, Cole, 119
Powell, Dick, 200–201
Powell, William, 92
Presley, Elvis, 4, 119, 127–28, 157, 189, 210; recordings, 2–3, 23
Price, Gloria, 172, 181
Prima, Louis, 72
Pryor, Roger, 91
Pudinger, Victoria, 156
Putnam, Bill, 78

Questal, Mae, 193

Rachmaninoff, Serge, 48
radio, 13–14, 18–23, 27, 64; ABC, 115, 154; CBS, 86–87, 106, 110, 119, 122, 151–53, 173, 183; NBC, 87–88, 90–91, 105–6, 145–46, 151, 179–82, 190–91, 193, 196–97, 199, 201–2, 204
Radio Corporation of America (RCA), 13; headquarters, 22.
ragtime, 6, 8–9, 45–48
Rambova, Natascha, 186
Rat Pack. *See* Clan
Razaf, Andy, 33
Reisman, Leo, 178, 193
Reneau, George, 56–57
Revelers, 28
rhythm and blues, 4, 128
Rhythm Boys, 36–37, 104–9. *See also* Bing Crosby; Al Rinker
Rich, Fred(die), 152, 167
Richman, Harry, 149
Riddle, Nelson, 156–57
Rinker, Al, 36, 100–10. *See also* Musicaladers; Rhythm Boys

Ritter, Louis Frederic, 6
RKO, 108–9, 147, 149
Robertson, Dick, 35
Robinson, Jackie, 121
Robison, Carson, 58
rock 'n' roll, 1–2, 4, 38
Rodgers, Jimmie, 171–72
Rogel, Yvette, 174
Rogers, Buddy, 31, 178, 193
Rogers, Roy, 183
Roger Wolfe Kahn and His Orchestra, 167, 169
Roland, Gilbert, 94
Rose, Fred, 33–34, 141, 183
Rose, Harry, 174
Rosenbloom, Maxie, 201
Ross, Shirley, 86
Rotter, Alma, 166
Rubinoff, David, 144, 201
Rupp, Carl, 59
Russell, Henry, 5
Russin, Babe, 89
Russo, Danny, 134–35

Sargent, Charles, 161–62, 166, 182
Sarnoff, David, 13, 22
Savoy Havana Band, 186
Savoy Hotel, 43, 186
Sawyer, Grant, 77
Scheuing, Edwin W., 192
Scott, Vernon, 157
Seaton, George, 118
Seeger, Pete, 7
Seeley, Blossom, 10, 34, 90
Segal, Harry, 78
Selvin, Ben, 165
Sennett, Mack, 109–10
Shapiro, Ted, 34
Shaw, Wini, 91
Shepherd, Donald, 99, 107–8
Sherman, Lowell, 94
Sherrell, Doris, 75–76
Sherrell, Grace, 75

Sherry, Diane, 122
Sinatra, Frank, 95, 114–15, 121–22, 126–27, 140, 157, 189
Sinnott, Rose Marie, 174
Slatzer, Robert F., 99, 107–8
Smalle, Ed, 167–69, 174–75
Smeck, Roy, 181
Smith, H. Allen, 62
Smith, Kate, 145, 150, 154, 164. 195
Smith, "Whispering" Jack, 14–16, 19–22, 27–28, 33–34, 36, 48, 58; recordings, 3, 30
Smythe, Billy, 46–48
Sousa, John Philip, 10, 99
Stanley, Aileen, 48, 57–58, 63, 167, 174
Stark, John, 47–48
Stept, Sam H., 141, 144
Stewart, Jimmy, 118
Sugarman, Elias E., 188
Sullivan, Ed, 154, 205
Sullivan, Joe, 89

Taylor, Glenhall, 107
Taylor, Vernon Wesley, 103, 108
Teal, Ray, 152
Tearle, Conway, 146
television, 22; ABC, 120, 122, 206, 211; CBS, 118, 125, 154, 205–6, 211; NBC, 77, 117, 122, 155–56, 204, 206, 211–13. *See also* Gene Austin; Bing Crosby
Theodore, Gigi, 77
Thompson, Charles, 102, 105, 110–11, 122, 128
Thorne, George, 162
Three Cheers Trio, 108, 124
Three Vagrants, 132
Tin Pan Alley, 9, 15, 49, 59, 146; composers, 8; recordings, 7; song pluggers, 14
Tiny Tim, 138, 155–56
Torme, Mel, 202

Trotter, John Scott, 112
The Troubadours, 167
Tubb, Ernest, 182
Tucker, Sophie, 9–10, 34, 71, 104, 145, 188
Turner, Ray, 102
Turpin, Tom, 47
Twentieth Century-Fox [film studio], 109, 114, 116, 122–23
Twentieth Century Pictures, 90

Ukulele Ike. *See* Cliff Edwards
Ukulele Luke, 166
Ulanov, Barry, 87, 99–100, 105
Underwood, Cecil, 90
United Artists [film studio], 109, 156, 202, 204, 206
United Artists [record label], 124
Universal Pictures, 91, 106, 152, 200

Vale, Jerry, 95
Valentino, Rudolph, 86, 110, 186
Vallee, Rudy, 12, 20–21, 24, 32–38, 40–42, 69, 85, 128, 131, 140, 145, 174, 178, 180; comments on Battle of the Baritones, 94, 110; bibliography, 300; biography, 185–215; death, 214–15; discography, 287–94; family members, 185–86; films, 92, 189–91, 193, 196, 198–204, 206, 210; legacy, 185, 215; marriage to Leonie Cauchois, 188; marriage to Fay Webb, 194; marriage to Bettejane Greer, 201; marriage to Eleanor Norris, 205; origin of nickname, 186; original name, 185; radio work, 111, 187, 190–97, 199, 201–2, 206–7; recordings, 186–89, 192, 195–99, 206, 208, 210, 212–14; television work, 205, 207, 209, 211–13; vaudeville performing, 187–88
Van & Schenck, 145, 188–89

Van Heusen, Jimmy, 113
Variety, 17, 31, 64–65, 121, 125–26, 136–37, 139, 143–44, 147, 149–52, 163, 165–66, 168–76, 178–81, 187, 191–95, 200, 211
vaudeville, 15–16, 149, 173, 179. *See also* Nick Lucas
Vernon Country Club Orchestra, 133
Victor [record company], 16, 26–29, 135, 159; Bing Crosby recordings, 104–6, 109, 111; Gene Austin recordings, 57–59, 61–62, 65–67, 77; Johnny Marvin recordings, 164–65, 167–71, 173–79, 181; Nick Lucas recordings, 133; orthophonic discs, 25; Rudy Vallee recordings, 187–89, 192, 195–99, 206; Russ Columbo recordings, 87; sound system, 69; Victrola, 27
Vincent Lopez and His Peking Five, 133
Vitaphone [film company], 34, 146, 173–74

Wald, Jerry, 181
Waldron, Billy, 141
Walker, Frank, 19, 26
Walker, Jimmy, 63
Wallace, Ken, 163
Waller, Fats, 33, 61–63, 65–67
Walsh, Jim, 23–24, 167
Walters, Eddie, 33
Ward, Sleepy, 187
Waring, Tom. 174
Warner Bros., 91–92, 145, 147–48, 152–53, 172, 174–75, 181, 196
Warren, Harry, 63, 90
Washington, George Dewey, 174
Weaver, Cicero, 177
Wehle, 73–75

Weintraub, George R., 164
Weitman, Bob, 87–88, 110
Welk, Lawrence, 155
West, Mae, 31–32, 71
Wheeler, Bert, 136
White, Lew, 144, 152
Whiteman, Paul, 36, 102–8, 111–12, 133, 171
Whiting, George, 62
Whitmark, Jay, 68
Whitney, Jock, 115
Wiedoeft, Rudy, 36, 41, 186
Williams, Andy, 125
Williams, Frances, 49, 90
Williams, Hannah, 89
Williams, Ted, 124
Winchell, Walter, 90
Wirges, William, 144
women as consumers, 11–12
women singers, 10–12
Wood, Natalie, 203
World War I, 161, 181
World War II, 113, 183–84, 201
Wrubel, Allie, 92

Xavier Cugat and His Orchestra, 202

Yale Collegians, 186–87
Yale University, 12, 186–87, 198
Yates, Harold, 171
Yorty, Sam, 156
Young, Loretta, 89
Young, Margaret, 11
Young, Victor, 150

Zanuck, Darryl F., 90, 145, 147–48
Ziegfeld, Florenz, 145
Zukor, Adolph, 111. *See also* Paramount
Zulueta, Cesar de, 126

About the Authors

Frank Hoffmann is a professor of library science at Sam Houston State University, in Huntsville, Texas. He teaches courses relating to information services, collection development, research methods, and popular music. He received his B.A. (1971) and M.L.S. (1972) from Indiana University, Bloomington, and Ph.D. (1977) from the University of Pittsburgh. He has written more than twenty-five books devoted to music, collection development, intellectual freedom, fads, and popular culture.

Michael Pitts has written numerous books on entertainment including *Famous Movie Detectives I & II*. He is also the co-author of Scarecrow Press's *The Great Pictures Series*.